Ethics Teaching in
Higher Education

THE HASTINGS CENTER SERIES IN ETHICS

ETHICS TEACHING IN HIGHER EDUCATION
Edited by Daniel Callahan and Sissela Bok

A Continuation Order Plan is available for this series. A continuation order will bring delivery of each new volume immediately upon publication. Volumes are billed only upon actual shipment. For further information please contact the publisher.

Ethics Teaching in Higher Education

Edited by

DANIEL CALLAHAN
and
SISSELA BOK

The Hastings Center
Hastings-on-Hudson, New York

PLENUM PRESS · NEW YORK AND LONDON

Library of Congress Cataloging in Publication Data

Main entry under title:

Ethics teaching in higher education.

    (Hastings Center series in ethics) ·
    Bibliography: p.
    Includes index.
    1. Ethics—Study and teaching (Higher)—United States. I. Callahan, Daniel,
1930-   II. Bok, Sissela. III. Series: Hastings Center. Hastings
Center series in ethics.
BJ66.E84   170'.7'1173   · 80-24002
ISBN 0-306-40522-9

© 1980 The Hastings Center
Institute of Society, Ethics, and the Life Sciences
360 Broadway
Hastings-on-Hudson, New York 10706

Plenum Press, New York
A Division of Plenum Publishing Corporation
227 West 17th Street New York, N.Y. 10011

Printed in the United States of America

Contributors

Sissela Bok has taught medical ethics at the Radcliffe Institute and at the Harvard–M.I.T. Division of Health Sciences and Technology. She received her Ph.D. in philosophy from Harvard University, and is the author of *Lying: Moral Choice in Public and Private Life.*

Daniel Callahan is the founder and Director of The Hastings Center. He received his B.A. from Yale and his Ph.D. in philosophy from Harvard. He has taught at Brown University, Temple University, and the University of Pennsylvania. He is the author or editor of 20 books and over 200 articles. His most recent books are *Abortion: Law, Choice and Morality; Ethics and Population Limitation;* and *The Tyranny of Survival.*

Arthur L. Caplan is Associate for the Humanities at The Hastings Center, and Associate for Social Medicine in the Department of Medicine, College of Physicians and Surgeons, Columbia University. He did his undergraduate work at Brandeis University, and received his Ph.D. in philosophy from Columbia University. He is the editor of *The Sociobiology Debate,* and the forthcoming *Concepts of Health and Disease in Medicine.*

Thomas Lickona is Associate Professor of Education at the State University of New York at Cortland. He recently held visiting appointments at Harvard and Boston Universities and served as Research Associate with the Danforth Foundation School Democracy Project. He received his Ph.D. in psychology from the State University of New York at Albany. His publications include the book *Moral Development and Behavior,* numerous writings on social and moral education, and a forthcoming book for parents on fostering moral development in the family.

Ruth Macklin is Associate for Behavioral Studies at The Hastings Center. She received her B.A. from Cornell and her Ph.D. in philosophy from Case Western Reserve University, where she taught for ten years before joining the staff of The Hastings Center. She is also Associate Professor of Community Health at Albert Einstein College of Medicine, where she teaches medical ethics. Dr. Macklin is one of several coeditors of *Moral Problems in Medicine,* and her book on the ethics of behavior control is scheduled for publication early next year.

William F. May is Professor of Christian Ethics at the Kennedy Institute of Ethics, Georgetown University. He has taught at Indiana University, and was former President of the American Academy of Religion. He cochairs the research group on Suffering, Death and Well-Being at The Hastings Center, and has taught summer seminars in management ethics and medical ethics under the sponsorship of the National Endowment for the Humanities. With the help of a Guggenheim Fellowship (1978–1979), he has been writing a book, *The Public Obligation of the Professional.*

Susan Resneck Parr is Associate Professor of English at Ithaca College, where she chaired her department, 1976–1979. She has just completed a year as a Visiting Associate Professor at Princeton. She received her A.M. from Wellesley, her M.A. from the University of Chicago, and her Ph.D. from the University of Wisconsin. Her recent publications include essays on Faulkner, Heller, Fitzgerald, and Sexton. At present, she is writing a book for teachers which demonstrates how to teach literature with an emphasis on moral dilemmas that are inherent in the works themselves.

Bernard Rosen is Associate Professor of Philosophy at Ohio State University. He received his B.A. from Wayne State University and his Ph.D. in philosophy from Brown University. He is the author of a recent book, *Strategies of Ethics.*

Douglas Sloan is Associate Professor of History and Education at Teachers College, Columbia University, and Editor of *Teachers College Record.* He received his Ph.D. in history and education from Columbia University. He is author of *The Scottish Enlightenment and the American College Ideal,* and most recently is editor of the book *Education and Values.*

Dennis F. Thompson is Professor of Politics at Princeton University. He received his M.A. from Oxford University and his Ph.D. from Harvard. He is the author of *The Democratic Citizen: Social Science and Democratic Theory in the 20th Century,* and *John Stuart Mill and Representative Government.* Since 1969 he has taught a course on political ethics and public policy in the Woodrow Wilson School at Princeton.

Contents

PART IV
SUMMARY RECOMMENDATIONS ON THE TEACHING OF ETHICS

Introduction

A concern for the ethical instruction and formation of students has always been a part of American higher education. Yet that concern has by no means been uniform or free from controversy. The centrality of moral philosophy in the undergraduate curriculum during the mid-19th Century gave way later during that era to the first signs of increasing specialization of the disciplines. By the middle of the 20th Century, instruction in ethics had, by and large, become confined almost exclusively to departments of philosophy and religion. Efforts to introduce ethics teaching in the professional schools and elsewhere in the university often met with indifference or outright hostility.

The past decade has seen a remarkable resurgence of the interest in the teaching of ethics, at both the undergraduate and the professional school levels. Beginning in 1977, The Hastings Center, with the support of the Rockefeller Brothers Fund and the Carnegie Corporation of New York, undertook a systematic study of the state of the teaching of ethics in American higher education. Our concern focused on the extent and quality of that teaching, and on the possibilities and problems posed by widespread efforts to find a more central and significant place for ethics in the curriculum. Over the course of the two-year project, ten extended meetings were held, a summer workshop of 150 participants was conducted at Princeton University, 30 papers and independent studies were commissioned, a large file of syllabi and curriculum material was accumulated, visits were paid to a number of schools, letters containing course information and opinions on the teaching of ethics were received from well over 1,000 teachers, talks were held with the officers of a number of professional and educational organizations, and advice on the project was sought from all quarters. The bulk of the work for the project was carried out by a group of 20 people, all of whom met together regularly over a period of two years, and most of whom prepared individual studies or papers for the project. An important reason for the formation of such a group to take part in the project from its beginning to its end was a desire to see whether some degree of agreement and consensus could be achieved on the main problems confronting the teaching of ethics in American higher education. The conclusions of that group are published in *The Teaching of Ethics in Higher Education* (Hastings-on-Hudson, N. Y.: The Hastings Center, 1980). The papers collected in this volume form much of the background for that report.

A number of motivations lay behind the decision of The Hastings Center to mount a serious study of the teaching of ethics in American higher education. Beginning in 1969, The Hastings Center devoted a considerable part of its own work to attempts to encourage the development of more formal programs on medical ethics in medical schools. At the same time, as that movement developed, the subject of bioethics gained increasingly prominent importance in the undergraduate curriculum. As it turned out, the teaching of bioethics was in many ways the forerunner of an interest in applied and professional ethics in other fields. By the mid-70s, it was clear that a broad concern for the teaching of ethics was beginning to manifest itself in almost all departments and divisions of the university. What, we asked ourselves, did this new development mean, and what problems and possibilities would it be likely to face? What are the appropriate purposes of courses in ethics? What kinds of student should such courses try to reach, and at what point in the curriculum? Who should teach such courses, and what sort of training ought they to have? How could one understand the curious fact that an interest in ethics was very high in some schools, moderate only in others, and nonexistent in still others? The work of The Hastings Center project was an effort to explore those questions, as confronted by those teaching ethics, interested observers in American higher education, and those in administrative positions wondering whether courses in ethics should be promoted within the university.

The papers in this book are addressed to the issues that we found to be the most critical. In his paper, Douglas Sloan explores the checkered history of the teaching of ethics in American higher education, 1876–1976. As his paper indicates, the place of ethics in the curriculum affords a significant and interesting way of understanding the shifts and turns in the very idea of a higher education, and the broader intellectual and social currents in the society as a whole. In his paper, Daniel Callahan takes up the question of goals in the teaching of ethics. Many different ones have been proposed, and the very plethora of suggested purposes in itself has been a major point of contention. In an appendix to his paper, Callahan also examines the question of appropriate qualifications for those teaching ethics. While a considerable portion of the teaching of ethics takes place within departments of philosophy and religion, taught by those with doctorates in those fields, probably the most significant development in the past decade has been the spread of courses beyond those disciplinary contexts. That spread, in turn, has posed significant questions concerning the qualifications and credentials of those teaching such courses.

Ruth Macklin addresses another difficult set of issues, those of indoctrination and pluralism. A major concern about the teaching of ethics has been whether, and to what extent, it is appropriate to teach courses on ethics in a pluralistic society, and whether it is possible to teach such courses without engaging in unacceptable indoctrination. Thomas Lickona addresses another problem encountered persistently throughout our project; i.e., does the field of moral psychology have a contribution to make to the teaching of ethics? That field has rapidly developed in recent years, and a great number of research findings have suggested that the perspectives of psychology can be illuminating. In his paper, Arthur Caplan considers the question of the evaluation of the teaching of ethics. Just as the problem of goals in the teaching of ethics has been troublesome, so also has that of evaluation—and the two general issues cannot be sharply separated.

The second set of papers, by Bernard Rosen, Susan Parr, and William May, approach the teaching of ethics from more specific angles. Bernard Rosen analyzes the role of formal courses in ethics in the undergraduate curriculum, discussing the types of problem encountered by undergraduate teachers of ethics, and the context in which that teaching takes place. He also provides his own recommendations concerning that teaching. Yet it is by no means the case that ethics arises only in formal courses so listed. A great deal of discussion of ethics also goes on in other places in the curriculum, particularly in the humanities and the social sciences. Susan Parr discusses some characteristics of such teaching, and examines some of the particular problems and possibilities that it poses. William May takes up the broad and difficult subject of the teaching of ethics in the professional school curriculum. He notes many of the problems encountered in that particular context, and discusses them in the larger setting of professional ethics.

Dennis Thompson and Sissela Bok contribute two substantive papers, on paternalism and on whistleblowing and professional responsibility. Their essays are meant not only to provide an analysis of these moral questions in their own right, but also as examples to show how certain broad ethical issues can arise in a variety of different teaching contexts. As topics for teaching, both paternalism and whistleblowing can be pertinent and useful in undergraduate institutions, as well as in professional schools.

Finally, we have included in this volume the summary recommendations of the group that carried out the project on the teaching of ethics. Although the individual authors of the papers were fully free to develop their own thoughts and ideas on their topics, the project as a whole drew heavily on those papers in formulating their final recommendations.

We would like to thank the Rockefeller Brothers Fund for the planning grant which enabled us to organize our project, and the Carnegie Corporation of New York for providing the two-year grant which enabled us to carry out the project as a whole. We are also very grateful to the contributors to this volume, to other members of the research project as a whole, and to the many people who assisted us in our meetings, and in particular read and criticized earlier drafts of these papers.

SISSELA BOK AND DANIEL CALLAHAN
Project Codirectors

Hastings Center Project
  on the Teaching of Ethics

CHAPTER 1

The Teaching of Ethics in the American Undergraduate Curriculum, 1876–1976

DOUGLAS SLOAN

This article is an attempt to look at main developments and issues in the teaching of ethics to undergraduates during the past century. Although I had suspected as much, it was not until I was well under way in working on the piece that I began to realize the extent to which a look at the teaching of ethics provides, as it were, a central window on the whole of American higher education. The teaching of ethics has been uniquely and inseparably connected with the most important issues of modern higher education, issues involving the curriculum, institutionalization, professionalization, epistemology, the "two cultures" split, the community—indeed, the very purposes of higher education. It is with this larger perspective in view that I have sought to understand the place and problems of the teaching of ethics, not only with respect to ethics courses as such, but also in the larger curriculum. Even as concern with the teaching of ethics has time and again flagged or even disappeared at one point in American higher education, it has without fail, and almost immediately, reappeared at another; for the issues with which it deals have been those integral to the entire enterprise.

 Two disclaimers are, perhaps, called for at the outset. The study does not presume to offer a systematic account of the development of ethical theory. Nor does it attempt to deal exhaustively with all influences on the teaching of ethics that have originated in the wider society and its institutions. I have endeavored, however, to take the theoretical and social-institutional contexts seriously, and to bring out those aspects of both that have borne directly on the problems of

DOUGLAS SLOAN ● Teachers College, Columbia University, New York, N.Y.

the teaching of ethics, or that, in my judgment, help to illuminate those problems most clearly.

MORAL PHILOSOPHY IN THE NINETEENTH-CENTURY COLLEGE

Throughout most of the nineteenth century, the most important course in
the college curriculum was moral philosophy, taught usually by the college president, and required of all senior students. The moral philosophy course was
regarded as the capstone of the curriculum. It aimed to pull together, to integrate, and to give meaning and purpose to the students' entire college experience
and course of study. In so doing, it even more importantly also sought to equip
the graduating seniors with the ethical sensitivity and insight needed if they were
to put their newly acquired knowledge to use in ways that would benefit not
only themselves and their own personal advancement, but the larger society as
well.[1]

Moral philosophy was not a newcomer to the college curriculum, but had
a long and respected tradition behind it. Moral philosophy had been part of the
arts course of the medieval university. Under the influence of the English and
Scottish universities, the early American colleges—Harvard, William and Mary,
Yale—continued to accord moral philosophy a prominent place in their teaching. It was not until about the time of the Revolution, however, that moral
philosophy began to assume the importance in the college curriculum that it
was to enjoy throughout most of the following century. It was then that the
colleges began to face entirely new tasks and problems. The expansion of
knowledge was beginning to demand that colleges introduce new professional
emphases, and a wide range of new subject matter in science, philosophy, and
literature alongside the core of the classics and mathematics. The need, moreover, to reconcile many of the philosophic and scientific influences of the
Enlightenment with traditional religious and ethical concerns was becoming ever
more pressing. Finally, as colleges increased in number after the Revolution,
they continued to carry a major responsibility for preparing leaders for the newly

---

[1]For two general discussions of nineteenth-century moral philosophy, see D. H. Meyer, *The
Instructed Conscience: The Shaping of the American National Ethic* (Philadelphia: University
of Pennsylvania Press, 1972); and Wilson Smith, *Professors and Public Ethics: Studies of North-
ern Moral Philosophers before the Civil War* (Ithaca: Cornell University Press, 1956). See also
George P. Schmidt, *The Old-Time College President* (New York: Columbia University Press,
1930); and Gladys Bryson, *Man and Society: The Scottish Inquiry of the Eighteenth Century*
(Princeton: Princeton University Press, 1945). For early American moral philosophy, see Norman S. Fiering, "Moral Philosophy in America, 1650–1750, and Its British Context" (Doctoral
dissertation, Columbia University, 1969).

developing society.[2] By the early 1800s, moral philosophy had begun to appear to be the central point in the college curriculum where these many new concerns could be pulled together and addressed as a whole.

The full significance and centrality of moral philosophy in the nineteenth-century college curriculum can only be understood, however, in the light of the assumption held by American leaders and most ordinary citizens that no nation could survive, let alone prosper, without some essential common social and moral values shared by all. For the creation of these common social values, Americans looked primarily to education. The faith in the power of education to build a sense of national community and purpose has been deeply ingrained in the thought of Americans from the beginning. We see it in Jefferson's conviction that an enlightened citizenry is essential to a democratic society—and by "enlightened" he did not mean merely being able to read and write in order to get ahead, but, rather, having the capacity to understand important social issues that confront all citizens, and to contribute to their solution. We see the same faith in the unifying purposes of education in Horace Mann's idea that the common school would be "the balance-wheel of the social machinery." This faith in education was certainly one reason, among others, for the explosion in the founding of educational institutions of nearly every kind during the years before the Civil War. Schools, colleges, churches, utopian communities, newspapers, literary and historical societies, academies, lecture series, and other educational agencies spread rapidly during the nineteenth century. In addition to serving more limited purposes, each of these was seen as contributing in its own way to what Perry Miller once described as a great search for national identity—for common social values in a culture that seemed in so many ways torn and fragmented.[3]

Within this larger educational expansion, the college was considered to have a special and leading role to perform. It was once fashionable to describe the early college as an institution much inferior to the modern university. Thanks to recent research, however, we are beginning to understand that the nineteenth-century college probably deserves far more respect than it has often received. We are learning that the colleges before the Civil War were not educationally backward, but that their curricular offerings were often relatively quite substan-

[2]On the role of the colleges in preparing national leaders, see James McLachlan, "The American College in the Nineteenth Century: Toward a Reappraisal," *Teachers College Record* 80 (1978), pp. 287–306. I have dealt with the response of the college to the intellectual and social challenges of the Enlightenment in Douglas Sloan, *The Scottish Enlightenment and the American College Ideal* (New York: Teachers College Press, 1971).

[3]Perry Miller, *The Life of the Mind in America from the Revolution to the Civil War* (New York: Harcourt, Brace & World, 1965). See also Lawrence A. Cremin, *Traditions of American Education* (New York: Basic Books, 1977); and Douglas Sloan, "Harmony, Chaos, and Concensus: The American College Curriculum," *Teachers College Record* 73 (1971), p. 221.

tial, up-to-date, and useful. We are becoming aware of the extent to which the colleges were open to more than a privileged upper-class elite, and were drawing fairly large numbers of poor and middle-class students. We are also beginning to recognize that the colleges were not usually narrow, sectarian institutions, but were more often community projects. Although they may have borne the name of one religious body, it is becoming increasingly apparent that they were probably more often than not supported by the entire community, were responsive to community needs, and were essentially community colleges.[4]

Also the early colleges had a national orientation. They were seen as part of a larger movement to shape the wider society and to provide common national goals and values. It was widely assumed that the man of learning, as such, exerts an uplifting and unifying influence on society. Jefferson had often spoken of the importance of having men of learning in positions of leadership. Higher education was to produce, in Jefferson's own phrase, just such an "aristocracy of talent and virtue." Underlying this view of higher education was the further assumption that the higher learning constituted a single unified culture in itself. The different branches of knowledge—literature, the arts, and science—were regarded as equals in a single culture of learning. Only if there existed such an intellectual unity among the different branches of knowledge could learned men provide effective cultural leadership for the wider society. Intellectual unity was thus regarded as an essential safeguard against cultural and moral chaos. It is against the background of these assumptions that moral philosophy acquired its central importance in the college curriculum.

The foremost task of the moral philosopher was to demonstrate to his students that human beings are fundamentally moral creatures, and that man's ethical striving is undergirded and sustained by a moral universe. The task was nothing less than to show that religion, science, and the human mind, all, if rightly understood, revealed and contributed to the highest values of the individual and of society. Thus, the philosophers took on the task of establishing a firm ground for the unifying moral principles considered so necessary for the health of the nation. In so doing, they were responding to the needs of a society that believed in progress, but feared the rapid changes the nineteenth century was daily thrusting upon it. The values to which moral philosophy pointed provided an anchor of stability for a nation in change, while promising continued progress to a people who strove for the realization of the highest ethical ideals.

---

[4]See David B. Potts, "American Colleges in the Nineteenth Century: From Localism to Denominationism," *History of Education Quarterly*, 11 (1971), pp. 363–380; David B. Potts, "College Enthusiasm! as Public Response, 1880–1860," *Harvard Educational Review*, 47 (1977), pp. 28–42; McLachlan, "The American College," pp. 287–306, Stanley M. Guralnick, *Science and the Ante-Bellum American College* (Philadelphia: American Philosophical Society, 1978); and Sloan, "Harmony, Chaos, and Consensus: The American College Curriculum," p. 221.

The effort of the moral philosophers was, as D. H. Meyer has written, "to shape and instruct an American public conscience, to create an ethical frame of mind that would direct a new nation seeking a moral as well as a political identity in a changing world."[5] Many of the leading academic philosophers—Francis Wayland, Mark Hopkins, Noah Porter, and others—became, through their public lectures and textbooks, teachers to the nation at large, giving instruction in the values and attitudes they thought necessary for the nation as a whole to share. Moral philosophy owed its importance in the nineteenth century not only to its being part of the college course of study, but to its being essential as well to the national curriculum.

Within the college itself, moral philosophy was important as more than merely another single course. Moral philosophy carried the task of preserving unity in the college curriculum, and, thereby of ensuring the existence of a unified and intelligible universe of discourse. Again moral philosophy represented a response to the needs of the times. Although it was assumed that all branches of learning constituted a single, unified culture, strains were already appearing early in the nineteenth century among the different fields, as science, literature, philosophy, and the arts each threatened to go its own way.[6] At the same time, new subject matter continued to make claims for inclusion in the college curriculum. Intellectual and curricular fragmentation threatened to destroy the very basis of reasoned, ethical discourse, and to lead directly to moral and ethical chaos.

Attempting to meet the challenge head-on, moral philosophers worked to preserve the unity of learning in two ways. First, they sought to provide a means of bringing together all the subject areas studied by the student, and, by relating these to higher laws, furnish an integrating principle for the entire curriculum. Mental philosophy and moral philosophy, for example, had always been closely connected, and the nineteenth-century philosophers stressed more than ever the role of the mind as a prime source of moral truth, whether through intuition and introspection, conscience and the "moral sense," or the use of ordinary reason. This emphasis on the mind also enabled the philosophers to draw connections between knowledge of moral laws and what it discovered about the laws of nature through science. Some moral philosophers, from John Witherspoon in the eighteenth century on, harbored the hope that moral philosophy could approach the same exactness as a mode of knowing as was enjoyed by

[5]Meyer, *The Instructed Conscience,* pp. viii-ix.
[6]For early conflicts between men of science and men of letters, see Howard S. Miller, *Dollars for Research: Science and the Patrons in Nineteenth-Century America* (Seattle: University of Washington Press, 1970, pp. 22, *passim;* and Frederick Rudolph, *Curriculum: A History of the American Undergraduate Course of Study Since 1836* (San Francisco: Jossey-Bass, Inc. 1977), pp. 107–109.

science.[7] Just as science was thought to reveal the divine handiwork in nature, so moral philosophy demonstrated moral purpose and design in human affairs. The moral law was considered to be as real and as inexorable as the law of gravity, and both pointed to a divine governor of the world. By emphasizing ethics and the moral law as also the common element of all religion, the moral philosophers represented a secularizing and moralizing of the religious impulses—an influence that was to become increasingly pronounced. At the same time, however, putting the emphasis on ethics rather than theology also made it possible for them to assert the underlying unity of religion at a time of mounting sectarianism and religious disagreement. They could argue that there were no fundamental conflicts among religion, science, and morality, and that all working together made possible the moral and material progress of society.

Moral philosophy also served to promote intellectual harmony by introducing into the curriculum a wide range of new subject matter, and attempting to exhibit for the student its ethical dimensions. Much of what we now recognize as the social sciences first appeared in the college curriculum in the moral philosophy course.[8] The attention given in moral philosophy to mental philosophy and social institutions as necessary to the construction of sound ethical theory also demanded the study of an increasing number of related fields. Moreover, the high value placed on scientific method—an introduction to scientific method, usually of a simplified Baconian type, was usually the first topic of the moral philosophy course—required increased precision in argument and greater delineation of related fields of study.

The results were threefold. First, moral philosophy became an important source for the origin and development of what later developed as political science, economics, philosophical ethics, psychology, anthropology, and sociology. Second, as these subjects split out of moral philosophy, they based many of their claims for autonomy on the very scientific status moral philosophy accorded them. Third, as these subjects became fields of study in their own right, they often carried with them the moral and ethical imperatives of moral philosophy. The later conflict within the social sciences as to whether they could

[7]John Witherspoon, President of Princeton, for example, told his senior class in moral philosophy, "Yet perhaps a time may come when men, treating moral philosophy as Newton and his successors have done natural, may arrive at greater precision." John Witherspoon, *Lectures on Moral Philosophy* (Princeton: Princeton University Press, 1912), p. 4.

[8]Ibid. In his moral philosophy lectures, Witherspoon touched on such topics as epistemology, political science, economics, jurisprudence, family and marriage, primitive customs, religion, personal and social morality, aesthetics, and others. For discussions of the relations between moral philosophy and the later social sciences, see Gladys Bryson, "The Emergence of The Social Sciences from Moral Philosophy," *International Journal of Ethics*, XLII (1932), pp. 304–323, idem, "The Comparable Interests of the Old Moral Philosophy and the Modern Social Sciences," *Social Forces*, 11 (1932), pp. 19–27, idem, "Sociology Considered as Moral Philosophy," *Sociological Review*, 24 (1932) pp. 26–36. See also Bryson, *Man and Society*.

remain both scientific and ethical was to become, as we shall see, one of the major questions in American higher education.

The final, and in some ways the most crucial and difficult, use of moral philosophy was to help form the moral character and disposition of the individual student. This required that the students' own ethical concerns be awakened, and that they be inspired to pursue their own continuing moral development. It also demanded that the theoretical underpinnings of ethics, which were a main component of the course, be presented, so as to confirm students in their own ethical striving. Furthermore, it meant providing concrete examples of ethical concern and conduct in the person of the moral philosopher himself. The scientific claims of moral philosophy were not taken to mean that the personal example of the teacher was unrelated to the content of instruction. It was the teacher's task to exhort, admonish, and inspire students to recognize that the demands of morality were real and all-encompassing. Although such things are difficult to measure, evidence in students' testimonials suggests that many moral philosophers may very well have made their greatest impact through the influence of their own personalities.[9] Others, by the same token, suffered their most important failure in their inability to bring their course to life, or to inspire through personal example.

It is important to point out, however, that moral philosophy was not expected to carry the whole burden of forming the students' characters and guiding their conduct. The entire college curriculum and environment had the same purpose. The classics themselves had long maintained their place in the curriculum in part because they were considered essential for understanding perennial ethical issues. Sermons in college chapel, and, not infrequently, evidences of religion drawn in a science class by a devout professor were intended to give further witness to the moral law. The mental discipline that study of the classics and mathematics was thought to impart was viewed as indispensable to the development and exercise of moral discipline. This discipline was further reinforced by the strict *in loco parentis* regimen of the college schedule. The entire college experience was meant, above all, to be an experience in character development and the moral life, as epitomized, secured, and brought to a focus in the moral philosophy course.[10]

---

[9]See Meyer, *The Instructed Conscience*, p. 126. "There is no part of the university work from which the student derives more real mental strength than from the course in philosophy under President Bascom," wrote one University of Wisconsin alumnus in 1885. "It is especially fortunate," he said "that Dr. Bascom is so thoroughly master of the subject; and along with a perfectly clear and adequate explanation of all obscure points, he imparts to the students a share of his own healthy enthusiasm." Quoted in Merle Curti and Vernon Carstensens, *The University of Wisconsin, A History, 1848-1929* (vol. I). (Madison: University of Wisconsin Press, 1949), p. 280.

[10]See Sloan, "Harmony, Chaos, and Consensus," p. 221.

This preeminence of moral philosophy in the undergraduate curriculum did not survive the nineteenth century, and the reasons for its decline were the result partly, though not entirely, of internal weaknesses. In retrospect we have become aware of many of the inherent problems of the moral philosophy course. For one thing, the desire for social unity and harmony was so consuming that the philosophers often studiously avoided issues that involved conflict. Consequently, they were sometimes blind to, or silent on, some of the most critical ethical problems of the times. Wilson Smith, for example, has pointed out that antebellum moral philosophers, with the exception of a few like Francis Wayland, almost entirely neglected the question of slavery.[11] The desire to seek harmony and avoid conflict also meant that their pronouncements often rose little above the level of truism—a tendency further encouraged by the exhortative, presumptuous, rhetorical style of the moralists.[12] The stress on harmony, the avoidance of conflict, the desire to promote progress—all gave to moral philosophy built-in conservative tendencies that lent themselves to the support of the status quo and the dominant interests of the society. It was no accident that the virtues and moral qualities cherished by the philosophers were also highly congenial to the solid citizen, the banker, the merchant, the respectable churchgoer.[13]

Perhaps the greatest weakness of moral philosophy was that the unity of the curriculum it strove to maintain was becoming illusory even by midcentury. It is ironic that the main proliferation of new subject areas in the college curriculum, besides those in natural science, came from precisely those areas that moral philosophy itself had first nourished. Moral philosophy had cast a false patina of unity over the curriculum, which it was powerless to maintain. The increasing fragmentation of knowledge signalled the rapid decline of moral philosophy. Intellectual disintegration also meant, however, as the philosophers had predicted it would, increasing neglect within American higher education of the ethical foundations of the pursuit of knowledge and of its moral uses.

Still, the nineteenth-century conception of moral philosophy did not simply disappear, for its influence and the concerns it had generated continued to be felt in American higher education. The old moral philosophy had emphasized the relation between society and morality, economics and ethics, science and value. This was a perspective that would resurface repeatedly among at least a few in twentieth-century American higher education, each time, its critics to the contrary notwithstanding, as the reassertion of a long and venerable American tradition. For all its conservatism and weaknesses, the old moral philosophy had a radical potential, as D. H. Meyer has clearly demonstrated.[14] In their under-

---

[11]Smith, *Professors and Public Ethics*, pp. 67–70.
[12]Meyer, *The Instructed Conscience*, pp. 74–75, 114.
[13]Ibid., pp. 104–107; and Smith, *Professors and Public Ethics*, pp. 3–4.
[14]Meyer, *The Instructed Conscience*, pp. 85–86, 119–20.

standing of the moral law as ultimately transcending politics, personalities, and conventional wisdom, the nineteenth-century moral philosophers established a tradition and provided resources for those who would continue to argue that social criticism and ethical deliberation lie at the heart of what it truly means to be an institution of higher education. Furthermore, the philosophers' view of the intimate relation between the unity of knowledge and the possibility of meaningful moral discourse appeared to receive continued confirmation. Finally, the nineteenth-century moral philosophers saw the essential unity of the three dimensions of the teaching of ethics: the cultural—the search for common values; the intellectual—the investigation of the philosophic ground of values and moral action; and the individual—the formation of character and conduct. The fracturing of this threefold unity was to remain a perplexing problem for higher education. If they fell far short in their undertaking, the nineteenth-century college moral philosophers, nevertheless, knew where many of the main problems lay. They had a clearer sense of the important issues in the relations between knowledge and values than they have often been given credit for.

ETHICS AND SOCIAL SCIENCE IN THE NEW UNIVERSITY

The decline of moral philosophy in American higher education was already well under way as early as the 1880s.[15] Yet many colleges continued for some time to hold out. In 1895, the Amherst College catalogue devoted the entire first page of the section on "The Course of Study" to a description of the course in ethics taught by the president of the college to the senior class.[16] But by 1905 ethics had disappeared from its front-page billing in the catalogue, and was to be found as merely one among several courses offered in Amherst's philosophy department as an elective for sophomores.[17] The fall of ethics from its exalted place in the Amherst curriculum, as indicated by these catalogue entries, is emblematic of a major change that had overtaken the whole of American higher education. So deep and thorough were the transformations taking place that even those institutions, such as Amherst, that would continue to regard themselves as the nation's major bulwarks of defense for traditional philosophies of higher education found themselves profoundly and permanently affected.

The passing of the older conception of moral philosophy did not mean

[15]Ibid., p. 130. According to D. H. Meyer, the last American textbook in moral philosophy of the traditional type was *Our Moral Nature*, written by James McCosh, President of Princeton, and published in 1892.

[16]Amherst College, *Catalogue*, 1895, p. 32. "The aim of the course," reads the catalogue, "is, by the philosophic study of the social and political relations of the individual to his fellow citizens and to the State, to promote that moral thoughtfulness ... which is the strongest element in true patriotism."

[17]Amherst College, *Catalogue*, 1905.

the immediate disappearance of a pervasive ethical perspective in American higher education. In many respects, in fact, the late nineteenth and early twentieth centuries witnessed an efflorescence of moral-reform activity, and with it an explosion outward into the whole society of the kind of moral enthusiasm and exertion that the earlier moral philosophers had taken it upon themselves to inculcate. In the face of mounting social problems in the late nineteenth century, the strong traditions of social-cultural reform established in America before the Civil War began to reassert themselves with renewed vigor. A myriad of social-cultural reform movements and activities began to appear in response to the increasingly complex problems of urban-industrial America.[18] The splintering of moral philosophy into many separate new subjects was in part a result of what today is sometimes called an explosion in knowledge; it also represented an extension outward of the reform spirit and moral concern that moral philosophy itself had helped to nourish. It was in this climate of social reform, moral uplift, and educational enthusiasm that the university movement of the latter nineteenth century was born.

The so-called rise of the university is too complex an affair to be captured and explained in a single phrase or formula. Much of the initial impetus for the university came from educational reformers who wanted an institution to do better what they felt the college and moral philosophy course had failed to do— train a generation of leaders imbued with a sense of responsibility and commitment to the nation. Daniel Coit Gilman, President of The Johns Hopkins, the model of the research university, spoke for most of his fellow university reformers when he said, "The object of the university is to develop character—to make men."[19] The university also took upon itself the task of providing training for the burgeoning career opportunities in an expanding industrial-managerial society. It coupled these functions with a commitment to support and lead scientific research, both in the faith that scientific expansion of itself promoted social progress, and that scientific methods of analysis were the tools most needed by a new generation of national leaders.

Soon a new social theory of higher education began to emerge to give direction to the university's diverse functions and to justify the leading role in

[18]This social-reform activity included the establishment and support of schools, universities, university extension, manual training and technical institutes, parks and playgrounds, settlement houses, institutional churches, women's study and social-science groups, civic improvement organizations, public museums and art institutes, libraries, and concert orchestras. In accounts of the time these activities were often lumped together and described variously as moral uplift, social reform, civic improvement, cultural uplift, and, in a popular phrase of the day, working for "the higher life." See Jane Allen Shikoh, "The Higher Life in the American City of the 1890s" (Doctoral dissertation, New York University, 1972); and Helen Lefkowitz Horowitz, *Culture and the City: Cultural Philanthropy in Chicago from the 1880s to 1917* (Lexington: The University Press of Kentucky, 1976).

[19]Quoted in Richard J. Storr, "Academic Culture and the History of American Higher Education," *Journal of General Education*, 5 (1950), p. 13.

society that was being claimed for it. The paramount need of American society, university spokesmen began to argue, was for guided social change under the direction of trained experts. The man of learning was still important, but he was now redefined as not so much a man of culture, and exemplar of a unified single culture of learning, as a specialized expert. This educated elite of experts, imbued with the ideals of social service and equipped with specialized knowledge, would apply its intelligence to the management of a society that had become too complex to be left to the direction of ordinary men.

Central to the institutionalization of this vision was the elective principle that, under the leadership of Charles W. Eliot at Harvard, became the main concept for organizing—or, as its critics claimed, for dismantling—the academic curriculum. The elective principle encouraged the expansion of knowledge, and, with the growth of university departments around the new disciplines, early undergraduate specialization, the proliferation of vocationalism and professional and graduate education, and an increasing emphasis on research.[20]

Equally important in institutionalizing the new theory of education was the formation during the 1880s and 1890s of learned societies based on specific fields of inquiry and supported institutionally by the growing departmental organization of the university. Increasingly, research specialization and scholarly approval by professional colleagues in the same field became the main criteria of academic appointment and promotion.[21] Professionally organized itself, and assuming the role of standardizing and certifying entry into all professions, academic and otherwise, the university was firmly secured in its prestige by the end of the century.[22] Although the universities were numerically a minority in comparison with the colleges, which the majority of students continued to attend, it was the university that increasingly set standards, and determined the goals of all of higher education.[23]

With the benefits of an enormous increase in knowledge and improvement of scholarly methods and standards, the specialization and professionalization of the faculty also brought problems. The vision of a unified curriculum and culture of learning was being abandoned, and the ethical, social, and character

---

[20]See Hugh Hawkins, *Between Harvard and America: The Educational Leadership of Charles W. Eliot* (New York: Oxford University Press, 1972).

[21]On the growing importance of university research and specialization, see Robert A. McCaughey, "The Transformation of American Academic Life: Harvard University, 1821–1892," *Perspectives in American History*, 8 (1974), pp. 237–332.

[22]On the role of the universities as certifiers and entries for the professions, see Burton J. Bledstein, *The Culture of Professionalism: The Middle Class and the Development of Higher Education in America* (New York: W. W. Norton, 1976); and Robert H. Wiebe, *The Search for Order, 1877-1920* (New York: Hill & Wang, 1967), p. 121.

[23]The impact of the university on the college curriculum and teaching is dealt with in George E. Peterson, *The New England College in the Age of the University* (Amherst, Mass.: Amherst College Press, 1964); and Willis Rudy, *The Evolving Liberal Arts Curriculum: A Historical Review of Basic Themes* (New York: Teachers College, Columbia University, 1960).

concerns once central to higher education were giving way to an emphasis on research and specialized training as the primary purpose of the university. With the new status and scholarly achievements of the faculties came an academic style that was becoming, in the words of Frederick Rudolph, "indifferent to undergraduates," "removed from moral judgment," and to an increasing degree "unrelated to the traditional social purposes of higher education."[24] The emphasis on the subject rather than the student, and on specialization rather than synthesis, were to be sources of strength, but also of large unresolved, often unaddressed problems.

At first the new social sciences and the learned societies that supported them carried both the ethical and the scientific orientation of moral philosophy in which they had been nourished and which they hoped to replace. Many of the new subjects and their corresponding professional bodies were founded expressly to apply the latest social-science methods and findings to the solution of pressing social problems. However, active social reform proved increasingly incompatible with the new canons of scientific objectivity, and with an academic career built on scholarly productivity. As a consequence, during their first years, the professional societies were racked by fierce disagreement over the place of ethics in a proper social science. The central question in the controversies, it should be stressed, was at first not so much whether social science had an ethical dimension, as what that dimension was, and how it should be expressed.

Many of the young social scientists—men such as economists Richard T. Ely, Henry Carter Adams, Simon Nelson Patten, and Edmund J. James— brought a strong ethical concern to their subject. Ely himself had been deeply influenced by his own college moral philosophy course, and he combined a commitment to Christian Socialism and an appreciation for the rights of labor with a stress on scientific method.[25] Most, like Ely, held to a conception of science shaped by evolutionary thought and the German historical school, which emphasized the uniqueness of each historical situation, and hence the possibility of social change guided by inductive empirical science. Their conception of an ethical social science committed most of them to actual social-reform activity outside the walls of the university, and to popularizing their science through books and lectures for the public. They also took the lead in organizing professional societies, as part of their larger effort to give effective institutional force to their ethical science and to combat older views, which they considered both socially conservative and unscientific. The American Economics Association, for example, was founded in 1885, primarily under the leadership of Ely, then a young professor at The Johns Hopkins, to make the ethical

[24]Rudolph, *Curriculum*, p. 157.
[25]Mary O. Furner, *Advocacy and Objectivity: A Crisis in the Professionalization of American Social Science, 1865-1905* (Lexington: University of Kentucky Press, 1975), pp. 49-54; and Benjamin G. Rader, *The Academic Mind and Reform: The Influence of Richard T. Ely in American Life* (Lexington: University of Kentucky Press, 1966).

ideal in economic life a reality, and to challenge the dominant position in academia of the classical *laissez faire* political economists.

By the mid-1890s, interestingly, nearly all of the originally more activist academics had begun to dissociate themselves from reform causes, and to emphasize instead their devotion to scientific research and their professional ties. They had discovered, for one thing, that their activities as popularizers and reform advocates—as ethics teachers to the nation at large—required precious time from their scholarly and scientific research. Because of their espousal of unpopular social causes, they found themselves embroiled in disputes with their university presidents and boards of trustees in ways that threatened the very existence of their still precarious academic careers. And, probably most important, they found themselves being criticized by social scientists of their own generation, who charged that their popularizing activities and their image as agitators and radicals called into question their standing as responsible, objective-minded scientists. During the latter 1890s, Ely severed almost all his connections with reform activity, as did most of the others.[26] As they retreated from reform, the professional organizations to which they belonged also ceased raising ethical questions, and began to concentrate almost entirely on detailed, carefully defined empirical research.[27]

The shift from advocacy and activism to an emphasis on "value-free inquiry" and professional organization was only partly the result of fears for the loss of newly won and very prestigious academic careers. It was also a rejection of the sentimental "do-gooder" attitudes prevalent at the end of the nineteenth century. Most important, it also reflected, as Robert L. Church has clearly shown, a growing consensus on the part of the social scientists as to how they might best, to use his phrase, "make a difference in the real world."[28] The shift represented a widening conviction among all the social scientists that they could make this "difference" and establish their authority most effectively by fully embracing the role of the indispensable expert who provided needed knowledge to those leaders in government and business who were in positions actually to shape public policy. Their unquestioning faith in the progressive nature of science enabled most of them to accept in good conscience the simplifications their emphasis brought to their personal and organizational lives, assuming that as scientific problems were solved the ethical issues would take care of themselves. The shift also was necessary for the internal unity and harmony required for the establishment of an authoritative professional community. Controversy threatened the credibility of the professionals in the eyes of the public, for, if the experts quarreled among themselves, who was to take their pronouncements

[26]Rader, *The Academic Mind and Reform*, p. 153.
[27]Ibid., pp. 130–158; and Furner, *Advocacy and Objectivity*, pp. 290–292, *passim*.
[28]Robert L. Church, "Economists as Experts: The Rise of an Academic Profession in America, 1870–1917," in Lawrence Stone, ed., *The University in Society*, vol. II (Princeton: Princeton University Press, 1974), see esp. pp. 573, 596.

seriously? Controversy also diminished the respect among peers so essential to the maintenance of professional standards. By dispensing with ethical questions, the academics also eliminated a major source of potential controversy.[29]

The withdrawal of the social scientists from active social reform did not mean their immediate abandonment of a concern for the ethical dimensions of their subjects. The majority still assumed that there was no fundamental conflict between ethical idealism and scientific objectivity. Indeed, as has been indicated, they had become convinced that it was as scientific experts that they could have their most effective influence on the world of affairs. Many of the most important figures in establishing the social sciences as university disciplines conceived of themselves as equally ethicists and scientists. They had entered their field in the conviction that the scientific study of society could give ethics a concreteness and a reality that neither the abstractions of their moral philosophy mentors nor the exhortations of contemporary social reformers could achieve.

The first two decades of the century witnessed a vigorous discussion in the social science literature regarding the relationship between ethics, on the one hand, and scientific research, technology, and social organization on the other. In the writings of such leading figures in the new social sciences as George Herbert Mead, Albion W. Small, James Mark Baldwin, James H. Tufts, John Dewey, and others, the theme was developed that ethics is not fixed once and for all, but, like mankind, is evolving, and that social science reveals the conditions and possibilities under which new ethical ideas can be created and realized.[30] The discussion was picked up and carried on also by lesser lights in the field.[31] Underlying this essentially evolutionary understanding of ethics and science was usually the assumption that man is basically an ethical being, or, in the

---

[29]The importance of internal harmony for the development and maintenance of modern professional communities is developed with respect to the study of early social sciences by Thomas L. Haskell, *The Emergence of Professional Social Science: The American Social Science Association and the Nineteenth-Century Crisis of Authority* (Urbana: University of Illinois Press, 1977), see esp. pp. 162–163.

[30]See, for example, James H. Tufts, "The Present Task of Ethical Theory," *International Journal of Ethics*, 20 (1910), pp. 141–152; George H. Mead, "The Philosophical Basis of Ethics," *International Journal of Ethics*, 18 (1908), pp. 311–323; Thorstein Veblen, "Christian Morals and the Competitive System," *International Journal of Ethics*, 20 (1910), pp. 118–185; Albion W. Small, "The Significance of Sociology for Ethics," *The Dicennial Publication of the University of Chicago*, vol. IV (Chicago: The University of Chicago Press, 1903), pp. 111–150; Charles H. Henderson, "Practical Sociology in the Service of Social Ethics," *The Dicennial Publication of the University of Chicago*, vol. III (Chicago: The University of Chicago Press, 1903), pp. 25–50; John Dewey, "The Evolutionary Method as Applied to Morality," *Philosophical Review*, 11 (1902), pp. 107–124, 353–371; and Charles A. Elwood, "The Sociological Basis of Ethics," *International Journal of Ethics*, 20 (1910), pp. 314–328.

[31]For example, Charles W. Super, "Ethics as a Science," *International Journal of Ethics*, 24 (1913/1914), pp. 265–281; G. Gore, "The Coming Scientific Morality," *Monist*, 14 (1904), pp. 355–377; J. W. Garner, "Political Science and Ethics," *International Journal of Ethics*, 17 (1907), pp. 194–204; and E. C. Hayes, "Sociology as Ethics," *American Journal of Sociology*, 24 (1918), pp. 289–302.

words of James H. Tufts, "a progressive being," whose science is itself a creative projection of creative potentialities.[32] This outlook portrayed the social sciences almost by definition as being integrating and ethical in nature.

Another outlook was also becoming more and more pronounced. This view stressed the notion of value-free, objective research, and the need to draw ever tighter the lines demarcating disciplinary boundaries. The evolutionary, ethical view of the social sciences, largely because of its uncritical, often utopian faith in science, was vulnerable to encroachments by the harder professional, objective notion of science, and, in fact, helped smooth the way for the latter's acceptance. By World War I, not only had social scientists disengaged themselves from direct social action, but their fields were becoming increasingly dominated by a stress on scientific method as ethically neutral, on a scientific, objective, and quantitative understanding of social-science research, and on tighter professional, organizational control. A conviction that ethics and social science were inseparable not only was yielding to confusion about the exact nature of the relationship, but this in turn was giving way to spreading embarrassment among professionals over colleagues who persisted in writing and speaking of the possibility of an ethically oriented science. This continuing shift is clearly apparent in psychology and sociology, two subjects closely connected originally with the teaching of ethics.

Long after moral philosophy and psychology had separated, the study of motives as the springs of human action had continued to furnish topics within the study of psychology and ethics alike. Mind, consciousness, and purposive striving continued for some time to be important concerns of psychology. The trend, however, was to eliminate ethics and value theory as integral parts of psychology.[33] By 1920, psychology as a field of study and an organized discipline had been thoroughly transformed.

---

[32]Tufts, "The Present Task of Sociology," pp. 148–149.

[33]This trend can be illustrated by a glance at the subject headings of *The Psychological Index*. Begun in 1894 as a bimonthly and edited for fifteen years thereafter by James Mark Baldwin of Princeton and James McKeen Cattell of Columbia, *The Psychological Index* was an extensive bibliography of the literature of psychology and its related subjects, and for years was a major research and reference guide in the field. J. Mark Baldwin and J. McKeen Cattell, eds., *The Psychological Review* and *The Psychological Index*, published bimonthly by Macmillan and Company. In the 1894 edition of the *Index*, "Ethics" held its traditionally high position within psychology as a subheading under the major topic of "Higher Manifestations of the Mind," along with such other subheadings as "Logic and Science," "Ideals and Values," "Theory of Knowledge," "Aesthetics," and "Feelings." Ethics maintained this position until 1906, when confusion seems to have begun to set in about the proper place of such topics in a psychological index. That year, although the subheading remained the same, the major heading was changed to "Philosophical Implications of Psychology," and within a few years the major heading was changed once again, to "Attitudes and Intellectual Activities," and the subheading from "Ethics" to "Psychology of Behavior and Morals." In 1915, the major topic heading changed once more, this time to "Social Functions of the Individual." The Index listings and the reinterpretations of ethics within psychology that they represented were, however, only mildly indicative of the profound changes that had been occurring within psychology.

The desire to imitate the exactness of the natural sciences led psychologists to want to eliminate the imprecision of research methods based on introspection, and the generality of such nonempirical notions as purpose and consciousness, and to seek instead complete objectivity and quantitative certainty. The behaviorist position in psychology, presented with great force by John Watson in his major writings between 1913 and 1919, tossed out all the talk about self and purpose that had been so much a part of the older psychology and of ethics as well.[34] The oft-quoted statement made by E. L. Thorndike in 1918, that "whatever exists at all, exists in some amount," symbolized the wholly physical, empirical, quantitative character of the new psychology.[35] Ethics was no longer a constituent part of psychology.

For a time, sociology presented something of a special case among the social sciences. Sociology preserved the connection between ethics and science longer than did such other fields as economics and political science. Sociology, however, was also burdened with its own peculiar difficulty, for, far more than the other fields, it lacked a clearly defined scientific focus and methodology. The place that sociology was to occupy in the curriculum and the task it was to perform remained, during the first decade of the century, open questions, and potential sources of creative debate about the place of ethics in the university. For that reason, it deserves a bit of special attention.

By 1900, sociology was being increasingly taught in American colleges and universities, but usually in connection with economics and political science departments, having yet to achieve autonomy as a discipline in its own right.[36] Probably the single person most responsible for the establishment of sociology as a university discipline was Albion W. Small. In 1880, as the newly appointed president of Colby College in Maine, Small altered the topics of the moral philosophy course he taught, replacing the "history of metaphysical philosophy" with "modern sociological philosophy." Small soon left Colby for the new University of Chicago, where, in 1892, he formed the first graduate department of sociology, and shortly thereafter launched the *American Journal of Sociology*, the first sociological journal in the United States.[37]

Small, like Comte, Spencer, and Lester Frank Ward before him, conceived of sociology as the unifying science of the study of man, and as a preeminently ethical science. He viewed sociology as a holistic science, one that would synthesize all the fields of knowledge and bring them to bear in the service of man.

---

[34]For an interesting discussion of the significance of behaviorism, see Edward A. Purcell, Jr., *The Crisis of Democratic Theory, Scientific Naturalism and the Problem of Value* (Lexington: University of Kentucky Press, 1973), pp. 34–35.

[35]See, for example, Lawrence A. Cremin, *The Transformation of the School* (New York: Alfred A. Knopf, 1962), p. 185.

[36]For a discussion of the development of sociology within Harvard's Department of Economics, see Robert L. Church, "The Economists Study Society: Sociology at Harvard, 1891–1902," in Paul Buck, ed., *Social Sciences at Harvard, 1860–1920* (Cambridge: Harvard University Press, 1965), pp. 18–90.

[37]Vernon K. Dibble, *The Legacy of Albion Small* (Chicago: The University of Chicago Press, 1975), pp. 2–3.

"Sociology in its largest scope, and on its methodological side," he wrote, "is merely a moral philosophy conscious of its task, and systematically pursuing knowledge of cause and effect within this process of moral evolution."[38] The whole point of science, Small argued, was to contribute to the enhancement of man's capacity to realize his highest values. "Science is sterile," he wrote, "unless it contributes at last to knowledge of what is worth doing. . . . Sociology would have no sufficient reason for existence if it did not contribute at last to knowledge of what is worth doing. . . . The ultimate value of sociology as pure science will be its use as an index and a test and a measure of what is worth doing."[39] Sociology would provide a scientific basis for an ethical perspective in life by studying the concrete context of human associations within which values are realized; in demonstrating the limited and parochial nature of all existing value judgments, sociology would press toward an evolutionary, universal ethic.[40]

For Small, as for many of his contemporaries, the absence of cultural and moral unity was the overriding tragedy of modern life, and the major ethical problem to be solved.[41] The university, he thought, had a special role to play in reestablishing cultural unity.[42] This, however, was a task it could not fulfill until it put its own house in order, for the moral confusion of modern culture was reflected in and exacerbated by the intellectual and ethical chaos of the university itself. If the university was to be true to its proper task, it would have to center itself around an ethical and unifying science of man—in short, around sociology as Small conceived it.

Despite his and others' contentions to the contrary, however, Small's vision of a synthetic, holistic social science was a misfit in the university of his day.[43] To those social scientists who were busy delimiting their own fields, the claims

[38]Albion W. Small, *Adam Smith and Modern Sociology* (Chicago: University of Chicago Press, 1907), p. 22.
[39]Small, "The Significance of Sociology for Ethics," p. 119.
[40]For my capsule account, I have relied especially on two studies of Small: Dibble, *The Legacy of Albion Small;* and Ernest Becker, "The Tragic Paradox of Albion Small and American Social Science," in *The Lost Science of Man* (New York: George Braziller, 1971), pp. 3–70.
[41]The deep concern among intellectuals of the period about the loss of common social values is dealt with in R. Jackson Wilson, *In Quest of Community* (Oxford: Oxford University Press, 1968); and Jean B. Quandt, *From the Small Town to the Great Community: The Social Thought of Progressive Intellectuals* (New Brunswick: Rutgers University Press, 1970).
[42]See Albion W. Small, "The Annual Phi Beta Kappa Address: The Social Value of the Academic Career," 1906, reprinted in Dibble, *The Legacy of Albion Small*, pp. 185–200. The address begins with the provocation: "If the world were governed by its wisdom instead of its selfishness, would universities be promoted?"
[43]Even though sociology had begun to find a focus in study of the social group, which was not far removed from Small's own emphasis on the interrelatedness of human associations, and even though many others voiced similar concerns about overspecialization and the need for integrating the special sciences, the pressures and rewards of scholarship ran in a different direction. On the emerging focus of sociology on the social group, see Furner, *Advocacy and Objectivity*, pp. 305–306. On the widespread expression of discontent with specialization and of sentiment for a larger synthesizing vision among social scientists, see Quandt, *From the Small Town to the Great Community*, pp. 102–125.

of a synthetic science sounded imperialistic and manifestly unscientific. The concept of an ethical science appeared, furthermore, to conflict with the canons of objective, value-free research. Small was fully aware of the problem. He knew that neither the university system itself nor the prevailing academic temper of mind provided much support for his view, and he sometimes criticized them on just that score.[44]

Yet Small was not always consistent. In his desire to see sociology acquire a disciplinary and professional base in the university, he was willing to trim his large claims for sociology, to keep a prudent silence about them, even to back down.[45] Owing much to Small's own indefatigable organizing labors, sociology was indeed established within the university, but at the price of having to abandon holistic, synthesizing pretensions, and of having to assume the much more humble position of one discipline among many, a discipline with its own focus, its own language, its own carefully delineated problems.[46]

To the end, Small still clung to the hope that sociology would take up its true task. The conception of sociology that triumphed, however, the only one that in his day could have, was set forth very clearly by William F. Ogburn in his presidential address to the American Sociological Society three years after Small's death in 1929. "Sociology as a science," said Ogburn, "is not interested in making the world a better place in which to live, in encouraging beliefs, in spreading information, in dispensing news, in setting forth impressions of life, in leading the multitudes, or in guiding the ship of state. Science is interested directly in one thing only, to wit, discovering new knowledge."[47] Sociology had at last come of age as a *bona fide* discipline.

The inward turn of the social sciences ensured the tightening of disciplinary boundaries, the development of increasingly esoteric bodies of knowledge accessible only to experts in each field, and a lack of concern, sometimes even of respect, for the general public and for the student. At the same time, it

---

[44]The decisive question in the university has usually been, he once wrote, "not what aspects of reality most urgently demand investigation, but with what sort of materials one could most certainly establish oneself as a teacher." Quoted in Becker, "The Tragic Paradox of Albion Small," p. 23.

[45]When, for example, Robert E. Park and Ernest W. Burgess, Small's associates at Chicago, published their *Introduction to the Science of Sociology* in 1921, setting forth their commitment to eschew systems and to provide a sociology based on "modest searching in the spirit of an inductive science," they had Small's blessing. See Robert E. L. Faris, *Chicago Sociology, 1920–1932* (Chicago: University of Chicago Press, 1967), p. 128.

[46]Becker argues that the tragedy of Small was that he never fully integrated in his own vision the concept of sociology as both synthesis and professional focus, and in the end opted for the latter, so that "one gained a new equality with other social sciences, but one lost social science." Becker, "The Tragic Paradox of Albion Small," p. 20. Dibble, on the other hand, argues, convincingly I think, that Small was internally consistent, but that his view was anachronistic in the university of his time and place. Both agree on the end result for sociology. Dibble *The Legacy of Albion Small*, pp. 149–153.

[47]Quoted in Becker, "The Tragic Paradox of Albion Small," p. 28.

brought the social scientists organizational security and authority, a base for widening involvement with government and business, and the conditions for scholarly achievement and recognition. It also meant that the social sciences could no longer be looked to as a primary source and stimulus for the teaching of ethics in the college and university curriculum. The hope of many at the turn of the century that the social sciences would embrace the ethical tasks of their moral philosophical heritage, but fulfill them in ways appropriate to the modern world as the old course never could, had been abandoned.

ETHICS IN DEPARTMENTS OF PHILOSOPHY: THE EARLY DECADES

Philosophy was always the first legatee of the teaching of ethics, particularly the branch of ethics concerned with the intellectual theory of moral thought and action. Once it was clear that the social sciences would not continue their moral philosophy tradition, the teaching of ethics as a formal subject was left for the most part—though not entirely, as we shall see—to departments of philosophy. What place ethics would occupy within departments of philosophy, what would be the dominant concern of ethics, how ethics would be related to other subjects, whether ethics would, for example, somehow step in to fill the vacuum left by the social sciences in their attempt to be value-free, whether ethics would seek to continue the full panoply of the earlier moral philosophy concerns, not only for the theory of ethics, but also for the actual formation of character and conduct—these remained open questions even into the 1920s, though by then certain definite trends in the teaching of ethics were becoming evident.

For a time, there appeared in the undefined territory between philosophy and sociology courses in social ethics—taught sometimes in philosophy departments, sometimes in sociology, sometimes as a course in religion, and, on occasion, within departments of social ethics. In the late nineteenth century, the American Social Science Association (ASSA) had attempted to encourage colleges to introduce social science courses and topics oriented toward the study of current American social issues of the times. In response to the growing social problems facing the nation after the Civil War, the ASSA had been founded in 1865 by influential persons drawn from business, the older professions, literary circles, and academia, persons who were concerned to encourage social reform and to develop better methods of studying and understanding social problems. The ASSA represented a practical extension and application of moral philosophy to actual social conditions, and, as part of its effort to improve the social consciousness of American leaders, it encouraged, during the 1870s and 1880s, the introduction into American colleges of courses in social science. In a survey conducted by the ASSA in 1885, over 100 colleges reported that they gave instruction in one or more topics in social science. Although one college, Wooster in Ohio, reported having just established a chair in morals and sociology, a close reading of the report suggests that most schools responding to the survey simply reported as social science topics those they were already giving in moral philosophy and political economy.[48] Little new came of these efforts, and it was not until the nineties and the early twentieth century that social ethics began to appear in higher education from other sources.[49]

One of the first major experiments in the teaching of social ethics was the development of Harvard's Social Ethics Department, under Francis Greenwood Peabody. The difficulty of establishing a subject area that lacked a clearly defined focus was well exemplified by the Harvard department. Peabody first began teaching ethics at Harvard in 1881, after some years as a lecturer on ethics at the Divinity School, and as a minister in Cambridge.[50] Throughout the 1890s he conducted one of the college's most popular courses among undergraduates, under the title "The Ethics of the Social Question." Sociology was also being taught within the Economics Department, but was still so closely tied to the methods and perspectives of that department that for many years there was little overlap or conflict.[51] And Peabody's own aim was not to develop sociology as such, but, essentially, to revive moral philosophy in a form he thought adequate to the problems of the day.

Peabody emphasized ethics and social science as a unity, combining his own social-gospel idealism with an attempt at empirical study and an emphasis on social action. David Potts has reported that by the end of the century over 400 Harvard students, products of "Peabo's drainage, drunkenness, and divorce," as they affectionately referred to his ethics course, were involved in various voluntary social work projects.[52] In 1906 Peabody organized the Social Ethics Department at Harvard, with courses offered in "Ethics of the Social Question," "Criminality and Penology," and "Practical Social Ethics."[53] The eclecticism of Peabody's approach, and his inability to be precise about the relation between ethics and social science, other than repeatedly to affirm it, resulted finally in social ethics becoming neither sociology nor moral philosophy. When Peabody retired in 1913, although the courses in the department were all listed as "social ethics," in their actual content the concern for ethics

[48]"Social Science Instruction in Colleges, 1886," *Journal of Social Sciences* (1886), pp. xxxv–xix.
[49]The attempt of the ASSA to establish closer relationships with the university, its rebuff by professionally minded academic sociologists, and its subsequent demise, are dealt with as part of the larger professionalization of the social sciences by Furner, *Advocacy and Objectivity;* and Haskell, *The Emergence of Professional Social Science.*
[50]For my discussion here of Peabody and the Harvard Social Ethics Department I draw mainly on David B. Potts, "Social Ethics at Harvard, 1881–1931: A Study in Academic Activism," in Paul Buck, ed., *Social Sciences at Harvard, 1860-1920,* pp. 91–128. See also, Jurgen Herbst, "Francis Greenwood Peabody: Harvard's Theologian of the Social Gospel," *Harvard Theological Review,* 54 (1961), pp. 46–52.
[51]See Church, "The Economists Study Society," pp. 18–90.
[52]Potts, "Social Ethics at Harvard," pp. 95–96.
[53]Harvard College, *Catalogue,* 1905–1906.

and values had almost totally disappeared, and had been replaced instead by an emphasis on practical, technical, bureaucratized social work.[54] Peabody had been attempting to revivify moral philosophy in the form of practical sociology, and to build an entire department around this notion. Because of its vagueness and lack of focus, social ethics, as Peabody conceived it, failed to become a profession itself, and at the same time was unable to resist the pressures and encroachments from another aggressive professionalizing group, the social workers.

Although few other schools, to my knowledge, attempted to follow Harvard's example under Peabody of trying to establish whole departments of social ethics as a form of revitalized moral philosophy, social ethics courses were introduced in many philosophy departments, to add a practical or applied orientation to the regular but more theoretic basic ethics course. Social ethics, in fact, would reappear throughout the century as a fairly staple offering in philosophy departments. Typical, for example, were the two elective ethics courses taught in the Department of Philosophy of the University of Wisconsin in 1905: the first a general introduction to ethics, and the second a course in "Social and Political Ethics," which examined "the rights of personal liberty, freedom of contract, property, national independence, and suffrage." In 1915 a third course, in "Business Ethics," was added, and remained a regular course with the other two well into the 1930s.[55] The Amherst College Department of Philosophy introduced a similar course in the early 1920s, entitled "Social and Political Ideals."[56] Social ethics, however, was a kind of floating topic that could surface in sociology and religion as well as in philosophy departments. The Religious Education Department at Macalester College, for example, provided a course in "The Social Teachings of the Bible," essentially a course in Christian social ethics that sought to apply "the social message of the Bible ... and its social principles to the solutions of current social problems," based on readings in the works of such leading social-gospel figures as Josiah Strong, Walter Rauschenbusch, Shailer Mathews, and Francis Greenwood Peabody himself.[57]

In 1910, the University of Utah offered an "Orientation through Social Ethics" course as an elective survey for freshmen.[58] In the early 1920s, professors of sociology at Dartmouth College and at the University of Illinois' sociology department wrote textbooks and taught courses in social ethics still based on a conception they shared with Albion Small, of sociology as a unifying science

---

[54]Harvard College, *Catalogue,* 1915–1916, p. 460. The Social Ethics Department continued in existence until 1931, when it was absorbed into the newly founded Department of Sociology, where any last vestige of ethics offerings disappeared.

[55]University of Wisconsin, *Catalogue,* 1904–1905, p. 102; 1915–1916, pp. 183–184; and 1935–1936, p. 183.

[56]Amherst College, *Catalogue,* 1925–1926, p. 95.

[57]Macalester College, *Catalogue,* 1915, p. 70.

[58]Russell Thomas, *The Search for a Common Learning: General Education, 1800–1960* (New York: McGraw-Hill, 1962), p. 76.

and a "scientific ethic."[59] What many schools did, in addition to offering individual social ethics courses in various departments, was begin to introduce, as
part of their increasing vocational orientation, courses in social work along the
narrow, practical lines that Harvard's Social Ethics Department later took. Even
small traditional liberal arts colleges often began to provide prevocational social-
work training. These, however, offered no ethics, and probably as little science.

During the first decades of the century, the role assigned to ethics in the
curriculum depended on the extent to which individual institutions had acceded
to university influences and the elective principle. In most of the universities,
ethics was taught as one possible elective among hundreds of others. Institutions
that attempted to preserve a liberal arts orientation and curriculum sometimes
made ethics a required course within a prescribed core curriculum. Macalester
College, for example, split its moral philosophy course into three—logic and
scientific method, psychology, and ethics—all required.[60] Other liberal arts colleges simply made ethics the major requirement for upper-class students in an
attempt to make ethics play a truncated version of the old moral philosophy.[61]
Still others, among them some like Amherst that were outspoken critics of the
university, abandoned ethics as a required course altogether.[62] By 1925, the pattern becoming prominent among universities and colleges alike was for ethics
as such to be offered as an elective within departments of philosophy.

Reading material available to students for the study of ethics was by 1900
diverse and increasingly rich, sometimes confusingly so. The classic texts by
America's nineteenth-century moral philosophers had all been almost totally
abandoned. Their place had been taken by leading British ethicists, whose works
were available to American classes for at least selected reading assignments in
the major ethical positions that set the context for turn-of-the-century theoretical discussion and debate: for instance, idealism in Thomas Hill Green's *Prolegomena to Ethics* (1883), intuitionism in James Martineau's *Types of Ethical
Theory* (1885), and intuitionism and utilitarianism in Henry Sidgwick's *Methods
of Ethics* (1874).[63] Moreover, a number of textbooks had appeared that presented a broad introduction to ethical thought, ancient and modern—texts such
as Friedrich Paulsen's *System of Ethics,* translated in 1899 by Cornell's Frank

---

[59]John M. Mecklin, *An Introduction to Social Ethics: The Social Conscience in a Democracy*
(New York: Harcourt, Brace & Co., 1920); and Edward Cary Hayes, *Sociology and Ethics: The
Facts of Social Life as the Source of Solutions for the Theoretical and Practical Problems of
Life* (New York: D. Appleton & Co., 1921.)

[60]Macalester College, *Catalogue,* 1900–1901, p. 42; 1909–1910, pp. 30–31.

[61]For example, Haverford College, *Catalogue,* 1905.

[62]Amherst College, *Catalogue,* 1915.

[63]All these books were on the reading list for the ethics course at Macalester College in 1900.
(Macalester College, *Catalogue,* 1900–1901, p. 42.) Thomas Hill Green, *Prolegomena to Ethics*
(Oxford: Clarendon Press, 1883); James Martineau, *Types of Ethical Theory* (Oxford: Claren-
don Press, 1885); and Henry Sidgwick, *Methods of Ethics* (London: Macmillan & Co., 1874).

Thilly, who the following year brought out a popular text of his own, *Introduction to Ethics;* Warner Fite's *An Introductory Study of Ethics* (1903); James Hyslop's *Elements of Ethics* (1895); S. E. Mezes' *Ethics: Descriptive and Explanatory* (1901); N. K. Davis' *Elements of Ethics* (1900); and others.[64] Some of these textbook writers—Mezes and Davis, for example—attempted to pull together and to present in condensed, simplified form some of the more daunting theoretical works. In addition, the teacher of social ethics had by 1910 at least three bibliographies of literature in that field to draw upon.[65] A collection of readings in ethics from Socrates to Martineau—the first instance in ethics I have found of a type of classroom aide that would later become extremely popular—was compiled and published the same year by Harvard's librarian, Benjamin Rand.[66]

The publication in 1908 of *Ethics,* by John Dewey and James H. Tufts, was a major event for the teaching of ethics. Both a text covering the whole field of ethics and Dewey's first full length statement of his own position in ethics, the book was extremely popular. Adopted by thirty colleges within six months of its publication, *Ethics* went through twenty-five printings before Dewey and Tufts revised it in 1932.[67] The main appeal of the book for teachers was the clarity of its discussion, and its three-part organization of the subject: part one covered the history of ethics, part two the theory of ethics, and part three, "The World of Action," discussed the application of ethics to concrete social problems. This was a model of organization that was to remain standard until the 1950s and 1960s, when the topics covered in Dewey and Tufts' part three would begin to disappear from the ethics textbooks. The book received immediate favorable notice, and many reviewers recommended it for the layman and general reader as well as for the student and "professional moralist."[68]

A random sampling of some of the texts used in the teaching of ethics

[64]Friedrich Paulsen, *System of Ethics.* (New York: Charles Scribner's Sons, 1899); Frank Thilly, *Introduction to Ethics* (New York: Charles Scribner's Sons, 1900); Warner Fite, *An Introductory Study of Ethics* (New York: Longmans, Green & Co., 1903); James H. Hyslop, *Elements of Ethics* (New York: Charles Scribner's Sons, 1895); S. E. Mezes, *Ethics: Descriptive and Explanatory* (New York: The Macmillan Co., 1901); and Noah K. Davis, *Elements of Ethics* (Boston: Silver, Burdett & Co., 1900).

[65]These included the Harvard bibliography in social ethics, *Teachers in Harvard University: A Guide to Reading in Social Ethics and Allied Subjects* (Cambridge: Harvard University Press, 1910); a bibliography in business ethics, R. H. Edwards, "Business Morals," *Studies in American Social Conditions,* no. 7, (Madison, Wisconsin, 1910), and a bibliography from the Fabian Society, *What to Read on Social and Economic Subjects* (London: King & Son, 1910).

[66]Benjamin Rand, *The Classical Moralists* (New York: Houghton Mifflin, 1909).

[67]This book has just been republished with a newly edited text by the Southern Illinois University Center for Dewey Studies: John Dewey and James H. Tufts, *Ethics,* Jo Ann Boydston, ed. (Carbondale and Edwardsville: Southern Illinois University Press, 1978). My references are to this edition.

[68]Ibid., "Textual Commentary," pp. 551–552.

during the first quarter of the century reveals the emergence of problems that
will appear familiar to the present-day reader. One problem was that of over-
coming the gap between theory and practice, between abstruse theoretical discussion and the actual needs and problems of students. "With the world calling
for moral power and efficiency, and with the adolescent of college years in the
nascent period of moral adjustment," wrote one early student of the teaching
of ethics, "how insufficient, foreign, barbarian, do the arid ethical logomachies
of most textbooks appear?" Despite this, the same writer conceded that,
although the theoretical terms of ethical instruction "stand for bewildering
mazes of controversy," they nevertheless "conceal very real problems."[69] The
question was how to give life to theory in such a way that it became more to
the student than mere speculation. It was just this problem, and his own conviction that ethics should be free of abstract theory, that prompted Francis Peabody at Harvard to begin his teaching of ethics "inductively," as a study of
specific social problems. It was a question also that continued to trouble textbook writers who felt that theoretical issues were important.

Almost all textbook writers not only indicated their awareness of the problem, but stated as one of their main purposes an attempt to strike a balance
between the theoretical and practical, and to speak meaningfully, as one put it,
to "concrete contemporary problems." "The purpose of a study of ethics," said
this writer, "is, primarily, to get light for the guidance of life."[70] Another writer
affirmed his hope that his book would make clear to every reader that "morality
is nothing more or less than the business of living."[71] And the opening sentence
of Dewey and Tufts' text in ethics was a statement that the true significance of
their work lay "in its effort to awaken a vital conviction of the genuine reality
of moral problems and the value of reflective thought in dealing with them."[72]
One way text writers could try to cope with the problem was, like Davis, an
earlier writer, to urge for all an introductory course in the fundamentals of ethics, and postpone treatment of theoretical controversies until later, and then only
for those who were interested. This, however, was easier said than done, if the
elementary course was to provide students with much more than obvious moral
truisms.[73] The better textbooks followed Dewey and Tufts's example by giving
attention to both theoretical and practical topics. Whether or not they actually
divided their work into separate sections as did Dewey and Tufts, most authors

[69]Edward S. Conklin, "The Pedagogy of College Ethics," *Pedagogical Seminary*, 18 (1961), pp.
427–428.
[70]Durant Drake, *Problems of Conduct, An Introductory Survey of Ethics* (Boston: Houghton
Mifflin, 1914), p. vi.
[71]Walter Goodnow Everett, *Moral Values: A Study of the Principles of Conduct* (New York:
Henry Holt & Co., 1926, p. vii.
[72]Dewey and Tufts, *Ethics*, p. 3.
[73]Davis, *Elements of Ethics*.

tried to make explicit the concrete problems, personal and social, to which they felt their ethical reflections applied.[74]

A second problem, closely related to the first and in many respects only a variation of it, had to do with the formation of the conduct and character of the individual student. In this the teachers of ethics still tried to fulfill what had been considered a main purpose of the nineteenth-century college and its moral philosophy course. Nineteenth-century moral philosophers had themselves achieved a questionable degree of success in the effort, and, with the greater freedom accorded students in the twentieth century, the task for the teacher of ethics appeared more formidable than ever. Nevertheless, if the textbooks can be taken as a true indication, it was an undertaking that teachers of ethics still saw as one of their most important jobs. G. Stanley Hall had early criticized the gap between the teaching of ethics and the actual moral ideas and conduct of students. He argued that ethics should be taught, not in a general course on the subject, but in courses that touched directly on the students' own personal interests and emotions. Writing late in the century, Hall indicated that his choice was personal hygiene:

> I have begun a course of ethics for lower college classes, and for two of three months have given nothing but hygiene; and I believe the pedagogic possibilities of this mode of introduction into this great domain are at present unsuspected and that, instead of the arid, speculative casuistic way, not only college but high school boys could be infected with real love of virtue and a deep aversion to every sin against the body.[75]

Although hygiene was a much discussed topic of the early twentieth century— often in connection with eugenics—few, if any, followed Hall's lead in making it the pedagogical focus for the teaching of ethics (it did provide a major topic of study in social ethics courses).

The problem of conduct and character, however, remained of concern to ethics teachers and writers. It is a problem that runs throughout Dewey and Tufts's *Ethics*—ethics they define as "the science that deals with conduct, in so far as this is considered as right or wrong, good or bad," and this is their reason for presenting the history of ethics before the theory.[76] To begin with the history of moral evolution, the development of actual moral principles and conduct, Dewey and Tufts felt, provided the student with a vivid sense of the reality and personal social setting of moral problems, which could only then be dealt with

---

[74]See, Drake, *Problems of Conduct;* and Everett, *Moral Values;* Warner Fite, *Moral Philosophy: The Critical View of Life* (New York: Lincoln MacVeagh, 1925); and Mary Whiton Calkins, *The Good Man and the Good: An Introduction to Ethics* (New York: The Macmillan Co., 1918).

[75]G. Stanley Hall, *Educational Problems*, vol. I. (New York: Appleton, 1911), Chapter 5.

[76]Dewey and Tufts, *Ethics*, p. 6.

analytically and theoretically in a meaningful way.[77] Other authors made personal conduct, or the ethics of the individual, the focus of their entire textbooks as a way of relating ethical theory, psychology, and sociology to the personal interests and concerns of the student.[78] Ironically, just as ethics teachers were making a last effort to keep alive an interest in the relation between theory and personal conduct, the triumph of the elective principle meant that in actuality the teaching of ethics was reaching only a relatively small percentage of students.

The growing isolation within the college and the curriculum and the practical ineffectuality of the undergraduate ethics course were symbolized by the blossoming of interest after 1910 in professional ethics. The ethics of the medical profession, of the law, of journalism, and of business were suddenly being discussed as never before.[79] On the one hand, this was a responsible and needed attempt to grapple with the problems posed by the new professional organization of American life. On the other hand, it represented something of a concession to a deepening sense that undergraduate instruction in ethics made little discernible difference in meeting the concrete problems of later life. If undergraduate instruction in ethics was lacking or failing, perhaps the moral dikes could be repaired later by arousing a professional ethical sensitivity. This made sense, but the temptation it carried simply to concentrate on professional ethics also meant a retreat, for a professional ethic was by definition a limited ethic, a stopping short of the universality that most thinkers had always maintained the highest ethical standards should seek to achieve.

During the 1930s and 1940s, the challenge to ethics by the dominant scientific conceptions about how we know, and about what we can and cannot know, began to produce a radical shift in the study and teaching of ethics. Although science had, indeed, posed problems for ethicists long before this, it would probably be inaccurate to speak of any kind of deep crisis of confidence about ethics before the late 1920s and early 1930s—if for no other reason than that, before then, the strength of evolutionary optimism and progressive idealism had helped to blur the seriousness of impending problems. Moreover, a certain skepticism had always been of the essence of a rigorous study of ethics; such questions as the reality of other selves, of universal standards versus the diversity of moral codes and practices, of intuitionism versus utilitarianism, of free will versus necessity, had all constituted the age-old, perennial issues of ethical discussion and debate. The growing force of scientific naturalism, however, began to appear to upset the balance in these venerable controversies, and to bias the

[77]Ibid., pp. 8–10.

[78]Drake, *Problems of Conduct;* Fite, *Moral Philosophy;* and Calkins, *The Good Man.*

[79]See Theodore Day Martin, "Instruction in Professional Ethics in Professional Schools for Teachers," (Doctoral dissertation, Columbia University, 1931); and Jesse Hickman Bond, "The Teaching of Professional Ethics in The Schools of Law, Medicine, Journalism and Commerce in the United States" (Doctoral dissertation, University of Wisconsin, 1915).

outcome irresistibly more in one direction than the other, more toward subjectivism, toward ethical relativism, toward functionalism, toward moral determinism. Within this larger intellectual context, and in reaction and response to it, the study and teaching of ethics took shape and acquired its own distinct problems and concerns. It is to this development and its consequences for the teaching of ethics from the 1930s through the 1960s that we now turn.

The Twentieth-Century Crisis in the Teaching of Ethics

During the 1930s, it became painfully apparent to ethical thinkers that the sciences, social and physical, rested on epistemological and methodological assumptions that threatened the very possibility of rational ethical discourse and action. Increasingly, scientific method was being regarded as the only valid mode of knowing, and the objects of science the only things about which genuine knowledge could be had. The outlook of science, with its exclusive focus on quantities, particulars, chance and probability, when transferred to other fields left qualities, wholes, purposes, and ideals, the subject matter of ethics, with no ground to stand on. From the point of view of the physical sciences, value qualities, the very thing ethical statements were presumably about, simply did not exist. It would be a gross oversimplification to say that this view was taken over wholesale and uncritically by the social sciences, and that there was no resistance to it. The general trend of thought, nevertheless, moved overwhelmingly in this direction.

The growing prestige of behaviorism has already been noted. By explaining all human behavior as either expressions of genetic endowment or responses to environmental influences, behaviorism left no room for the autonomy, self-deliberation, and volitional activity on which the conception of man as a moral agent depends.[80] The notion of a deliberating, deciding, and freely acting subject was often regarded as an unscientific myth, or at least as an imprecise designation for phenomena that could only be truly understood by breaking them down to their environmental and physiological components. In anthropology and sociology, the tendency to view all beliefs, religions, and values as expressions of more fundamental biological and economic needs of social groups was pronounced. In an important article in 1926, Bronislaw Malinowski gave to this approach of the social sciences the name "functionalism." Although the notion has been much criticized, refined, and made more precise since, it signified for

---

[80]In attempting to make sense of the very complex developments dealt with summarily in this and the following paragraphs, I have found two discussions especially helpful for both interpretational and bibliographical leadings: Purcell, *The Crisis of Democratic Theory;* and Frederick A. Olafson, *Ethics and Twentieth Century Thought* (Englewood Cliffs, N.J.: Prentice-Hall, 1973).

Malinowski, as for most of his contemporary social scientists, the general view that any social practice, custom, or belief was to be understood not by any intrinsic meaning, rational or moral, that it might have in itself, but only with reference to its consequences for the larger social group.[81]

Sociologists, perhaps more than others, tended to preserve the tension between the older reformist, value-oriented role of social science and the newer objectivist, empirical, and strictly disciplinary orientation; and during the 1930s and 1940s there remained sociologists who continued the attempt to counteract the dominant objectivistic, value-free conception of sociology.[82] As Edward A. Purcell has indicated, however, it is significant that even those social scientists who endeavored to keep questions of value and meaning alive in their discipline were severely handicapped because they also shared with their opponents one all-important assumption, namely, that though ethical values could be asserted and affirmed, genuine knowledge and rational justification were possible only of the empirical data with which science dealt.[83] By the late thirties the possibility of establishing and validating ethical norms and values was one that few social scientists would have defended, had they been interested.

Most social scientists held not only that social science is a totally objective, value-free enterprise, but also that ethical values themselves are expressions of subjective preferences. Ethical values were seen as noncognitive, nonrational, frequently as mere epiphenomena of underlying biological, economic, and social forces. Some objectivist scholars did acknowledge that researchers often could not avoid bringing their own value judgments into their work, but since these represented merely irrational biases and lapses, their primary task was to weed them out as completely as possible.

This is not to say that social scientists were uninterested in leading an ethical life as individuals, or in contributing to the creation of a more humane society. At least three positions were taken by objectivist social scientists in relation to ethical ideals and values. By far the most common response among them was simply to accept the conventional values of society uncritically and without question. Many were committed as individuals to humane and democratic ideals derived from religious and cultural sources they were no longer able or willing to recognize, ideals for which they would have found it difficult to provide a rational evaluation and defense had they been asked. The alleged neutrality of social-science research did not raise for these social scientists any disturbing questions about the traditional ideals of American life that they took on

[81]Bronislaw Malinowski, "Anthropology," *Encyclopaedia Britannica*, 13th ed., suppl. I (Chicago: Encyclopaedia Britannica, Inc., 1926).

[82]Sociology has continued to produce at least a minority of important scholars who have continued to raise ethical, normative questions from within and about sociology itself. One thinks of a line running through Albion Small, Robert Lynd, Robert McIver, Pitirim Sorokin, Gunnar Myrdal, C. Wright Mills, Alvin Gouldner, Peter Berger, and Robert Bellah.

[83]Purcell, *The Crisis of Democratic Theory*, pp. 44–45.

faith. Another position that usually went hand in hand with the first was to continue to view science itself as by nature progressive, and as leading irresistibly toward a more harmonious and humane social order. As with the first position, however, scientists would have been hard-pressed to give a justification for this faith that would have satisfied their canons of objective, scientific knowledge. Nor was there any contradiction between these attitudes and the determination of many social scientists to concentrate, in what was thought to be the manner and the key to the success of the physical sciences, on developing the methodology of their discipline, ignoring any substantive and normative questions about its meaning and application.

Appealing directly to the physical sciences as his model, the social scientist George A. Lundberg said in 1929:

> It is not the business of a chemist who invents a high explosive to be influenced in his task by considerations as to whether his product will be used to blow up cathedrals or to build tunnels through the mountains. Nor is it the business of the social scientist in arriving at laws of group behavior to permit himself to be influenced by considerations of how his conclusions will coincide with existing notions, or what the effect of his findings on the social order will be.[84]

The putative value-neutrality of the social sciences allowed the scholar to hold to his own value preferences uncritically, and, at the same time, absolved him of any responsibility for the uses others might make of his research results.

It was within this larger intellectual context that, beginning in the late 1920s and becoming fully manifest in the 1930s, major shifts in the field of ethics occurred. Ethics, however, took much longer than did the social sciences to reflect the pervasive influence of scientific ways of knowing. One reason for this was the lingering strength in American philosophy of late nineteenth- and early twentieth-century idealism, not only within philosophy departments, but among the informed public as well.[85] Common to almost all forms of idealism, both popular and professional, was a threefold conviction that mind is the fundamental reality, that ideas, therefore, are in some ways as real or more real than the objective world, and that a community of thought joins the individual, society, and nature. Although idealism appeared to provide a solid epistemological ground for ethical evaluations and judgments, it was unable to withstand the new intellectual pressures.

In the first place, idealism tended all too often in practice to become a form of subjective idealism in which ideas and ideals served not so much to change reality as to justify and sanction it. This made idealism especially vul-

---

[84]G. A. Lundberg, R. Bain, and S. Anderson, eds., *Trends in American Sociology*, 1929, quoted in Robert K. Merton, *Social Theory and Social Structure* (Glenco, Ill.: The Free Press of Glencoe, 1963), p. 543.

[85]On the many schools of idealistic philosophy that flourished in America during the early twentieth century, see Herbert W. Schneider, *A History of American Philosophy* (New York: Columbia University Press, 1946), pp. 454–496.

nerable to those functionalist interpretations of the social sciences that viewed ideas and values as mere rationales for subjective preferences and group interests. In the second place, idealism had real difficulty in finding an adequate place within its outlook for the biological and psychological elements of human behavior that science was uncovering. In the third place, idealism stressed community of thought and culture precisely at a moment when the culture of learning was fragmenting, and scholars, including, ironically, idealistic philosophers themselves, were enjoying the protective boundaries of disciplinary compartmentalization. Finally, idealism was linked with the values and purposes of the humanities at a time when the prestige of the humanities was in decline. Throughout the 1920s and into the 1930s idealism still exerted a strong influence on the teaching of ethics, but this situation was rapidly to change.

For a time, so-called philosophic naturalism, represented preeminently by John Dewey, offered another possible direction for ethics to take. Throughout his long life, whether he was dealing with political and social philosophy, education, aesthetics, logic, or with ethics itself, Dewey returned again and again to questions of morality and value. Dewey insisted that there exists an integral, inseparable relationship between knowledge and action, research and its consequences, science and ethics, the natural world and human values. Dewey preserved the moral idealism, reform orientation, and synoptic vision of the earlier social science, but attempted to bring these, shorn of their metaphysical overtones, into conjunction with modern science and the problems of the modern world. "Moral science," Dewey said, "is not something with a separate province. It is physical, biological, and historic knowledge placed in a human context where it will illuminate and guide the activities of men."[86]

Because Dewey himself has frequently been portrayed as an uncritical champion of modern science, a brief closer look at Dewey's understanding of the relationship between science and ethics is in order. It is true that Dewey usually spoke of science as synonomous with organized intelligence, and throughout his life urged this conception of science as the model for all thinking. But there was another side to his thought that was critical of modern science. Because Dewey himself never fully developed this aspect of his thought, it has been frequently overlooked, and Dewey cannot be held blameless for often being regarded as an unquestioning defender of modern science. A look at this other, somewhat furtive strain in Dewey's thinking may help to throw light not only on why Dewey's naturalistic ethics did not find wider acceptance, but also on why ethical theory and teaching took the turn they did. If it seems that inordinate attention is given to Dewey here, it is because Dewey's work, perhaps more than that of any other, helps bring into sharp focus some of the

---

[86]John Dewey, *The Quest for Certainty*, 1929, quoted in Mary Warnock, *Ethics Since 1900* (London: Oxford University Press, 1960), p. 77.

central problems that have been involved in the study and teaching of ethics in the modern world.

Central to Dewey's writing was his concern to overcome the widening gap between scientific knowledge and morality. "Certainly," he wrote, "one of the most genuine problems of modern life is the reconciliation of the scientific view of the universe with the claims of the moral life."[87] The split had arisen, Dewey was convinced, because, on the one hand, ethics had failed to keep pace with the advances of physical science and its technological applications, and, on the other hand, because science often was improperly conceived and practiced. Dewey devoted much of his writing to showing the correct view of science that he thought was demanded by an understanding of the relational character of experience.

Dewey's understanding of the interconnectedness of all experience— reflected in those key phrases, "interaction," "transaction," and "community," that are hallmarks of his work—ran counter to many assumptions held by scientists and social scientists. In the first place, it denied the subject–object dichotomy that positivistic science took for granted. From Dewey's standpoint, there was no place for the notion of a detached onlooker coolly observing the world and serving up the facts about it with neither he nor they being affected in the process. Furthermore, it challenged the assumption that an adequate understanding of complex phenomena is to be attained by reducing them analytically to their parts, rather than seeing that they can only be understood with reference to the whole. Finally, a relational view of the world brought to light the importance of the initially noncognitive as an essential element in experience and a potential source of genuine knowledge. Here Dewey was attacking the fundamental problem posed to ethics by an atomistic, positivistic science. He was attempting to establish that qualities and ideals could be given a status in knowledge fully as solid as that enjoyed by the numbers, measurements, and energies of physical science. Failure to recognize that the initially noncognitive can in itself be a source of genuine knowledge was a primary reason, Dewey felt, why every form of knowledge except scientific knowledge is constantly on the defensive. In his writings in the 1930s, he began to make this position explicit. "It tends to be assumed," he wrote, "that because qualities that figure in poetical discourse and those that are central in friendship do not figure in scientific enquiry they have no reality, at least not the kind of unquestionable reality attributed to the mathematical, mechanical, or magneto-electric properties that constitute matter." And, again: "That esthetic and moral experience reveal traits of real things as truly as does intellectual experience, that poetry may have a metaphysical import as well as science, is rarely affirmed."[88] In this view, ideals

---

[87]John Dewey, *Philosophy and Civilization* (New York: Capricorn Books, 1963), p. 43.
[88]John Dewey, *Experience and Nature* (London: George Allen & Unwin, Ltd, 1929), p. 19.

need not, indeed, must not, be regarded as mere epiphenomena of material processes.

It is not often pointed out how disturbed Dewey seemed to be at times about the way science was actually conceived and practiced. For there to be a unity of science and ethics, science could not, in Dewey's view, be too far removed from everyday, common experience. And yet science seemed in actual fact to be moving farther and farther away. As a consequence, Dewey criticized what he considered to be misinterpretations of scientific concepts, and even began in the 1930s to argue on occasion for a fundamental reconception and reorientation of science itself.

Although Dewey had great appreciation for the abstractive power of science, he warned against what he called "the fallacy of selective emphasis," his version of Whitehead's "fallacy of misplaced concreteness." The "fallacy of selective emphasis" is committed whenever scientific concepts, which, for Dewey, are properly only instruments of control, are identified with reality itself.[89] Mistaking the concepts of science for something actually in nature, or, worse, making them into a general world picture, Dewey argued, had disastrous consequences. "Since all value traits are lacking in objects as science presents them," he explained, "it is assumed that *Reality* has not such characteristics."[90] In place of a living, multileveled, complex world, there is substituted one which, by definition, has no place for enjoyment, purpose, creativity, meaning, or moral striving. By introducing the kind of simplification that has proven so effective for science into social and moral subjects, Dewey warned, "We eliminate the distinctively human factors—reduction to the physical ensues."[91] Dewey was very clear: science has its own proper but limited domain, within which its power is second to none; extended beyond, unintentionally or by design, it lays waste.

Strictures against "the fallacy of selective emphasis," however, were not enough. Dewey began to sense that not all conceptions of science were compatible with his own point of view. When he contemplated the highly abstract and arcane character of most actual natural science, he became uncomfortable. He recognized the procedural necessity for abstraction, but he was suspicious of its remoteness from common experience. Dewey considered the distinction between pure science and applied science to be artificial and pernicious in its consequences. It fostered an esoteric knowledge inaccessible to the public and controlled by an elite few, who because of the actual connection between science and technology threatened to become not merely an intellectual elite, but a power elite also.[92] Furthermore, the undemocratic tendencies of abstract sci-

---

[89]Ibid., pp. 25–28.
[90]Dewey, *The Quest for Certainty*, p. 137.
[91]Ibid., p. 216.
[92]John Dewey, *The Public and Its Problems* (Chicago: The Swallow Press, Inc., 1927), pp. 173–178, 208.

ence were not its only danger. It threatened also to alienate man from his own true nature. Science divorced from the common experience, from "the primacy and ultimacy of the material of ordinary experience," creates "a world of things indifferent to human interests."[93] To avoid the alienating tendencies of modern abstract science, Dewey began to edge toward a reconception of science that would keep it connected with human interests and the qualities of everyday experience.

When Dewey began to think in this way, he took as his model for the scientist, not the mathematician and logician, but the old craftsman, the artisan, and "the intelligent mechanic."[94] The scientist as craftsman, as artisan, deals with problems that arise out of everyday experience. He produces knowledge that feeds back into the life of the community, and is accessible to its control. His is a knowing by doing. This was all strictly in keeping with Dewey's pragmatic, instrumentalist conception of the relation between knowing and action, and it preserved the unity of knowledge; but it was not modern science. It is revealing that Dewey was emphasizing a practical, workshop notion of science precisely when scientists were actually ascending to ever higher and more rarified levels of abstraction. It was in this latter direction, not Dewey's, that ethics would follow.

During the 1930s, just as Dewey was broadening his explorations of the relationships between empirical knowledge and ethics, the movement of thought known as logical positivism began to exert a strong influence on American philosophy. Although on the surface the positivists appeared to have much in common with Dewey, they constituted in actuality an alternative and a direct challenge to Dewey and other naturalists like him. Their influence was to give a decisive new direction to ethical theory, and, with it, to the teaching of ethics. Whereas Dewey had begun to search for a redefinition of science in order to find support in it for his conception of ethics, the logical positivists accepted fully the outlook and canons of modern science, and undertook instead to redefine ethics.

Logical positivism increasingly became a force in American intellectual life through the work of a number of European thinkers who, originally concentrated in Vienna, began during the 1930s to assume university positions in the United States. Taking its leads directly from science, logical positivism accepted both the scientific emphasis on empirical data that naturalists like Dewey also prized, but at the same time emphasized the abstract logic of science that Dewey was beginning to find objectionable. Furthermore, they categorically rejected any form of ethical naturalism, such as Dewey's, that posited an inseparable connection between descriptions of the natural world and ethical values.

[93]Ibid.; and Dewey, *Experience and Nature*, pp. 25–28.
[94]Dewey, *Experience and Nature*, pp. 25–28; and John Dewey, *Art as Experience* (New York: Capricorn Books, 1958), pp. 5–6. (originally published 1934)

Two philosophers, G. E. Moore and Ludwig Wittgenstein, whose work the logical positivists drew upon for support, were to assume ever greater importance in twentieth-century ethical thought, and, hence, deserve here at least passing note. In his *Tractatus Logico-Philosophicus*, published in 1922, Wittgenstein, seeking to purify and cleanse language by showing what it can and cannot do, insisted that the chief function of language is to describe the structure of the empirical world, and that any nonempirical, nonverifiable language is nonsense. This the positivists interpreted as bolstering both their own concern with the use of language and their view that only the empirically observable and verifiable is real. Likewise, the earlier work of G. E. Moore was selectively hauled into service to provide backing for the positivists' cause. As with Wittgenstein, the positivists found in Moore an emphasis on clarifying ethical concepts that fitted well with their own preoccupation with the analysis of logic and language. At first glance, however, the substance of Moore's thought might seem to have made him an unlikely source of support for the positivists and those who followed them. In his *Principia Ethica* (1903) Moore had labeled as "the naturalistic fallacy" any attempt to define, describe, or analyze ethical qualities in terms of the properties of characteristics of things in the natural observable world. His purpose in repudiating naturalism was to secure the autonomy of ethics against all efforts to reduce goodness, the chief ethical quality with which he was concerned, to something other than the indefinable, immediately intuited reality he considered the good to be. Moore's own primary intentions, therefore, were quite different from those of the positivists. The latter, however, had only to reject Moore's intuitionism to find in his notion of "the naturalistic fallacy" arguments for their own view not merely that, as Hume had put it, "is" does not imply "ought," but that, more radically, all talk about those nonempirical entities with which the oughts of ethics had traditionally been thought to deal simply had no warrant.[95]

There are, the positivists argued, only two kinds of true or meaningful statement. One kind, exemplified in mathematics and logic, is true by definition

---

[95] It may be worth observing that those who drew most on Wittgenstein and Moore, the positivists and the analysts who succeeded them, seem to have been able to do so only by bypassing or misinterpreting central elements in both. Wittgenstein appears not only to have changed his mind about the primary function of language as set forth in the *Tractatus*, but also, from the very beginning, to have repudiated both logical positivism and linguistic philosophy. Only temerity would lead one to pronounce unhesitatingly on the true interpretation of Wittgenstein, around whose work an enormous literature of comment has grown. The bibliography of K. T. Fann's book on him, for example, is 65 pages long. "I must confess," Professor G. E. M. Anscombe, one of his students, has written, "that I feel deeply suspicious of anyone's claim to have understood Wittgenstein. That is perhaps because, although I had a strong and deep affection for him, and, I suppose, knew him very well, I am very sure that I did not understand him." K. T. Fann, *Wittgenstein's Conception of Philosophy* (Oxford: Blackwell, 1969); Paul Engelmann, *Letters from Wittgenstein with a Memoir* (Oxford: Blackwell, 1967). On the highly selective use of Moore by the analysts who have claimed him as one of their own, see Warnock, *Ethics Since 1900*.

and logical deduction, but has no necessary connection with the empirical world. The other kind of meaningful statement is that which can be tested by experiment and verified by sense experience. From the point of view of their radical empiricism, all metaphysical, religious, poetic, and ethical concepts that are incapable of scientific verification were clearly meaningless. In the phrase of A. J. Ayer, whose 1935 book, *Language, Truth, and Logic,* was perhaps more influential than any other in setting forth most starkly the implications of logical positivism for ethics, ethical statements were "pseudoconcepts"; they had no cognitive significance. Ethical statements served at most to express or arouse emotions of approval or disapproval.[96]

Presented at first iconoclastically and in mere outline by such spokesmen as Ayer, this emotive theory of ethics, as it came to be called, came under immediate attack from critics. Nevertheless, its influence grew. Probably the most important representative of the emotive theory in American philosophy has been Charles L. Stevenson. In articles published in the late 1930s and then in 1945 in a book, *Ethics and Language,* which has been dubbed "the bible of emotive theory," Stevenson made refinements and distinctions that produced a much more complex and sophisticated version of the emotive theory than had hitherto existed.[97] Perhaps Stevenson's main difference, among several, from earlier emotivists was his insistence that the central function of ethics was not so much to express emotions as to influence other people. At bottom, however, ethical judgments rested as much for Stevenson as for other positivists on subjective feelings and attitudes. In the final analysis, ethical statements were subjectivistic, relativistic, and ultimately arbitrary, because they could not be rationally validated or justified, only asserted.

Although the emotive theory as formulated by Stevenson was quickly subjected to criticism, its influence helped to give a decisive new direction to ethical theory, and eventually to the teaching of ethics. With the positivists and the emotivists there came a shift toward an increasing emphasis on the analysis of ethical terms and their meanings, and a diminishing attention to normative questions and practical problems. For the emotivist, the main task of the ethicist was to analyze the terms and "pseudoconcepts" of ethics to show that they had no connection with science, and to uncover the real psychological and sociological meanings hidden within them. Although by the mid-1950s there seem to have been few proponents of a pure emotive theory, linguistic analysis had become a dominant concern in ethics. Increasingly the term metaethics, as contrasted with normative ethics, came to be used to describe the central task of ethics as one of analyzing the meanings of ethical terms and judgments and their justification.[98]

[96] A. J. Ayer, *Language, Truth, and Logic* (London: Victor Gollanez, 1936).
[97] See Charles L. Stevenson *Ethics and Language* (New Haven: Yale University Press, 1944); and Warnock, *Ethics Since 1900,* p. 75.
[98] For a comprehensive definition of metaethics, see Roger N. Hancock, *Twentieth Century Ethics* (New York: Columbia University Press, 1974), p. 2.

By baldly denying the rationality of ethical statements, the positivists and emotivists had laid down a challenge and set the agenda of subsequent ethical inquiry. If the emotivists were not correct, how and in what way could ethical judgments in fact be said to have a rationality and integrity in their own right? This substantive problem, as much as the awareness that, as the emotivists had indeed demonstrated, many terms in ethics are often employed indiscriminately and with careless disregard of their precise meaning, helps account for the increasing emphasis among all those who followed them on analysis and metaethics. If only the language of ethical discourse could be clarified, so the hope seemed to be, the true subject matter and rational standing of ethics would finally emerge.

What was the impact of all this on the actual teaching of ethics? Evidence, such as class notes, course syllabi, and reading lists, that might shed light on what was in fact taking place in classrooms is hard to come by. Again, however, textbooks may at least provide some clues. A glance at textbooks indicates that throughout the 1940s–1960s the actual teaching was probably much broader and more eclectic than a history of main currents of ethical theory might suggest.[99] No one system or outlook dominated the scene. The emotive theory was

[99]My comments on the teaching of ethics from roughly World War II through the mid-1960s are based on a survey of topics dealt with in a random sampling of popular texts and readers. These include: 1940–1959: Charles A. Baylis, *Ethics and the Principles of Wise Choice* (New York: Henry Holt & Co., 1958); Richard Brandt, *Ethical Theory* (Englewood Cliffs, N.J.: Prentice-Hall, 1959); A. C. Ewing, *The Definition of Good* (New York: The Macmillan Co., 1947); Stuart Hampshire, *Thought and Action* (London: Chatto & Windus, 1959); R. M. Hare, *The Language of Morals* (Oxford: Clarendon Press, 1952); Oliver Johnson, ed., *Ethics* (New York: Dryden Press, 1958); C. I. Lewis, *Knowledge and Valuation* (La Salle, Ill.: Open Court, 1946); Wayne A. R. Leys, *Ethics and Social Policy* (New York: Prentice-Hall, 1941); A. I. Melden, ed., *Ethical Theories: A Book of Readings* (New York: Prentice-Hall, 1950); A. I. Melden, ed., *Essays in Moral Philosophy* (Seattle: University of Washington Press, 1958); Edwin T. Mitchell, *A System of Ethics* (New York: Charles Scribner's Sons, 1950); Alan Montefiore, ed., *A Modern Introduction of Moral Philosophy* (London: Routledge & Kegan Paul, 1958); P. H. Nowell-Smith, *Ethics* (Baltimore: Penguin Books, 1954); Charles H. Patterson, *Moral Standards: An Introduction to Ethics* (New York: Ronald Press, 1952); William Henry Roberts, *The Problem of Choice: An Introduction to Ethics* (Boston: Ginn & Company, 1941); Wilfred Sellars and John Hospers, *Readings in Ethical Theory* (New York: Appleton-Century-Crofts, 1952); Charles L. Stevenson, *Ethics and Language;* Harold H. Titus, *Ethics for Today* (New York: American Book Company, 1947, 2nd ed.; 1st ed. 1936); Stephen E. Toulmin, *An Examination of the Place of Reason in Ethics* (New York: Cambridge University Press, 1950); and Philip Wheelwright, *A Critical Introduction to Ethics* (New York: The Odyssey Press, 1949, rev. ed.; 1st ed. 1935. For the years 1960–1969: Raziel Abelson, *Ethics and Metaethics* (New York: St. Martin's Press, 1963); Robert E. Dewey et al., eds., *Problems of Ethics* (New York: The Macmillan Co., 1961); Joel Feinberg, ed., *Moral Concepts* (London: Oxford University Press, 1969); Phillipa Foot, ed., *Theories of Ethics* (London: Oxford University Press, 1962); Harry K. Girvetz, ed., *Contemporary Moral Issues* (Belmont, Calif.: Wadsworth, 1963); Thomas English Hill, *Contemporary Ethical Theories* (New York: The Macmillan Co., 1960; 1st ed., 1950); John Hospers, *Human Conduct: An Introduction to the Problems of Ethics* (New York: Harcourt, Brace & World, 1961); W. T. Jones et al., eds., *Approaches to Ethics* (New

discussed, evaluated, and criticized as one highly influential outlook among others. Much attention, however, was also being given to existentialism in its various forms, and the writings especially of Sartre, Heidegger, and Kierkegaard stirred new excitement. At the same time, the more traditional theories and positions of an older generation of American philosophers—the intuitionism of a Wilbur Marshall Urban, the idealism of a William Ernest Hocking, the naturalism of a John Dewey—were still represented, along with linguistic analysis and the newer religious and existentialist ethics. Moreover, the perennial problems of ethics, for example, the controversy concerning free will and determinism, the issue of ethical relativism, particularly as this had been raised by anthropologists and social psychologists, and the problems of social ethics, all continued to receive attention.

Striking in the texts is the prominence given throughout the 1940s and 1950s to normative ethics and practical problems. Along with the attention devoted to theoretical ethics, the texts dealt with such topics as "the nature of capitalism and business ethics," "the ethics of physical and mental health," "professional ethics," "ethics and the media of communication," "morality and race relations," "marriage and the home," "religion and ethics," "education and ethics," and others. Most of the textbooks were still marked by a concern, as one author said, "to deal with the actual problems which men and women face in the world today," and by a conviction that the study of ethics will be of value to students in their later lives, to enable them, as another author put it, "to live at their best in a society of free men and women."[100] Some authors continued to express the hope that they were writing, not for a small professional group, or even for college students, but for the general educated public.[101] The eclectic nature of the texts and the range of topics they covered should caution against making simple generalizations about the dominance of one viewpoint or approach in the teaching of ethics during the decades of the 1940s and 1950s. Nevertheless, despite the hopes and pieties of textbook authors, the trend toward an ever more exclusive emphasis on analysis, metaethics, and curriculum isolation was continuing, and would become fully apparent during the turbulent decade of the 1960s.

York: McGraw-Hill, 1962); Joseph Katz et al., eds., *Writers on Ethics* (Princeton: N.J.: D. Van Nostrand, 1962); Joseph Margolis, ed., *Contemporary Ethical Theory* (New York: Random House, 1966); Milton K. Munitz, *A Modern Introduction to Ethics* (Glencoe, Ill.: The Free Press of Glencoe, 1961, 2nd printing; 1958, 1st printing); Andrew Oldenquist, ed., *Readings in Moral Philosophy* (Boston: Houghton Mifflin, 1965); Evelyn Shirk, *The Ethical Dimension* (New York: Appleton-Century-Crofts, 1965); Paul Taylor, ed., *The Moral Judgment* (Englewood Cliffs, N.J.: Prentice-Hall, 1963); Judith J. Thompson and Gerald Dworkin, eds., *Ethics* (New York: Harper & Row, 1968); and W. H. Werkmeister, *Theories of Ethics: A Study of Moral Obligation* (Lincoln, Neb.: Johnson Publishing Company, 1961).

[100]Titus, *Ethics for Today*, p. v; and Patterson, *Moral Standards*, p. v.

[101]Patterson, *Moral Standards*, p. vii; and Hill, *Contemporary Ethical Theories*, p. vii.

By 1965, three tendencies in ethics, each directly affecting teaching, were clearly apparent. First, the central theoretical task of ethics remained that of discovering some rational grounding for morality. Or, to use an older formulation with which the newer theorists, to be sure, would not have felt fully comfortable, the task still remained that of trying to establish and secure "the place of value in a world of fact." In this effort, the work of British ethicists—such persons as R. M. Hare, Stephen Toulmin, P. H. Nowell-Smith, Philippa Foot, Stuart Hampshire—had become highly influential.[102] The positivist and emotivist positions, if they had not been entirely discredited, no longer threatened to hold the field. Analysis remained the main preoccupation of the philosophers, nevertheless, and the names of Moore and Wittgenstein, because of what was taken to be their pioneering work in the analysis of language, were prominent as seldom before.[103] The emphasis of the new analysts, however, had shifted increasingly from the analysis of the meaning of ethical terms to the analysis of the logic and structure of moral reasoning as a whole. Ethics, it was being argued, constitutes a language and meaning structure in its own right, which cannot be determined by or reduced to something else, as the positivists and emotivists had wanted to do. Ethical discourse, they pointed out, is for the purpose of guiding conduct, and close attention to the nature of ethical reasoning, they insisted, disclosed definite rules of procedure that make possible and give direction to moral discussion and activity.

The possibility of showing the existence of such rules of conduct, and of spelling out the criteria by which they were to be properly applied in regulating and justifying moral activity, offered the hope of establishing the autonomy of ethics on a firm foundation all its own. Some of the newer ethicists were also beginning to argue, however, that this could be done without Moore's repudiation of naturalism, and were returning to one key notion of Dewey and other naturalists—that facts and values are related.[104] One of the ways we establish

[102]The development of ethical theory during the past quarter century has been extremely complex, and the distinctions separating one ethicist from another are often drawn exceedingly fine. To help me wend my way through this very intricate thicket, I have relied heavily on Warnock, *Ethics Since 1900;* Olafson, *Ethics and Twentieth Century Thought;* Hancock, *Twentieth Century Ethics;* Razial Abelson and Kai Nielson, "History of Ethics," and Kai Nelson, "Problems of Ethics," in *The Encyclopedia of Philosophy,* vol. 3 (New York: Collier Macmillan, 1967) pp. 81–117, 117–134. William J. Frankena, "Ethical Theory," in Roderick M. Chisholm *et al.,* ed., *Philosophy* (Englewood Cliffs, N.J.: Prentice-Hall, 1964), pp. 345–464; and G. J. Warnock, *Contemporary Moral Philosophy* (New York: St. Martin's Press, 1967).

[103]The posthumous publication of Wittgenstein's *Philosophical Investigations* in 1953 had given a boost to this interest. For some of the newer analysts, Moore's notion of "the naturalistic fallacy," as well as his interest in the analysis of philosophical terms, lent impetus to the growing concentration on metaethics and to the neglect of normative ethics.

[104]For criticisms of antinaturalism from within the analytic perspective, see, for example, Philippa Foot, "Moral Beliefs," *Proceedings of the Aristotelian Society,* 59 (1958–1959), pp. 83–104, reprinted in Philippa Foot, *Theories of Ethics* (New York: Oxford University Press, 1967), pp. 83–100; and Warnock, *Contemporary Moral Philosophy,* pp. 62–72.

the morality of any action, some maintained, is by giving "good reasons" for it, reasons that in part describe the results, the factual outcomes, of that action. The emphasis on rules of procedure and on the need to justify moral statements and actions with persuasive reasons also underscored the social and public character of ethics in a way that had been lost to the positivists and emotivists.

And yet, there were those who were unconvinced that the new analysis had really achieved what it had claimed, that is, rescued ethics from positivism. Deriving rules of moral conduct from the internal logic of language systems peculiar to some existing community of discourse seemed to some critics to suggest that the analysts had at best succeeded in grounding ethics only in social and institutional convention. And why in the end an appeal to the mores and rules of conduct of a particular moral community should be any less arbitrary and subjective than the cruder formulations of the emotivists was not entirely clear. Moreover, the inability or reluctance of ethicists even to talk about the ultimate reality or nonreality of moral qualities or value properties—much in the manner that natural science extruded such qualities from its purview—suggested to some that the ethicists had after all still not overcome the separation between fact and value. Scientific naturalism continued, as it had throughout the century, to cast a shadow over the ethical enterprise. Despite the increasing sophistication and the refinements made in ethical theory, deep uncertainty about the actual status of ethics prevailed.[105]

Second, consequently ethics had become dominated by a concern with metaethics to such an extent that both normative questions and concrete problems were almost totally ignored. Textbooks and anthologies, though giving customary coverage to the traditional schools of thought, the great thinkers, and the perennial problems, approached even these more and more from the perspective of analysis and theory. Ethics was increasingly presented as a self-contained field of study with but a tangential connection with other disciplines and practical issues. Social thought and the concrete social problems of the earlier textbooks, when they did not disappear altogether, were treated primarily as material for metaethical analysis.[106] In 1964, William Frankena wrote that

---

[105]Types of criticism of the ethical theory of the 1950s and 1960s may be found in Olafson, *Ethics and Twentieth Century Thought, passim,* esp. pp. 23–24; more specifically from within the analytic tradition in Warnock, *Contemporary Moral Philosophy,* from a naturalist point of view in *Hancock, Twentieth Century Ethics.* pp. 87–163; and from a metaphysical position in Henry B. Veatch, *For an Ontology of Morals* (Evanston, Ill.: Northwestern University Press, 1971), pp. 19–56.

[106]For a more detailed discussion of recent ethics textbooks and pedagogical trends, which also notes the exceptional texts of the period, see Jim Giarelli, "Primers in Ethics: Reflections on a Changing Field" (Paper presented at the meeting of the Southeastern Philosophy of Education Society, Atlanta, February, 1977). Unfortunately, Professor Giarelli's paper came to my attention after my study was complete, but I have drawn on it to the extent that this has been possible. I think that I am correct in finding substantial agreement in our conclusions regarding the texts of the sixties.

> American philosophers have been relatively unpreoccupied in their official capac-
> ities with the practical and cultural problems of the day, a fact that has often
> disturbed their readers, as well as some of their own number. . . . They have usually
> contented themselves with offering general principles for the solution of such
> problems, and a very influential school of thinkers has disowned even the respon-
> sibility of doing this.[107]

For some this was a regrettable but unavoidable state of affairs. Only a few
years after Frankena's observations, Kai Nielson noted that

> It is felt by many philosophers that the logical status of moral utterances and the
> nature of moral reasoning are so unclear that we cannot profitably do normative
> ethics until we have a far more adequate metaethics than we have at present.
> Because of such convictions, a central and pervasive question in metaethics is
> whether a normative ethics is possible.[108]

Others were quite willing to make a virtue of the situation by affirming that the
sole task of philosophy is analysis, and that this is quite enough. As one philosopher said, for example, in introducing his own textbook of readings in ethics
for college students, one of the few that did, in fact, attempt to relate metaethics
to normative and practical issues, "Philosophy is not practical wisdom. . . . At its
best, it can improve the clarity of our thought and the consistency of our reasoning—and this is a great deal."[109]

    Third, ethics had become more isolated than ever within the college cur-
riculum. This was not a new situation, but one that was exacerbated by the two
characteristics of ethics that have just been examined. It is probably worth pointing out that the emphasis on analysis and metaethics fitted well with a certain
conception of professionalization that would make disciplinary boundaries
watertight by focusing primarily on methodological problems and concerns.[110]
Be this as it may, ethics had become increasingly a subject that would appeal
mainly to philosophy majors and the occasional stray student from other fields
seeking to fulfill a humanities requirement. Small liberal arts colleges, which
usually had resources for only one general ethics course, and, perhaps, a seminar
for majors, were, ironically, probably worse off in this regard than the larger
universities, which could offer a richer spread of courses. Among the several
courses a large university was capable of providing were some that would deal

[107]Frankena, "Ethical Theory," pp. 437–438.
[108]Nielson, "Problems of Ethics," p. 119.
[109]Abelson, *Ethics and Metaethics,* p. vii.
[110]The propensity of philosophers during this period to speak mainly to one another and to
worry little about the wider consequences and applications of their work has frequently been
explained as the result of a heightened guild mentality within academia. Whatever truth there
may or may not be to this charge, it should be remembered that in the case of ethics, as with
the social sciences as we have seen earlier, what may appear as professionalization is inseparable from the conception and focus of the discipline itself. The substance of philosophy and
the structure of the profession have gone hand in hand, and an enquiry into the one must
entail a looking into the other as well.

with social problems and social theory in ways that would certainly raise broad ethical questions, although they were not offered specifically as ethics courses. Amherst, for example, in the mid-1960s offered one ethics course in its philosophy department as an elective for sophomores.[111] The philosophy department of the University of Wisconsin, on the other hand, provided three ethics courses as such, the additional courses "Introduction to Social Philosophy," "Man, Religion, and Society," and "Social Philosophy of John Dewey," and also a course that had been a regular offering of the department for a decade, the "Social Problems of Contemporary Art," which examined such ethical issues as censorship, freedom, and the social uses of art.[112] Nevertheless, regardless of how broadly the ethics course might be defined, within the overall college curriculum the study of ethics was for the few.

A 1964 article presenting a sampling of 100 college and university catalogs—representing institutions of all types, large and small, public and private, religious and secular—found that only 27 institutions "required any philosophy at all for graduation with the bachelor of arts degree." And ethics was only one among several fields within philosophy itself. The author of that study noted that in his own institution of 12,000 students the enrollment in ethics averaged 11 students per year.[113] His institution was probably fairly representative. By the mid-1960s the teaching of ethics was in deep trouble.

Generalizations about a period as recent as the last two or three decades must be offered tentatively, and in the awareness that we may still be too close to judge in proper perspective. Two final observations about the period just examined are, therefore, in order. In the first place, it could be argued that, in devoting themselves to metaethics, the philosophers were in a real sense dealing with the most practical problem of all, the intellectual difficulties that had made the theoretical foundations of all ethics so uncertain in the twentieth century. The question was whether metaethics as it was conceived was helping to reduce or to make worse that uncertainty. At the same time, developments in ethical theory, and their implications for teaching, were not static. We have depicted the fifties and sixties with broad strokes of the brush, highlighting major trends characteristic of the period, but by necessity ignoring hints of possible new departures, including some within the analytic school itself.[114] We will return to some of these that appear to have surfaced in the seventies in the concluding pages.

[111]Amherst College, *Catalogue*, 1965–1966. Amherst also offered one ethics course at this time in the religion department.
[112]University of Wisconsin, *Catalogue*, 1964–1965, pp. 260–265. This course was still being offered ten years later. *Catalogue*, 1972–1974.
[113]George Henry Moulds, "The Decline and Fall of Philosophy," *Liberal Education*, 50 (1964), pp. 360–361.
[114]To an historian writing in the year 2000, it may be precisely these, or, to us still more hidden aspects of the sixties, that will emerge as the most important marks of the period.

The Teaching of Ethics in the Larger Curriculum

Professional ethicists have not been the only persons in twentieth-century American higher education concerned with the teaching of ethics, nor has this teaching been the sole province of departments of philosophy. A full study of the teaching of ethics in the undergraduate curriculum, for example, would have to examine the continuing efforts to raise ethical issues in traditional humanities courses and in the social sciences. How often have students, for instance, enrolled in psychology—or literature, or history, or political science and government—courses, in hopes, of which they have been perhaps only half conscious, of finding there some enlightenment or guidance for pressing personal and social problems? To what extent have these disciplines addressed, bypassed, or suppressed these needs? Another area requiring further inquiry has to do with the ways in which ethics instruction has figured in undergraduate professional and vocational curricula. Have the "foundations" courses in undergraduate education programs, for example, or the "business and society" courses for undergraduate business majors, served in reality as forms of required moral philosophy courses? To deal with these intriguing areas and questions adequately would require a more extensive study than, unfortunately, is possible here, but to point to them may at least help to indicate the presence of the ethical dimension, even when ignored, throughout the undergraduate curriculum.

There have been other areas, however, that have been consciously and directly concerned with the teaching of ethics. Spokesmen for the variety of curricular reform described under the heading of general education have almost all viewed moral education as one of the prime purposes of undergraduate instruction. And some of the most lively teaching of ethics, at least since World War II, has taken place within departments of religions. Both, therefore, warrant a brief look.

The General Education Movement

General education has represented in part a reassertion of the older liberal arts tradition that the teaching of ethics should properly be the responsibility not merely of a single course or department but of the entire institution of higher education and its curriculum. General education, however, has always been something of a rearguard action to keep alive the liberal arts within hostile or indifferent circumstances, and has had by necessity to exist as a compromise—and often compromised—movement. Consequently, it has been made to serve many purposes, not all of them compatible with one another. At its strongest and most vital, general education has presupposed that ethical concerns lie at the heart of the educational task, and that the moral uses of knowledge and the integration of knowledge are intimately connected. In its weaker times, general education has sunk to being little more than an administrative and rhetorical device for putting some order into a curriculum that has gotten entirely out of hand. Not surprisingly, general education has frequently found itself under fire from two sides: on the one, from reformers who feel that it makes too many concessions to traditional academic departments; on the other, from specialists who disdain it for being superficial. Yet, despite its weaknesses, general education has been a source of some of the most interesting critiques and reform proposals in modern American higher education.

Early in the century a variety of attempts began to be made to stem the splintering of the curriculum that the elective principle and intensive specialization had produced. By the late 1930s, virtually every type of curricular reform that has been attempted in the twentieth century had in one form or another made its appearance. There were first the introduction and adoption by most colleges and universities of the concentration and distribution system, and the spread of the popular but frequently criticized survey and orientation courses. Then, during the twenties and thirties, there began those experiments that made up what has been known as "the general education movement" itself: the founding of new experimental colleges—Bennington, Sarah Lawrence, the new program at St. John's at Annapolis, the major curriculur reorganizations of Columbia, the University of Chicago, and Reed College, and the organization of entirely new units within existing institutions, as with the General College of the University of Minnesota, the General College of Boston University, and the Experimental College at the University of Wisconsin, among others.[115]

The foundation on which general education was based varied considerably among the different institutions: the two-year Contemporary Civilization and Humanities sequence at Columbia, the lower-college prescribed courses in the humanities and the natural, physical, and social sciences at the University of Chicago under President Robert Hutchins, the arts curriculum at Bennington, the ill-fated but imaginative two-year reading and group discussion program led by Alexander Meiklejohn at the Experimental College of the University of Wisconsin, based on an intensive study of Greek culture in the freshmen year and contemporary culture in the sophomore year, and the so-called Great Books Program at St. John's College in Annapolis. Despite such differences, however, the major advocates of these experiments all indicated that their central concern was moral education, the turning out of persons with the breadth of knowledge, intellectual discipline, and ethical sensitivity needed to grapple with the personal and social problems of the modern world. Looking back many years later, Harry

---

[115]Excellent accounts of the broad history of general education may be found in Russell Thomas, *The Search for a Common Learning: General Education, 1800–1960* (New York: McGraw-Hill, 1962); Daniel Bell, *The Reforming of General Education: The Columbia College Experience in Its National Setting* (New York: Columbia University Press, 1966); and Earl J. McGrath, *General Education and the Plight of Modern Man* (Indianapolis: The Lilly Endowment, Inc., n.d.).

Carman described the motives that had led him and a group of young faculty members at Columbia University in 1917 to convert the course, "Issues of the War," begun to acquaint students with the causes and purposes of the war, to a "peace issues" course which as "Contemporary Civilization" laid the basis for the development of Columbia's full-scale general education program over the next three decades. "The college, we agreed," wrote Carman,

> should be concerned with education for effective citizenship in a democratic society: citizens with broad perspective and a critical and constructive approach to life, who are concerned about values in terms of integrity of character, motives, attitudes, and excellence of behavior; citizens who have the ability to think, to communicate, to make intelligent and wise judgments, to evaluate moral situations, and to work effectively to good ends with others.[116]

This was the theme that in various formulations was common to all the pioneer experiments in general education.

Lacking, however, was consensus on what should be the integrating principle of the curriculum. In 1922, President Alexander Meiklejohn of Amherst published an article analyzing the tasks and difficulties facing those who would seek a unified curriculum. Meiklejohn, since his inauguration at Amherst in 1912, had been a major voice in criticizing the elective principle and in calling for common purposes in the liberal college; he argued that there could be no genuine unity in the curriculum without an underlying unity of knowledge itself, the very thing that, as yet, no one had been able to supply. He argued that the fragmentation of learning was the result of the overbearing influence of natural science. "First," he said, "it is chiefly Natural Science which is responsible for the opinion that knowledge has no unity. Second, it is chiefly that view which has brought our college teaching into incoherence and confusion."[117] The problem, then, was nothing less than to discover and defend a philosophical foundation for the curriculum that would by definition challenge the very conception of knowledge and knowing dominant in the university. This was general education's most formidable obstacle, and one its proponents have as yet never successively overcome.

By the mid-1930s at least four different positions on the problem had emerged. One was based on course content, and sought to find the unity of the curriculum in the humanities and the humanistically oriented social sciences. This was the solution represented, for example, by the General Education Program at Columbia University. The strength of this position was that, so long as the humanities commanded respect, they could bring to bear on the curriculum the weighty ethical and value heritage of Western civilization. Because the valid-

---

[116]Quoted in McGrath, *General Education*, p. 29. See also James Gutman, "The Pioneers of Columbia's General Education Curriculum," *Columbia College Today;* (1979), pp. 11–13.

[117]Alexander Meiklejohn, "The Unity of the Curriculum," *New Republic* 32 (1922), pt. 2, pp. 2–3; quoted in Thomas, *The Search for a Common Learning*, p. 71.

ity of these values, however, was in the main simply accepted without question, when they were seriously challenged the general education based on them had little defense to fall back upon. Moreover, this conception of general education was to suffer deep erosion as the models for knowing and professionalization within the humanities themselves were increasingly drawn from natural science.

A second position was to locate the integrating principle of the curriculum, not in subject matter or content, but rather in the method to be employed in dealing with significant cultural problems. This was Meiklejohn's own position, and he argued that this method was not the same as the techniques of scholarly research, but rather "a common unspecialized form of study" that cuts across all specialized interests and inquiries and that combines analysis and synthesis, the past and the contemporary, the humanities and science, interpretation and empiricism. Meiklejohn called this form of study "intelligence." The prescribed course at the Experimental College devoted to the study and discussion of significant cultural problems sought to show that "intelligence" in this sense was a reality, and that it provided both the goal and the means of a liberal college education. Meiklejohn's hostility to graduate research, his rejection of the disciplinary classification of knowledge, and his holistic conception of intelligence did not favor widespread acceptance of his position. Nevertheless, Meiklejohn anticipated many reform proposals that were to be made later.[118]

A third position was that taken by Dewey and his followers, which attempted to find the unity of the curriculum in the solution of concrete life problems through the method of science. This bore resemblances to Meiklejohn's outlook, but, unlike his, was, on the one hand, hostile to prescribed courses, and, on the other, more narrowly programmatic in its insistence that the method of intelligence was the method of the natural sciences. If general education be identified, not with a prescribed course of study, but, more accurately, with the attempt to establish a unifying principle and ethical orientation in the curriculum, Dewey clearly was part of the "search for a common learning." As Laurence Veysey has observed, Dewey's approach could be interpreted in two opposite ways, either as favoring a planned program based on "life situations," or as fostering total individual elective freedom—the one leaning toward more prescription than Dewey favored, the other threatening to augment the very fragmentation that Dewey, like others, wanted to overcome.[119] The deeper problems of Dewey's approach we have examined in detail.

The fourth position made metaphysics the basis for an integrated curriculum. In 1936 Robert Hutchins published an essay, *The Higher Learning in*

---

[118]Alexander Meiklejohn, *The Liberal College* (Boston: Marshall Jones, 1920); and Alexander Meiklejohn, *The Experimental College* (New York: Harper & Brothers, 1932). There is an excellent brief discussion of Meiklejohn's experimental curriculum in Laurence Veysey, "Stability and Experiment in the American Undergraduate Curriculum," in Carl Kaysen, ed., *Content and Context: Essays on College Education* (New York: McGraw-Hill, 1973), pp. 54–57.
[119]Veysey, "Stability and Experiment," p. 54.

America, in which he effectively marshalled most of the current criticisms of American higher education, calling it to task for its commercialism, its vocationalism, its curricular confusion, its antiintellectualism, and its ethical relativism. The fundamental problem for Hutchins, however, was the skepticism of scientific naturalism, which made all talk about truth and value impossible. There was little that was radically new in this criticism, although Hutchins had advanced it with much verve and provocation. Where Hutchins did deviate dramatically from others was in saying that only a thoroughgoing metaphysics— and Hutchins embraced the Aristotelian–Thomistic natural-law tradition— could bring order to knowledge, and provide a solid foundation and justification for ethical values.[120]

Hutchins' essay touched off a rarity in the history of American higher education, an intense public dialogue on the purposes and philosophy of education. Hutchins' position was immediately subjected to a many-sided criticism, both from major spokesmen for the university and from John Dewey, who actually agreed with much of Hutchins' diagnosis of the university's ills, but abhorred his recommendation for a remedy. Hutchins' appeal to tradition was condemned as antiquarian and irrelevant to the solution of contemporary problems. His assertion of the existence of a higher, nonempirical level of reality was judged inconceivable by modern canons of knowledge. And, finally, his claim that the problems of the modern university and world could be put right only by a recognition of absolute metaphysical principles was deemed, especially by Dewey and his followers, as authoritarian and reactionary.[121] Whatever the merits or weaknesses of his own solution, Hutchins had forced attention to the central question: How necessary was an integrating principle within the curriculum, and on what grounds could it be established? The outbreak of the war brought the debate to an end as the nation and the universities turned from trying to justify the values of democracy to the more immediate task of defending them. It would be some time before the debate would be resumed.

Just as in World War I "war aims" courses had given an impetus to the beginnings of general education, so also World War II helped touch off a renewed surge of interest in the movement. This time Harvard University took the lead. In 1943, President James Conant of Harvard appointed a committee to study "the objectives for general education in a free society." Two years later the committee issued its report under the title *General Education in a Free*

---

[120]Robert Hutchins, *The Higher Learning in America* (New Haven: Yale University Press, 1936).

[121]In fact, in an increasingly rancorous debate each side succeeded in associating the other with fascism: the scientific naturalists were charged with abetting Hitler because of their ethical relativism; the metaphysicians because of their alleged authoritarianism. See, for example, John Dewey, "President Hutchins' Proposals to Remake Higher Education," *The Social Frontier*, 3 (1937) pp. 103–104; and Mortimer J. Adler, "God and the Professors," in his *Science, Philosophy, and Religion, A Symposium* (New York: n.p., 1941), pp. 120–137.

Society. [122] Reflecting wartime anxiety about the stability of democratic society in the face of fascism and the rising threat of communism, as well as concern about possible postwar social disorientation at home, the report stressed the role of education in the creation of common social values. Foreseeing continual growth and diversification of higher education after the war, the report sought to avoid any further fragmentation of the curriculum and of American cultural values that this might entail.

The aim of general education was viewed primarily as one of training up intelligent and capable citizens committed to the values necessary for a full and responsible participation in democratic society. The integration of the curriculum would center in a combination of the religious and humane values of the Western cultural heritage with the methods of the physical and social sciences taught as the means of implementing those values. Through a program of general and specific courses distributed among the three areas of the natural sciences, the social sciences, and the humanities, general education would prepare students "to think effectively, to communicate thought, to make relevant judgments, to discriminate among values." This was traditional enough, but somewhat unique to the report was the notion that general education must be a continuing ethical education. "Unless," wrote Conant in his preface to the report, "the educational process includes *at each level of maturity* [his italics] some continuing contact with those fields in which value judgments are of prime importance, it must fall far short of the ideal." In other words, general education as the formation of ethical discernment and capacity for action must extend throughout all education and all of life. [123]

For all of its several virtues, *General Education in a Free Society* lacked in important respects the precision and sharp analysis of the problems of moral education that had begun to be evident in the general education programs and debates of the 1930s. The report accepted without question the humane values of Western culture as the center of the curriculum, as though their validity were self-evident and beyond challenge. It assumed equally without question that these given values were fully compatible with the critical methods of modern science and philosophy, and only awaited transmission to the students. "The impulse to rear students to a received idea of the good," read the report, "is in fact necessary to education. It is impossible to escape the realization that our society, like any society, rests on common beliefs, and that a major task of education is to perpetuate them." The report sought to avoid any suggestion of implied indoctrination in such a manner of speaking by invoking the spirit of John Dewey, pragmatism, and scientific experimentation. [124] The report sought

---

[122] *General Education in a Free Society: Report of the Harvard Committee* (Cambridge: Harvard University Press, 1945).

[123] Ibid., pp. vii–ix.

[124] Ibid., pp. 46–47.

an easy and eclectic amalgamation of the traditional and the modern, the humanities and science, the "spiritual" and the "material," the given and the experimental, in the faith that by presenting both together an integral balance between them would of itself be achieved and maintained. This unexamined faith, however, simply meant staving off the hard questions that sooner or later would have to be faced, once the values embodied in the report and the justi-fication for them had been challenged, or, just as fatal to the program, ignored.

The immediate response, however, was a renewed enthusiasm for general education throughout the country. As they spread, general education programs varied considerably from campus to campus. Many were little more than a reshuffling and expansion of previous distribution requirements; some, like the senior seminar and symposia at New College in Florida, Bowdoin College, Macalester, and other institutions, appeared very much like full-fledged modern versions of the old moral philosophy course; others, like those at Columbia, Harvard, and other institutions, attempted to be more thoroughgoing recon-structions of the curriculum.[125] In *The Journal of General Education,* founded in 1946, the movement had its own voice and forum for the exchange of ideas. By 1955, Earl McGrath has observed, probably half the colleges of the nation were experimenting with some form of general education.[126]

The decline of postwar general education, however, was even more rapid than its rise. The erosion of general education began in the late fifties, and within little more than a decade the movement was nearing total collapse.[127] The response to the launching of Sputnik in 1957 brought enormous prestige and funding to scientific and technological research, at the expense of the humani-ties, and encouraged colleges and universities to return to the specialized ori-entation of the old distribution system. That same year a widely discussed, if controversial, study of the influence of college teaching raised serious questions about the very ability of higher education to affect student values in any sub-stantial way whatsoever.

In a broad survey of student attitudes and assumptions, entitled *Changing Values in College: An Exploratory Study of the Impact of College Teaching,* Philip E. Jacob concluded that colleges had little, if any, effect on student values.[128] In ordinary times, the data and conclusions presented by Jacob might well have supplied arguments for the champions of general education. Coming as it did, however, at the height of the postwar general education experimentation, it may—we can only speculate here—very well have taken the heart out of efforts

[125]Macalester College, *Catalogue,* 1953–1955; and Rudolph, *Curriculum,* pp. 248–249.

[126]McGrath, *General Education,* p. 23.

[127]Ibid., pp. 20–49. Earl McGrath documents in detail the erosion of the general education programs at Harvard, Columbia, and Chicago during this period.

[128]Philip E. Jacob, *Changing Values in College: An Exploratory Study of the Impact of College Teaching* (New York: Harper & Brothers, 1957).

to defend the importance of teaching and to resist the resurgence of research specialization and concentration.[129]

The decline of general education, however, would not have been so rapid had not even deeper problems already begun to manifest themselves—problems that cast grave doubt on general education as any kind of effective source for the teaching of ethics and values. First, the essential question of establishing a genuine integrating principle for the curriculum had never been answered, and since World War II had scarcely been addressed. As a result, many of the general education schemes were little better than administrative efforts to balance a variety of competing faculty interests. Second, the lack of such an integrating principle left general education vulnerable to serving simply the distribution needs of the traditional subject-matter disciplines. When this happened, prescribed general education courses were accorded low priority and relegated to graduate teaching assistants, and became merely an ordeal to be endured by students on their way to fulfillment of nonmajor requirements. This was exactly one charge brought against such courses by dissident students and critical faculty during the 1960s.[130] Finally, the deeper philosophical problems that had begun to be raised during the thirties regarding the very possibility and justification of moral education in the university had not been rigorously dealt with within the postwar general education movement. Indeed, it seemed that at times they had been deliberately ignored. As a consequence, although it could still function as a means of softening and mitigating the worst excesses of extreme early specialization, general education had been nearly deprived of its own ultimate justification. In retrospect, it is hardly surprising that the sixties and early seventies witnessed a veritable rush to dismantle prescribed courses and programs of every kind.

Experiments with the undergraduate curriculum continued throughout most of the 1960s, but these were mainly administrative rearrangements of no real consequence.[131] Although he presented a fascinating analysis of higher education, Daniel Bell, in his 1964 effort at Columbia to restate the case for general education, aroused no interest even at his own university. By making methods of disciplinary inquiry the basis for integrating the curriculum—a much different, and narrower, conception of method than that proposed by Meiklejohn and others thirty years earlier—Bell's proposal may have seemed to

[129]For a contemporaneous discussion of Jacob's study, see John E. Smith *Value Convictions and Higher Education* (New Haven: The Edward W. Hazen Foundation, 1958). For discussions on the problems of values in higher education still reflecting the influence of the Jacob study a few years later, see Jack F. Cully, ed., *Contemporary Values and the Responsibility of the College* (Iowa City: State University of Iowa, 1962).

[130]Harold Taylor, *Students Without Teachers; The Crisis in the University* (New York: McGraw-Hill, 1969), pp. 131–163.

[131]Paul L. Dressel and Frances H. DeLisle, *Undergraduate Curriculum Trends* (Washington, D.C.: American Council on Education, 1969).

the traditional advocates of general education like handing them over to their enemies and to the specialized research interests, who were in the ascendent anyway; a bit like carrying coals to Newcastle.[132] "By 1976," Frederick Rudolph has written, "concentration was in charge of the curriculum."[133]

Already the pendulum has swung, and today, once again, there is a resurgence of interest in general education. One expression of this interest appears in the larger context of the kind of concern that motivated Jacob's study, mentioned earlier, regarding the influence of the total college experience on student values. The nineteenth-century conception of "the college as a community" has never entirely disappeared. And recent years have witnessed a mounting number of efforts to take yet another look at the impact of "college life" on students.[134] Some investigators, such as Theodore Newcomb and Kenneth Feldman, have concluded, like Jacobs before them, that, all told, the college has relatively little effect in altering student values; others, such as William Perry, have presented evidence suggesting that the actual and potential impact of the college experience may be very important indeed.[135] As yet interest in studies of this sort continues strong.

General education has also experienced a resurgence among those involved in reconceiving a "liberal core" in the undergraduate curriculum as a means of countering excessive specialization and curricular fragmentation.[136] As we have seen, this is a problem endemic to the modern university, and reform

[132]Bell, *The Reforming of General Education.*

[133]Rudolph, *Curriculum,* p. 248.

[134]Among the most important works of a voluminous and growing literature are Arthur W. Chickering, *Education and Identity* (San Francisco: Jossey-Bass, Inc., 1972); Kenneth Feldman and Theodore M. Newcomb, *The Impact of College on Students,* 2 vols. (San Francisco: Jossey-Bass, Inc., 1976); Douglas H. Heath, *Growing Up in College* (San Francisco: Jossey-Bass, 1968); Joseph Katz et al., *No Time for Youth* (San Francisco: Jossey-Bass, Inc., 1969); William G. Perry, *Forms of Intellectual and Ethical Development in the College Years* (New York: Holt, Rinehart, & Winston, 1968); and Harold Webster et al., "Personality Changes in College Students," in Nevitt Sanford, ed., *The American College* (New York: John Wiley & Sons, 1962). See also Martin Trow, "Higher Education and Moral Development," *AAUP Bulletin* 62 (1976) pp. 20–27.

These represent latter-day manifestations of what in actuality has become a rather long-standing interest among values-interested social scientists. For some early examples of the genre, see Harry William Foot, "A Psychological Approach to the Problem of Character-Training in Institutions of Higher Education" (M.A. Thesis, Columbia University, 1932); G. J. Dudycha, "The Moral Beliefs of College Students," *International Journal of Ethics,* 43 (1933), pp. 194–204; A. Snyder and K. Dunlap, "A Study of Moral Evaluations by Male and Female College Students," *Journal of Comparative Psychology,* 4 (1924), pp. 289–324; and W. H. Crowley and W. Walker, "A Study of Student Life," *Journal of Higher Education,* 6 (1935), pp. 132–142.

[135]See footnote 134. Mine is a gross summary of some very intricate studies.

[136]See, for example, Malcolm G. Scully, "Tightening the Curriculum: Enthusiasm, Dissent, and 'So What Else Is New?'" *The Chronicle of Higher Education,* 18 (1978) pp. 1, 12; and Gerald Grand and David Riesman, *The Perpetual Dream: Reform and Experiment in the American College* (Chicago: The University of Chicago Press, 1978), pp. 355–382.

efforts intended to deal with it wax and wane with cyclic regularity. Curriculum reforms of this sort, however, as has also been observed, concentrate less on keeping ethical concerns and values questions alive in higher education than on providing students with cross-disciplinary understanding and methodological breadth. It remains to be seen whether the most recent attempts in this regard will preserve at their center any notion of "the educated person," including "the ethical person," or whether they will devolve, at best, into a streamlined refurbishing of the old system of distribution, or, at worst, into the politics of departmental representation.

A final, and still different, call for general education has come from those who seek an issue-oriented curriculum, as distinct from either the content- or method-oriented approaches of other general-education attempts. There are antecedents of this issue orientation, but the main impetus for the present proposal has come from issues raised by student protesters in the sixties, and, now more recently, from those who see the possibility of addressing those issues directly within higher education. "The point of departure," Earl J. McGrath, one of the main spokesmen for the issue orientation, has written, "must be the problems with which this and succeeding generations must deal—ecology, energy, crime, hunger, war, and the rest."[137] The hope of making issues the focus of a reformed curriculum is to unite once again relevance, moral commitment, and knowledge, and to avoid having the movement captured by the subject-matter interests of the faculty and the existing divisions of the curriculum.

The main problem that has continued to plague both the teaching of ethics and general education has been the modern tendency to regard only scientific knowledge as genuine, and to look upon other concerns as somewhat out of place in the university. It will have achieved little to make issues the central focus, if in the end the scientific and technological solutions to them are the only ones that enjoy philosophic and social standing. Unless this problem is addressed, one may expect continuing problems for the present movement. In the meantime, the vision of a meaningful general education will continue to appeal to many who would insist on raising questions concerning the moral uses of knowledge and who seek a concrete arena within which personal and social ethics can be taught in relation to the whole curriculum.

RELIGION AND ETHICS

Throughout the twentieth century the teaching of ethics in American higher education has maintained vestiges of the special relationship with religion that it enjoyed in earlier periods. This relationship finds expression, for example, in the familiar phrase "religion and ethics," still sometimes used to describe, not

---

[137]Earl J. McGrath, *Values, Liberal Education, and National Destiny* (Published by The Lilly Endowment, Inc., n.p., 1975), p. 36.

always with approval, the domain of moral concerns within higher education. One difficulty, in fact, in identifying the sources of the teaching of ethics in higher education is that religious programs and courses, even when they lack a specific emphasis on ethics as such, have almost invariably been taught with ethical aims in view. Thus, courses in Biblical studies, in the philosophy and psychology of religion, and in comparative religion have often been justified, not only as being culturally important, but also as providing a necessary framework within which to understand the most important problems of personal and social life.

During the first half of the twentieth century, most of the teaching of religion in higher education was concentrated within private colleges sponsored by religious bodies, mainly Protestant and Roman Catholic, but including a few explicitly Jewish institutions. Private nonsectarian colleges, many of which had originated as denominational schools, often bent over backward to exclude religious courses from their curriculum programs, in their desire to establish their autonomy and status as independent institutions. State universities, however, which had a much longer and closer connection with the teaching of religion than is often supposed—many of them in their earlier years were nearly indistinguishable from other nineteenth-century church-related colleges in being suffused with pan-Protestant values and religious concerns—were actually more flexible than many nonsectarian private schools. Concern about church–state conflicts inhibited the inclusion of religion courses and departments within the regular curriculum of public institutions during the late nineteenth and early twentieth centuries, but gradually more and more schools of this sort began to make provision for the study of religion, in a variety of different programs.[138] A major study of the teaching of religion in American colleges and universities, conducted in 1936, concluded that in Roman Catholic colleges all students received religious instructions, in Protestant colleges one out of two students did so, and in private nondenominational colleges and state universities and colleges the respective figures were one out of eight and one out of twenty. In all these programs courses in ethics were among the major offerings, though a still smaller number of the students enrolled in religious studies would have taken courses specifically in ethics.[139]

---

[138]See John F. Wilson, "Introduction: The Background and Present Context of the Study of Religion in Colleges and Universities," in Paul Ramsey and John F. Wilson, eds., *The Study of Religion in Colleges and Universities*, (Princeton: Princeton University Press, 1970), pp. 3–22.

[139]The study reported that in public institutions three groups of courses competed closely for first place in being most frequently offered in religious programs: biblical studies, ethics, and philosophy of religion. Among Protestant schools, explicit ethics courses were prominent, but ranked along with Biblical studies, the life and teachings of Jesus, and religious education; though again, within these last, it would undoubtedly be difficult to draw a hard and fast line between the ethical and nonethical dimensions of what was taught. Only two subjects stood

The two decades following World War II witnessed a dramatic growth of religion departments within private, nonsectarian schools and within state universities. By 1950, Clarence Shedd reported, nearly 60% of state universities and land grant colleges were offering instruction in religion on an academic credit basis, and their number continued to increase.[140] The proliferation of religious programs was just as rapid among private nonsectarian institutions. This surge in the intellectual study of religion reflected in part a growing awareness of the religious dimensions of many other fields of study, such as sociology, psychology, anthropology, and literature. It was also due in part to the availability of highly trained graduates from interdenominational seminaries—Yale, Harvard, Duke, Union–Columbia, Chicago—to staff the new programs. These graduates were imbued with the intellectual and religious excitement stemming from the theological renewal of the 1930s through the 1950s—often associated in Protestantism with so-called neoorthodoxy, but actually limited neither to Protestantism nor neoorthodoxy—in which these seminaries had played a leading part. One hallmark of the newer theological outlook was an intense appreciation of the central intellectual and ethical importance of the Judeo-Christian tradition in the development of Western culture.

The result for the teaching of ethics was threefold. First, the treatment of ethical and moral questions in their broadest political, social, and philosophic dimensions was accorded a central position in the study of religion. Both religious ethics—stimulated by the theological works of such persons, among others, as Paul Tillich, Karl Barth, Reinhold and Richard Neibuhr, Jacques Maritain, Nicholai Berdyaev, and Martin Buber—and nonreligious ethical viewpoints—such as that of Jean Paul Sartre—were dealt with as bearing directly on the ultimate concerns of man. Second, a main characteristic of this theological renewal was its concern with the large problems of political and social ethics, rather than with a narrow, individualistic interpretation of religious morality. As a consequence, normative ethical issues and major social issues

out prominently within Roman Catholic colleges: doctrine and ethics. (Gould Wickey and Ruth A. Eckhart, *A National Survey of Courses in Bible and Religion in American Universities and Colleges*. Printed for the Indiana Council on Religion in Higher Education, 1936.) With the exception of Roman Catholic colleges and universities, much more data than is now available is needed to assess the exact nature of these religiously based ethics courses. A more complete study would have to look in much greater detail than has been possible in this paper at the tradition of the teaching of ethics in Roman Catholic institutions.

[140] Clarence Prouty Shedd, "Religion in the American State Universities: Its History and Present Problems," in Henry E. Allen, ed., *Religion in the State University: An Initial Exploration*, (Minneapolis: Burger Publishing, 1950), p. 25. A copious literature soon developed to deal with the issues raised by the rapid growth of religious studies. Among some of the more useful examples are Ramsey and Wilson, *The Study of Religion*, which contains an extensive bibliography; Clyde A. Holbrook, *Religion, A Humanities Field* (Englewood Cliffs, N.J.: Prentice-Hall, 1963); and Robert Michaelson, *The Study of Religion in American Universities* (New Haven: The Society for Religion in Higher Education, 1965).

probably received much more attention during the 1950s and 1960s within the teaching of ethics in religion departments than within departments of philosophy.[141] Third, an existentialist outlook and attitude was, likewise, probably much more prevalent in religion departments than in departments of philosophy, both because of the importance of existentialism in much twentieth-century religious thought, and because it combined intellectual analysis with a call for commitment in dealing with crucial ethical issues of the day. Although existentialism made personal decision the sole basis for authentic moral action, and was, therefore, for the most part unabashedly subjective, perhaps its being taught within the framework of a religious perspective may have seemed to provide it with a foundation it lacked in the more analytic and positivistic climate of departments of philosophy. At any rate, it would probably be safe to conclude that during most of the 1950s and 1960s some of the most vital teaching of ethics in American higher education took place within departments and programs of religion.[142]

At present the situation seems to have changed. The theological renewal of the midcentury was unable to stem the fundamental modern skepticism about religious knowledge, and, consequently, a religiously based teaching of ethics also appears to have lost the promise it held out for a time of being able to command the attention and respect of a wide audience. Compounding the problem is that, in their desire to establish the full academic status and respectability of their fields, members of departments of religion were, perhaps, even more zealous than others to adopt the standards of graduate-school-oriented professionalism, with all of the unresolved, perhaps unavoidable, problems of curriculum isolation and compartmentalization that this has historically entailed. However, to assess the degree to which the combination of these two factors has actually affected the teaching of ethics in departments of religion would require a much more extensive analysis of present programs than is possible here.

RETROSPECT AND NEW DEPARTURES

Two things happened during the nineteenth and twentieth centuries that were to have momentous consequences for higher education and modern society in general, as well as for the teaching of ethics in particular. Both were

[141]It is probably no accident, for example, that one of the exceptional texts of the early sixties that focused entirely on concrete ethical problems opened with readings from the theological-ethical perspectives of Karl Barth and George F. Kennan, and contained substantial sections on "Church and State" and "The Church and Social Reform," with readings from the Niebuhr brothers, John Courtney Murray, and others. Girvetz, *Contemporary Moral Issues.*

[142]A comprehensive discussion of the content and issues of Christian ethics is the bibliographic essay by James Gustafson, "Christian Ethics," in Paul Ramsey, ed., *Religion* (Englewood Cliffs, N.J.: Prentice-Hall, 1964), pp. 285–354.

centuries-long developments that reached a kind of culmination in the 1890s, although it was not for several decades thereafter that their full impact and implications began to become clearly manifest. One development was the splintering of the culture of learning into many different, self-contained disciplines of knowledge. We have considered some of the main aspects of this development, and the so-called professionalization process that accompanied it, as these affected the decline of moral philosophy and a widening separation of the social sciences from the teaching of ethics. The other development—essentially much more important than the first—was that one of these branches of knowledge, namely natural science, began to be regarded as the one and only valid mode of knowledge.

As this conception of knowledge became increasingly dominant, it began to make extremely difficult any consideration of values other than those already embedded in natural science and its technological application. The eventual impact of this attitude on the teaching of ethics—in fact, on all attempts to determine the very place of ethics in higher education—was profound. Subjects that traditionally had most to do with values and meaning—art, religion, literature, and philosophy—were increasingly called into question as sources of genuine knowledge. The growing conviction that science alone dealt with an objective world of knowledge meant that these nonscientific subjects were more and more regarded, not as modes of knowing or sources of new knowledge, but as, at best, merely expressions of subjective feelings and preferences, or as repositories of folk customs and social habits, or as ideological manifestations of group interests. They even began to have difficulty finding a place within the university, except insofar as they sought to model themselves after the natural sciences. Doing this, however, meant the sacrifice of their own integrity and identity as independent sources of value and ethical judgment.

From the beginning there have been surges of awareness that other values besides the scientific and technological are essential to a humane society. Periodically, throughout the twentieth century, there have been attempts to redress the balance by introducing consideration of values into the university curriculum. In effect, the loss of the role played by the old moral philosophy courses has been keenly felt, and attempts have repeatedly been made to find some meaningful substitute for it—usually to little avail. Programs for general education, for the study of professional ethics, for renewing the arts and humanities, have come and gone again and again during the past seventy-five years.

Today we are experiencing a rebirth of concern for moral philosophy and the teaching of ethics, of an extent and magnitude perhaps unprecedented in modern American education. The reasons for this renewal are many and complex. The multiplicity and enormity of problems demanding moral decision and action confronting humankind today have become simply unavoidable. Student demands of the last decade for "relevant" courses, whatever else their effects, challenged faculties to reexamine the connection between knowledge and values, between the discovery of knowledge and its ethical applications. And mounting concerns, and doubts, regarding the ethical sensitivity and commitment of public leaders have spurred professional groups and educators as seldom before to grapple with the tasks of moral education.

This renewed attention to the teaching of ethics is manifest at nearly every point in the curriculum. Professional philosophers and ethicists themselves have begun on a wide front to deal with pressing normative and practical problems. Leading philosophers, many of them directly within the analytic tradition itself, have frequently been at the forefront in reflecting on such issues as social justice, equality, personal and social freedom, war, and the ethical problems of science.[143] Perhaps the persistent involvement of the analytic school with language has itself helped foster within its once narrow and technical domain the reestablishment of connections with the great classical traditions of humanistic political and social theory.[144] The founding of new publications has signaled the desires of philosophers to deal with a variety of specific problems only recently out of fashion; ethics textbooks and anthologies of readings for undergraduates have begun increasingly to make normative and practical issues a central focus of instruction.[145] Moreover, not only within philosophy, but also within the other humanities and the sciences as well have appeared a growing awareness of the ethical dimension and devotion to the pedagogical problems of moral education.[146]

Perhaps most important, across a broadening spectrum are to be glimpsed indications that some of the most fundamental theoretical problems underlying the teaching of ethics are once again being addressed.[147] Within psychology, for

[143]For example, see Richard M. Hare, *Applications of Moral Philosophy* (Berkeley: University of California Press, 1972); Thomas Nagel, *The Possibility of Altruism* (Oxford: Clarendon Press, 1970); Robert Nozick, *Anarchy, State, and Utopia* (New York: Basic Books, 1974); John Rawls, *Theory of Justice* (Cambridge: Harvard University Press, 1971), and Kersten J. Struhl and Paula R. Struhl, eds., *Ethics in Perspective* (New York: Random House, 1975).

[144]See, for example, John Rawls, *Justice.*

[145]Among recently founded journals especially noteworthy in this context are *Philosophy and Public Affairs* and *Journal of Medicine and Philosophy.* For examples of new approaches and emphases among texts and anthologies, see Raziel Abelson and Marie-Louise Friqueqson, eds., *Ethics for Modern Life* (New York: Random House, 1975); A. K. Bierman and James A. Gould, eds., *Philosophy for a New Generation* (New York: Macmillan Co., 1970); Thomas A. Meppes and Jane S. Zembaty, eds., *Social Ethics: Morality and Social Policy* (New York: McGraw-Hill, 1977); Carl Wellman, *Morals and Ethics* (Glenview, Ill.: Scott, Foresman & Co., 1975. See also, for example, Thomas Nagel *et al.*, eds., *War and Moral Responsibility* (Princeton: Princeton University Press, 1974); Thomas Nagel *et al.*, eds., *The Rights and Wrongs of Abortion* (Princeton: Princeton University Press, 1974); Thomas Nagel *et al.*, eds., *Equality and Preferential Treatment* (Princeton: Princeton University Press, 1977); and Thomas Nagel, *Philosophy, Morality, and International Affairs* (New York: Oxford University Press, 1974). See also Giarelli, "Primers in Ethics."

[146]The Hastings Center Study of the teaching of ethics is eloquent testimony to this growing interest.

[147]Some aspects of these developments are discussed in Carl Wellman, "Ethics Since 1950," *Journal of Value Inquiry,* 6 (1972), pp. 83–90; and Donald S. Klinefelter, "The Place of Value in a World of Fact," *Soundings,* 58 (1975), pp. 363–379.

example, the work of such persons as Piaget, Lawrence Kohlberg, and William Perry suggests to some that moral issues are part and parcel of the basic process of education. A revised concern with general education has again called attention to the inseparable connection between the moral uses and the unity of knowledge. And especially promising are the voices within science who are calling, like Dewey at one point, though not along his lines, for a reconception of science that would recognize the all-important role of creative insight and the value of the knower in all knowing. From this last perspective comes the suggestion that a fundamental unity joins scientific insight, artistic insight, and moral insight, and that the vision of an ethical, intellectual, and integral curriculum may yet be a genuine possibility.[148]

ACKNOWLEDGMENTS

I wish to thank the Hastings Center Institute of Society, Ethics and the Life Sciences, for whom this study was prepared and whose support made possible the research on which it is based. I am also indebted to Philip M. Phenix, Lawrence A. Cremin, Trygve R. Tholfsen, and to the members of The Hastings Center and the participants in The Hastings Center Project on the Teaching of Ethics in Higher Education for their helpful criticisms of earlier drafts. Any errors of fact and of interpretation remain my sole responsibility.

[148]Klinefelter, "Place of Value," pp. 363–379. See Michael Polanyi, *Personal Knowledge* (Chicago: University of Chicago Press, 1958); see especially the articles by the theoretical physicist David Bohm, "Imagination, Fancy, Insight, and Reason in the Process of Thought," in Shirley Sugarman, ed., *Evolution and Consciousness: Studies in Polarity* (Middletown, Conn.: Wesleyan University Press, 1976), pp. 51–68; and David Bohm, "On Insight and Its Significance for Science, Education, and Values," *Teachers College Record*, 80 (1979), pp. 403–418. Also provocative and relevant in this context is Huston Smith, "Excluded Knowledge: A Critique of the Modern Western Mind Set," *Teachers College Record*, 80 (1979), pp. 419–445.

PART I

General Issues in the Teaching of Ethics

CHAPTER 2

Goals in the Teaching of Ethics

DANIEL CALLAHAN

Any discussion of possible goals in the teaching of ethics must begin by facing a number of formidable difficulties. The very phrase "the teaching of ethics" has a variety of connotations in our culture, and so for that matter does the term "ethics." One can never be certain just what people hear when they encounter the notion of "teaching ethics": for some, it means instructing people not to break the law, or to abide by some legal or professional code; for others, it means an attempt to improve moral character or to instill certain virtues; for still others, it primarily means imparting special skills in the handling of moral argumentation. Moreover, clarity is by no means guaranteed by the standard method of simply stipulating one's own definitions or viewpoints. Someone who was once "taught ethics" by harsh and repressive methods of gross indoctrination may have trouble understanding "the teaching of ethics" in any more benign sense, however carefully one may point out other possibilities.

If merely trying to get clear what one is talking about is sometimes difficult enough, the range and multiplicity of settings and contexts for the teaching of ethics in higher education introduces a further complexity. Consider only a sample of the possibilities: teaching ethics to college freshmen (and to freshmen at very selective institutions versus those where even basic literacy is in question); teaching prelaw students; teaching third-year law students; teaching medical students (or nurses, or paramedical students); teaching college sociology majors; teaching graduate students in philosophy or religion; and so on. Ethics can be taught to the widest range of students with the widest range of backgrounds at the widest range of institutions. Each setting will dictate somewhat different pedagogical techniques, different assumptions about student capacities, and different teacher preparation. An emphasis on problem solving and dilemma resolution can be an appropriate goal at the professional-school level, and an

---

DANIEL CALLAHAN ● Director, The Hastings Center, Institute of Society, Ethics and the Life Sciences, Hastings-on-Hudson, New York.

emphasis on theory construction and critique may be a perfectly reasonable goal in some types of undergraduate courses. Some teachers and some students are more comfortable with a case method approach, while others find an analysis of moral principles together with illustrative cases more attractive.

The most obvious questions to ask of any proposal to "teach ethics" are (1) why should one want to undertake such a venture in the first place? (2) what could or should be accomplished by such teaching? and (3) what is the nature of the subject matter, ethics? A relatively simple answer can be given to the first question. Courses in ethics should be taught because morality is part of any reflective personal life, and because ethical perspectives and specific moral rules are part of any cultural and civic life. That is only to say that ethical problems are inescapable. Whether explicitly or implicitly, it is difficult to think of any aspect of personal or public life that will not be determined or conditioned by moral values. Ethical problems arise at all stages of life, and are part of all professions, disciplines, and jobs. A consideration of them is as appropriate and necessary at the advanced graduate and professional level as it is at the undergraduate level.

What could or should courses in ethics accomplish? There is one fairly broad answer. At the very least, courses in ethics should make it clear that there are ethical problems in personal and civic life, that how they are understood and responded to can make a difference to that life, and that there are better and worse ways of trying to deal with them.

The third question raises the most difficulties. Both the term "ethics" and the realities to which it purports to refer are highly problematic in our society, subject to seemingly endless disagreement and lack of resolution. That is not to say that there is no agreement whatever, or that total confusion reigns. It is perfectly possible within some contexts—that of contemporary philosophical ethics, for example—to find a rough agreement on the domain and subject matter of ethics: that ethics includes a descriptive, a normative, and a metaethical dimension; that morality or "morals" customarily refer to specific rules of conduct, and so on.

But it is no less obvious that once one moves outside of the narrow circle of conventional definitions and into the substance of the matter, many disagreements characterize the field. A common public perception of ethics is that there is, in principle, no way to resolve the disagreements, and that taste or bias or some kind of arbitrary existential choice in the end reigns supreme. That the general public—or those from disciplines that claim greater precision and decisiveness—should be doubtful about the status and value of ethics is thus hardly surprising. If they take the trouble to press those who make a profession of studying ethics in the hope that their perception is wrong, they are not likely to be instantly reassured.

The awkward truth is that the skeptical public perception is, by and large, accurate. As Alasdair MacIntyre has noted:

> It is impossible in our culture now to find a systematic way of using such words

as "ethical" and "moral" which does not already embody not merely a particular morality but a particular contentious morality which is at war with its rivals.... Because disagreements among moral philosophers parallel and reflect the disagreements among moral agents themselves—moral philosophers turn out to be merely the most articulate and systematic examples of moral agents—philosophy cannot as of now resolve these rivalries in any logically compelling way.... Our reply to a request for an account of *the* concept of morality, or *the* meaning of "ethical," would have to be: there no longer is such a concept or such a meaning. Instead, we are forced into a task of conceptual reconstruction. Any such reconstruction will ... itself be morally partisan. Philosophers can no longer be comfortable in the claim that they are only exhibiting in clear form the contents of the ordinary agents' moral consciousness.[1]

To be sure, Professor MacIntyre puts the contemporary situation in exceedingly doleful terms. A less pessimistic, more balanced, account would also have to note that there are many shared values and many moral rules that command general agreement—rules against lying, stealing, murder, discrimination, and so on. That there are many borderline problems concerning those rules (when they apply, and what are legitimate exceptions, for example) should not obscure the fact of their general acceptance. Frequently enough, it is not a practical and specific moral rule that is in contention. Instead, the disagreement will surface in the search for a theoretical basis for the rule, and people who can agree on its validity for daily life can fundamentally disagree on its ultimate foundation or grounding. One can, for example, base the rule against lying on utilitarian grounds (that it leads to the greatest happiness of the greatest number), or on an ethic of respect for persons (which emphasizes inherent individual good rather than aggregate communal good). Thus, for all the practical agreement on many issues, the existence of widespread dispute on the foundations of ethics lends strong validity to Professor MacIntyre's viewpoint.

The special contemporary hazard of ethical analysis is that of begging the question. One can make no moral assertions that do not depend upon certain assumptions. Precisely because ethics forces a confrontation with basic premises about human nature and life, it always works at the edge of an abyss. In societies marked by a common set of assumptions and agreed-upon ethical principles and moral rules, ethical analysis and the making of decisions can proceed more easily—not everything needs to be questioned. Quite the opposite is often true in pluralistic societies. Even if most people would subscribe to the view that lying is wrong, and stealing bad, and murder immoral, no contemporary teacher of ethics can assume that his or her students know why they hold such views, whether they have reasons to support them, and whether, for that matter, all students even accept such views without reservation.

Teachers of ethics will constantly be forced, to use Professor MacIntyre's phrase, "into a task of critical reconstruction" with their students. This can be interesting and challenging in some contexts (advanced undergraduate or grad-

---

[1]"How to Identify Ethical Principles," in *The Belmont Report*, Washington, D.C.: Department of Health, Education and Welfare Publication No. (OS) 78-0013, pp. 10-31, 10-40.

uate courses in ethical theory), but enormously frustrating in those circumstances where students desperately want assistance in resolving very specific kinds of moral dilemmas (a course in a medical or law school, for example). The latter circumstance calls for an exercise in casuistry, that of applying specific rules of conduct in particular circumstances. But effective casuistry is hardly possible in the absence of some agreement on general principles. Thus the course itself, if it is to have any solidity, must make room for some consideration of more general questions about the nature and foundations of ethics, a difficult and arduous business under the best of circumstances. Of course, a teacher can evade that task and simply present one more partisan position. But even if it is a reputable enough position, and the teacher openly declares his or her allegiance to it, he or she will be failing to provide the students with the whole truth about contemporary ethics, and thus failing them at a critical juncture.

The teacher of ethics will always be faced with both moral and practical dilemmas: to do full justice to ethics, on the one hand, and to cope with the limitations of time, student interests or capacities, or institutional demands, on the other. That is hardly a problem unique to the teaching of ethics, but it has a special poignancy when the conceptual foundations of the field itself are a central issue. Students characteristically come away from courses in ethics with the sense that they have moved constantly in circles, chasing and biting their own moral tails. Yet that is and should be the mark of a good course in ethics— full of self-critical awareness and dogged attempts to avoiding begging the question. It takes very good teaching to make that kind of regimen palatable, much less enjoyable. Ethics is an austere pleasure.

The argument of this paper is that the goals of the teaching of ethics can be divided into three general classes: those (1) that are important for all courses in ethics, whatever the educational level or context; those (2) that are doubtful for all courses; and those (3) that will, as special topics, be either optional or important, depending upon the context. Moreover, there are some alleged goals that I consider to be of doubtful validity; they will also be examined. Although the primary emphasis in this discussion will focus on formal courses in ethics, there are many other contexts, short of full courses, in which ethics both is, and can be, taught—as parts of other courses, as segments of field work, and so on. The goals proposed here should be adaptable to those contexts, which may be as frequent as formal courses.

IMPORTANT GOALS IN THE TEACHING OF ETHICS

STIMULATING THE MORAL IMAGINATION

A course in ethics can be nothing other than an abstract intellectual exercise, unless a student's feelings and imagination are stimulated. Students must be provoked to understand that there is a "moral point of view" (Kurt Baier's phrase), that human beings live their lives in a web of moral relationships, that a consequence of moral theories and rules can be either suffering or happiness (or, usually, some combination of both), that the moral dimensions of life are as often hidden as visible, and that moral choices are inevitable and often difficult. For purposes of teaching, one may think of this as the "premoral" stage, a necessary (but not sufficient) condition for any serious moral discourse and reflection at all. But if one sees the moral imagination as the very source of a drive to get straight on ethics, it will continue to have a place even in the most advanced courses in ethics. A lively moral imagination is the only real corrective to the conceptual and logical analysis that is equally necessary for advanced work in ethics; it is as important at one end of the spectrum as it is at the other. Imagination without analysis is blind; analysis without imagination is sterile.

Yet even if it is true that imagination and analysis need each other, imagination should have an initial priority in introductory courses. The emotional side of students must first be elicited or evoked—empathy, feeling, caring, sensibility. Even here, though, the cognitive must quickly enter: to discern hidden assumptions, to notice consequences of thought and behavior, to see that pain or pleasure do not merely happen. The use of novels, plays, and films can be very effective at this point, often far more successfully stimulating the imagination than can be done with ordinary reading fare in philosophical or theological ethics. Care must be taken here, however. Courses that depend almost exclusively on visual or fictional material can swamp the imagination while starving the mind. It is always a temptation to wallow in feeling and passion; it can become an end in itself, and be nothing other than mere sentimentality. Our feelings of sorrow, pity, anguish, or outrage may be delivering true moral messages—but that can never be taken for granted, and a minimal perception to be conveyed to students is the possible difference between what they *feel* to be right or good, and what *is* right or good.

RECOGNIZING ETHICAL ISSUES

A very fine line separates a stimulation of the moral imagination and a recognition of ethical issues. There is good psychological evidence to suggest that all emotional responses embody a degree of appraisal and cognitive judgment; there can be no sharp distinction between feeling and thought. Thus I would want to specify the goal of a recognition of ethical issues to be a conscious, rational attempt to sort out those elements in emotional responses that represent appraisal and judgment, however inchoate at first. How should one characterize and rationally articulate a felt response of injustice, or the violation of a person's autonomy, or the nature of the anguish felt in the face of a decision about whether to keep a severely defective child alive? Part of such an attempt will require the examination of concepts, of prescriptive moral statements, and of ethical principles and moral rules. Those are the tools of rationality in ethics, the means whereby some order is given to the relatively untutored deliverances of experience and previous conditioning. If our emotional responses embody an appraisal, how are we to judge the validity of that appraisal? That is the kind of question that ought to be put to those whose moral imaginations have been stimulated.

ELICITING A SENSE OF MORAL OBLIGATION

However ridiculous such an attempt may seem, it is conceivable that a course on ethics could be taught that paid no attention to volition or action. One could merely analyze the logical implications of moral propositions. But apart from that kind of exercise, a major point of ethics is that of the guidance of conduct, not only how I ought to direct my behavior toward others, but also what I ought to be able to claim from others in their behavior toward me. A necessary condition for moving outside of our minds and emotions into the realm of behavior is that (1) we recognize action as an outcome of ethical judgment (and praise and blame can be seen as a form of action), and (2) that we *will* to act on the basis of our judgment. Can one speak legitimately of a *desire* to do good, or of a willed *intention* to act benevolently or with justice toward others? It would seem very odd if one could not speak that way, as if what we will or intend has no bearing on what we actually do; that would fly into the face of experience.

Yet even if one agrees that there is an intimate relationship between reasoning, willing, and acting—and something obviously to be discussed in a class on ethics—to what extent should it be acceptable to stimulate positively an intention to do what is good, right, and just? And can that even be done, without moving across the border that separates education from indoctrination? The answer to the question lies, I think, in the necessity of making clear in any course in ethics the centrality of freedom and personal responsibility. These are the heuristic premises of any conceivable moral life. I call them "heuristic" only to leave open the old questions of free will and determinism, environment and heredity, and the like, questions that should be confronted at some point in a course in ethics. But for all practical purposes, it makes no sense to talk of ethics unless it is presupposed that individuals are free to make moral choices, and that they are responsible for the choices they make.

"To elicit a sense of moral obligation" is only to highlight with students an internal requirement of ethical thinking: that it calls us to act in the light of what we perceive to be right and good. I call it an "internal requirement" to indicate its formal structure, one that says nothing whatever about what counts as the substance of a right or good act. It is not "indoctrination" to point out that requirement; it is only a way of signaling the inherent dynamism of ethical decision making. The perception of what one takes to be good or right carries with it a strong and profound question: ought I not act upon my perception? The broader question here, "Why ought I be moral?", is basic, and not to be neglected in a course on ethics. But whether that question has been answered satisfactorily or not, once one begins to engage in the process of ethical analysis and judgment—thus conceding *some* kind of answer to the question—the dynamism of moral obligation takes over. The only wholly effective way to keep ethical analysis separate from a sense of moral obligation is to stay away from the subject altogether.

DEVELOPING ANALYTICAL SKILLS

If concepts, rules and principles are the tools of rationality in ethics, then skills must be developed in using them. The definition of concepts, the import and consequences of moral rules, and the meaning and scope of general ethical principles will all have to be explored. If that is done well, the stage will of course be set for the kind of frustration inherent in ethical inquiry. "Justice," "rights," "good," unfortunately, all are disputed concepts. Who says that moral rules are necessary, and anyway, aren't all moral rules subject to exceptions? Why do we need general ethical principles, and aren't most of them so general and controverted as to be vacuous anyway? Thus the thicket of ethics, from which few escape without cuts, bruises, and the bewilderment of often operating without a compass.

As much as anything else, the development of analytical skills will be simply the development of logical skills. Coherence and consistency are minimal goals, both in the analysis of ethical propositions and in their justification. Ethical principles and moral rules have implications both of a logical and of a practical kind. Ways must be found to trace out those implications, an exercise requiring both reason and imagination. Moral choices will have consequences for the individual making the choice and for those affected by them. That needs to be pointed out, if it is not immediately obvious enough. But are the consequences of moral choice and action the only pertinent criteria in judging their validity? An old question, but one that every student of ethics will have to wrestle with; and the sooner the better. Is it by right actions alone that one is moral, or are good intentions enough? And so on. Just how deeply a teacher should attempt to press such questions, or emphasize analytical skills, strikes me as a matter of personal judgment and student capacity. But since such skills are a fundamental part of more advanced work in ethics, all students should be put on notice about their importance; they cannot be left out of even the most introductory course.

TOLERATING—AND REDUCING—DISAGREEMENT AND AMBIGUITY

What often separates ethics from other kinds of intellectual analysis is the necessity of constantly examining the most basic premises of the entire enterprise. There are profound questions of jurisprudence in the law, and difficult issues of inductive logic and theory construction in science, and enormous conceptual puzzles about the meaning of "health" and "illness" in medicine. But the daily business of law, science, and medicine can proceed without directly confronting those questions. That is not true in the case of ethics, where every serious moral dilemma should force a grappling with the nature of the moral life itself. Moreover, though, law, medicine, and science can make do with a number of accepted conventions, the profundity of disagreement in ethics (both theoretically and practically in pluralistic societies) makes it difficult to find undisputed conventions that can serve to avoid the necessity of arguing each and every issue down to its roots.

That is the frustrating part of ethics, and the aspect most likely to alienate students. Why bother with ethics when there are so many other interesting disciplines or ways of looking at the world, where the existence of accepted conventions and methodologies obviates the need to engage in constant "critical reconstruction," and where decisions can be made and actions taken without an obsessive turning back on oneself in the process? Disagreements exist in all fields, and uncertainty is not confined to ethics. But ethics takes most of the prizes in that respect, and if students are not prepared to accept and live with that reality, they will not be able to make the progress that is possible in ethics.

A considerable part of that possibility lies in the reduction of ambiguity and disagreement. For, if toleration is necessary, no less important is an effort to reduce conflict, to seek out points of agreement, and to clarify that which is opaque or vague. Some disagreement in ethics is inevitable, but some is not; only great care and attention will make it possible to sort out the difference, whether it is a matter of ethical theory or the resolution of concrete moral dilemmas. Leaning to argue without rancor, and to disagree without personal invective, are important skills to be developed.

Bernard Rosen has proposed a final important goal also, one that takes up and subsumes many of the points I have made above:

> 1. Means. Provide a general means for each person to arrive at justified moral judgments; a means applicable to personal and professional life.
> 2. Action. Work out a strategy of teaching that makes it likely that action on the basis of the decision arrived at will occur.... One desirable result of education, in whatever the area and whatever the subject, is the dispensability of the teacher ... the "dispensability criterion."[2]

Rosen notes the difficulty of achieving such goals, and particularly the difficulty of finding a method for doing so. Nonetheless, he concludes that "The highest state of dispensability is reached when your student not only does not need you to arrive at justified judgments, but does not need you to arrive at the method that is used to arrive at justified judgments" [personal communication].

I would only want to add one clarifying stipulation to Rosen's formulation.

---

[2] *Goals in the Teaching of Ethics* (Unpublished paper prepared for a meeting on the Teaching of Ethics Project of The Hastings Center, 1978, p. 2).

There is surely a fundamental sense in which all moral judgments must be our own individual judgments, the consequences of which are our personal responsibility. At the same time, however, there is no such thing as a wholly idiosyncratic moral judgment. We gain our ethical concepts from the society in which we live, the moral options open to us are finite, and it is always wise to consult the moral opinions of others before making our own judgments. This is only to say that we are not wholly isolated moral agents, able to invent our own private worlds *de novo*. We live in human communities, and whatever we, as individuals, decide to do will represent the outcome of our interaction with those communities.

DOUBTFUL GOALS IN THE TEACHING OF ETHICS

In the foregoing section, I have tried to lay out and explicate some important goals in the teaching of ethics, applicable to all courses and at all levels of higher education. It should be noted that they are "goals," that is, ends to be sought. To what extent they can be achieved will be a function of the talents of the teacher, the receptivity and capabilities of the students, and the general ethos of the educational institution. I have prudently refrained from presenting any recipes for the most effective means of pursuing those goals in the classroom. I doubt that there are any simple formulas that can guarantee success. But then, there are no formulas available for the teaching of any subject that will guarantee success.

If there are some goals in the teaching of ethics that are always important, and others that are optional or context-dependent (as will be discussed below), there are also some alleged goals that I want to argue are doubtful.

It is often said that one test of the success of teaching ethics would be a change in the moral behavior of students, and that a central goal should thus be an attempt to change behavior. If ethics bears on conduct, then the point of teaching ethics should be to influence conduct. That seems clear and simple enough. Upon closer inspection, however, this is an exceedingly dubious goal. First, even if a course could change behavior, it is hard to see how, short of constant reinforcement of the new behavior, its effect could be long or surely sustained once out of the classroom; other influences would play their role, and no course can be a permanent antidote against them. Second, in most types of course in applied or professional ethics, the students will not yet have had an opportunity to behave one way or another; there is nothing to change, since their moral behavior, for better or worse, still lies before them.

Third, even if a short-term change in behavior can be effected, one can hardly assume that the behavior of all students in all circumstances is immoral or bad. It would make no sense to set as a goal the changing of moral behavior regardless of what the present behavior is; that could do as much harm as good. Fourth, the whole point of an ethics course would seem to be that of inquiring

into what should count as good behavior. The purpose of an ethics course—
that of critical inquiry—would be begged by a preestablished blueprint of what
will count as acceptable moral behavior. Far from encouraging the dispensability
of the teacher, that kind of a goal would make the teacher indispensable.

Having raised these objections, however, it may be possible to specify at
least one sense in which courses on ethics should set the stage for behavioral
change. If they are any good at all, they should make a change in the ways in
which students *think* about ethical issues, and possibly also in the way they *feel*
about those issues. They should, at a minimum, provide students with the skills
necessary to change their verbal behavior, i.e., by providing them with the tools
for a more articulate and consistent means of justifying their moral judgments,
and of describing the process of their ethical thinking. To be sure, the verbal
behavior may represent nothing more than clever sophistry; bad moral positions
can be skillfully defended. That danger must be run in order that students learn
the necessity of providing public and articulated reasons for their ethical
conclusions.

With respect to behavior, however, the most important goal would be that
of providing the student with those ingredients of ethical analysis and self-crit-
icism, such that he would, *if* the analysis seemed to require it, both recognize
the importance of changing behavior, and be prepared to change. The question
is not whether courses should automatically change behavior, but whether the
course would help a student to know the importance of changing his or her
behavior if that was what a moral judgment seemed to entail. It is not change
per se that should be the goal, but the potentiality for change as a result of
ethical analysis and judgment.

Another doubtful goal is that of the self-presentation of the teacher of
ethics as a role model. While it is almost certain that teachers as well as other
adult or authority figures are often seized upon as role models, it is quite another
matter for a teacher to deliberately attempt to be a role model. For one thing,
not all teachers will have the personal skills or attractiveness to make that possible, even if they try. To require that teachers be role models would, therefore,
be to impose upon them a burden many simply could not discharge. For another
thing, given a goal of teacher dispensability, too strong a role model would
obviously undermine that possibility. In ethics—as in a healthy psychological
life generally—a person must develop his own self-image and personal sense of
integrity. No person can entirely model his life on someone else's; it is neither
practically possible nor psychologically desirable.

Is this to say that a teacher should ignore or be utterly indifferent to the
kind of personal impact that he or she will have on students? That would be
naive, for surely students will notice whether a teacher exemplifies the spirit of
ethical inquiry that the teacher professes to be espousing. A teacher whose mode
of pedagogy patently contradicts the substance of what he or she is trying to
communicate can hardly be a very credible figure. Let me venture a proposal in

this respect. The first person that a teacher of ethics has to educate is himself, and the indispensable goals of the teaching of ethics suggested above are also the indispensable goals of the teacher's own self-education. And it is an education that must be lifelong, never once and for all completed. Students who see their teachers educating themselves before their very eyes will have a helpful role model, yet one that points no less effectively to the dispensability of the teacher as that model.

The foregoing comments can all be taken as ways of casting doubt upon the validity of what has been called "moral education," at least at the level of higher education. I am not certain that there is any single agreed-upon definition of the term "moral education." Generally speaking, however, I take it to mean an educational process with the goal of improving moral behavior, instilling certain virtues and traits of character, and developing morally responsible persons. So put, these seem to be goals that are laudatory enough, assuming that one can accomplish such things in the classroom—and, of course, parents try to do this kind of thing all the time with their children.

They are, however, doubtful goals in the undergraduate or graduate classroom. No teacher of ethics can assume that he or she has such a solid grasp on the nature of morality as to pretend to know what finally counts as good moral conduct. No society can assume that it has any better grasp of what so counts as to empower teachers to propagate it in colleges and universities. Perhaps most importantly, the premise of higher education is that students are at an age where they have to begin coming to their own conclusions and shaping their own view of the world. It is the time and place to teach them intellectual independence, and to instill in them a spirit of critical inquiry.

I would stress that last point in order to make it clear that I do not want to endorse an easy ethical relativism. That no teacher can have a full grasp of final moral truth does not imply that there is no final moral truth. It is only to say that, at the college or professional school level, the point of an ethics course is to set students forth on their own quest of whether there is such a truth, and what it is. No teacher should conceal his or her own moral convictions, whatever they may be. But it is not right for a teacher methodically to aim to have those convictions shared by his or her students, however generally acceptable and even benign they may be. It is the task of the teacher to help students form their *own* \
moral convictions. That cannot be accomplished unless the teacher supplies the student with those tools of ethical analysis that will enable him to examine and be in a position to reject not only his own present moral convictions, but also those of the teacher. A legitimate goal in the teaching of ethics is to help students develop a means and a process for achieving their own moral judgments. If "moral education" means something more than that—an education in specific moral rules, or specified traits of character—then it is illegitimate. That some students will end by sharing the convictions of their teachers is no evidence in itself that they have been unduly influenced. The real question is whether the

students have come to those convictions by means of the use of analytical tools and skills that might have led them in other directions. Undue influence is present when no option other than that proposed by the teacher is possible. In a word, indoctrination is wholly out of place, if by that term is meant a conscious attempt to lead students to accept one and only one system of ethical theory and moral values.

OPTIONAL AND CONTEXT-DEPENDENT TOPICS IN THE TEACHING OF ETHICS

I have tried to make a case that some goals are important in all courses in ethics; and all bear on the development of skills, perspectives, and attitudes. There are, however, a number of special topics for different types of ethics courses, all of which would count as legitimate enough, but some of which are optional in some contexts yet would be important in others. Since I assume that there is nothing particularly controversial (or, at least, there ought not to be) about these context-dependent topics, I will provide only minimal commentary.

ADVANCED ETHICAL INQUIRY

In this category I include those elements of ethical inquiry required for the pursuit of the subject with full rigor. While it is important that even beginning students be introduced to these elements, the extent to which they should be pursued in detail will be context-dependent. They would be mandatory in some types of course (any *advanced* course, or even any introductory course specifically advertised as dealing with ethical theory), but could legitimately be optional in others (e.g., an introductory course in ethics and journalism).

1. An understanding of, and ability to analyze, ethical concepts (e.g., rights, justice, liberty, autonomy).

2. Familiarity with the history of the development of ethical theories and with the examinations to which those theories have been subjected (e.g., utilitarianism and the objections leveled against it).

3. Familiarity with metaethical issues (e.g., the justification of moral judgments).

THE SOCIAL AND PSYCHOLOGICAL SETTING OF ETHICAL SYSTEMS AND MORAL BEHAVIOR

This category presupposes that there are a number of disciplines outside of philosophy and theology whose findings and perspectives can be illuminating to ethical inquiry. Ethical theories do not arise in a cultural vacuum, moral rules are normally fashioned to meet particular political and social needs, and moral judgments are made by human beings with both rational minds and emotional responses. These goals would be important for any advanced course, at least as issues to be touched upon. They would also be important for any course in professional ethics, since it can be assumed that the codes and mores of specific professions have a specific cultural and political history. They would be optional goals in most other types of ethics course.

1. An understanding of the general cultural, social, and political context that can lead to, and sustain, particular ethical theories and modes of ethical reasoning, and which will help to explain the particular moral rules, mores, and practices of a given historical period or culture.

2. Familiarity with the general theories and findings of moral psychology.

3. Familiarity with those aspects of sociology and anthropology that are concerned with the development of ethical and value systems and practices.

ELEMENTS OF APPLIED ETHICS

In this category are included those elements necessary for the grappling effectively with actual problems of normative decision making. By "applied ethics" I mean any attempt to make use of ethical theory and moral rules to arrive at concrete moral judgments in specific circumstances. One example may help to clarify my point, that of moral decision making in professional life. Questions of professional decision making can arise both directly and vicariously. They arise directly when a professional practitioner is faced with a moral dilemma, and where there are significant consequences whatever the decision. They can arise vicariously in those courses designed to introduce preprofessionals, or even those who will never be professionals, to the kinds of moral problem and the dilemmas faced by practitioners (e.g., an undergraduate course in bioethics). Yet it would be a mistake to reduce applied ethics in a professional context, direct or vicarious, simply to matters of personal morality. Students should also be led to understand the cultural, economic, political, historical, or other factors which can cause or condition the types of dilemmas that have to be faced. The possibility or necessity of a radical critique of social systems as a whole should be an available option, to be resorted to when it becomes clear that the available moral choices reflect unnecessarily narrow possibilities.

Issues of applied ethics must be confronted in any course on professional ethics. While they should be at least touched upon even in introductory ethics courses, they are optional in all courses save those designed specifically to elucidate problems of professional practice.

A. General

1. A detailed understanding of the official codes, and unofficial mores, of whatever discipline or profession is the subject of a course (e.g., the Code of Hippocrates for medical students).

2. A general understanding of the historical origin and social significance of the pertinent professional code or codes, and a critical awareness of the objections leveled against the codes.

3. An understanding of any contrast between provisions of the code (or accepted mores) and the more general morality of the society, and a capacity to analyze the provisions of a code both from the perspective of the profession, and the perspective of the broader society.

B. Specific

1. An understanding of the pertinent factual components that need to be considered in professional decision making (e.g., medical and biological data pertinent to bioethical decisions, or economic and social-science data pertinent to ethical issues of public policy decision making).

2. An understanding of the explicit or implicit values or ethical premises of the characteristic methodologies employed by particular disciplines and professions (e.g., the value assumptions of cost–benefit analysis in public policy, or the use of deception in some forms of social-psychology research).

3. An understanding of the characteristic ethical problems that face particular professions or disciplines (e.g., informed consent in medical and social-science research, conflict of interest in law, business, and accounting, risk–benefit analysis in medicine and engineering, privacy and confidentiality in law, medicine, and journalism, and the political uses and abuses of research findings in the social and policy sciences).

A final, general point should be made, about both the general goals and the context-dependent topics in the teaching of ethics. Except perhaps for the necessity of beginning with a stimulation of the moral imagination in introductory ethics courses, I do not think that there is any special order in which the goals should be pursued in individual courses, or any special way of working toward them. Whether it is best to begin with case studies, followed by considerations of theory, or vice versa, strikes me as a matter of prudential judgment, based on the teacher's assessment of what would be most effective. The same can be said about particular topics: whether, say, in a course in professional ethics the code of a profession or the social setting and history of the profession should come first, or other more general issues of ethical theory. The important point is that a method of teaching should be sought that will work steadily toward the chosen goals, neglecting none that are important, and introducing topics that are optional when the occasion makes that seem appropriate.

Appendix

Qualifications for the Teaching of Ethics

Who is qualified to teach a course in ethics? Both the general goals and the context-dependent topics proposed above would seem to presuppose some qualifications. On the face of it, the question would appear simple to answer: anyone who has received a graduate education in the field of ethics. That answer, however, is too easy. First, there are a number of academically solid courses in ethics being taught by those who do not have graduate training in the field. Second, effective courses in applied and professional ethics usually require knowledge of material drawn from a wide range of other fields and disciplines, e.g., law, medicine, the social sciences. Third, credibility in the teaching of applied and professional ethics seems, on occasion, to require not only academic knowledge, but also personal experience of the kinds of moral problem encountered in personal or professional decision making. Fourth, a case might be made that in at least some circumstances personal traits and unusual pedagogical skills are more important than academic credentials. Fifth, just what is "the field of ethics"? There are at least two important streams in Western ethics itself, one stemming from religious and the other from philosophical traditions. Moreover, within many professions there are independent traditions and mandated practices stemming from professional codes and time-honored mores.

The prevalence of these complications is readily discernible. They can be seen in the often ill-disguised skepticism of practicing physicians or lawyers when faced with a philosopher. The latter, it is charged, may have a head full of theories and armchair opinions, but never has and never will treat a patient or counsel a client. The philosopher often reciprocates the doubt: neither a medical education nor the care of hundreds of patients will reveal the finer points of utilitarian theory, much less develop well-honed skills in ethical analysis. Defending clients in a court room is a good way to understand the way in which the legal system works; but it is not adequate for an understanding of competing philosophical theories of justice and liberty. Those with a degree in moral theology can expect little professional respect from those allegedly so much more fortunate as to have received a degree in philosophy. And, of course, it is far more respectable to have been philosophically trained in the more rigorous modes of Anglo-American analytical philosophy than in the softer modes of continental existentialism and phenomenology.

Examples of mutual disrespect need not be multiplied. They can be found within the field of ethics itself, and in the relationships between those trained in ethics and those from other fields. I will make my own task easier here by putting to one side some of these squabbles. No one would dispute the contention that the best training for teaching an undergraduate or graduate course in theoretical philosophical ethics is a graduate degree in philosophy. Nor is anyone likely to dispute the notion that those working in applied and professional ethics should have some knowledge of the technical and professional subject matter of those fields to which they bring their training in ethics. For the purposes of this appendix, I will also assume that those trained in moral theology or moral philosophy (and any recognized school in moral philosophy) are equally qualified to teach ethics. Finally, I will also assume that, though it is conceivable that superb personal traits and pedagogical skills can on rare occasions suffice for very brief introductory teaching, they are not adequate substitutes for a firm academic grounding in the subject matter of ethics.

Even if one can accept these assumptions, many difficult questions remain. The principal reason for considering the qualifications of those teaching courses in ethics is a concern for the quality of the teaching. A course in ethics should be taught with the same rigor as any other course; hence, qualifications are critical. The recently renewed interest in ethics, at the undergraduate and professional-school level, has drawn heavily on those trained in ethics. But it has also attracted those with no obvious formal academic qualifications at all, especially in courses and programs outside of established philosophy and religious studies departments. There is more than a suspicion on occasion that the teaching of ethics by those with inadequate training can enhance the possibility of indoctrination and defective ethical analysis. Whatever the shortcomings of, say, a training in philosophical or theological ethics, that training may be expected to provide some well-established criteria for the assessing and justifying of moral arguments, and some body of developed theory to provide a grounding for applied ethics; there are disciplinary standards of rigor and quality. Enthusiasm, good will, and interest are not sufficient qualifications for teaching courses in organic chemistry, microeconomics, or Greek literature. There is no reason why they should be thought sufficient for the teaching of ethics, a difficult subject with a long history.

It is no less important to point out that good training in the technical aspects of biology, law, or public policy, even supplemented by considerable practical experience, do not automatically confer any special skills in analyzing or resolving the moral dilemmas arising in those fields. It is of course seductive to think that they do. Most thoughtful practitioners will in fact have wrestled with moral problems, will have discussed them with colleagues, and may well, in their undergraduate education or their own efforts at self-education, have given some thought to ethical theory and analysis. Nonetheless, even that is not sufficient for the teaching of a course in ethics—any more than the personal experience of having balanced a checkbook, backed up by undergraduate exposure to Paul Samuelson's textbook and a daily perusal of the financial section of the newspaper, qualifies one to teach a course in economics.

What, then, would count as adequate qualification? I want to reject at the very outset that form of disciplinary chauvinism which contends that *only* those with advanced degrees in moral philosophy or moral theology are properly qualified. That is correct in only one respect: they, and only they, are properly qualified to teach courses that fall strictly and entirely within their own disciplines. But the matter is very different for the teaching of applied and professional ethics. It is at that point that the field becomes, of necessity, interdisciplinary, requiring knowledge both of ethics and of the other field or fields to be analyzed from an ethical perspective. It is ethics *and* law, ethics *and* biology, ethics *and* journalism, and so on. A person trained exclusively in ethics will not be fully qualified to teach such courses; other knowledge will have to be acquired. Yet, by the same token, someone trained in a discipline other than ethics can become qualified to teach ethics, if, in addition to training in his or her own field, he or she acquires the necessary ethical training. The philosopher without any exposure to the field of journalism is not qualified to teach ethics and journalism— and an expert in journalism is not qualified to teach the subject either, without some exposure to philosophy. A traditional distinction should make the point perfectly clear: when the teaching of ethics requires the knowledge of two or more fields, it is a necessary but not sufficient condition that there be a full grounding in one of the fields; a sufficient condition will be some degree of grounding in the other field as well.

In an earlier study carried out by The Hastings Center on the teaching of bioethics, we made that distinction by introducing the idea of the "competent amateur."[1] By that phrase, we meant to characterize the degree of training and sophistication that should be achieved by someone working in a field other than the one in which he or she was originally trained. A person trained in moral theology or philosophy, for example, and interested in teaching a course in law and ethics, should become a "competent amateur" in the field of law. Ideally, perhaps, someone who teaches such a course should have both a Ph.D. in philosophy and a law degree. But that is not often a practical solution, and is usually not necessary.

[1] *The Teaching of Bioethics* (Hastings-on-Hudson, N.Y.: The Hastings Center, 1976).

Let me say more about the concept "competent amateur" than was said in that earlier study. A competent amateur may be defined as one who has a broad familiarity with the language, concepts, and characteristic modes of thinking of another discipline. To this familiarity should be added an understanding of the modes of analysis or the methodology of the other discipline—what that discipline considers to be an appropriate way of framing issues that arise in its field, how it makes use of and evaluates evidence or data, how it distinguishes between good work and bad, between the brilliant and the average. How much training or self-education is necessary for one to become a "competent amateur?" I would propose that about one year of education would be at least the minimal requirement, whether gained in one block or cumulatively. I doubt that self-education is ever sufficient—courses or formal training programs seem far preferable.

No less importantly, the "competent amateur" should have a decent sense of the internal dynamics and folkways of the other discipline. It is evident, for example, that all disciplines display a gap between the theoretical or idealized version of their work and what actually occurs in practice. Writings on the philosophy of science are not necessarily good guides to what researchers actually do in laboratories; nor do textbooks on differential diagnosis fully reveal the mixture of art, intuition, and experience that mark the first-rate diagnostician. Just as practicing lawyers take pleasure in pointing out to new law clerks the difference between the "real world" of law and what they learned in school, so too almost all practitioners in all fields make analogous points. Only some degree of personal exposure—for example, some clinical experience for those who want to teach bioethics—can help the "competent amateur" to bridge that gap. Not only is it necessary, then, to have some familiarity with the theories of another field; it is equally important to have a familiarity with practical moral problems as they arise in the work or professional context.

An important practical problem here is that of finding ways to become a "competent amateur" in another discipline. At present, there are comparatively few formal ways to do so—most teachers of ethics are reduced to informal reading on their own, and to the usually no less informal seeking of advice and guidance from colleagues in other fields. An expansion of those programs that seek to provide interdisciplinary training outside of the customary degree route would seem imperative for the future welfare of applied and professional ethics. These include, for example, post-doctoral fellowships, summer workshops and seminars, and special nondegree, accelerated courses.

Although I wish to deny the necessity of a full graduate training in ethics as a condition for teaching courses in applied and professional ethics, I do want to contend that the field of ethics must have a privileged place in the background and preparation of any teacher. By a "privileged place," I mean simply that one can claim no competence whatever to teach ethics without some familiarity with the history, the modes of reasoning, and the concepts of moral philosophy and moral theology.[2] That would seem such an obvious point that one may wonder whether it needs making at all. Unfortunately, those coming to ethics from other fields are often so put off by the writings of moral philosophers that they frequently cease trying altogether to understand. The professionalization of philosophy, the tendency of philosophers to write only for each other, and the lingering disinterest on the part of philosophers in normative, much less applied, ethics, probably accounts for some of that disenchantment. But it is also often the case that those trained in other disciplines find the shift to different modes of reasoning extremely difficult; some never develop a capacity for it at all.

At least for those teaching applied and professional ethics, nothing would seem more important than developing the skills necessary to move out of the comforting circle of professionalism into a world of more general discourse. That much said, I would nonetheless underscore a strong point: whatever the literary or other failures of moral philosophers, those coming to ethics from other disciplines must wrestle with their writings. They should feel free to rail against the jargon and the apparent irrelevance on many occasions to most human lives; but the works must be read, and the best of them should be included in the syllabi of courses in applied and professional ethics.

A common solution to the problem of credentials is that of team-teaching. Its attractions are obvious. It provides those teachers lacking specialized training in another discipline the opportunity to rely upon a colleague to provide to students that knowledge they do not have. It can also provide for students a vivid sense of what it means to try combining two or more disciplines in pursuit of a common problem and mutual insights. There are also some drawbacks. It is an expensive solution, and often an impractical one because of the departmental structure of most colleges and universities; and it is excessively dependent upon finding professors who can work well together. Perhaps its main drawback, however, is that it is prone simply to present material from different disciplines in a parallel, side-by-side way, with little effort to achieve a full integration.

Two conditions would seem imperative for good team-teaching. The first is that the courses be structured in a way that weaves together as tightly as possible the technical material from the nonethics discipline with the material that is squarely in the field of ethics. The second is that those engaged in team-teaching be fully prepared themselves to grapple with the material from their

---

[2] I would also contend that those trained in moral philosophy are only half-educated in ethics if they are ignorant of the main lines and schools of moral theology. At the least, as teachers, they are bound to be somewhat insensitive to those whose moral outlook has been shaped by a religious tradition; at most, they will be grossly overlooking a major source of Western values and moral concepts. Those trained as moral theologians are almost always given a decent exposure to philosophical ethics. Graduate departments of philosophy rarely return the compliment.

colleague's discipline. The initial goal of team-teaching efforts should be that of the mutual education of the instructors. If they cannot find ways of educating each other, it is hardly likely that their students will be able to make the necessary connections. Team-teaching should not become a substitute for the more important task of a teacher's developing into a "competent amateur" in another field. Team-teaching can enhance that possibility, but, given the practical and other difficulties of organizing and sustaining on a permanent basis interdisciplinary courses, most teachers will eventually be forced to go it alone.

Any consideration of the question of qualifications for the teaching of ethics should take account of two broad points. The first is the need for those teaching ethics to be qualified to do so. It is a field no more to be lightly wandered into than any other. Both the future reputation of the field, and the welfare of those taught ethics, depend upon high and rigorous standards. The second point, however, is that an obsessive emphasis upon credentials has done much to contribute to an excessive professionalization in our society, and to the development of an intellectual sterility in many disciplines. The future development of the teaching of ethics will depend upon both improvement in the training of those who want to teach ethics, and avoidance of the pitfalls of credentialism.

CHAPTER 3

Problems in the Teaching of Ethics: Pluralism and Indoctrination

RUTH MACKLIN

INTRODUCTION

We in the United States live in an ethically pluralistic society. Why should that pose a problem for the teaching of ethics? One major worry stems from the fact that moral convictions issue in actions. They also govern social and legal institutions and practices, and influence the formation of public policy. If moral beliefs were confined merely to what people think, they would not impinge on the lives of society's members in quite the same way. But it is precisely because cooperative or competitive activities are regulated by moral convictions that ethical pluralism gives rise to opposition to the teaching of ethics.

"Pluralism" sometimes refers to a descriptive thesis, depicting the existing array of moral and political values in our culture. It can also serve as a normative doctrine, expressing a positive commitment to the preservation of these diverse values. Either interpretation can produce concerns about the teaching of ethics. For some, recognition of the mere facts of ethical pluralism carries with it the obligation to be tolerant of the variety of moral viewpoints abroad in the land. The obligation of tolerance embodies a subsidiary duty to refrain from doing things that might undermine the existing plurality of values. There are some who fear that to teach ethics in educational institutions necessarily endangers the pluralistic fabric of our society. An even stronger objection to the teaching of ethics is voiced by those who espouse the normative doctrine of pluralism. To hold that ethical pluralism is a good thing is to have a commitment to allowing diverse value positions to play themselves out in the social and political workings of society. Proponents of this view argue that the natural interplay of

RUTH MACKLIN ● The Hastings Center, Institute of Society, Ethics and the Life Sciences, Hastings-on-Hudson, New York.

value forces is likely to be thwarted by the imposition of moral beliefs or the preaching of ethical doctrines in the classroom. On either interpretation of ethical pluralism, some who see it as a hallmark of our culture worry that the teaching of ethics in higher education will contribute to its erosion.

The chief worries about teaching ethics in a pluralistic society will be explored below. The argument will be in the form of objections and replies— objections to the teaching of ethics in a pluralistic society, and my replies to those objections. The conclusion that I shall attempt to support is that there is nothing to fear from the teaching of ethics, if the fears derive from the pluralistic character of our society. But before turning to the objections and my replies to them, a few initial premises need to be made explicit.

THE TEACHING OF ETHICS VERSUS INDOCTRINATION

The teaching of ethics is a pedagogical activity that involves critical skills, analytical tools, and techniques of careful reasoning. This activity is nonetheless wholly compatible with putting forward a particular normative doctrine—say, egalitarianism, liberal democratic ideals, altruism, or whatever. Teaching ethics is not preaching morals. Nor is it tantamount to indoctrination. But it need be neither a mere rehearsal of all the alternative ethical theories or principles, nor a dry examination of the meaning of "good" or "right" or other metaethical niceties. A teacher of ethics may well have a commitment to one or more ideologies or normative theories, and yet hold that tolerance for the values of others requires that we let a hundred flowers bloom on the plains of value. Put succinctly, the first premise about the nature of teaching ethics that I invite the reader to accept is this: *The teaching of ethics neither rules in, in principle, nor rules out, in principle, espousal of a particular moral viewpoint.*

A second premise that needs to be made explicit at the outset relates to the scope both of ethical pluralism and of the teaching of ethics, as those topics are discussed in what follows. In referring to a plurality of values in our culture, I mean to include everything people actually claim as moral values, regardless of how specific or general they may be. This takes in everything from broad theories of justice and political ideologies, such as democracy or socialism, to specific moral judgments about truth telling, abortion, whistleblowing, or reverse discrimination in hiring or admissions policies.

To recognize the truth of the descriptive thesis of ethical pluralism is not to accept without reservation all of the values in the pluralism. In defending the teaching of ethics against the charge that it erodes traditional values or tends to destroy pluralism in our society, one needs to distinguish systematically those values in the pluralism that should be preserved from those that should not. The teaching of ethics could hardly be defended if it turned out to support an ethical pluralism whose chief elements included racism, political repression, intolerance of religious minorities, and other views of that ilk. In arguing that the teaching of ethics is wholly compatible with sustaining pluralism, I still need to show that the kind of pluralism to be sustained is a desirable one. The following account is incomplete, then, insofar as it fails to provide theoretical criteria for indicating what values ought to be included in pluralism.

Fears about the impact of ethics teaching on the pluralistic nature of the American system of values must be predicated both on what ethics courses are like, and on what ought to be the goals in the teaching of ethics. If no such link is made with the purposes embodied in ethics courses and their success in achieving their stated goals, then objections to the teaching of ethics are bound to lack credibility. The familiar philosophical distinction between *is* and *ought* thus arises here: it cannot be assumed that the way ethics courses are actually taught succeeds in living up to the ideals prescribing how they ought to be taught. To complicate matters further, disagreement exists over what the ideals themselves should be.

To give some concreteness to what tends to be a rather abstract discussion, I shall accept without further explication here the general goals in the teaching of ethics put forth by Daniel Callahan in Chapter 2.[1] Since I shall revert periodically to these goals in stating my replies in the next section, it would be well to list them first here:

1. Stimulating the moral imagination
2. Recognizing ethical issues
3. Developing analytical skills
4. Eliciting a sense of moral obligation and personal responsibility
5. Tolerating and reducing disagreement and ambiguity

As goals, these are necessarily ideal. Some teachers of ethics who strive to reach these goals may nonetheless fail to attain some of them all of the time and all of them some of the time. Moreover, some teachers of ethics probably do not consciously espouse all or even some of these goals. But we must start somewhere, and if these goals are either not sought or not achieved (or both), then perhaps there is more to fear from the teaching of ethics in a pluralistic society than my replies to the objections suggest. But there is much less to fear from teachers of ethics who fail to attain these five goals than from a range of other faculty members in the university: incompetent teachers, indifferent teachers, unscrupulous academic researchers, professors bent on self-aggrandizement, older, tenured faculty who would rather write than teach, and younger, untenured faculty who care less about their students than they do about publishing— lest they perish.

Beyond the acceptance of Callahan's goals, more needs to be said about what ethics teaching ought to be like. Although I think that there is room for

[1]Daniel Callahan, "Goals in the Teaching of Ethics," this volume, pp. 61–80.

a good deal of latitude in methods, course content, and approaches to the subject matter, several features serve to distinguish the teaching of ethics from the wholly different activity of indoctrination. Since a number of the objections to follow rest on an assumption that teaching ethics to students and indoctrinating them are indistinguishable, it would be well to make a few preliminary remarks stating my views about the nature of ethics teaching and how it differs from indoctrination.

One of the chief characteristics of philosophical inquiry is its emphasis on justification and reasoning. The logical relationship between premises and conclusions, questions about what counts as evidence in support of a conclusion, and a rational adjudication among competing theories, are central concerns in all branches of philosophy. A longstanding problem in philosophical ethics is the relationship between facts and values—whether "ought" statements can be derived from premises containing only factual, or "is" statements. Another eternal question is whether reason alone can provide a system of morality, and, if not, what other factors are necessary for the constructing of a well-grounded system of ethics. In exploring these topics, teachers usually conduct a critical examination of classical and modern texts, as well as students' own views presented orally in class, in written assignments, and on examinations. Developing the skills to reason clearly and soundly about moral matters and becoming familiar with the chief ethical positions are the main achievements that teachers of ethics should expect from their students. One way of accomplishing this is for the teacher to confront the class with alternative ethical theories and genuine ethical dilemmas, pointing out that reasonable people sometimes disagree profoundly on questions of value. A critical, reflective examination of ethical beliefs and theories, as well as a look at past and present social practices and institutions, is the approach actually taken by most teachers of philosophical ethics.

In sketching what courses in ethics ought to be like, as well as indicating how they are usually taught, I have focused mainly on the pedagogical enterprise I know best: the teaching of philosophical ethics. Rigorous training in logic and emphasis on the construction of sound arguments are core elements in the education of most philosophers. As a result, they are better equipped than scholars in other disciplines to recognize invalid arguments, formal and informal fallacies in reasoning, and semantical and syntactical ambiguities. It is not that others are unable to perform such tasks, or fail to possess these and valuable complementary skills. Rather, it is that these are central to the nature of philosophical inquiry.

In contrast to the emphasis on reasoning and justification in the teaching of philosophical ethics, the process of indoctrination tends to avoid critical analysis and the use of rational methods. Attempts to define the concept of indoctrination, however, have been fraught with difficulty. Even a cursory look at recent writings on the subject of indoctrination reveals that there is lack of agreement among those who have discussed the concept in the context of education.

On one major view, what makes a practice one of indoctrination is largely an epistemological matter. According to John Wilson:

> The concept of indoctrination concerns the truth and evidence of beliefs.... If we are to avoid indoctrination, therefore, the beliefs we teach must be rational. They need not be certain ... it may only be that the general weight of evidence is in their favor.... What they *must* be is backed by evidence: and by "evidence" of course we must mean publicly accepted evidence, not simply what sectarians like to consider evidence.[2]

Contesting this view, R. M. Hare argues that the essence of indoctrination is to be found in the *aim* of the indoctrinator. Hare criticizes Wilson's view on the grounds that it distinguishes only between *method* and *content* in trying to arrive at an adequate characterization of indoctrination. But there is a third possibility to consider: the intention of the teacher. Hare distinguishes between education and indoctrination on the basis of aim:

> The educator is waiting and hoping all the time for those whom he is educating to start *thinking*.... The indoctrinator, on the other hand, is watching for signs of trouble, and ready to intervene to suppress it when it appears, however oblique and smooth his methods may be. Again, the aim of the educator is to work himself out of a job, to find that he is talking to an equal, to an educated man like himself—a man who may disagree with everything he has ever said; and, unlike the indoctrinator, he will be pleased.[3]

Criticizing both Hare and Wilson, Antony Flew argues that an adequate notion of indoctrination must include reference *both* to content and to aim. The concept of indoctrination Flew himself urges (where indoctrination is taken to be a bad thing) is as follows:

> Indoctrination ... is a matter of trying to implant firm convictions of the truth of doctrines which are in fact either false or at least not known to be true; usually, of course, though not necessarily, the indoctrinator himself believes mistakenly that the doctrines in question are both true and known to be true.[4]

Flew calls this the "primary sense" of the term, and identifies a "second sense" as well. About this sense he claims:

> Indoctrination would be a matter of trying, in any sphere whatever, to implant beliefs, even those which are true and known to be true, by certain disfavoured methods. And the general objection to indoctrination in this sense would presumably be that such methods are in some way incompatible with the production of

---

[2]John Wilson, as quoted in Antony Flew, "Indoctrination and Doctrines," in I. A. Snook, ed., *Concepts of Indoctrination*, (Boston: Routledge & Kegan Paul, 1972), pp. 68–69.
[3]R. M. Hare, as quoted in Flew, p. 69.
[4]Ibid., pp. 86–87.

a proper understanding of what is taught and of a critical appreciation of its
logical and epistemological status.[5]

A view encompassing a number of these features of indoctrination, yet
adding an interesting new twist, is that put forward by Gerald Paske. Paske
claims that Hare's emphasis on the aims of the indoctrinator misleads him into
thinking that the crucial issue is whether a particular aim is accomplished, rather
than what effect is actually occurring in the individual subjected to indoctrination.[6] Paske also questions the definition of indoctrination that makes the content of beliefs inculcated by this process the central feature. He notes that "it is
extremely tempting to define indoctrination in terms of content, and to castigate
those who use procedures quite similar to ours on the grounds that we are
teaching the truth whereas they are indoctrinating false values."[7] Paske thus
rejects both Hare's and Wilson's final characterizations, though recognizing the
partial correctness of their accounts. Paske's own "rough definition" of what he
calls "cognitive indoctrination" is as follows:

> ... It is the process of getting a person to commit himself emotionally to a doc-
> trine independently of his understanding of any rational justification of that doc-
> trine. "Emotional commitment" must be understood to refer to a psychological
> association between the doctrine and the person's evaluation of his own worthi-
> ness such that he *feels* that his own worthiness is dependent upon the truth of the
> doctrine so that he responds to threats and challenges to the doctrine as though
> they were threats to himself. It is this psychological association that allows the
> indoctrinator eventually to allow his victim to "decide for himself," for the victim
> is emotionally incapable of ever objectively reviewing his commitments.[8]

It is beyond the scope of this paper to adjudicate among these contending
interpretations of the concept of indoctrination. I think Paske's account is the
most illuminating, generally, and especially for the attempt to distinguish the
teaching of ethics from the activity of indoctrination. Taken together, these several views cite features of indoctrination that are incompatible with the five general goals in the teaching of ethics presupposed here. Those whose aim is to
indoctrinate rather than educate will *suppress* the moral imagination, rather than
stimulate it; they will *announce* what counts as an ethical issue rather than try to
get students to recognize ethical issues; they will *not* strive to develop analytical
skills; they may elicit a sense of moral obligation, but in a narrow and circum-
scribed way, as prescribed by the doctrine they strive to implant; and they will
most certainly not tolerate disagreement and ambiguity.

Further worries that the teaching of ethics might amount to a form of
indoctrination are discussed in the objections and replies below. The following

[5]Ibid., p. 87.
[6]Gerald Paske, "Education and the Problem of Indoctrination," *Proceedings of the Philosophy
of Education Society,* Philosophy of Education Society, 1972, p. 94.
[7]Ibid., p. 95.
[8]Ibid., p. 98.

objections include ones that people have actually stated, as well as possible objections lurking behind some vague disquiet that surfaces on occasion.

OBJECTIONS AND REPLIES

OBJECTION 1

The basis of morality lies in religious teachings. The Constitutional provision of freedom of religion, along with the separation of church and state, precludes the teaching of religious doctrines in schools. Since ethics must be based on religious underpinnings, its inclusion in nondenominational educational institutions, whether public or private, is inappropriate.

REPLY

The first mistake in this objection lies in the first sentence. It is simply false that the basis of all morality lies in religious teachings. Although it is surely true that the origins of at least some contemporary Western ethical beliefs and moral principles are found in Judaic and Christian religious sources, this is not the same as identifying the basis of morality with a religious underpinning. But it is not an uncommon mistake, in spite of the fundamental error involved in linking ethics and religion in an essential way. Even if it is true that much of our contemporary Western system of morality had its origins in Judeo-Christian teachings, it is an instance of the genetic fallacy to assert that, because things started that way, there must still remain a religious basis to morality.

Other writers have made similar replies to this sort of objection. In a paper on the same topic as the present one, Peter Caws discusses the reluctance in ethics courses to teach the elementary principles dogmatically. Caws writes:

> I wonder whether this reluctance may not be partly due to a fear that to insist on any particular maxims in secular institutions of learning would be to violate the constitutional provision about the separation of church and state. For there is a very widespread belief that ethics and religion are somehow connected. If something like this is at work—if it is covertly felt that the teaching of morality, to be effective, must somehow involve, even implicitly, an appeal to a higher system of belief—then no wonder moral standards have declined....The teacher of ethics should in my view explicitly disavow the connection of religion, construed as a present reliance on any belief in the transcendent. This does not mean being antireligious, or denying the immense debt that we owe to the moral imagination of religious thinkers in the past; it means only that a secular morality must rest on a secular basis.[9]

---

[9]Peter Caws, "On the Teaching of Ethics in a Pluralistic Society," *Hastings Center Report*, (1978), p. 34.

The second mistake in Objection 1 lies in the assumption that teaching ethics is the equivalent of teaching religious doctrines. Even when the content of ethics courses includes a study of theological ethics, or early Christian writings on ethics, the way in which the subject matter should be taught bears little resemblance to religious instruction in church schools or seminaries. At least two of the goals in the teaching of ethics discussed by Daniel Callahan are incompatible with the way in which religious doctrines are usually promulgated. Goal 3—Developing analytical skills—requires that courses attend to "the definition of concepts, the import and consequences of moral rules, and the meaning and scope of general ethical principles."[10] Callahan notes further that "as much as anything else, the development of analytical skills will be simply the development of logical skills. Coherence and consistency are minimal goals, both in the analysis of ethical propositions and in their justification."[11] Goal 5—Tolerating and resisting disagreement and ambiguity—seems precisely the opposite of what courses intended to inculcate doctrinal religious beliefs would aim for. As Callahan observes:

> What separates ethics, and probably philosophy in general, from other kinds of intellectual analysis is the necessity of constantly questioning the most basic premises of the entire enterprise.... Moreover ... the profundity of disagreement in ethics (both theoretically and certainly in pluralistic societies) makes it difficult to find undisputed conventions that can serve to avoid the necessity of arguing each and every issue down to its very roots.[12]

Although a number of the precepts of religious ethics may be identical with those of secular ethics, it does not follow that the foundations of morality derive from religious teachings. Objection 1 can, therefore, be dismissed as resting on a mistaken belief about the nature of philosophical ethics as a discipline.

OBJECTION 2

Since a pluralist society contains a number of diverse religious viewpoints, the teaching of ethics must invariably include some, while overlooking others. This result is patently unfair to students whose religious beliefs fail to get addressed in ethics courses.

REPLY

The reply to this objection can take one of two different tacks. The first and harsher response simply reasserts that the teaching of ethics need not be the teaching of religion, so that teachers of ethics are under no obligation whatever to see to it that all viewpoints in religious ethics are fairly represented. A course

[10]Callahan, p. 67.
[11]Ibid.
[12]Ibid., 67–68.

in religious ethics should, perhaps, strive for completeness within the domain it aims to cover. But the content, scope, and methods of nonreligious instruction in ethics need not attend to the full range of religious viewpoints, in the name of tolerance for the plurality of ethical values or anything else.

The second and kinder response to this objection takes the form of a plea for understanding the time constraints and priorities in ethics courses, as elsewhere in the curriculum. There simply is not time to give comprehensive (or even brief) coverage to every ethical theory or moral perspective ever held. This is so for philosophical ethics as well as religious ethics. Someone's views are bound to be left out, no matter what the orientation of an ethics course. So those who advance Objection 2 need to reflect on whether their discontent lies solely with the omission of religious perspectives in ethics courses, or whether they would argue just as strongly for the inclusion of all secular viewpoints in a pluralist society. Either way, total comprehensiveness in the subject matter of any course is an impossible goal.

OBJECTION 3

Ethics may not rest on a religious foundation; even so, there is a right to moral freedom, just as there is to religious freedom. Shouldn't a free society honor separation of morality and state, as well as of church and state?

REPLY

I think not. Notice that separation of church and state itself operates within moral limits; we do not and should not allow such things as sacrifices of young children, even if they are motivated wholly by religious reasons. Moral freedom is similar in that its legitimate exercise is limited by certain moral principles. It is different, however, in that its central element is a negative right not to be coerced to hold certain moral views, rather than a positive right to engage in practices that accord with one's views.[13]

Some further points deserve to be made in reply to this objection. First, it is wrong to suppose that teaching ethics at any level of education is the equivalent of having a state religion. It was that prospect that moved the founding fathers to ensure the separation of church and state in America. What moral theory or set of principles might one fear could become tantamount to a state religion, if ethics is taught in the schools? Given the wide-ranging views of individual teachers—even if they did teach ethics in a manner analogous to the way religion is usually taught, it is unlikely that a single, predominant view could ever take hold.

But, the objector might retort, it is not the promotion of a single, predom-

---

[13]Robert Audi, "Tolerance without Relativity: A Perspective on Moral Education," Paper presented at the Values Issues in Education Conference, Center for the Study of Values, University of Delaware, Newark, October 25–28, 1978, p. 15.

inant view that is to be feared, so much as the arrogation of responsibility by schools of what properly should be the task of the home or of religious institutions. It is not the proper business of colleges, universities, or secondary schools to engage in moral instruction.

To reply to this formulation, it is necessary to make a distinction between the teaching of ethics, on the one hand, and moral instruction, on the other. Moral instruction is an activity whose overriding aim is to get students to accept and act on a specific set of moral beliefs or principles. Unlike formal ethics teaching, it usually does not involve a critical examination of alternative principles, or any attempt to develop moral reasoning. Once the distinction between the teaching of ethics and moral instruction is made clearly, little remains of Objection 3.

There is, however, a lingering air of paradox about Objection 3. Separation of church and state, and, hence, the teaching of religious doctrines, are topics addressed by the U. S. Constitution. But not only is separation of morality and state not prescribed by that document; if anything, the Constitution itself mandates certain forms of conduct, and proscribes others, *on moral grounds*. The Bill of Rights is the embodiment of a number of basic moral rights, and other Constitutional amendments guarantee specific freedoms as well as equality for all persons under the law. Although law and morality do not always coincide, there are surely many laws, at every level of government, that are enacted or rescinded for moral reasons. So far from its being the case that a free society should honor separation of morality and state, as Objection 3 proposes, our own liberal democracy rests on moral foundations, and embodies moral precepts in statutes and in judicial decisions.

OBJECTION 4

Granted that ethics does not necessarily rest on a religious foundation; that is precisely the problem with teaching ethics in educational institutions. It undercuts the religious foundations of ethics by teaching morality as a secular enterprise.

REPLY

But morality *is* a secular enterprise, just as much as it is a religious enterprise. To deny this is to take a narrow view of ethics, and one that is mistaken, besides. Take, for example, that part of morality that has to do with justice. Judaic and Christian religious teachings did have something to say about retributive justice (in fact, as is well known, the Old and the New Testament differ on that subject), but neither Judaism nor Christianity, in the ancient writings, even addresses the topic of distributive justice. Another gap in classical religious and philosophical teachings is the whole subject of human rights. Neither the ancient Greeks nor the major Western religions had a concept of individual rights as we are familiar with that concept today. One of the marks of a good general course in ethics is that it points out the different emphases, theories, and concepts of various historical and contemporary approaches to ethics.

More important, to teach morality as a secular enterprise is in no way to undercut its religious foundations. It would be just as dishonest for a teacher of ethics to deny the historical foundations in religion of some modern ethical precepts as it would be for religious ethicists to deny the numerous and influential secular contributions to the field of ethics. Some less-than-scrupulous *teachers* of ethics may attempt to undercut the religious foundations of ethics in one way or another. But the teaching of ethics as a secular pedagogical enterprise could not by itself yield that result.

OBJECTION 5

Those who teach ethics are likely to use their courses to press their own private political and other value agendas. Even if this is done under the guise of "consciousness raising," teachers will more than likely use the occasion to emphasize their own particular versions of value issues. The result will be a distortion of the very nature of ethics, as well as of the range of legitimate value positions.

REPLY

First of all, a teacher need not be teaching ethics to seize an occasion to press his or her own political value agendas. Faculty members in departments of history, literature, or any of the social sciences can find ample opportunity, using the subject matter of their own discipline, to put forward moral or political views, even when the course ostensibly has nothing to do with ethics. Beyond that, in times when social and political issues of great moral weight are in the news and on everyone's lips, faculty members whose area of specialization has nothing to do with ethics, politics, or religion are often among the most vociferous spokesmen for social change, political activism, or opposition. Anyone associated with universities during the 1960s saw professors of physics leading sit-ins (not solely in protest against the bomb), organic chemists organizing teach-ins, and civil engineers urging civil-rights activism. Many members of the faculty and administration argued at the time that the university is not the proper place to engage in social protest, and that academe should not serve as a political forum.

Regardless of the merits or demerits of that position, there remains a singularly appropriate place within the university for discussion of just and unjust wars, paternalism on the part of the government, the ethics of lying in the alleged interest of national security, the morality of brutality to suppress agitators for social change. That place is the ethics classroom. If an ethics teacher strives to attain the five general goals in the teaching of ethics, and, what is more, has succeeded in at least some of these goals, then students will be equipped to evaluate the teacher's own moral arguments, and even to rebut them if they are unsound.

If there is a tendency for those teaching ethics to use their classroom as a forum to expound their personal value systems (and I have suggested that such tendencies, when they exist, are not limited to those who teach ethics), it will not be confined to faculty members of only one moral or political persuasion. Although college professors may, in the aggregate, fall slightly more to the left along the political spectrum than the population at large, it is surely not the case that professors of moral philosophy, religious ethics, politics, or any other discipline where ethics is taught all occupy positions from the liberal left to flaming radicalism. This is largely an empirical matter, and one that deserves careful, systematic study if this objection to the teaching of ethics is to have any weight at all.

OBJECTION 6

Regardless of any connections (or lack thereof) between ethics and religion, the teaching of ethics is tantamount to indoctrination. There is good reason to question the place of indoctrination in any educational setting. But it is surely out of place in the curriculum of colleges and universities in a pluralistic society.

REPLY

To raise this question is to deny explicitly or to ignore the first premise with which we began, namely, that teaching ethics is not at all the same thing as preaching a doctrine, promoting an ethical code, or foisting an ideology on unwitting students. Rather, it should be a pedagogical activity involving the use and transmission of critical skills and analytical tools, and imparting knowledge of traditional and contemporary ethical theory. As already noted, this is compatible with putting forward a particular normative doctrine, but only if it is done in a rational, critical manner. Teachers of ethics in higher education do use methods of instruction that differ radically from those employed by people whose aim is to indoctrinate. And the content of ethics courses is bound to differ in a number of respects from efforts to indoctrinate or promote a specific ideology. Courses in religious as well as philosophical ethics include an examination of a number of different ethical theories, political doctrines, and moral perspectives.

For example, in a course devoted to a study of theories of justice, it is common to include the seventeenth-century political and economic position known as libertarian theory, along with its twentieth-century version; the classical utilitarian view; a welfare-state liberal theory such as the detailed, scholarly treatise by John Rawls; more radical egalitarian conceptions of justice; and perhaps even the very first work on justice in the Western philosophical tradition— Plato's *Republic*. This is obviously quite different from a course that masquerades as a general course in ethics, in which all of the readings are from the New Testament or the Koran or the *Communist Manifesto* or *The Prince*. But even courses devoted to a thorough examination of one major work or one man's writings or one ideological viewpoint need not amount to a form of indoctrination. Would those who urge Objection 6 to the teaching of ethics wish to ban seminars or independent study devoted to a scholarly exploration of a single topic in ethical or political theory? If so, it is not pluralism that they are defending, but a form of censorship in the university.

Recall again Callahan's five general goals in the teaching of ethics. If we accept the notion that a central goal is that of analysis, clarification, and the critical examination of ideas, then there is surely nothing to fear from a careful and critical exposure to a wide variety of ideas. Students will be armed with the techniques of reasoning and rational argument with which to assess ideologies and doctrines. Today one could not teach the Old Testament or *The Wealth of Nations* or Locke's *Second Treatise* if the examination of a variety of doctrines in the history of traditional and modern thought were either banned or required "equal time" from every competing view.

OBJECTION 7

The replies to Objections 5 and 6 are convincing, as far as they go. But they do not meet all of the worries about indoctrination and the teaching of ethics in pluralistic society. What about the teacher who introduces an ideological bias in the very selection of material? Or the teacher who asserts that the "only important moral issue" or the "real" issue is racism, or capitalist exploitation of the workers, or the environmental crisis? Although these tendencies do not constitute a blatant form of indoctrination, they can have the same effect in influencing students. The issues selected for study are the chief moral issues in the eyes of that teacher of ethics, but not in the larger, pluralistic society.

REPLY

Although this objection does cite a potential problem for the teaching of ethics, it is not really a problem of indoctrination. The discussion in the previous section laid out a number of features of indoctrination—features that do not seem to be present in the tendencies described in Objection 7. These tendencies require a substantially different explanation and analysis from considerations of indoctrination. The concerns expressed here are much closer to the worry behind Objection 5—that of teachers who grind their own moral axes in the classroom. This is bound to be more subtle than straightforward indoctrination, since the method of teaching is often the same as that in courses where the selection of material is not ideologically biased. In other words, a teacher who concentrates on a particular moral issue of the times may well choose readings and conduct a careful inquiry with all of the balance, rigor, and scholarship of a course that is not similarly biased. How can we protect against these subtle forms of influencing students' values?

First of all, it needs to be emphasized that bias in the selection of materials is not limited to the ethics classroom. Teachers of economics, history, sociology, literature—virtually every subject except, perhaps, the physical sciences and engineering—necessarily introduce a value bias into the selection of material. This is so even when the subject matter is not directly concerned with moral issues. Take economics, for example. There is just as much bias in the selection of materials for general courses in economics that wholly ignore a Marxist analysis as there is in courses that purport to be basic courses but are totally given over to Marxist interpretations. The same holds for selection both of subject matter and texts in history or in political science. Unless the objector is urging, once again, a form of censorship that would limit the items of curricular study in universities to those interpretations according with the ideals of liberal democracy, there must be considerable latitude granted to faculty to choose topics, texts, and emphases for their courses. This is what academic freedom is all about.

Second, and more to the point, granting faculty this latitude seems to be perfectly compatible with the tenets of ethical pluralism. If courses in ethics or any other subject are taught in such a way that they avoid the features of indoctrination cited in the previous reply, then there is little to fear in the way of an erosion of pluralism as a result of the teaching of ethics. Shouldn't we have more to fear from overprotection or isolation of students from radical, minority, or skewed value biases—when these are clearly present in the larger society—than from exposure to them in the halls of learning?

All of us who have taught in colleges or universities have some topics that we think are more important than others in our area of specialization. Each of us has value biases, of one sort or another, that will be conveyed to students, wittingly or unwittingly. In my view, the best way to deal with this matter is for teachers to put their value biases up front, so to speak, by acknowledging them explicitly in the classroom. Second best is for teachers to be left free to impart whatever biases they hold by the selection of texts and topics, whether in ethics courses or elsewhere. In the long run, in a pluralistic society, these value biases will balance out. Least preferable, I would argue, is to prohibit courses devoted explicitly to ethics or to institute some form of higher control over course contents or texts. To maintain the fiction of value neutrality is both dishonest and shortsighted. In the end, it is contrary to the ideals of ethical pluralism.

OBJECTION 8

If teaching ethics is not the same as engaging in a form of indoctrination, then it must be left, in the end, to the students to arrive at their own substantive moral judgments. But this approach fails to recognize (a) the essential human condition of fallibility, and (b) the result that ethics courses will turn out to be morally wishy-washy.

REPLY

Since there are two parts to this objection, I shall take up each part in turn.

The objection (a) from human infallibility is voiced by Carl Bereiter, who mounts a many-pronged attack on moral education in the public schools. Although his stated objection is to values education in secondary schools, the same points might be raised against the teaching of ethics in higher education. The present objection is most likely to be voiced by those who view morality as essentially linked to religion. Indeed, Bereiter's statement of this objection indicates as much. In discussing the position that it is a good idea for everyone to form moral opinions, Bereiter cites Roman Catholic doctrine as a primary source for the contrary view:

> Human beings, presumably at any level of moral development, can arrive at mistaken conclusions. Where the matter is one of spiritual consequence, the Church intercedes with its own wisdom, which, while not infallible either, is supposed to be a lot less fallible than the wisdom of the isolated individual. The new moral educators do not, of course, deny human error, but it seems that the only correction they allow for is self-correction or by peer influence.[13]

What is the alternative to allowing or urging individuals to come to their own moral conclusions? Presumably, issuing moral judgments that stem from some acknowledged authority, be it the Church, the predominant view of the government in power, or even the teacher. A curiosity in the objections to the teaching of ethics emerges clearly at this point. Ironically, the entire set of objections to the teaching of ethics in a pluralistic society stems from two opposing worries; that students will be influenced *too much* by the value biases of their teachers (Objections 5, 6, and 7); and that students will receive *too little* guidance in the formation of their moral judgments (the present objection). The fact that these essentially opposite worries are voiced, and that both need to be taken seriously in defending the teaching of ethics, strikes a note of confidence in pluralism.

There is little danger that students will flounder helplessly in the search for

[13]Carl Bereiter, "The Morality of Moral Education," *Hastings Center Report*, (1978), p. 23.

moral convictions. The schools are not the sole influence in the formation of an individual's system of values. It is probably true that the schools constitute the weakest influence—behind the home, religious instruction for those who are exposed to it, peers, and the community. The argument from human fallibility, if taken seriously, would have a pernicious effect on higher education. It would shut off opportunities for students to learn to think reflectively and critically. It would lessen the tendency for students to put forward their own moral viewpoints and have them subjected to critical scrutiny by teachers and fellow students. An educational policy that would minimize opportunities for self-correction, as this objection seems to promote, is intellectually pernicious, and at odds with the tenets of a pluralistic society.

As for the objection (b) that ethics courses will turn out to be morally wishy-washy if they are not tantamount to some form of indoctrination, here again we face the curious irony of polar oppositions to the teaching of ethics. But what does it mean to charge a course with being "morally wish-washy"? Does it mean that the course does not provide univocal answers to all the hard moral choices and ethical dilemmas confronting individuals in their ordinary life or professionals in their practice? Does it mean that there are no moral presumptions in favor of truth telling instead of lying, acting from duty rather than self-interest? Or does it mean that students are taught to analyze moral arguments and to develop sound reasoning in favor of whatever viewpoint they may wish to adopt, so that courses in ethics are reduced to instruction in how to win at moral argumentation?

It may mean any or all of these things. In this objection, as in earlier ones, the problem seems to lie in the prospect of bad teachers doing inappropriate things in the classroom. A teacher of ethics who fails to impart to students the idea that some courses of action are in general morally better than others (truth telling over lying, for example), with readings, exercises, and ample class discussion to illustrate the point, suffers an intellectual as well as a moral failing. Further, a teacher who emphasizes *winning* in moral arguments, instead of trying to arrive at morally superior conclusions, should have chosen a career teaching law rather than ethics. A course in ethics that fails to demonstrate to students that moral reasons for acting are superior, in an important sense, to reasons of self-interest or expediency is a course that need not have been taught at all, from a pedagogical as well as from a moral point of view. The difficulty, then, lies in the prospect of inadequate teaching or morally obtuse instructors, not with the enterprise of the teaching of ethics.

OBJECTION 9

Even if the teaching of ethics need not amount to a mode of indoctrination, how are we to decide just what moral principles, moral values, or ethical viewpoints to teach?

REPLY

Now we get to the heart of the matter. The short answer to this question is: teach the major ones, the important ones, those prominent in our culture or in today's world. But that answer is both too general and too glib. I look for more precise formulations from others who have thought about the matter.

Peter Caws, in his paper "On the Teaching of Ethics in a Pluralistic Society," notes that America is "the great *Aufhebung* of conflicting traditions and beliefs, but does that mean that we are obliged to make room for cultures in which lying and fraud and murder are the norm ...?" Caws observes that "on reflection it seems to me that ours is clearly not a morally pluralistic society ... and I think that that is because it is not a rationally pluralistic society."[14] Caws notes in this connection that we do not accept the notion of ethnic arithmetic or regional logic. By the same token, we do not accept the view that race or religion excuse people from observing ethical norms. The trick lies in squaring the obvious pluralism of *values* in our society with what is really a fundamental *moral* agreement on principles of conduct, human rights, and a range of social practices.

Similar points are made by Robert Audi in a paper entitled "Tolerance without Relativity: A Perspective on Moral Education." In answer to the question posed in Objection 9, Audi replies:

> In a free and democratic society, we need to decide which are basic and concentrate on teaching them, and, to a lesser degree, subsidiary principles, values, and rights.... [S]uch principles as those prohibiting murdering, harming, enslaving, lying to, and stealing from, others, and those requiring us to treat People "equally" ... are all examples of what I would call basic moral principles, and I believe that many basic moral principles, basic moral values, and basic moral rights are expressed in the U. S. Constitution.[15]

Other, somewhat broader moral principles appear in a quotation from R. S. Peters: impartiality, the consideration of interests, freedom, and respect for persons.

In replying earlier to Objection 3, I argued that one reason *not* to seek a "separation of morality and state" is that the Constitutional basis for our own political system embodies a set of basic moral precepts. That point is reiterated in replying to the present objection. Surely we cannot go wrong in our pluralistic society by including in ethics courses an examination of the fundamental moral values that lie at the heart of our liberal democracy: freedom, equality, justice, tolerance, respect for the privacy and autonomy of persons. To the extent that these values sometimes come into conflict with one another, as they inevitably do in the practical sphere, then it is the task of teachers of ethics to conduct a rational and informed inquiry into these conflicts. It is no threat to ethical plu-

[14]Caws, p. 35.
[15]Audi, pp. 22–23.

ralism to draw conclusions in favor of one or another of our most cherished moral precepts, when one must take precedence over another in the formation of policies or in making social choices.

OBJECTION 10

Even though we live in a pluralistic society, it is a mistake to think that the plurality of values people adhere to are all correct. Some come into conflict with others, and incompatible beliefs cannot simultaneously be correct. But there *is* a set of universally valid moral principles, although not everyone believes in their truth. Therefore, any attempt to teach ethics in a nonpartisan or value-neutral fashion will be misleading, dishonest, or pernicious.

REPLY

The key point in this objection is the assertion that there *is* a set of universally valid moral principles. In one extreme form, this claim can be expanded into the doctrine known as "moral absolutism." This is not itself a normative ethical thesis; rather, it is a metaethical position about the nature of moral judgments or moral principles. In one version, the thesis holds that there exists a universally valid set of duties and moral obligations, which has a correlative set of rights. In another version, it holds that there exist one or more timeless, exceptionless, or universally valid moral principles. In whatever version, this position has been the subject of unending debate among moral philosphers. It is not at all clear what could count as conclusive evidence for its truth or falsity. It is surely beyond the scope of this paper to address this long-standing metaethical dispute. To the extent that Objection 10 gains its force from one of these opposing stances in the debate over the truth of ethical absolutism or its contradictory thesis, normative ethical relativism, it is not an objection that can fruitfully be taken up in this paper. Its ultimate reply must await the resolution of the metaethical controversy on which it rests.

In the meantime, there is all the more reason to plunge ahead with the teaching of ethics. Any decent course in ethics—whether philosophical, religious, or applied—should devote some time to a study of the debate over ethical absolutism versus ethical relativism, and the detailed arguments in support of each. Absolutists who voice Objection 10 can then remain hopeful that, if ethics continues to be taught, perhaps some brilliant student will come up with a demonstration of the truth of the absolutist contention.

OBJECTION 11

Normative ethical relativism is the correct philosophical position. Since there are no moral absolutes—or even any interpersonal moral truths—no doctrine of any sort should be taught in schools. In a pluralistic society, people gain their values from whatever interest group or subculture they happen to belong to. But since teachers of ethics can not hope to include all ethical, political, religious, and social ideologies or theories, and, in any case, are not likely to present all divergent views fairly, ethics should not be included in the curriculum.

REPLY

This objection, the weary reader might still be able to discern, is the obverse of the previous objection. Just as Objection 10 gains its force from the truth of some version of ethical absolutism, the present objection relies for its force on the correctness of normative ethical relativism. This position holds that the only meaning assignable to notions of right and wrong, good and bad, derives from the particular cultural norms, standards, or values in which such moral concepts are embedded. There are no cross-culturally valid ethical norms or principles. There are no universally valid moral theories. In its extreme form, ethical relativism holds that it is impossible even to make interpersonal moral judgments, since no two persons completely share a common set of values.

To the extent that this objection rests on the truth of normative ethical relativism, we are faced with the same problems in replying to it as we confronted in the previous objection. A satisfactory reply must hinge on the resolution of the absolutism–relativism controversy, so we may proceed straightaway to the next objection.

OBJECTION 12

Even though we live in a pluralistic society, it is a mistake to think that the plurality of values people adhere to can all be correct. Since incompatible beliefs cannot simultaneously be correct, a teacher must come down on one side or another when ethical conclusions come into conflict. But there exists no agreed-upon method for resolving fundamental ethical disputes; so to select any one moral view and argue for it would be arbitrary, doctrinaire, or contrary to sound philosophical practice.

REPLY

This objection appears to be a variant of Objection 11. But here the metaethical force behind the objection lies in the lack of a satisfactory method for the rational resolution of value disputes. This objection would have us await yet another metaethical advance before undertaking to teach ethics at any level. Although it may begin to sound like an article of faith, it is worth repeating once again the point made earlier: the more students who take courses in ethics,

the greater the likelihood that one will stumble on a solution to the chief unresolved epistemological problem in metaethics—an agreed-upon method for set-
tling ethical disagreement. But there are other points worth making in reply to
this objection.

The objection assumes that teachers must come down on one side or the
other when ethical stances come into conflict. But, in fact, many teachers fail to
take a stance, for one reason or another; it is not always the case that a particular
moral position is adopted by the teacher. Previous replies have dealt with objections to the failure of teachers to draw moral conclusions in the course of teaching ethics, and no further remarks need be added here.

More important, it is neither arbitrary nor doctrinaire nor contrary to sound
philosophical practice to offer arguments in support of one or another moral
view in the teaching of ethics. It is not arbitrary, because some moral positions
are clearly more defensible than others. It is not arbitrary to defend freedom
against most forms of coercion; to defend equality of persons against various
forms of economic or political exploitation; to defend the promotion of the
general welfare against the power and authority of the ruling few. To the extent
that philosophy can distinguish good reasons from bad, and better arguments
from worse, in support of a moral position, it is not arbitrary to select one moral
view and argue for it. Nor is it doctrinaire to offer arguments in support of one
or another moral view, if the teacher accepts and strives to obtain the important
goals in the teaching of ethics. Only when the teaching of ethics lapses into a
form of indoctrination can the adoption of a particular moral viewpoint by a
teacher be correctly termed "doctrinaire."

Finally, to adopt a reasoned argument in support of a particular value
stance is not contrary to sound philosophical practice; it is an instance of it.
There are few areas of philosophy where there is universal agreement among
scholars or recognized giants in the field. Philosophy thrives on unresolved problems and disagreements about the foundations of inquiry. Philosophical ethics
is no exception. We might as well close the doors on the philosophical study
of epistemology, metaphysics, philosophy of science—perhaps even some areas
of logic—if lack of an agreed-upon method for resolving disputes were sufficient reason to cease teaching the subject. What is important is to bring to the
forefront of teaching the uncertainty and disagreement that remain in these
methodological and epistemological matters. This should be part of the subject
matter of courses in ethics, rather than something to sweep under the rug or to
count as a reason to abandon the pedagogical enterprise. It would be enlightening, both to students and to many faculty members in other disciplines, to
learn that epistemological and methodological uncertainty and disagreement
exist in science as well as in ethics. No one argues (cogently) that we ought to
abandon the teaching of the natural sciences or the social sciences when fundamental disagreement remains. Why should it be any different for ethics?

CONCLUSION

There is a final point of opposition—in the form of a metaobjection—to all of my replies. "These replies are all very well and good in theory; but, in the end, the teaching of ethics will only be defensible against the objections if those who teach ethics succeed in adhering to the five general goals. Some may fail because they refuse to acknowledge the stated goals in the first place. Others may accept the goals, but fall short through incompetence or human weakness. Since we cannot ban from teaching ethics any of these types, it is better not to take the risk. Therefore, ethics ought not be taught in a pluralist society."

I disagree. It is better to take the risk. Where laudable goals or worthwhile ideals exist in human endeavor, it is better to strive to achieve them and fall short than never to seek these goals at all. It is better to approximate such goals in the teaching of ethics than to refuse to embark on the task because of possible failure. If the goal of careful analysis of moral arguments, clarification of ethical theories, and critical examination of ideas is approximated to some extent, then there is little to fear in a pluralistic society from exposing students to a wide variety of ideas. Even assuming that there are teachers who engage in some manner of indoctrination, or who violate the spirit of pluralism in some other way, it is still better to take the risk.

The burden is on those who think that ethics should not be taught to advance convincing arguments why this subject matter should be exempted from the curriculum in a liberal education that includes courses in religious studies, politics, economics, and sociology. Perhaps the motto that serves best here is: Let the buyer beware. If parents fear that their own religious or ideological beliefs will be undermined by their son or daughter's taking courses in ethics in undergraduate school, perhaps those parents and their unfortunate offspring should seek a college or university with advance knowledge of its curriculum and any ideologies that may be embedded in it. But these same parents and students should also remain alert to the fact that, even if no ethics courses were taught on any college campus, there would remain role models, peer groups, books of all persuasions, the mass media, commercial advertising, political campaigns, and whatever other influences exist in daily life. The unique value of good ethics teaching in the domain of higher education is that both its method and its subject matter are much more likely to be balanced, informed, well-reasoned, and scholarly than any of the other modes of transmitting values that impinge on everyone's life in a pluralistic society.

CHAPTER 4

What Does Moral Psychology Have to Say to the Teacher of Ethics?

THOMAS LICKONA

The psychological study of morality, like the teaching of ethics, has suffered fluctuating fortunes. Like ethics, the systematic study of moral development and behavior was largely neglected for much of this century. In recent times, however, both ethics teaching and moral psychology have made a comeback. Although it is safe to say that between the two disciplines there are ample opportunities for mutual learning, my assignment here is to look at half of that exchange. What does moral psychology have to say to the teacher of ethics?

"Moral psychology" is a wide tent. Under it gather an assortment of types who are no more agreed about the basic issues that define their enterprise than ethicists presumably are about the issues that define theirs. Different moral psychologists operate with different models of man, different ideas about what is important to study, and different research methodologies. There are cognitive developmentalists, who study structural stages in the development of moral thinking. There are social psychologists, who focus on the impact of situational variables on moral behavior. There are old-style learning theorists who reduce morality to a matter of conditioned or reinforced responses, and social-learning theorists who place more emphasis on social models and the vast amount of learning that occurs by watching what other people do and what happens to them. There are also cognitive learning theorists, who are interested in how people learn moral rules or concepts. And there are personality theorists, such as ego-psychologists or psychoanalysts, who see moral development and behavior as being governed by deep psychic needs, such as the need to feel safe or esteemed.

I would like to focus on the first two of these approaches—cognitive-

THOMAS LICKONA • Department of Education, State University of New York at Cortland, Cortland, New York.

developmental stage psychology and social psychology—since these seem to me to have important implications for ethical education at the undergraduate and graduate levels. What do these two schools of moral psychology teach us about moral development and behavior? And what does this psychological knowledge suggest about the goals and methods of the teaching of ethics?

THE PSYCHOLOGY OF MORAL DEVELOPMENT

Morality *develops*. The verification and elaboration of that basic idea will no doubt stand as one of the central contributions of the twentieth-century study of morality. Originally articulated by Plato, the idea that moral under-standing progresses through a series of stages, each more mature than the pre-ceding, gained its first empirical validation through the work of Jean Piaget and his associates. Piaget's pioneering book, *The Moral Judgment of the Child*,[1] reported his observations of how children constructed and understood the rules of a game of marbles, and how they responded to his "clinical interviews" about moral questions and stories (e.g., What is a lie? What should you do if someone walks up to you on the street and punches you? Who is naughtier—a boy who broke 15 cups by accident, or a boy who broke one cup when he was stealing some jam?) On the basis of this work with 5 to 13-year-old children, Piaget postulated three overlapping stages of moral development: a "heteronomous morality" based on unilateral respect for the rules of adult authority; a morality of cooperation and strict equality based on mutual respect among social peers; and a morality of equity based on a flexible, Golden-Rule consideration of the needs of individuals in particular situations. Although his research was limited to Swiss children, the basic outline of Piaget's description, and many of the details, have been confirmed by scores of independently executed studies carried out over several continents.[2]

Lawrence Kohlberg, as a doctoral student at the University of Chicago in 1955, picked up where Piaget left off. Kohlberg began a still-continuing lon-gitudinal study of 50 working and middle-class males, then 10 to 16 years old. Like Piaget, Kohlberg adopted the basic developmentalist-structuralist assump-tions that the life of the mind is organized into *holistic structures*, that these organized patterns of thought are *constructed* by the individual through inter-action with the environment, and that such psychological structures develop in a natural *sequence of stages* which occur, like biological differentiation and inte-gration, in human cultures everywhere. Like Piaget, Kohlberg defined moral

[1] J. Piaget, *The Moral Judgment of the Child* (New York: Random House, 1965).
[2] For a review of these studies see T. Lickona, "Research on Paiget's Theory of Moral Devel-opment," in T. Lickona, ed., *Moral Development and Behavior* (New York: Holt, Rinehart & Winston, 1976) pp. 219–240.

judgment according to how an individual reasons (structure), rather than according to what he thinks (content). To try to lay bare the structure of a person's moral reasoning, Kohlberg conducted in-depth interviews about moral dilemmas. For example: Should a doctor mercy-kill a fatally ill woman who pleads to be put out of her pain? Why or why not? Does the woman have the right to make such a request? And so on.

Kohlberg reinterviewed his subjects every three years. He used several different dilemmas to probe their thinking about 10 value issues that he maintains all people, regardless of class or culture, deal with in their social relations: punishment, law, property, affection, authority, the value of life, liberty, truth, sex, and justice. Of the six moral stages that Kohlberg has postulated (see Table I),[3] the first five have been confirmed by his longitudinal research. He reports: "At every 3-year interval, subjects either remained at the same stage or moved one stage ahead," with some subjects moving all the way from Stage 1 to Stage 5.[4]

The six stages of moral reasoning are perhaps best illustrated by successive views of justice, the central issue in Kohlberg's concept of morality. He holds that a person's view of justice permeates his approach to defining human rights and obligations and to solving any moral conflict.

The concern for justice, like thinking about other moral issues, is given a new and wider definition at each higher stage. At Stage 1, the conception of justice is a primitive "mechanical equivalence," an eye for an eye and a tooth for a tooth. At Stage 2, the individual becomes aware that he and others have different viewpoints and interests of which they are mutually aware, and justice takes a positive dimension: you help me and I'll help you, let's make a deal. At Stage 3, justice becomes ideal reciprocity, the Golden Rule applied to interpersonal relations; here, being fair means being a nice guy, putting yourself in the other guy's shoes, and living up to the expectations of significant others, like friends and family.

At Stage 4, the relatively simple Stage 3 morality of interpersonal relations is broadened. The Stage 4 thinker reasons that getting along in a complex society, with just distribution of rights and duties, requires a social system of roles, authority, and law. Kohlberg's research indicates that only a minority reaches Stage 4 by the end of high school, and fewer than 20% of adults ever move beyond it. The problem with that state of affairs is that Stage 5 is required for the full understanding of the morality of respect for individual rights that underlies a constitutional democracy. At Stage 5, the person reasons that morality is higher than or prior to law; that the social-legal order does not dispense

---

[3]Table I is adapted from L. Kohlberg, "Moral Stages and Moralization," in T. Lickona, ed., *Moral Development and Behavior* (New York: Holt, Rinehart & Winston, 1976), pp. 31–53.
[4]L. Kohlberg and D. Elfenbein, "The Development of Moral Judgments Concerning Capital Punishment," *American Journal of Orthopsychiatry* 45 (1975), pp. 614–640.

Table I
Kohlberg's six moral stages[a]

Level and stage	Conception of the right
Level I: Preconventional Stage 1: Heteronomous morality	To avoid breaking rules backed by punishment, obedience for its own sake, and avoiding physical damage to persons and property.
Stage 2: Individualism, instrumental purpose, and exchange	Following rules only when it is to someone's immediate interest; acting to meet one's own interest and needs and letting others do the same. Right is also what's fair, what's an equal exchange, a deal, an agreement.
Level II: Conventional Stage 3: Mutual interpersonal expectations, relationships, and interpersonal conformity	Living up to what is expected by people close to you or what people generally expect of people in your role as son, brother, friend, etc. "Being good" is important and means having good motives, showing concern about others. It also means keeping mutual relationships, such as trust, loyalty, respect and gratitude; golden rule.
Stage 4: Social system and conscience	Fulfilling the actual duties to which you have agreed. In order to maintain the system, laws are to be upheld except in extreme cases where they conflict with other fixed social duties. Right is also contributing to society, the group, or institution.
Level III: Postconventional or principled Stage 5: Social contract or utility and individual rights	Acting so as to achieve the "greatest good for the greatest number." Being aware that people hold a variety of values and opinions, that most values and rules are relative to your group. These relative rules should usually be upheld, however, in the interest of impartiality, and because they are the social contract. Some nonrelative values may be upheld in any society, and regardless of majority opinion.
Stage 6: Universal ethical principles	Following self-chosen ethical principles. Particular laws or social agreements are usually valid, because they rest on such principles. When laws violate these principles, one acts in accordance with the principle. Principles are universal principles of justice: the equality of human rights and respect for the dignity of human beings as individual persons.

[a]Adapted from Kohlberg, 1976.

rights to individuals, but exists by a social contract between the government and the governed to protect the inalienable rights of all. Stage 4 will sometimes violate individual rights for the sake of maintaining order in the system, as Watergate participants did when they carried out burglaries in the name of national security. From a Stage 5 perspective, such actions make no logical or moral sense, since the very legitimacy of a democratic system is to maximize individual rights.

At Stage 6, Kohlberg's highest stage, a person is able to articulate universal ethical principles underlying the assertion of human rights, such as the principle that persons should be treated as ends, not merely as means. Although Kohlberg's longitudinal subjects are all now adults in their 30s, none of them has manifested Stage 6 thinking. Kohlberg now views Stage 6 as a philosophical position, espoused by some philosophers and other individuals, rather than as a natural psychological stage in moral development.

Kohlberg has made the claim that each of the successive stages of moral reasoning is "objectively preferable to or more adequate than an earlier stage" according to both psychological and philosophical criteria.[5] From a psychological standpoint, he argues that the higher stages are better because they are more "equilibrated," more capable of handling diverse moral conflicts within their problem-solving framework. From a philosophical standpoint, Kohlberg maintains that each higher stage does a better job of measuring up to the long-standing criteria of reversibility, consistency, and universalizability that Kant,[6] Rawls,[7] and other "formalist" philosophers have viewed as the essence of rational moral judgment.

CRITIQUES OF KOHLBERG

Kohlberg's scheme[8] is supported by a variety of longitudinal, cross-cultural, and experimental evidence that is, by social-science standards, impressive. Nevertheless, as the leading theory of moral development, his work has drawn fire from many camps. He has been taken to task for centering too much on justice in defining the moral;[9] for being culturally biased in his definition of

[5]For an elaboration, see L. Kohlberg, "From Is to Ought: How to Commit the Naturalistic Fallacy and Get Away with it in the Study of Moral Development," in T. Mischel, ed., *Cognitive Development and Epistemology*. (New York: Academic, 1971), pp. 151–235; and L. Kohlberg, "The Claim to Moral Adequacy of a Highest Stage of Moral Judgment," *Journal of Philosophy*, 70 (1973), pp. 630–646.
[6]I. Kant, *Critique of Pure Reason*, in *Great Books of the Western World*, vol. 42 (Chicago: Encyclopedia Britannica, 1952).
[7]J. Rawls, *A Theory of Justice* (Cambridge: Harvard University Press, 1971).
[8]For more detail on the theory and research, see L. Kohlberg, "Stage and Sequence: The Cognitive-deveopmental Approach to Socialization," in D. A. Goslin, ed., *Handbook of Socialization: Theory and Research*. (Chicago: Rand-McNally, 1969), pp. 347–480; and Kolhberg, "Moral Stages and Moralization," pp. 31–53.
[9]See J. B. Orr, "Cognitive-developmental Approaches to Moral Education: A Social-ethical Analysis," *Educational Theory*, 24 (1974), pp. 365–373; R. S. Peters, "Moral Development: A Plea for Pluralism," in T. Mischel, ed., *Cognitive Development and Epistemology* (New York: Academic Press, 1971); R. S. Peters, "Why Doesn't Lawrence Kohlberg Do His Homework?" *Phi Delta Kappan*, 56 (1975), p. 678.

morality;[10] for being sex-biased in studying an exclusively male sample and for defining the stages in ways that emphasize "masculine" themes of rights and justice and neglect "feminine" themes of responsibility and love;[11] for going from a description of what moral development is to a prescription of what it ought to be;[12] for devaluing conventional morality;[13] for overestimating the role of reasoning in moral functioning, and underestimating the role of other factors, such as affect, personality, habit, and expectations of consequences;[14] for failing to take into account adequately the impact of the particular nature of the moral dilemma on the stage of moral reasoning elicited from a subject;[15] for lack of sufficient validity and reliability of his research methodology;[16] for having insufficient evidence for his two highest stages;[17] and for failing to respond to his critics.[18]

All of these criticisms, I think, have some merit, and they have been a healthy stimulus for the ongoing development of Kohlberg's theorizing and methods of research. In some circles, however, the chorus of Kohlberg criticism has been taken to mean the death knell for moral-stage theory and its educational applications. Underlying this view, I think, is a failure to see Kohlberg's work in a wider context. What critics sometimes miss is that Kohlberg's work does not stand alone, but rather rides on the back of a larger tradition of structural-developmental psycholgy that has never been healthier. In America, at least,

[10]See E. Simpson, "Moral Development Research: A Case of Scientific Cultural Bias," *Human Development,* 17 (1974) pp. 81–106; E. Sullivan, *A Study of Kohlberg's Structural Theory of Moral Development: A Critique of Liberal Social Science Ideology* (Toronto: Ontario Institute for Studies in Education, 1977); R. W. Wilson, "Some Comments on Stage Theories of Moral Development," *Journal of Moral Education,* (1976), pp. 241–248.

[11]C. Gilligan, "In a Different Voice: Women's Conception of the Self and of Morality," *Harvard Educational Review,* 47 (1977), pp. 481–517.

[12]W. P. Alston, "Comments on Kohlberg's 'From Is to Ought'," in T. Mischel, ed., *Cognitive Development and Epistemology* (New York: Academic Press, 1971), pp. 269–284.

[13]C. M. Hamm, "Dialogue with Don B. Cochran," *Moral Education Forum,* 1 pp. 3–7; Peters, "Lawrence Kohlberg", p. 678.

[14]See Alston, "Kohlberg's 'From Is to Ought'," pp. 269–284. note 12; J. Aronfreed, "Moral Development from The Standpoint of a General Psychological Theory," pp. 54–69; W. Mischel and H. Mischel, "A Cognitive Social-learning Approach to Morality and Self-regulation," pp. 54–69; E. Simpson, "A Holistic Approach to Moral Development and Behavior," pp. 159–170, all in T. Lickona, ed., *Moral Development and Behavior* (New York: Holt, Rinehart & Winston, 1976).

[15]C. Levine, "Role-taking Standpoint and Adolescent Usage of Kohlberg's Conventional Stages of Moral Reasoning," *Journal of Personality and Social Psychology* 34 (1976), pp. 41–46.

[16]W. Kurines and E. Grief, "The Development of Moral Thought: Review and Evaluation of Kohlberg's Approach," *Psychological Bulletin* 81 (1974) pp. 453–470.

[17]J. Gibbs, "Kohlberg's Stages of Moral Judgment: A Constructive Critque," *Harvard Educational Review,* 47 (1977), pp. 43–61.

[18]Peters, "Lawrence Kohlberg," p. 678; B. Sichel, *Can Kohlberg Respond to His Critics?* Paper presented to the annual meeting of the Jean Piaget Society, Philadelphia, June, 1976; Sullivan, *Kohlberg's Structural Theory.*

stage theory is currently the dominant approach to making sense out of human development, and new stage sequences for this or that area of functioning are appearing all the time.

Piaget, who started it all, not only identified childhood moral stages, but also has done more than 50 years of research to demonstrate the existence of four stages of cognitive development, ranging from infancy to adolescence.[19] More recently, William Perry[20] of Harvard has defined, on the basis of his interviews with Harvard and Radcliffe undergraduates, a series of "stage-like levels" which represent shifts in personal epistemology and identity from dualism to relativism to commitment. Robert Selman[21] has identified stages of "social understanding," tracing the evolution in children and adolescents of the capacity to take the perspective of others in increasingly complex ways. William Damon,[22] using hypothetical and real-life dilemmas designed especially for children, has produced a much more refined account (*three* stages, each with two substages) of childhood moral development than either Piaget or Kohlberg had given us. Jane Loevinger[23] has mapped stages of ego development in childhood, adolescence, and adulthood, and finds in the successive transformations of the self's relationship to the world a moral progression very much like Kohlberg's. James Fowler,[24] studying subjects ages 4 to 80, has gone beyond ego to describe stages in the development of "faith": the way people reason about the meaning of life. Fowler, too, finds in his data a moral progression very much like Kohlberg's.

When one steps back from the Kohlberg canvas to consider its broad strokes, it is hardly surprising that other researchers and theorists have painted a similar picture of moral growth. Kohlberg calls his first two stages "preconventional," his middle stages, 3 and 4, "conventional," and his highest stages, 5 and 6, "postconventional." In other words, the developing person begins by being premoral, centered on meeting the concrete needs of the self with little regard for the needs of others. In the move to conventional morality, the person joins the world, learns the rules, plays the game; he becomes "moral" in the

[19]J. Piaget and B. Inhelder, *The Growth of Logical Thinking from Childhood to Adolescence* (New York: Basic Books, 1958), J. Piaget, *Six Psychological Studies* (New York: Random House, 1967).

[20]W. G. Perry, *Forms of Intellectual and Ethical Development in the College Years: A Scheme* (New York: Holt, 1970).

[21]R. Selman, "Social Cognitive Understanding: A Guide to Educational and Clinical Practice," in T. Lickona, ed., *Moral Development and Behavior* (New York: Holt, Rinehart & Winston, 1976), pp. 299–316.

[22]W. Damon, *The Social World of the Child* (San Francisco: Jossey-Bass, Inc: 1977).

[23]J. Loevinger and R. Wessler, *Measuring Ego Development* (San Francisco: Jossey-Bass, Inc. 1970).

[24]J. Fowler, "Faith and the Structuring of Meaning," in J. W. Fowler and A. Vergate, *Toward Moral and Religious Maturity: The First International Conference on Moral and Religious Development* (Morristown, N.J.: Silver Burdett Co., 1980).

conventional, conformist sense of trying to meet the expectations of others, either interpersonal others like family or friends (Stage 3), or impersonal others like one's community, institutions, or nation (Stage 4). In the move to postconventional morality, the individual is no longer wholly identified with or imbedded in the conventions—the roles, rules, and regulations—of the prevailing social system. Now he can step outside that system, evaluate it, change it if necessary, operating from an autonomous moral perspective. Is the system just? Does it fully respect human rights? Does it adequately promote human welfare? You can argue with how Kohlberg gathers or reads his data, or with how he characterizes the upper reaches of moral thought. But the basic sweep of moral development—from preconventional to conventional to postconventional morality—seems to me be be both logically self-evident and empirically established.

IMPLICATIONS OF MORAL DEVELOPMENT FOR THE TEACHING OF ETHICS

If you take seriously the idea of stages of moral development, what are the implications for education in general and ethics teaching in particular? The implications, I think, are far-reaching.

1. Kohlberg and other developmentalists have argued, with John Dewey, that development should be the central aim for education.[25] Development is of two kinds: (a) *vertical development*—to more comprehensive, more consistent, more integrated stages of logical and moral functioning; and (b) *horizontal development*—the application of one's highest stage to an ever widening realm of one's life experience. Both kinds of development are taken as offering "non-relative" educational goals, which are not culture-dependent and the desirability of which rational people can agree on. Developmental moral education does not seek to inculcate particular moral beliefs. Rather it seeks to provide the conditions that stimulate progress through a natural sequence of stages of moral reasoning toward autonomous, principled morality, toward increasingly universalized respect for persons.

2. The pedagogical implications of moral-development theory flow from a single premise: *that the major impetus for movement through the moral stages is the person's own activity as a problem solver, as called forth by challenging interactions with the environment.* Kohlberg and his colleagues have spelled out six kinds of experience that they believe stimulate the active problem-solving efforts necessary for development:

(a) Being in a situation where seeing things from other points of view is encouraged—important because upward stage movement is a process

[25]L. Kohlberg and R. Mayer, "Development as the Aim of Education," *Harvard Educational Review* 42 (1972), pp. 449–496.

of getting better at reconciling conflicting perspectives on a moral problem

(b) Engaging in logical thinking, such as reasoned argument and consideration of alternatives—important because one cannot attain a given stage of moral reasoning before attaining the supporting Piagetian stage of logical reasoning

(c) Having the responsibility to make moral decisions and to influence one's moral world (e.g., through participation in group decision making)—necessary for developing a sense of moral agency and for learning to apply one's moral reasoning to life situations

(d) Exposure to moral controversy, to conflict in moral reasoning that challenges the structure of one's present stage

(e) Exposure to the reasoning of individuals whose thinking is one stage higher than one's own—offering a new moral structure for resolving the disequilibrium caused by moral conflict

(f) Participation in creating and maintaining a just community whose members pursue common goals (e.g., learning, school reform, the amelioration of a social problem) and resolve conflict in accordance with the ideals of mutual respect and fairness

Clearly, there are some basic similarities between developmental moral education and the teaching of ethics. They appear to share, first of all, a rejection of ethical relativism; both appear committed to the idea that some forms of moral or ethical reasoning are more adequate than others. Moral-stage theory holds that higher stages are more adequate than lower stages. The notion of adequacy seems to me to be endorsed in Daniel Callahan's "Goals in the Teaching of Ethics" when he says, "At the very least, courses in ethics should make it clear that there are ethical problems in personal and civic life ... and that *there are better and worse ways of trying to deal with them.*"[26] Ethicists, it seems to me, can find in the data of developmental psychology a kind of validation of their philosophical rejection of relativism. In the course of human development, as people move from one stage to the next, they are in fact rejecting their former stage as inadequate, less fair, less consistent, than their new stage. Even children, if offered advice at a stage lower than their own, will reject it as "silly" or "not a good reason."[27]

In the realm of pedagogy, developmental moral education and contemporary ethics teaching are also compatible bedfellows. The "new look" in ethics instruction recognizes that you can't teach ethics (any more than you can develop morality) by simply lecturing about it. It recognizes that a good ethics class will be the one that has many of the ingredients of the developmental recipe for moral education: encouragment to see things from a variety of view-

[26]D. Callahan, "Goals in the Teaching of Ethics," this volume, p. 62. (Italics added).
[27]L. Kohlberg and E. Turiel, "Moral Development and Moral Education," in G. S. Lesser, ed., *Psychology and Educational Practice* (Glenview, Ill.: Scott Foresman, 1971), pp. 410–465.

points; systematic, logical examination of arguments and alternatives; immersion in moral controversy; and exposure to a mix of moral reasoning by peers, some of which, at least some of the time, is likely to be more sophisticated, more adequate, than one's own.

I say all of this about contenporary ethics teaching, not as an insider, but as someone reading the literature coming out of an enterprise like The Hastings Center, literature that eschews the old dry-as-dust didactic theory courses in favor of rigorous debate about concrete moral questions that "put moral reflection to the test of practical living."[28] From the standpoint of moral-development theory, such a turn of instructional events can only be applauded. As they pursue their new pedagogy, ethical educators may wish to reflect upon some of the findings of developmental moral educators over a decade of interventions. In offering these findings, I do not mean to equate the systematic study of ethical theories and their application with the fostering of moral development, though I think that the parallels are provocative. Rather I mean to share what moral-developmental psychology learned when it "went to school," in the hope that ethics teachers can extrapolate where it makes sense to do so.

LESSONS LEARNED FROM THE RESEARCH IN MORAL EDUCATION

1. Socratic questioning makes a difference. In a year-long study of 32 high-school social-studies courses in Boston and Pittsburgh, only one teacher behavior separated those classes that showed significant moral-stage advance from those that did not: the teacher's use of Socratic questioning to draw out and challenge students' moral reasoning.[29] The obvious implication: developmental moral educators, and perhaps ethics teachers as well, should make a deliberate effort to use Socratic questioning in their classrooms. This kind of questioning is a complex skill that takes most people much time and practice to develop—and a skill that one does not commonly find in the college classroom. Those who are drawn to ethics teaching may be better at this skill than most, but it would seem wise to ask what kinds of faculty-development program may be useful in helping to refine this and related techniques that make for effective teaching.

2. The more the mix, the better. In the same study just cited, classes showing stage change were more likely to contain a mixture of three stages in the moral reasoning of students than were no-change classrooms. At the high-school level, this finding argues against tracking. At the university and professional school level, it suggests that professors should strive to elicit the full range of reasoning present among their students.

[28]S. Bok and D. Callahan, "Teaching Applied Ethics," *Radcliffe Quarterly* 65:2 (June 1979), 30–33.
[29]A. Colby, L. Kohlberg, E. Fenton, B. Speicher-Dubin, and M. Leiberman, "Secondary School Moral Discussion Programmes Led by Social Studies Teachers," *Journal of Moral Education* 6 (1977), 90–111.

3. *Groups are more effective with a leader.* This is one of those findings that have earned psychologists the appellation "apostles of the obvious." A study of junior and senior high-school students[30] found that moral-dilemma discussions led by adults produced three times as much stage change in students as peer-led discussions, where an adult was present but remained largely passive. This result dovetails with the study underscoring the importance of the teacher's Socratic questioning. The teacher, of course, need not necessarily be the one who leads. At the university or professional-school level, it would seem desirable for students to move into the leadership role at some point. What appears to be important is that someone be responsible for insuring that the discussion probe the moral issues in the problem at hand.

4. *Students need skills.* Teachers who attempt moral discussion at the elementary or high-school level invariably report that, at least initially, their students are sorely lacking in basic skills needed for good discussion: listening; the ability to paraphrase another's point; the capacity to connect with a previous speaker's comment; the ability to disagree without "putting down"; and simple courtesy (e.g., not interrupting). Undergraduate and graduate students are not likely to come to blows, as some high-school students have done, when they disagree about a moral dilemma. My experience, however, is that university students, like most adults, show plenty of room for improvement in the kinds of communication skills that make for a cohesive and productive discussion. If such skills are neglected, one creates an educational and ethical contradiction: talking about morality without practicing it in the human interactions of the classroom.[31]

5. *Change is small.* A spate of studies[32] has shown the average advance generated by moral reasoning programs to be modest: about one-third of a stage. The amount of change varies from student to student, some not changing at all, some moving up half a stage, and a few advancing a full stage over the course of a year. For the vast majority of those who do progress, the change is small.

6. *Change may be slow.* A corollary of the small-change phenomenon, this finding is further evidence that structural development proceeds gradually—and sometimes does not appear at all until after the intervention is over. One ambitious Canadian intervention[33] to stimulate principled moral reasoning among high-school students found no stage gains after the year-long program, but a small, significant superiority of the experimental subjects over the control

---

[30]M. Blatt and L. Kohlberg, "The Effect of Classroom Moral Discussion Upon Children's Level of Moral Judgment," *Journal of Moral Education* 4 (1975), pp. 169–172.

[31]For suggestions on developing discussion skills, see R. Hersh, D. Paolitto, and J. Reimer, *Promoting Moral Growth: From Piaget to Kohlberg* (New York: Longman, 1979).

[32]For a careful review, see A. Lockwood, "The Effects of Values Clarification and Moral Development Curricula on School-age Subjects: A Critical Review of Recent Research," *Review of Educational Research* 48 (1978), pp. 325–364.

[33]E. Sullivan, *Moral Learning* (New York: Paulist Press, 1975).

group one year later. A program in developmental moral education, or a class in ethics, may have this "sleeper effect": creating a different set of mind in students that subsequently interacts with other experiences to produce developmental progress.

7. *The greater the interest, the greater the change.* Blatt's study[34] found a close relationship between how much interest a student expressed in the moral discussions (e.g., "I liked them because they really made you think hard"), and how much stage advance he made. The implication for teachers: follow a discussion where the students' interests lead it; select problems that students will be interested in discussing; and monitor the interest level of the class with periodic verbal and written evaluations. One of my doctoral students this year found that high-school students participated the most when discussions were about dilemmas that the students had written themselves. Ethics courses might do well to invite students, perhaps working in pairs or small groups, to prepare cases of their own choosing for class discussion.

8. *Too many moral dilemmas make a poor academic diet.* Some teachers have initiated moral-discussion programs with an excess of zeal, serving up one dilemma after another to their students, who soon protest their fate. I suspect that ethics teachers using case studies run the same risk. A colleague lamented his one-shot experience in teaching a summer course in medical ethics. The medical students, he said, expressed frustration and fatigue in the face of a long series of wrenching moral dilemmas, none of which, they complained, appeared to have any "right" solution. Any teaching strategy, used too often, has diminishing returns. With ethical dilemmas, where the cognitive strain is at a consistently high level, the need for a change of pace, a mental rest (of the kind that a "clear case" can provide), seems especially important.

9. *Role playing promotes role taking.* A dissertation study[35] with 11-year olds found that role playing—casting the children as characters in a moral dilemma and having them ad-lib their lines, speaking from the character's viewpoint—was far and away the most effective method of stimulating the interest and involvement of the children. I have found much the same thing in running moral discussions with adults. In a normal discussion, asking people to take the perspective of the various parties to a moral conflict may inspire only the thinnest kind of intellectual role taking. With role playing, however, you don't merely imagine how a given character would think or feel; you *become* that character. People typically comment afterward that they gained a much deeper sense of how it would feel to be in the shoes of the person they played.

10. *The peer group doesn't always help.* One can get the impression from Piaget's and Kohlberg's theoretical emphasis on social exchange as a catalyst for moral growth that the peer group always operates as a force for moral

[34]Blatt and Kohlberg, "Classroom Moral Discussion," pp. 169–172.
[35]P. Grimes, *Teaching Moral Reasoning to 11-Year Olds and Their Mothers.* Unpublished Doctoral Dissertation, Boston University School of Education, 1974.

maturity. In practice, it can have a "depressor effect." Sullivan[36] reports that, in their high-school program in Ontario, they often found that the stage of moral reasoning individual students revealed in their written assignments was higher than the stage they displayed in classroom discussions with peers. Sullivan's interpretation: students were afraid to sound too "goody-goody" in front of their classmates. Samson[37] reports that high-stage students reverted to lower stages in discussions of sexual moral dilemmas when their initial arguments were laughed at by their lower-stage peers. I suspect that ethics teachers may encounter a more subtle version of this problem even among more mature students: discomfort with unabashedly moral language, with explicit references to "right" or "wrong," and a preference for the hard-headed vocabulary of pragmatism, of costs and benefits—what Michael Walzer[38] calls "body-count morality," or the application of economic models to moral life. Ethics teachers are probably already well aware of this particular danger. One way to meet it is head-on: by asking students to discuss why it is that people are so often embarrassed by being moral.

11. *A person's hypothetical reasoning and real-life reasoning are not necessarily the same.* Leming[39] asked 8th- and 12th-graders to judge classical moral dilemmas like the Heinz story. Predictably, he found the 12th-graders using higher-stage reasoning. Then he asked both groups to respond to *personally relevant dilemmas:* e.g., "A girl wonders whether she should lie to her parents about where she is going in order to attend a party her parents have forbidden. What would you do?" In both groups Stage 2, self-interest reasoning came to the fore; now there was no difference in average stage of reasoning for the 8th- and 12th-graders. The lesson here (a familiar one): Don't assume that because people use high-level thinking about hypothetical moral problems, they will use high-level thinking to solve real-life problems in their personal experience. Acting on that knowledge, ethics teachers might ask students to reflect (perhaps in a journal) on how they apply the ethical principles they are studying to the moral situations they encounter in their own lives.

12. *Action works better than talk.* Rundle's[40] 1977 dissertation study compared the effect of talking about other people's moral dilemmas with the effect of solving and acting on the real-life dilemmas of the classroom. Over a

---

[36]Sullivan, *Moral Learning.*

[37]J. Samson, *The Public Schools and the Teaching of Sexual Values.* Lecture delivered to the Summer Institute for Teacher Education, Simon Fraser University School of Education, Vancouver, British Columbia, Canada, 1978.

[38]M. Walzer, "Teaching Morality," *The New Republic* 178:23 (June 10, 1978), pp. 12–14.

[39]J. S. Leming, "An Empirical Examination of Key Assumptions Underlying the Kohlberg Rationale for Moral Education." Educational Resources information Center (ERIC), ED 093–49, 1974.

[40]L. Rundle, *The Stimulation of Moral Development in the Elementary School and the Cognitive Examination of Social Experience: A Fifth-grade Study.* Unpublished Doctoral Dissertation, Boston University School of Education, 1977.

12-week period, 5th-graders who merely discussed hypothetical dilemmas showed no significant gains in moral reasoning, whereas students who debated and resolved issues of classroom management showed an unusually large gain of half a stage. One implication: the wise moral teacher makes his own classroom part of the moral curriculum. Kohlberg and his colleagues reached a similar conclusion on the basis of their prison interventions: conducting discussions with inmates about moral dilemmas did not improve their prison behavior; democratizing the prison did.

13. *Working together is better than working alone.* Both Piaget and Kohlberg have stressed that morality is inherently social, and that its development requires social interaction and social relationships. The common school procedure of "shutting the child up in work that is strictly individual," Piaget said, "helps more than all the family situations put together to reinforce the child's spontaneous egocentrism" and is "contrary to the most obvious requirements of intellectural and moral development."[41] Reports of grade-obsessed university students sabotaging each other's laboratory work and razoring out required articles from library journals indicate that individualistic, competitive learning may be as inimical to moral development among young adults as Piaget says it is for children. One study at the college level bears on the importance of the cooperative search for truth: An individualized, programmed learning approach to fostering moral reasoning proved inferior to an approach that involved students in open, interactive discussion of moral issues.[42] At the college level one can also use team projects, and even team testing, as ways of fostering cooperative morality and what Dewey spoke of as "the realization that knowledge is a possession held in trust for furthering the well-being of all."[43]

"EXPERIENTIAL ETHICS": MAKING MORALITY A LIVED EXPERIENCE

The last three research findings—that hypothetical reasoning does not necessarily get applied to personal moral decisions, that solving real-life moral problems stimualtes more growth than discussing fictional dilemmas, and that cooperative social interchange is an important nutrient for moral development—all suggest the wisdom of an "experiential" approach to moral and ethics education. In the developmental moral-education movement, there has been a clear and strong shift away from merely talking about morality to creating opportu-

[41]J. Piaget, *Moral Judgment of the Child*, p. 405.

[42]A. C. Bennett, "A Cognitive-developmental Orientation Toward Moral Education: An Experimental Study in 'Developing Moral Judgment' Through the Compable Efforts of Two Teaching Strategies," (Unpublished Doctoral Dissertation, The Pennsylvania State University, 1975).

[43]J. Dewey, "The Need for a Philosophy of Education," in *The New Era in Home and School* 15 (1934), pp. 211–214. Reprinted in R. Archambault, ed., *John Dewey on Education* (New York: Random House, 1964), pp. 12–13.

nities for students to live out their developing moral values. "Developing the independence of the person," Piaget wrote recently, "and respect for the rights and freedoms of others ... demand a return by their very make-up to a *lived experience* and to *freedom of investigation,* outside of which any acquisition of human values is only an illusion."[44]

The need for an experiential approach to moral and ethical education is suggested by a college student's evaluation of an Introduction to Ethics course:

> We started talking about different ethical systems, and the question of morality become irrelevant. It was a question of how you thought about ethics, and was evil necessary to have good? And how would you define God? And then there was a big discussion of determinism versus free will—and that was interesting, but it was only fun. It was only, you know, mind games. And I could have gotten the same kind of thinking out of math, where you just set up a set of definitions and manipulate them for all they're worth. But for me, the interesting thing about morality is ... how ambiguous it is, the fact that it doesn't provide neat answers ... and you didn't make judgments.[45]

The professor of this course would probably be glad to hear that this student learned that morality doesn't provide neat answers. But I suspect he would be troubled to learn that the student came away thinking that ethics was just a pleasant form of moral gymnastics, something on a par with math games. How does one avoid this unhappy outcome? How do you get students to make the moral *judgments* that this student says they didn't make? How do you get them to take ethics seriously, to see it as something relevant to making moral decisions in the real world and to leading a good life? How to stimulate the moral feelings and imagination of students, as Callahan[46] has urged, so that an ethics course is not merely "an abstract intellectual exercise"?

Experiential ethics is one way to try to do all of these things. The course or the academic program becomes a kind of laboratory for making ethics the lived experience that Piaget says is central to the acquisition of human values. This can be done in a variety of ways.

1. *One can conduct a democratic classroom*—allowing students to participate in decisions about "fairness issues" (What are fair course requirements? How should grading be determined?), instructional issues (How should classes be run?, What should be the balance of theory and application? Lecture and discussion?), and even curriculum issues (What should be the goals of the course? What should be studied?). One ethics instructor, for example, begins his course with a discussion of three questions: (1) What are we doing here? (2)

[44]J. Piaget, *To Understand Is To Invent* (New York: Grossman, 1975), pp. 125–126 (italics added).

[45]D. Boyd and L. Kohlberg, "Medical Ethics: An Antidote for Sophomoritis," in *Teaching Biomedical and Health Care Ethics to Liberal Arts Undergraduates.* (Chicago: Associated Colleges of the Midwest 1977), pp. 38–49.

[46]Callahan, *op. cit.* "Goals in the Teaching of Ethics," pp. 64–65.

What am I looking for from you? and (3) What are you looking for from me? This discussion of course goals leads to a contractual agreement between the professor and the students. He comments: "I found that if the students have one agenda and I another, the course is a waste of everybody's time." I would add that his democratic procedure is not only pragmatic; it is also sound educational practice from the standpoint of moral-development theory. Democratic decision making demands the consideration and reconciliation of varied perspectives, which is what the moral stages are all about; and it provides an opportunity for students to make moral decisions that have real consequences in their lives.

2. One can democratize the wider program or school.   Students can be given opportunities to have input into decisions about course requirements, program policies, and the like. Depriving students of such opportunities may seriously undercut the effectiveness of the educational effort. At one university, where at least part of the program promoted democracy in the public schools, students were heard to complain bitterly that they had no chance to participate democratically in shaping the department's graduate program to meet their needs. One can imagine students in a medical-ethics course becoming cynical about the gap between the ethics that are studied in courses and those they perceive to be practiced in the running of the medical school.

3. One can provide opportunities for students to step into roles of social responsibility for real-world problems in the wider community.   A good case can be made that, to involve students fully, to engage their will and their emotions as well as their minds, every ethics course should have a *practicum,* a field experience of some kind that guarantees an interplay between ethical theory and the practice of morality. Every student's personal life, of course, offers one kind of practicum, but there is also great value in having students involved collaboratively in wider social responsibilities that require confronting ethical problems and making ethical decisions. A model of what this looks like at the secondary level is provided by Fred Newmann's work in citizenship education, involving students in selecting, analyzing, and in some systematic way ameliorating a social problem like pollution, vandalism, or discrimination against the poor.[47]

At the postsecondary level, Alverno College, a small liberal arts college for women, has designed a six-step process for developing the student's competence of "forming value judgments within the decision-making process." The program requires every student to "formulate goals from a complex of issues, identify the values underlying those goals, and then work through the process of accomplishing them in a decision-making plan of her own design" for "acutal use in field projects."[48] At the professional and preprofessional levels, there may be

[47]F. Newmann, *Education for Citizen Action: Challenge for Secondary Curriculum* (Berkeley, Calif.: McCutchan, 1975).
[48]*Liberal Learning at Alverno College* (Milwaukee: Alverno Productions, 1976), p. 24.

similar opportunities for practicums in ethics. Bok and Callahan point out that many medical and premedical students have worked in hospitals, homes for the aged or retarded, or neighborhood clinics, and "are likely to keep courses related to actual moral choice and to bring up issues ignored in class."[49] I am suggesting that this kind of real-world contact *not be left to chance, but be built into the course or program as an integral part of the student's experience.* The reason, once again, is not only to keep class discussions anchored in the concrete and relevant, but also, and more fundamentally, to enable students to develop the kind of applied ethical understanding and sense of moral agency that comes from having to put theory into practice in their own lives.

SOME OTHER APPLICATIONS OF MORAL-DEVELOPMENT THEORY

Before turning to social psychology and its educational implications, I would like to describe two more ways that I think moral-development theory may be useful to the teacher of ethics. First of all, it provides a framework for understanding students—where they are coming from developmentally, and what the next step for them is in the developmental sequence.

Most students coming to college, for example, will be operating at the conventional level, Kohlberg's Stages 3 and 4. The task of the introductory ethics teacher will be to dislodge them from their unreflective conventional morality, to shake them loose from their unexamined assumptions and values. That kind of freeing up is one way to facilitate the transition from conventional to postconventional, principled morality—the kind of moral reasoning required for the construction and evaluation of ethical theories. A sizable and growing number of students, however, both at the undergraduate and the graduate levels will come to an ethics course, not as conventional thinkers, but as relativists, sometimes died-in-the-wool relativists who hold to their relativism as vehemently and aboslutely as any ideologue ever clung to his creed. Here, for example, is an 18-year-old relativist that Kohlberg interviewed, responding to the Heinz dilemma:

> There's a million ways to look at it. It depends on how he is oriented morally. If Heinz thinks it's worse to steal than to let his wife die, then it would be wrong what he did. It's all relative. What I would do is steal the drug. I can't say that's right or wrong, or that it's what everyone should do.

Kohlberg's longitudinal study found in fact that 20% of his middle-class sample, between late high school and the second or third year of college, adopted a radical relativism. These were the same persons who in high school had been the most morally advanced on Kohlberg's scale, "all having a mixture of conventional (Stage 4) and principled (Stage 5) thought. In their 'college

[49]Bok and Callahan, "Teaching Applied Ethics," p. 33.

sophomore phase,' they kicked both their conventional and their Stage 5 moral-ity and replaced it with hedonistic relativism, jazzed up with philosophical and sociopolitical jargon."[50] One person, for example, had been the high school student council president, but as a college sophomore considered himself a "Nietzschean," espoused a Social Darwinism racism, and took to stealing to teach people what the world was really like.[51]

One of my doctoral students, in an autobiographical essay, reconstructed her own experience of relativism. Her account suggests that the breakdown of a conventional world view can have profound affective as well as cognitive consequences:

> Graduation from high school was bliss. I walked on golden clouds, relishing my new status as a well-educated, free adult who had her universe well together, with a firm grasp on what the world is like. The minute I walked onto the college campus, this world shattered into a thousand pieces. It dawned on me that I knew nothing about anything at all, an intuition which grew with frightening speed to a conviction, fueled by the courses which had no beginning and no end and offered no right answers. The confrontation with the very diverse student body contributed greatly to this process.... The experience of relativism was at the same time enormously liberating and confusing: the world had no boundaries anymore at all; everything was possible, and many, many more things were accept-able and desirable than before....

How does moral-development theory help the ethics teacher deal with stu-dent relativism? First, it tells him not to worry; for some students, aggravated relativism is a natural part of the process of moving from conventional to postconventional morality. The data—both Kohlberg's and Turiel's—show rad-ical relativists eventually moving to the principled thinking of Stage 5.[52] Second, a developmental perspective tells one not to treat student relativism as mere posturing. It may be that, but it may also be a genuine developmental transition, with a deeply felt psychological reality. Third, a developmental viewpoint cau-tions against teaching ethics in such a way as to exacerbate relativism—for example, by making ethics appear to be rather arbitrary "mind games," or by never making it clear that, however complex an issue, ethics is for making moral

[50]L. Kohlberg, "Continuities and Discontinuities in Childhood and Adult Moral Development Revisited," in L. Kohlberg, *Collected Papers on Moral Development and Moral Education* (Cambridge, Mass.: Center for Moral Education, Harvard University, 1973), p. 17.

[51]For a fine-grained analysis of the nature of adolescent relativism, see E. Turiel, "Conflict and Transistion in Adolescent Moral Development," *Child Development* 45 (1974), pp. 14–29; and E. Turiel, "Conflict and Transition in Adolescent Moral Development, II," *Child Development* 48 (1977), pp. 634–637.

[52]See Kohlberg, "Continuities and Discontinuities," p. 17; and Turiel, "Conflict and Transition," pp. 634–637. This is not to imply tbat all relativists will automatically develop into principled thinkers. The relativists that Kohlberg studied were all among the most advanced moral think-ers in his sample before they moved into relativism. It may not be possible to generalize from this group's developmental pattern to the increasingly large number of college students who show relativistic thinking. Whether they develop principled morality or remain relativists is not known.

decisions and taking moral stands. Finally, a cure for relativism is suggested by the developmental postulate that morality must be constructed and reconstructed by the person through his own active problem solving. Boyd describes how he used a college course, entitled "Moral Development: The Search for Reflective Equilibrium," to prod relativists in the direction of principled thinking. One of his strategies was to suggest to relativists that if they didn't come around, he would flunk them. "You can't do that!" they protested in disbelief. "Why not?" the professor asked. "It's not fair!" they said—and, as they heard what they were saying, came the dawn. Grading in the course became a real-life problem that the students and instructor grappled with and democratically resolved. Said one student in a final evaluation:

> We didn't just cover the material in this class—we dealt with it. It's one thing to talk about something; it's another thing to actually do it. . . . If you talk about it *and* do it, then you're going to . . . *know* what it is. In this class, we were learning morality from the inside.[53]

GIVING AWAY THE THEORY

One final "application" of developmental theory: If I were teaching a course in ethics, I would teach Kohlberg's moral-development theory as grist for the moral mill. For many students, the discovery of Kohlberg's theory of moral stages has a considerable impact. They speak of viewing the world through a moral lens; of seeing moral dilemmas where they didn't see them before; of hearing examples of the moral stages at every turn. The theory gives them an organized way of thinking about moral development, a way of making sense out of other people's behavior, and a way of understanding their own moral growth. Ethics students, I think, would profit in similar ways. Moreover, they could examine ethical theories in the light of data about how people do in fact develop morally (at least according to Kohlberg's research), and in turn could examine Kohlberg's system in the light of ethical theories. All of this stands to add an exciting psychological dimension to the study of ethical theories, and to help move ethics to the center of a student's consciousness and moral life.

Let me turn now to some of the findings of social psychology and their implications for the work of ethical educators.

THE SOCIAL PSYCHOLOGY OF MORAL BEHAVIOR

Whereas developmental psychologists like Kohlberg began with an interest in how people reason about moral problems, and turned later to look at how reasoning related to behavior, social psychologists began with an interest in

---

[53]Boyd and Kohlberg, "Medical Ethics," p. 49.

behavior. How would people behave in real moral situations, and how would their behavior change as the situation changed? Would personality measures predict a person's conduct, or would situational variables be the overriding determinants?

THE GOOD SAMARITAN REVISITED

Some of the best modern social-psychological research was inspired by the tragic death of Kitty Genovese, murdered in Kew Gardens while 38 of her neighbors ignored her screams for help. Much of this research is reported in the excellent book, *The Unresponsive Bystander: Why Doesn't He Help?*[54]

A typical study was carried out by Darley and Batson[55] with students at a respected theological seminary in the northeast. The study began by seeking to assess the professed nature of the seminarians' religiosity. Were they committed to religion largely as a means to other ends (e.g., personal security), or was their commitment based on the intrinsic value of religion as a quest for meaning ("I try hard to carry my religion over into all my other dealings in life")?

Each student, upon arriving for the experiment, was told he was to deliver a lecture from prepared notes on one of two topics: the parable of the Good Samaritan, or the job opportunities for seminary graduates. Half of those assigned to each of the lectures were told that they would have to hurry to be on time, while the other half were informed that they had more than ample time. On the way across campus, the students came upon a person in distress (actually an actor), who sat slumped in a doorway, coughing and groaning. The experimenters' question: How would the seminarians respond, confronted with this opportunity to be Good Samaritans themselves?

Of the 40 subjects, only 16 stopped to help the man in distress. Most of those who helped were from the group told that they had plenty of time to get to their lecture. Most surprising was the finding that seminarians about to give a lecture on the Good Samaritan were no more likely to help than those prepared to lecture on job opportunities. Noted the experimenters: "Indeed, on several occasions, a seminary student going to give his talk on the parable of the Good Samaritan literally stepped over the victim as he hurried on his way." Finally, seminarians' behavior bore no relation to the expressed nature of their religiosity.

These were astonishing results: Individuals ostensibly committed to a life of upholding religious and moral values, functioning in an institutional context

---

[54]B. Latané and J. Darley, *The Unresponsive Bystander: Why Doesn't He Help?* (New York: Appleton-Century-Crofts, 1970).

[55]J. Darley and C. Batson, "'From Jerusalem to Jericho': A Study of Situational and Dispositional Variables in Helping Behavior," *Journal of Personality and Social Psychology* 27 (1973), pp. 100–108.

ostensibly dedicated to those same values, having prepared a speech on a man whom Christ held up as exemplifying those values, nonetheless failed to act upon those values in a real human situation. Only the luxury of having extra time had any influence on whether they paused to help a fellow human being in need.

The bystander research focused on our sins of omission, the good that we fail to do. Other research, more disturbing still, turned a light on the evil we are willing to do when the situation seems to demand it.

STANLEY MILGRAM'S STUDIES: THE ANATOMY OF OBEDIENCE

In 1963, Stanley Milgram of Yale University published the results of an experiment that has by now become famous. Milgram ran an ad in the New Haven newspaper that said he would pay $5 to anyone who would volunteer for an experiment on "learning." He got volunteers from all walks of life and all age levels. Their task was straightforward: to give an increasingly intense electrical shock to a "learner" each time the learner made a mistake in remembering word assocaitions. Shock levels ranged from 15 to 450 volts, in increments of 15 volts.

The learner actually received no shocks at all, but what the "teacher" heard through the wall were dramatic and convincing "responses" to the shocks. The learner first complained about his discomfort, then screamed in pain, then pleaded to be released, then protested that he had a heart condition and could stand it no longer, and finally fell silent. When they heard the screams from the other side of the wall, most subjects showed visible conflict about obeying instructions to continue. Reports Milgram: "Subjects were observed to sweat, tremble, stutter, bite their lips, frown, and dig their fingernails into their flesh. These were characteristic rather than exceptional responses." Whenever subjects expressed hesitation about continuing, the experimenter replied with words such as, "You have no choice, teacher. The experiment requires that you go on."

Twenty-six of the 40 subjects did as they were told, and gave the full 450 volts. Despite a good deal of controversy about the ethics of his experiment, Milgram repeated it, as did other psychologists in other settings, some of them using college students as subjects. The results were always depressingly similar. Summarizing a series of his studies, Milgram wrote:

> With numbing regularity, good people were seen to knuckle under to the demands of authority and perform actions that were callous and severe. The results raise the possiblity that the kind of character produced in American democratic society cannot be counted upon to insulate its citizens from brutality and inhumane treatment at the direction of malevolent authority.[56]

---

[56]S. Milgram, "Behavioral Study of Obedience," *Journal of Abnormal and Social Psychology* 67 (1963), pp. 371–378.

The curious thing about Milgram's findings is that no one was able to predict them. Prior to conducting the experiment, Milgram described his procedure to various groups—undergraduates, psychologists, psychiatrists—and asked for their judgment both about the morality of obeying the experimenter and the percentage of people they thought would obey to the end. All of these groups said the same thing: that it would be morally wrong to deliver the highest level of shock, and that fewer than 1% of subjects would do so. Those who did, they said, would be psychologically disturbed.

And yet, two-thirds of the subjects did deliver the strongest shock. Roger Brown, a social psychologist who has written thoughtfully about the dynamics of moral behavior,[57] speculates that a similar percentage of those who were asked to make predictions about subject behavior would have obeyed had they been the subjects. Judging from outside the experiment, Brown says, these persons formed a conception of the situation which emphasized the autonomy of the subject and his sensitivity to the person receiving the shocks. This conception proved to be grossly out of touch with the conceptions that arose from *inside* the experiment, when the situation was real. Most subjects who did participate in the experiment said, when interviewed later, that they had felt that they were doing their moral duty in carrying out the experimenter's instructions, even though it was painful for them to do so. What was most central to their in-the-situation conceptions was not a sense of their own autonomy, but rather a sense of being an agent of the experimenter, of being responsible to him and to the experiment. The depth to which they would feel this kind of responsibility, and the degree to which it would override concern for the victim's welfare, was simply not anticipated by anyone outside the actual situation.

THE ROLE OF MORAL REASONING IN MORAL BEHAVIOR

As moral and ethics educators, we might ask, what develops the ability to know from the outside what a situation is like on the inside? That kind of knowing is the work of moral imagination, which most of us get little practice in developing. But perhaps our moral imaginations are inherently limited and will never be able to do their task very well. If we cannot, standing outside a situation, really know what it is like on the inside, we may change the question and ask: What provides the ability to stand outside a situation when you are inside it? What enables a person to maintain moral perspective in the face of strong situational pressures?

Moral-development theory offers one answer: A principled moral stage, unlike lower-stage reasoning, defines moral obligation on the basis of autonomous moral principles, rather than on the basis of shifting situational factors like the expectations of others. By that logic, principled subjects in Milgram's

[57]R. Brown and R. Herrnstein, *Psychology* (Boston: Little, Brown & Co., 1975).

experiment should have been more likely to disobey then lower-level subjects. Kohlberg[58] interviewed Milgram's subjects, and confirmed this hypothesis.

Other studies on the relationship of moral reasoning to moral behavior have yielded similar results: higher-stage subjects are less likely to cheat on a test than lower-stage subjects,[59] more likely to resist the instructions of authority in order to help someone in distress,[60] and more likely to honor a commitment.[61] Michael Bernhardt, the only soldier to refuse to participate in the My Lai massacre, was scored as a postconventional thinker in a Kohlberg moral-judgment interview. Said Bernhardt:

> The law is only the law, and many times it's wrong. It's not necessarily just, just because it's the law. My kind of citizen would be guided by his own laws. These would be more strict, in a lot of cases, than the actual laws. People must be guided by their own standards, by their self-discipline.[62]

It is reassuring to know that moral reasoning makes a difference in moral behavior. But a question remains: Why don't high-stage reasoners *always* act in high-stage ways? Kohlberg's interviews with Milgram's subjects, though they provide some comfort, also reveal a frightening fact: two of the six subjects who scored at the principled level, possessed of the most sophisticated grasp of universal human rights, nevertheless obeyed to the last. An even more sobering reality is the fact that *no subject*, not even those who finally rebelled, quit the experiment prior to administering 300 volts.

THE POWER OF THE CONTEXT TO SHAPE BEHAVIOR

There is something in human moral behavior that must be given its due, something that may be even more compelling than the best understanding of morality. And that is the *ecological context* of the behavior, the web of situational factors in which the action is enmeshed. Context, to a disturbingly great degree, appears to shape thinking, feeling, and conduct. As evidence of just how profoundly it can affect all of these, let me cite one last social-psychological experiment.

Haney, Banks, and Zimbardo,[63] characterizing prisons—with their recidivism rates of up to 75%—as social, economic, and humanitarian failures, set out

[58]Kohlberg, "Stage and Sequence," pp. 347–480.
[59]P. Grim, L. Kohlberg and S. White, "Some Relationships Between Conscience and Attentional Processes," *Journal of Personality and Social Psychology* 8 (1968), pp. 239–252.
[60]S. McNamee, "Moral Behavior, Moral Development, and Motivation," *Journal of Moral Education*, 7 (1977), pp. 27–31.
[61]D. Krebs and A. Rosenwald, "Moral Reasoning and Moral Behavior in Conventional Adults," *Merrill Palmer Quarterly*, 23 (1977), pp. 77–87.
[62]P. Scharf, *Moral Education* (Davis, Calif.: Responsible Action Press, 1978), p. 64.
[63]C. Haney, C. Banks, and P. Zimbardo, "Interpersonal Dynamics in a Simulated Prison," *International Journal of Criminology and Penology*, 1 (1973), pp. 69–97.

to study the effects of the "social-psychological milieu" of prisons on human behavior. They selected 24 subjects from a pool of 75 college males who answered a newspaper advertisement asking for male volunteers to participate in a psychological study of "prison life" for $15 a day. Volunteers were carefully screened in order to select the *most* prosocial, mature, and physically and mentally stable individuals to participate. No subject selected had any known history of emotional disability, crime, or other antisocial behavior.

Half of the subjects were randomly assigned to the role of "prisoner," the others to that of "guard." They were to spend the next week in a mock prison environment at Stanford University which "physically constrained the prisoners in barred cells and psychologically conveyed the sense of imprisonment to all participants." Role instructions to the subjects were deliberately vague. Guards, for example, were told only "to maintain the reasonable degree of order within the prison necessary for its effective functioning," but that they must not use any kind of physical punishment. All guards were outfitted in uniforms of plain khaki shirts and trousers, a whistle, a police nightstick, and reflecting sunglasses. Prisoners wore loosely fitting muslin smocks, with an identification number on the front and back. Guards were instructed to refer to prisoners only by their identification numbers.

The daily routine and rules and regulations of prison life were specified by a "warden," played by a research assistant. Prisoners were served three bland meals a day, allowed three supervised toilet visits, and given two hours daily for reading or letter writing. Three times a day, prisoners were lined up by the guards for a "count."

How did the "guards" and "prisoners" respond to such an elaborate simulation? Although there were individual differences (some guards trying to be "tough but fair," some prisoners standing up under the regime better than others), both groups, the experimenters report, showed "extremely pathological" reactions. Guards harassed prisoners, insulted them, threatened them, and even used physical punishment, despite the experiment's prohibition against it. The most hostile guards on each shift quickly moved into leadership roles of giving orders and deciding on punishment, and were emulated by other members of the shift.

> After the first day of the study, practically all prisoners' rights (even such things as the time and condition of sleeping and eating) came to be redefined by the guards ad "privileges" which were to be earned for obedient behavior. Constructive activities such as reading and watching movies were arbitrarily cancelled until further notice by the guards—and were subsequently never allowed.[64]

One guard even attempted to keep an "incorrigible" prisoner "in the hole" all night, in violation of the guards' own rules and in concealment from the experimenters, who were thought to be "too soft on the prisoners."

[64]Ibid., p. 94.

Prisoners, confronted with this loss of their identity and arbitrary control of their lives, at first expressed disbelief, then rebelled, then tried to work within the system through an elected grievance committee. When all of these efforts failed, self-deprecation and deprecation of each other became the characteristic pattern. Half of the prisoners coped with the situation, the experimenters say, by becoming "emotionally disturbed."

> Five prisoners had to be released before the end of the experiment because of extreme emotional depression, crying, rage, and acute anxiety.... Others became excessively obedient in trying to be "good" prisoners. They sided with guards against a solitary fellow prisoner who coped with his situation by refusing to eat.... As the days wore on, the model prisoner reaction was one of passivity, dependence, and flattened affect.[65]

Because of the unexpected intensity of the subjects' reactions, the experiment was terminated after six days. Those prisoners who remained at that point were "extremely delighted with their good fortune." In contrast, most of the guards seemed to be distressed by the decision to stop the experiment. In fact, on several occasions, guards had "remained on duty voluntarily and uncomplaining for extra hours—without additional pay." Only one guard reported being personally upset by the suffering of the prisoners, but he did nothing to act upon that feeling.

At the end of the experiment, guards and prisoners were interviewed for their reflections on the experience. Here are sample statements:

PRISONERS

"I realize now that no matter how together I thought I was, my prison behavior was less under my control than I realized."

"I began to feel I was losing my identity, that the person I call _____, the person who volunteered to get me into this prison, was distant from me, was remote, until finally I wasn't *that* person, I was 416. I really was my number."

"I learned that people can easily forget that others are human."

GUARDS

"They (the prisoners) didn't see it as an experiment. It was real and they were fighting to keep their identity. But we were always there to show them just who was boss."

"I was tired of seeing the prisoners in their rags and smelling the strong odors of their bodies that filled the cells. I watched them tear at each other, on orders given by us.

"Acting authoritatively can be fun. Power can be a great pleasure."

"Most dramatic and distressing to us," the experimenters conclude, "was the observation of the ease with which sadistic behavior could be elicited in

[65]Ibid., p. 95.

individuals who were not 'sadistic types,' and the frequency with which acute emotional breakdowns could occur in men selected precisely for their emotional stability."[66]

IMPLICATIONS OF SOCIAL-PSYCHOLOGICAL RESEARCH FOR THE TEACHING OF ETHICS

It is with some ambivalence that I have reported these various probes into the darker side of our character, so readily elicited by manipulations of the situational context. The experimental procedures—the deception of subjects, the subjection of participants to stress far greater than anything they anticipated, the use of pressure to keep subjects in the experimental situation, the involvement of subjects in experiences that may have left them less moral at the end of the experiment than they were at the beginning—all these methods are open to ethical challenge. (The researchers, in their own defense, have cited long-range follow-ups with subjects whom they say show no lasting detrimental effects from participation.) I report these studies, not to applaud the ethics of their methodology, but to offer for reflection the knowledge about moral behavior which these investigations produced. What are the implications of this knowledge for the teacher of ethics?

They are, I believe, essentially the same as the central implications of the theory and research in moral development. There I suggested that ethics students would benefit from knowing about moral-stage development and the gap that sometimes yawns between hypothetical and real-life reasoning. Just as ethics students may profit from looking at moral reasoning as developmental psychologists, so, too, may they profit from looking at moral behavior as social psychologists. Some acquaintance with the enormous impact that the situation can have on the way people behave may better prepare students to deal morally with the situational pressures they will inevitably encounter in their own careers and lives.

A social-psychological perspective also directs our attention to the natural experiments afforded by the laboratories of business, medicine, law, politics, and the like. How do decisions really get made out there in the world? We all know something about the decisions we have been part of, and these experiences, where possible, should be brought to light in ethics courses for whatever they can teach us about the role of ethical deliberation in real life, or the lack of it. We can also learn a good deal about the psychology of decision making from history. An especially enlightening historical record is provided by David Halberstam's story of the men who ran the Vietnam War during the Kennedy and Johnson eras. If Halberstam's account in *The Best and The Brightest* is right,

[66]Ibid., p. 89.

the decisions about the war were not moral decisions; morality never entered the discussion. Even dissenters like George Ball "did not talk about doing good, or put Johnson off by discussing the moral thing to do."[67] People who wanted to be on the team talked the cold, tough language of pragmatism. And real men, in the Johnson Administration, did not have doubts. Hearing that one member of his administration was becoming "dovish" on Vietnam, Johnson said, "Hell, he has to squat to piss." In this institutional ethos, all the splendid intellects from Harvard, the brilliant rationalists, all surely capable of high-stage reasoning on hypothetical moral dilemmas, spoke of military costs and benefits, of the political consequences of this or that policy, of whether we could win the war—never of whether it was right or wrong.

Or look at John Dean's *Blind Ambition* for an account of how institutions socialize people into playing the roles that need to be played. When Dean was brought on, Haldeman gave him his job definition: "Doing whatever you goddam lawyers do for those who need you."[68] Murray Chotiner then advised Dean that, if he wanted to get along with the president, he had better not ask any questions. Dean's first assignment was to send the IRS after *Scanlan's Monthly* as retribution for a satire it carried on Spiro Agnew. His second was to facilitate the implementation of the "Huston Plan," whereby the president "removed most of the legal restraints on gathering intelligence on left-wing groups"—authorizing wiretaps, mail intercepts, and burglaries. Dean carried out the first assignment without protest. When he balked at the second, he was told that "there are people around here who think you have some little old lady in you." In the Nixon White House, as in Johnson's, it was weak and unmanly to be moral. After that, Dean worked hard to look tough. In an interview at the Boston University Law School, he said,

> I had never pictured myself getting into trouble before I began working at the White House. It was a very rude awakening to see how easily I was tempted to cross over the line. I had one set of perceptions when I was working as part of the criminal justice process (in the Justice Department), and quite another later on.[69]

The interviewer asked Dean, "Do you think that the outcome of your career might have been different had law school focused on questions of professional responsibility to a greater extent?" Dean replied,

> No, I don't think so. I must say that I knew that the things I was doing were wrong, and one learns the difference between right and wrong long before one enters law school. A course in legal ethics wouldn't have changed anything.[70]

[67]D. Halberstam, *The Best and the Brightest* (New York: Random House, 1969), p. 645.
[68]J. Dean, *Blind Ambition* (New York: Simon & Schuster, 1976), p. 17.
[69]D. Goldman, "Exclusive Interview with John Dean," *Comment*, Boston University School of Law (February 1979), p. 7.
[70]Ibid., p. 1.

Jeb Magruder would probably agree with Dean; he took William Sloan Coffin's ethics course.

Dean's statement echoes a theme of both the moral-development and the social-psychological research: to know the right is not necessarily to do it. Socrates gave us only half the truth when he said that to know the good is to do the good. St. Paul gave us the other half when he said, "The good that I would do, that I do not do. The evil that I would not do, that I do." Knowledge of the good is clearly a necessary condition for doing it, but it is, equally clearly, not sufficient.

DEVELOPING THE WILL TO DO THE RIGHT

How, then, do we get people to do the good they know they should do? The old construct of *will*, always important in theology, deserves a place in our moral psychology and education. How do you develop the will to act in morally responsible ways, to keep your moral principles when all about you are losing theirs?

Aristotle said it was a matter of practice. We get better at being good by being good. In presenting the educational implications of moral-development theory, I stressed the importance of the person's activity, both as a way of developing better moral reasoning, and as a way of learning to put that reasoning into practice. The social-psychological research points to the same conclusion: If we bend so easily before the winds of situational pressures, then we need opportunities during development, if not to face the strongest winds, as least to deal with some of the complexities and pressures of real situations. Bok and Callahan have written that ethics courses permit consideration of "moral choices that will be encountered in later life but without all the pressures and risks that accompany these dilemmas in the real world."[71] From a psychological standpoint, that is precisely the problem. Ethics done only in the safety of the classroom, never put to the test of real decision making, may fail to develop the moral will, the commitment to the right, that is the necessary bridge between thought and action.

I do not mean to suggest that all learning must be experiential, that all ethical inquiry must be tied somehow to first-hand action. In discussing Vietnam and Watergate, I tried to indicate that much can be learned about ethics in the real world from the example, the prior experience, of others. I remember a comment in this vein at a Harvard seminar on ethics teaching sponsored by the Hastings Center. One gentleman observed:

> Most people will become functionaries in large institutions, subject to the decisions of others rather than making decisions. Do we merely raise their anx-

---

[71]Bok and Callahan, "Teaching Applied Ethics," p. 32.

ieties by talking about ethics? We must open their eyes to the opportunities for ethical choices—show them how given institutions, say, have reconciled profit and a concern for human welfare. Let people see examples of opportunities to do good in the world and still work within the organization.

From this perspective, part of preparing to be an ethical person in the real world is thinking about the contexts, the institutional settings, where ethical decisions will be made or not made. How can people make those contexts more receptive to ethical thinking? How can ethics become part of business as usual, so that ethical thinkers will not be in the position of one economist, who told Callahan, "I've been interested in ethics personally for years, but every time I bring it up with my colleagues, they think I'm losing my grip, going soft in the head"?[72] What institutional structures or processes need to be changed to get ethics on the agenda? To examine questions like these is to try to develop a practical sociology as a tool in the service of applied ethics.

Let me say, too, that ethics needs to be on the daily agenda, not reserved only for matters of great moment. Momentous moral decisions about nuclear energy, the distribution of fuel, genetic screening, and human conception in the laboratory are obviously great challenges before ethics, but they are rare events, not the stuff of our day-to-day moral lives. Whether to declare everything on our income tax when money is tight and the government wastes a lot of it, whether to conserve fuel when it is inconvenient to do so, whether to be democratic when it is easier to make the decision ourselves, whether to give someone time when our time is short, whether to object to small corruptions when silence is more expedient, whether to be decent to our subordinates and fair with our children—these are the moral choices that, taken together, determine the quality of moral life in society. There is a need to cultivate an "ethics of the everyday," a morality of minor affairs, that translates respect for persons into small deeds of kindness, honesty, and decency. In short, I think that ethics courses, to be credible, must come down on the side of "cleaning up our act." Decency and integrity in our everyday encounters are both important in themselves and likely to be important in strengthening our disposition to be moral when we face the big decisions. If we do not nurture ethics on the small scale, we may not get it on the grand scale either.

In his position paper, "Goals in the Teaching of Ethics," Daniel Callahan states unequivocally that "The whole and final point of ethics is that of the guidance of conduct.... Ethics calls us to act in the light of what we perceive to be right and good."[73] That viewpoint has served as the underlying premise for the suggestions I have offered in this paper. For if students learned to "do ethics" and didn't become better people, if they merely learned to talk a good game in the confines of a course, if their human relations, their work, their

[72]D. Callahan, "The Rebirth of Ethics," *National Forum* 9 (Spring 1978), p. 12.
[73]Callahan, "Goals in the Teaching of Ethics," this volume, Chapter 2.

stance in the world remained untouched, would not the whole huge effort to teach ethics in our colleges and professional schools be judged a cruelly disappointing failure, deepening intolerably the already prevailing cynicism about the gap between what people say and what they do? Certainly ethics courses cannot try to teach particular moral behaviors; that would be indoctrination. But if the movement to teach ethics is serious about developing not only the capacity to think ethically but also the commitment to act ethically, then it will have to find ways to fire the will as well as the intellect, to engage the heart as deeply as the mind, and to put will, intellect, and feeling to the test of behavior. Armchairing alone won't do the job. Engaging and developing the whole person is unquestionably a tall order, more than any one-semester course can do adequately, perhaps more than many educational institutions are prepared to tackle. But that, from the standpoint of moral psychology, is the size of the task.

CHAPTER 5

Evaluation and the Teaching of Ethics

ARTHUR L. CAPLAN

THE "NEED" FOR EVALUATION IN EDUCATION

During the past decade, extraordinary pressures have been exerted upon governmental bodies and regulatory agencies to become more cost-effective. As a result, policymakers charged with controlling public funds and with their expenditure for public projects have become increasingly concerned with the demonstrable effects and visible products of investments in research and social welfare programs. The need to legitimate the expenditure of public monies has become particularly pressing in the academic and scientific research sectors, where the difficulties of securing funds for basic research in the natural sciences and clinical medicine are familiar policy issues. Those seeking government grants for the arts and for higher education are now confronted by the same difficulties.

In response to these budgetary pressures, educators and scientists have chosen to justify the expenditure of large sums of money for scientific research by pointing to its useful technological and medical products. The "bottom line" legitimation of basic research outlays is, in the researchers' own arguments, the improvements in health, transportation, communication, defense, and agriculture which science has and will continue to provide for humankind. Whether or not one agrees with the assessment of basic research, an instrumentalist justification of basic research activities has been a rather successful policy strategy for securing public monies in support of research.

One interesting outcome of the heightened concern with demonstrating results in the domain of education is the growing emphasis on evaluation. Most federal agencies, such as the National Endowment for the Humanities and the National Institute of Education Association, now require an evaluation com-

ARTHUR L. CAPLAN ● The Hastings Center, Institute of Society, Ethics and the Life Sciences, Hastings-on-Hudson, New York and Department of Medicine, College of Physicians and Surgeons, Columbia University, New York, New York.

ponent as an element of any grant application. The field of educational evaluation studies has blossomed, partly in direct response to the perceived need to satisfy bureaucrats and public officials that monies spent on higher-education projects will not be "wasted" or "frittered away."

Pressures to develop appropriate evaluation measures for innovative or experimental programs in the field of education do not issue solely from external funding agencies and federal officials. Administrators within the university setting require some means for evaluating curricular innovations. Both the faculty members directly involved in new offerings and those involved in curricular revision and in setting school and departmental requirements are faced with the need for objective assessments of the merit and impact of new courses and programs.

How to evaluate courses and programs becomes especially acute when new areas of inquiry and research are proposed for the academic curriculum, or when revisions of program requirements and core courses are considered. Competition for student time within and between departments is intense, and proposals for new courses or programs are likely to meet with a less than enthusiastic reception from faculty members concerned with obtaining minimally adequate time for their own particular areas. Any new curricular program or revised course requirement is likely to receive more critical scrutiny than traditional parts of the undergraduate or professional school curricula. Moreover, the current educational concerns with evaluation are further exacerbated by forces other than the competition for scarce course time and faculty resources.

The course content of American colleges and universities has not been immune to changing fads and fancies in the philosophy of education. In the late nineteen-sixties, for example, there were drastic revisions in the course offerings and requirements of many schools. In the seventies there has been considerable curricular retrenchment, as many of the new offerings and new elective freedoms of the sixties have become casualties of changing political, ideological, demographic, and cultural forces. These recent experiences in curriculum innovation and change have made educators acutely aware of the need for objective criteria and standards for assessing the curricula of colleges and universities. The need for "objective" means of evaluation is further heightened in that declining enrollments, shrinking budgets, and unstable economic conditions have led some educators to question whether peer review and administration assessment are viable or appropriate vehicles for molding course and program content. Not surprisingly, administrators and curriculum committees have begun to turn more and more to evaluation experts for "impartial" guidance and advice.

The evaluation of new courses and programs in the teaching of ethics must be viewed in light of the widespread emphasis on evaluation in education, science, and the arts. However, the teaching of ethics has received unusual evaluative scrutiny, even for an area which is new and possibly trendy, and requires significant amounts of faculty and curricular time.

The question of whether ethics deserves greater emphasis in the undergraduate and professional-school curriculum has not received a univocal answer among students and faculty. The diversity of methods and means for achieving this new emphasis almost guarantees passionate debate and disagreement. In such a situation, the temptation to turn to "impartial," quantifiable, "objective" standards of evaluation becomes overwhelming and understandable.

Moreover, ethics and values courses fall within the province of the humanities, which as a whole have not been faring well in terms of course enrollments and faculty security. Thus, new curricular proposals in the humanities are often subjected to evaluative scrutiny that may be neither appropriate nor necessary. The vulnerability of new courses on ethics or values to stringent evaluation is exacerbated by the fact that humanists as a group have not been particularly adept at articulating or defining the evaluative standards that they feel ought to obtain in this area.

Courses on ethics or values have no real home in departments in professional schools, and some applied-ethics courses and programs at the undergraduate level come perilously close to infringing on the territories of existing course offerings; this, too, contributes to the cry for more evaluation of the success and impact of ethics and values courses. The dependence of these offerings on "soft" funding and high enrollments also adds to the perception that courses in medical ethics, business ethics, engineering ethics, environmental ethics, and the like, should receive especially careful critical scrutiny.

The emerging concern with evaluation in education generally, and with new course offerings in ethics and values in particular, has sent many humanists into a frenzied scramble to locate the perfect questionnaire or test instrument, and to seek operationally minded social scientists who can provide graphs, scales, and numbers that will bedazzle the grants officer or department chairperson. Tests and questionnaires designed to measure moral abilities and ethical attitudes are proliferating as the pressures to evaluate and legitimate a renewed emphasis on ethics and values teaching in American higher education increase. This combination of political, academic, and financial forces has thrust evaluation to center stage as one of the key educational issues for proponents as well as critics of ethics teaching in higher education.

GOALS, EVALUATION AND THE TEACHING OF ETHICS

It may appear that the only way to establish standards for evaluating courses in ethics or values is to clarify the specific goals of such courses. Despite the many different rationales for moral education, individual instructors and courses on ethics and and values usually are based in a set of explicit or tacit goals that guide instruction. Were it possible to agree upon a minimum set of goals for ethics teaching, these would provide a starting point for a consideration of appropriate evaluation techniques.

That course goals must be determined prior to a discussion of appropriate modes of evaluation is frequently espoused in theory, but forgotten in practice. Grants officers tend to be impatient with ethicists who, because of ignorance or a repugnance for measurement and quantification, incessantly proclaim that ethics is not the sort of subject that can possibly be evaluated.[1] Some instructors simply yield in the face of powerful pressures, and half-heartedly supply the kinds of tests and measures that are thought to be sought. Others fall back on the truism that ethics is different from physics or medicine. Still others note that ethics, unlike medicine or law, has no facts and accepted professional standards, and that there is nothing to measure in courses on ethics and values.

Even the claim that a discussion of the acceptable goals of ethics teaching must precede a discussion of evaluation in teaching ethics is not accepted as a self-evident truth. Some argue that there should be no instruction on any topic before the effect of such an enterprise can be difinitively measured and/or understood.[2] If no agreed-upon method exists for evaluating what we are doing in the classroom, then we might be better off not doing anything at all.

In the evaluation of a course on any subject, the following issues must be addressed. First, *what* is to be evaluated: student course performance, course content, course organization, teacher skills, student comprehension, the retention of course information, behavioral performance subsequent to instruction, student attitudes, cognitive abilities, emotional capacities, student development and growth, etc.? Second, *for whom* is the evaluation being conducted: students, funders, teachers, professional societies, society, academic peers, etc.? And third, *why* is the evaluation being conducted at all: to satisfy academic regulations, establish competence, certify competence, assess adequacy, discover inefficiencies, etc.? These questions illustrate the diversity of things to evaluate, potential evaluators, and possible rationales for assessing an educational endeavor. The questions also show that, in order to make an evaluation, one must know the purpose of both the evaluation itself and the activity being evaluated. Only by explicating these goals can we make sense of the concept of evaluation in the context of education.

Other factors complicate the relation between goals and evaluation in the teaching of ethics. There are, for example, two distinct rationales for evaluation. The purpose of a *formative* evaluation is to monitor a course, in order to provide

[1] Mary Warnock makes much the same point in her essay "Towards a Definition of Quality in Education," in R. S. Peters, ed., *The Philosophy of Education* (Oxford: Oxford University Press, 1973).

[2] Such arguments appear in W. J. Popham, *Instructional Objectives* (Chicago: Rand-McNally & Co., 1969); R. J. Kibler, L. L. Barker, and D. T. Miles, *Behavioral Objectives and Instruction* (Boston: Allyn & Bacon, 1970); and M. Rokeach, *The Nature of Human Values* (New York: The Free Press, 1973).

feedback to those being evaluated, as well as the evaluators. This reciprocal interaction is intended to allow the goals of a course or program to evolve under the scrutiny of the evaluators. In this type of evaluation, best exemplified by initial funding decisions by peer reviewers, the distinction between goals and methods for evaluating their attainment tends to become blurred, since the evaluation process is intended to guide and influence the selection of goals as a program or course begins and evolves.

A *summary* evaluation is conducted *post facto*, upon the completion of instruction. Through questionnaires, site visits, or reports, a summary evaluation assesses the successes and failures of a completed instructional enterprise. Both summary and formative evaluations are used for ethics and values teaching, and it is important to understand that the aims and goals of a course in this area may not be equally clear at all times during the evaluation process.

A second complicating factor is the distinction between evaluations for quality, i.e., those undertaken to assess the quality of courses, and evaluations for existence, i.e., those undertaken to determine whether a course or program ought to exist in the curriculum at all. Quality assessment may be irrelevant to this latter type of evaluation. An ethics instructor may give an excellent course on engineering ethics; yet this evaluation may have little bearing on whether the course is retained as an offering in the engineering school.

Evaluating for existence is particularly difficult because most existing modes of evaluation pertain to quality assessments. The criteria used to decide about the viability of any course may vary widely—from enrollment figures to historical tradition. Most evaluations in the educational arena do not concern content, pace, clarity, and utility, or faculty reviews of curriculum adequacy and student performance. Since the purpose of course evaluation is often to decide whether existing courses should continue or new ones be instituted, the existing modes of course evaluation do not necessarily transfer well from evaluations of quality to the task of evaluating for existence. Despite these problems, it may still be possible to determine the kinds of variables to which evaluations of ethics and values courses should be sensitive, provided there can be agreement about the desirability and undesirability of various goals in such courses.

Behavior as an Evaluative Measure in Ethics Teaching

In his paper "Goals in the Teaching of Ethics," Daniel Callahan describes some of the acceptable and unacceptable goals for ethics teaching.[3] He argues

---

[3]"Goals in the Teaching of Ethics," (This volume, Chapter 2). See also R. T. Hall and J. U. Davis, *Moral Education in Theory and Practice* (Buffalo: Prometheus Books, 1975; and David Durpel and Kevin Ryan, *Moral Education: It Comes With the Territory* (Berkeley, McCutchan, 1976).

that any course in ethics, if it is to be a "serious" course, must attend to at least five general goals:

1. Stimulate the moral imagination
2. Provide ability to recognize ethical issues
3. Develop analytical skills
4. Elicit a sense of moral obligation
5. Promote the tolerance of ambiguity and disagreement

Significant by its absence from this list of goals is behavioral change, which Callahan terms a "doubtful" and "inappropriate" goal for ethical instruction. Since a good deal of current evaluational methodology in the area of ethics and values in education uses behavioral measures to determine the success or failure of moral instruction (as do the evaluations of many academic and nonacademic onlookers), this disparity between goal and test raises some serious issues as to the adequacy of present evaluation activities.

The question of whether behavioral change is an appropriate measure of success for instruction in ethics is widely and hotly debated. Callahan, among others, argues that behavioral change is not an acceptable pedagogical goal for ethics teaching. And it is difficult not to agree with his assessment. After all, there are many faster and more efficient ways to produce desired behavior than instruction in ethics courses.

Nevertheless, the question still remains open as to whether behavioral change might be an appropriate goal for ethics teaching in certain settings such as within religious communities. And, though behavioral change may be inappropriate as a goal of ethical instruction, it may, unfortunately, play a prominent role in the assessments made of ethics courses by administrators and evaluators. Perhaps part of the reason underlying the attention given to behavior in evaluation can be traced to a confusion between the use of behavior as evidence and the use of behavior as a goal for ethical instruction.

Even if behavioral change *per se* is not an appropriate pedagogical goal in ethics teaching, it is possible that behavioral change may serve as evidence to measure other plausible goals of moral instruction. For any of Callahan's five goals, for example, it is relatively simple to construct plausible behavioral indices that may provide *evidence* for a "stimulated moral imagination," or indicate the presence of "the ability to recognize ethical issues." Although the distinction between proof and evidence is patent, the concepts are not always kept distinct in thinking about the role behavioral changes might play in educational evaluations.[4] This is not to say that there are no problems confronting those who wish to use behavior as evidence, rather than as a final proof of success or failure in ethics teaching; and some of these problems will be considered in the last

[4]T. F. Daveney, "Education: A Moral Concept," in G. Langford and D. J. O'Connor, eds., *New Essays in the Philosophy of Education* (London: Routledge & Kegan Paul, 1973).

section of this essay. First, however, let us turn to other criteria which may be used to assess the impact of ethical instruction upon students.

There is a relatively new and growing emphasis on changes in student and professional conduct in professional settings. In medical schools, for example, the question often asked is whether students behave more ethically, or display a more considerate attitude toward patients, as a result of specialized instruction in medical ethics. In business schools, the criteria for success frequently include the levels of lying, stealing, cheating, whistleblowing, and bribery that are manifest among businessmen who have taken a course in ethics, as opposed to those who have not. Similar behavioral measures could be described for students in schools of law, journalism, engineering, accounting, and public policy. Anyone who doubts that changes in student behavior or professional conduct are the primary evidence for the evaluation of the quality and utility of the teaching of ethics in professional schools need only look at the reasons advanced for introducing ethics into the curriculum:[5] Watergate, Koreagate, Viet Nam, "ghost" surgery, etc. Consider also the "conclusive" argument against ethics teaching in professional schools advanced by the dean of the Stanford Business School— "There are a lot of people in jail today who have taken courses in ethics."[6]

To the best of my knowledge, there are no widely accepted test instruments for measuring behavioral change subsequent to ethics teaching in professional schools. However, some schools have introduced examinations involving hypothetical or real case examples, in an effort to assess the moral commitments and likely behavioral propensities of students. These tests, and similar attempts to discern the probable professional conduct of students subsequent to school, raise questions about the validity of using conduct or attitudes as evidence for evaluating the impact and worth of ethical instruction.

It is probably true that hypothetical cases presented in classroom settings can shed only a little light on the future behavior of professionals in actual settings.[7] Students quickly discern what teachers hope to find in examination answers, and readily supply these responses. But these criticisms skirt the heart of the matter: Is behavior or even prospective behavior a variable worthy of consideration for evaluating the teaching of ethics?

One drawback to focusing on behavioral change as evidence for evaluating the attainment of pedagogical goals in teaching ethics is that such a measure unavoidably skews the assessment in the direction of the effects, rather than the causes, of behavioral change. Changes in professional conduct subsequent to a

[5]Derek Bok, "Can Ethics Be Taught?" *Change* 8 (October 1976), pp.26–30; Daniel Callahan, "The Rebirth of Ethics," *National Forum*, 58 (Spring, 1978), pp. 9–12; Andrew L. Kaufman, "Law and Ethics," *Hastings Center Report*, 7 (December, 1977), pp. 7–8.

[6]Quoted in E. B. Fiske, "Ethics Courses Now Attracting Many More U. S. College Students," *New York Times*, 20 February 1978.

[7]R. B. Bloom, "Discipline: Another Face of Moral Reasoning," *College Student Journal*, 1979. Also California Professional Responsibility Examination of the State Bar of California, 1975.

course in ethics do not support inferences about the causes of the changed behavior. No matter how behavioral change is defined, an emphasis on improved behavior can saddle the ethicist with a goal that was not intended, or credit a course for results that are not deserved. There are multiple explanations for any particular action. Fear, opportunity, self-interest, and circumstance can all combine to produce behavior that is legitimately describable as laudable or desirable, but does not issue from any real concern with ethics, morality, or professional responsibility.

The assumption that an action deemed moral is necessarily the result of having taken a course in ethics would seem to represent an instance of the logical fallacy *post hoc, ergo propter hoc.* To make the connection, it would be necessary to establish a causal link between moral instruction, conscious volitional choice, and moral behavior. Behavioral change alone is only one possible element of what is surely a complex etiology between instruction and action. In addition, a focus on behavior can foster a commitment to behavioral change for change's sake, when there is no real reason for so acting. The ease with which behavior can be measured in some contexts can lull instructors into the false belief that it is simply the behavior, rather than the underlying reasoning, that should be the locus of moral teaching.

But, most importantly, behavior is easily abused as an evaluative standard. The demand to show positive effects as a direct consequence of ethical instruction can force teachers to adopt goals that are inconsistent with both acceptable moral practices and espoused educational philosophies. The lures of creating highly moral professionals and more virtuous professional conduct can overwhelm efforts to aim at other instrumental or intrinsic educational goals. For example, one reason for introducing ethics into the professional-school curriculum may be to counteract the negative effects of early professionalization, or the powerful forces of professional socialization. Worthwhile goals such as this can all too easily be forgotten in the effort to guarantee "good" professional conduct. Although behavioral change may, in principle, be a valuable index of evaluation in assessing the impact of moral instruction relative to certain goals, its utility in that context is directly proportional to the availability of sound theories of human action, learning, and conduct, and to the legitimacy and purpose of the educational goals that motivate the instruction.

TESTING MORAL COMPETENCE

Evaluation of moral instruction at the undergraduate level does not usually manifest the same attention to conduct as does evaluation in the professional-school setting. For the most part, evaluations of student performance and course success follow what I have termed the traditional modes of evaluation in college teaching: examinations, quizzes, papers, interviews, dissertations, etc. However, in recent years there has been a rise in interest among educational and developmental psychologists in developing more refined methods of evaluating and testing moral capacities and knowledge. Some persons involved in programs or courses explicitly devoted to values teaching, moral development, or applied ethics have been quick to utilize these new test instruments, in the hope of proving the importance and legitimacy of what are often new or experimental ethics or values programs. The work of Lawrence Kohlberg, Sidney Simon,[8] and their followers is cited with increasing frequency in the evaluations and tests administered by teachers and administrators who want to prove the efficacy of ethics teaching to skeptical faculty members and funding sources, and to each other.

Tests and measures for moral skills and abilities are proliferating. One test in particular, explicitly designed for use with college and graduate students, has gained a rather broad following among educators in these settings—James Rest's Defining Issues Test (DIT). Because the DIT is not only typical of the evaluation tests presently available, but also represents a relatively sophisticated example of an evaluative methodology, it will serve as a convenient focus for a discussion of behavioral evaluation at the college level of ethical instruction.

Rest's DIT is designed to measure the ways in which subjects identify "the important issues of moral dilemmas."[9] To test moral judgment, subjects are asked to read hypothetical moral dilemmas and select from a series of statements that describe possible moral issues raised by the cases. Subjects then rank the issue statements in terms of a scale of perceived importance, which is interpreted by Rest as a mode for evaluating the importance of various Kohlbergian moral-stage characteristics in viewing moral dilemmas. The ultimate aim of the DIT is to see whether a "standardized, objectively scorable measure of moral judgment may be devised."[10]

After administering the test to thousands of subjects in high schools, colleges, and graduate schools, Rest reports a number of interesting findings.[11] High school students score noticeably lower on the DIT than graduate students in philosophy. High correlations exist between DIT scores and various cognitive-capacity measures, as well as various attitudinal measures of value commitment and affective stage development. Retest scores are highly stable, and students do poorly when asked to "fake" high scores on the DIT.

The main value of the DIT is as a developmental measure. Scores on the

[8]This is born out by our research on the teaching of ethics and the evaluations used at colleges such as Notre Dame, Fordham, UCLA, Goucher, Haverford, Washington and Lee, etc.

[9]J. R. Rest, "Recent Research on an Objective Test of Moral Judgment: How the Important Issues of a Moral Dilemma are Defined," in D. J. DePalma and J. M. Foley, eds., *Moral Development: Current Theory and Research* (Hillsdale, N. J.: Lawrence Erlbaum, 1975), p. 76.

[10]Ibid., p. 76.

[11]Ibid., pp. 79–86. Also J. R. Rest *et al.*, "Development in Judging Moral Issues." Minnesota Moral Research Projects, Technical Report #3, 1977.

DIT are correlated with Kohlbergian stages of moral development. These correlations are used as evidence to show that "as subjects develop cognitively, they come to define moral dilemmas more complexly, and to place greater importance on principled moral thinking than do the less cognitively advanced subjects."[12] Principled moral thinking—that is, moral judgments which appeal to normative principles, the need for structure in morality, and the value of institutional and social norms—is held to be the key characteristic of advanced moral thinking.

One of Rest's students, Panowitsch,[13] has studied changes in the DIT scores of college students enrolled in logic and ethics courses. Not surprisingly, the DIT scores of the students in the ethics course showed significant improvements well beyond the changes in scores observed in students taking logic courses in pretest/posttest situations. The DIT test is particularly sensitive to demarcating those items thought to be indicative of principled moral reasoning—a key stage in the development of moral judgment. Philosophy graduate students perform very well on the DIT, especially with reference to this category of moral judgment.

Researchers using the DIT admit that it has a "few problems, as do most psychological measures,"[14] but argue that the advantages of the test in enabling "researchers to use a standardized assessment of moral judgment, to objectively score their data, and to compare their results"[15] far outweigh any methodological problems. Rest himself is rather cautious in his claims about the uses to which the DIT and its ilk ought to be put. He notes that the DIT is intended solely as a measure of moral judgment, not of moral worth, or of likely moral conduct.[16]

Nonetheless, because of growing pressures for evaluations of curricular offerings, especially new ones, the climate is ripe for misuse of the kind of evaluation the DIT represents. Moreover, societal concerns with group differences, crime, social standing, and personal worth could result in the misinterpretation and abuse of test results which would far outweigh the benefits to be derived from this sort of psychometric evaluation methodology.[17] Still, it might be

[12]Rest, "Recent Research on an Objective Test," pp. 87–88.

[13]Reported in J. R. Rest et al., "Development in Judging Moral Issues," pp. 5–9.

[14]D. J. DePalma, "Research and Theory in Moral Development: A Commentary," in D. J. DePalma and J. M. Foley, eds., Moral Development: Current Theory and Research (Hillsdale, N. J.: Lawrence Erlbaum, 1975, p. 188.

[15]Ibid., p. 188.

[16]These disclaimers are carefully noted in the mimeographed letter Rest sends in response to all inquiries about the DIT.

[17]The most familiar contemporary controversy over the dangers of psychometric testing is the debate surrounding the use of intelligence tests. Excellent introductions to ethical and methodological objections to such testing can be found in N. J. Block and G. Dworkin, eds., The IQ Controversy (New York: Pantheon, 1976) and L. J. Kamin, The Science and Politics of IQ (Potomac, Md., Lawrence Erlbaum, 1974).

argued that the probability of misuse is not an argument against the validity of a moral test. Since there are valid reasons for concern about the worth of this mode of evaluation on methodological grounds, the philosophy and methodology of psychometric moral testing deserves some comment.

We have already noted the grounds for skepticism about the prospects of developing an objective, standardized test to evaluate the efficacy of moral instruction in the teaching of ethics to undergraduates and professional-school students. The diversity of possible goals for courses in ethics, and the value-laden nature of the arguments necessary to pursue a particular goal, make it unlikely that a single measure of moral change, i.e., Rest's DIT test for moral judgment, will be of much utility in the evaluation of courses on ethics and values. Most educational psychologists, including Rest, build their hopes for an objective testing methodology on the availability of standardized test items that do not depend upon the subjective opinions of the evaluator for their identification or scoring. But standardization does not solve the testing problems posed by the diversity of plausible, normatively grounded goals for moral instruction. To use a test like the DIT to evaluate a variable such as moral judgment would require a complete explication of the nature of moral judgment, and a normative argument as to the validity of taking the maximization of this specific variable as a worthwhile aim of moral education. Such arguments are rarely forthcoming from either moral measurement theorists or test users.

In addition, there is a plethora of problems surrounding the value biases in a test like the DIT (i.e., the emphasis on principled moral reasoning). It is particularly difficult to decide how to interpret a change in a test score measuring moral judgment, in the absence of a causal theory about the sources of such shifts. High scores are not to be valued merely for their high numbers, but, presumably, because they represent shifts in valued moral properties, traits, or skills. Changes in test scores subsequent to instruction in ethics are difficult to interpret—particularly if uncertainty exists about the native abilities and capacities of students, and the willingness or amenability of students in providing the kinds of response that will result in higher scores on such tests.

Finally, there are serious methodological problems with evaluation measures such as the DIT. Standardized test items used in the DIT and other test instruments tend to narrow the range of possible student response. Moreover, the use of test items that are loaded in the direction of a particular theory of moral development, for instance a Kohlbergian paradigm, raises serious problems of circularity in the interpretation of test results. If test items are initially selected on the ground that they are indicative of various stages of development in moral judgment, then it should come as no real surprise that students who score well on such tests will have demonstrated a higher degree of moral judgment and development. A "forced choice" among preselected test items on an evaluation test considerably narrows the type and range of result and interpretation that can be obtained. For example, it is unlikely that sophisticated moral skeptics or committed ethical intuitionists would fare very well on a test that leaves no room for the expression of the complex moral reasoning that can be the source of such views, and is strongly weighted in favor of principled moralities that are incompatible with other views of ethics and the teaching of morality.

I think it fair to say that many teachers of ethics and values would be unhappy with the use of overt measures of morality, such as student behavior or student test scores, in evaluating the efficacy and worth of their instruction. An emphasis on the overt, observable effects of teaching on students would, for many teachers, inappropriately undervalue the vitally important role of reasoning in coming to act upon or maintain a set of value beliefs. "Right" reasons, rather than "right" answers or "right" conduct, is the measure likely to concern instructors who have only limited time and access to students.

This is not to say that no empirical evaluative measure is useful in assessing moral instruction. If one is concerned to show that teaching ethics in college or professional schools has some effect on students, then many empirical indices can admirably fulfill this goal. But, since ethical teaching is motivated by different educational concerns, and occurs within highly diverse academic environments, the prospects are not good for pinpointing a single test or behavioral dimension as *the* measure of worth in the teaching of ethics. At best, if used with caution, standardized tests or behavioral surveys can serve as valuable adjuncts to the traditional modes of evaluating student performance and course effects. But the traditional modes—examinations, interviews, observations, peer review, essays, quizzes, etc.—still seem to provide the greater evaluative flexibility requisite for the proper assessment of diverse goals, educational philosophies, pedagogical methods, student abilities, and academic environments.

TRADITIONAL MODES OF EVALUATION

Even if it is possible to agree on a set of minimal goals for the teaching of courses on ethics and values, important choices about strategies remain. If the goal of evaluation is to assess both the importance and the quality of course instruction in ethics for students, the following questions seem especially relevant to any decisions as to methodology:

1. Are traditional modes of evaluation in the humanities appropriate for courses on ethics and values?
2. Is ethics as a subject matter unique or special in its evaluation difficulties?
3. Can objective evaluations of any course in the humanities be conducted?

Most humanists would agree that standards for the evaluation of student course performance do exist. Humanists are no different from other scholars in their proclivity to judge student performance and assess student work. Anyone who has ever taken a course in philosophy, theology, or literature soon recognizes that standards of competence and excellence do indeed exist in these fields, and this is equally true of the subareas of ethics and values. Classroom discussions, tests, and writing assignments provide students with ample opportunities to have their nascent analytical ethical skills and beliefs critically assessed by faculty. Classroom performance, tests, and written papers are the traditional modes of evaluation in the humanities in general, and in courses on ethics and values in particular. The question, then, is not whether modes of evaluation exist,[18] but whether they are sufficient for instruction in ethics.

The traditional modes of evaluation seem as adequate for ethics and values as for other instruction. Classroom discussion and written work are reasonable tests of a student's mastery of ethical knowledge. The instructor who carefully attends to what students say in class and on paper can assess the student's ability to identify ethical issues, the skill with which ethical theory is applied to the analysis of problems, and the liveliness of the moral imagination. In the ethics course, as elsewhere, evaluation must focus around thought, and not action.

Some will argue that time and enrollments do not permit close faculty supervision of students, or that science or business students will not sit still for ethics courses that require term papers or erudite review essays. But neither of these worries impugns the validity of the traditional modes of student evaluation in humanities courses: the first concern pertains to the mechanics of successful teaching (small classes, lots of discussion time), and the second to the kinds of topics and cases that must be used to rivet the less-than-enthusiastic student's attention. Still, a persistent critic of traditionalism in evaluation methodology might protest that the discussion of evaluation misses the point: neither students nor faculty know what counts as good or bad work in ethics. Whether an instructor uses case studies, papers, classroom debates, or special videotapes, no one will know what makes for good work in matters ethical or valuational.[19]

This concern is really a worry about the possibility of objective evaluation in ethics. Although modes of evaluation exist, it is not clear that taste, personal idiosyncrasy, prejudice, and mood do not combine in one very fickle criterial jumble of evaluative assessment.

Much could be said about objectivity and evaluation in the context of courses on ethics and their impact on students, but two points are particularly germane. One is that the concern about objectivity, if raised selectively about

---

[18]But see Carl Bereiter, "The Morality of Moral Education," *Hastings Center Report* 8 (April 1978), pp. 20–25; William J. Bennett and Edwin J. Delattre, "Moral Education in the Schools," *The Public Interest* 50 (Winter 1978), pp. 81–98; Edwin J. Delattre and William J. Bennett, "Where the Values Movement Goes Wrong," Change (February 1979), pp. 38–43; and Martin Trow, "Higher Education and Moral Development," *AAUP Bulletin* (Spring 1976), pp. 20–27, for some concerns about the morality of evaluation.

[19]Carl Bereiter, *Must We Educate?* (Englewood Cliffs, N. J.: Prentice-Hall, 1972), and "The Morality of Moral Education," pp. 20–25.

evaluations in ethics, is really a disguised version of that old chestnut of positivism—ethical emotivism. There is no reason to assume that objective judgments of students' ethical reasoning and skills are either more or less problematic than such judgments in other disciplines. Competent instructors can recognize good arguments, legitimate value puzzles, and perky moral imaginations.

The second point is that objectivity becomes of particular concern when there is a reason to suspect a lack of impartiality on the part of the evaluator. This is why program evaluations by colleagues and peers are often suspect. But instructors are, happily, in a better position to assess their impact on students, and vice versa. Consequently, objective quality assessment can be fostered by mechanisms to insure this much needed impartiality ("blind" grading of papers, steering away from articles written by the instructor, etc.).

Most people working in the field of ethics and values already believe in those evaluation strategies, and use them regularly. But a defense of traditionalism in the evaluation of the impact of ethics and values courses may seem less banal when juxtaposed with a discussion of some views of the evaluation of student performance and teaching success that are currently gaining some favor in certain academic circles.

WHAT ARE THE BEST CRITERIA FOR EVALUATION?

The problem still remains of deciding exactly how to go about the process of evaluation in an ethics course. Here the focus has been on the traditional modes, but there are obviously important issues involving the evaluation of student performance, pedagogical techniques, and professional conduct which need to be addressed as well.

Let us turn now to concrete suggestions about the modes of evaluation one might use in analyzing the worth of various pedagogical techniques in the ethics classroom. Although much of what I have to say will be easily transferable to other evaluational contexts, I want to emphasize that there are no quick and easy answers to the puzzle of evaluation in the teaching of ethics. Since many people advocate many different goals in undertaking such teaching, and since many different motives underlie the evaluation enterprise, it is unlikely that any single set of modes and criteria will serve as a panacea for all the practical difficulties. Moreover, any evaluation is only as sound as the rationale that supports it. The most that evaluation can provide is evidence. It cannot provide, and should not be used by itself to obtain, proof of the efficacy or inadequacy of any teaching endeavor. The evidence must be interpreted, weighed, and analyzed, and there are no hard and fast rules for carrying out these complex tasks.[20]

[20]See Israel Scheffler's *Conditions of Knowledge: An Introduction to Epistemology and Education* (Chicago: University of Chicago Press, 1965).

There are at least seven ways to acquire information about the efficacy and utility of teaching ethics in a course or program. Some of these modes are traditional techniques in the humanities for making judgments and evaluations. Others are newer and less well-articulated. Both types may be useful, and the inexperienced teacher of ethics may do well to try them all.

TRADITIONAL SOURCES OF INFORMATION

1. *Classroom observation.* The performance of students and teachers in classroom settings is an important index for the assessment of teaching. Do students participate in discussions? Are the instructor's views questioned and challenged? Do students incorporate course readings and lecture material in their discussions? Do students seem eager and willing to engage in discussion and debate about substantive moral issues?

2. *Written evidence.* Can students analyze moral problems in a clear and cogent manner in written assignments? Does their writing about ethical issues reflect increased sensitivity to course content as the course progresses? Are the students able to construct their own analyses of moral problems, and present plausible interpretations or solutions to these problems? Are students able to go beyond the lectures and readings in constructing their interpretations and solutions?

3. *Interviews.* In direct conversation with instructors, can students integrate classroom material into their everyday lives? Do students have opinions as to the quality and utility of lectures and readings? Are they able to conduct a reasonably coherent discussion about a moral problem or ethical issue of public moment?

4. *Games and simulations.* Are students capable of analyzing hypothetical or idealized moral problems? Can they "take sides" in a debate, and articulate the reasons (if any) underlying various moral points of view? Can the student put himself or herself "in another person's shoes," and see moral problems from something more than a personal perspective?

NONTRADITIONAL SOURCES OF INFORMATION

5. *Peer interviews.* What do friends and associates of students say about their attitudes, beliefs, and modes of behavior relative to moral matters subsequent to course or program instruction? Do students tend to show increased sensitivity to the existence of moral issues? Do they tend to articulate and defend moral points of view more readily than prior to classroom instruction? Are they better able to aid their peers in analyzing moral problems?

6. *Observation outside the classroom.* Do other teachers notice any shifts in the attitudes, beliefs, or arguments of students subsequent to or during the ethics course or program? Do students raise issues concerning moral problems in appropriate circumstances outside the ethics classroom?

7. *Tests.*   There are a number of tests presently available for measuring the level of moral reasoning of individuals. Many of these tests have not been applied at the college level. Nonetheless, a standardized test or scale, e.g., Rest's DIT, may provide evidence of cognitive or affective change as a consequence of ethical instruction. Although there are numerous difficulties in interpreting the results of such tests, they may provide useful information if one's interest is confined solely to the measuring of cognitive or affective change subsequent to classroom instruction.

No single mode is distinctively *the* best way of obtaining information about the teaching of ethics. Some of the most effective measures of educational efficacy require the application of these techniques to students who have left university life and are well along in their postacademic careers. Some of the most sensitive techniques for the observing of subtle changes in abilities, knowledge, skills, and behavior involve levels of observation and interaction that are often difficult to achieve for a variety of reasons.

CRITERIA

There are many levels of teaching, and many settings for the teaching of ethics. Thus, no universal set of criteria can be adduced to guide evaluation and assessment in this area. Moreover, because the evaluation criteria that are utilized must remain sensitive to the goals and purposes motivating ethical instruction, there will, of necessity, be a large variation in the types of criterion deemed relevant by instructors, students, administrators, and peers. Nonetheless, it may be useful, especially to those not experienced in the teaching of ethics or humanities, to have examples of the considerations utilized in many ethics classrooms. The criteria described below have proved useful in my own teaching.

1. *Quality of arguments for moral views.*   There is a large difference between assessing the "correctness" of a given moral position, and assessing the quality of a moral argument. Sound positions in ethics ought to be supported by good reasons. Students should be sensitive to the difference between moral conclusions and the assumptions and premises of moral argument. Familiarity with a broad range of moral theories, and ability to relate moral beliefs to these theories and their constitutive rules and principles, form the heart of competence in ethics. Students in any ethics course should be able to articulate, verbally and in written assignments, coherent moral arguments rooted in moral theory.

2. *Mastery of theories and principles of ethics.*   As in any other discipline or field, there is a body of theory and knowledge in ethics which students must master. The difficulty confronting the instructor is that there is, usually, much too much material available for a single course. Moreover, instructional competence will vary over the range of available material, and students must not be overwhelmed by a barrage of names, traditions, qualifications, and schools of thought. Despite these difficulties, it seems reasonable to require that all students

be able to demonstrate a high degree of familiarity with the range and scope of ethical traditions presented in the classroom, and that the basic concepts and terms of ethical analysis and argument (i.e., utility, principle, duty, rights, etc.) introduced in discussions and readings be mastered.

3. *Identification of moral issues.* Students should be able to identify various sorts of moral issues. The ability should extend beyond classroom examples and case studies, to materials or discussions drawn from other disciplines, fields, and nonclassroom sources.

4. *Ability to argue both sides of a position.* All students should be prepared to take moral views and defend them for the sake of argument, to demonstrate the ability to "see the other side" of an argument and empathize with the moral points of view of others. By the end of a course, students should be willing and eager to engage in moral debate and theoretically inspired ethical argumentation.

It is, of course, possible to evaluate using many more criteria than the four discussed here. But these seem minimally necessary as standards for any course on ethics. When combined with the various modes of gathering information discussed earlier, they should provide a solid basis for evaluation.[21]

CONCLUSION

The subject of evaluation is an irritating topic to many individuals involved in the teaching of ethics and values in colleges and universities. This is partly a consequence of the fact that many of the hard questions about ethical instruction—what counts as ethics, what are the legitimate goals of ethics teaching, how can indoctrination be avoided, etc.—are often left in the hands of those charged with making evaluations. In addition, many people feel that courses on ethics and values are singled out unfairly for evaluative scrutiny: no one, they say, evaluates the quality of freshman physics teaching, or asks whether anatomy belongs in the medical school curriculum.

Some of the irritation is rooted in a general distaste for the existing modes of course evaluation. As one foundation official has complained, "Everyone knows evaluation studies are worthless, so why bother to do them or even talk about them!"

There is some validity in all these concerns with evaluation in ethics and values teaching. Nonetheless, the reality of the present situation is that ethics and values courses are not like other subjects in the curriculum. These courses touch upon subjects and views that many people find disturbing, and even

[21]John Lachs in describing his NEH Summer Seminar arrives at similar conclusions as presented here. See the report on this seminar by Susan V. Lawrence, "Individual Rights and the Public Good: No Easy Answers," *Forum on Medicine* 2, no. 10 (October 1979), pp. 671–687.

inappropriate to college or professional education. In many cases, course offerings are new, or the content is radically revised to meet new perceptions of need and demand. Either situation can result in special attention to the quality and merit of these courses. Finally, not everyone in academia finds current evaluation methodologies "worthless." Those who do should neither demand nor perform them. But those who think that evaluation has a legitimate role to play in both quality and efficacy assessment (myself among them) are faced with the need to do something.

I have argued that the traditional means of evaluation for both the quality and the efficacy of humanistic teaching should be viewed as more than adequate. Diverse educational objectives and diverse course goals demand evaluative techniques that are flexible, and sensitive to teacher and program intentions. Papers, quizzes, case-study analyses, and active classroom discussions seem to meet these requirements better than behavioral measures or psychometric tests of attitudes or judgments. Whether these traditional evaluation modalities will meet the demands of critics of the teaching of ethics in the university, or of the various sources of funding for such efforts, remains to be seen. But, since the same can be said about the new burst of interest in ethics and values teaching in general, perhaps this evaluation is the most that one can reasonably expect.

PART II

The Teaching of Ethics in the Undergraduate and Professional School Curriculum

CHAPTER 6

The Teaching of Ethics in American Higher Education: An Empirical Synopsis

HASTINGS CENTER STAFF

METHODS OF RESEARCH

An important part of the work of the Teaching of Ethics project was the collection of information about activities in this area at the college and professional-school levels. There is a significant amount of activity at present in the area of ethical instruction. Indeed, the number of persons and schools involved in ethics education is so large, that any description of activities and programs will by necessity be somewhat incomplete and out of date. Ethical instruction is undergoing rapid development at many schools, and new programs and courses are constantly being added to the curriculum.

Upon confronting the enormous task of describing the broad range of activity that currently exists in the teaching of ethics, our research group seized upon several strategies for sampling the available data. First, we solicited information through advertisements in various scholarly journals and newsletters. As a result, we were able to develop a list of approximately fifteen hundred persons actively engaged in ethics instruction at institutions at the college or professional-school level. Second, we conducted a sample survey of college catalogues from institutions in the United States to determine the number, distribution, and variety of ethics courses currently being taught (1978). Third, we used a mailed questionnaire to survey a random sample of ten percent of the law professors listed in the ABA Guide to Legal Education who gave their area of teaching expertise as professional responsibility or legal ethics. Fourth, we established

HASTINGS CENTER STAFF • The Hastings Center, Institute of Society, Ethics and the Life Sciences, Hastings-on-Hudson, New York.

contact with such academic professional societies as the American Association for the Advancement of Science, the American Council of Learned Societies, the American Philosophical Association, the Modern Language Association, the American Association for the Advancement of the Humanities, the American Bar Association, and the American Historical Association, in order to ascertain the extent of teaching activity in the area of ethics among members of these organizations. Fifth, we drew upon our own previous work in surveying the areas of medicine, nursing, and allied health as to medical ethics education. Sixth, we conducted site visits to schools, including the University of Florida, Pace University Law School, Marist College, Fordham University, Vassar College, the United States Military Academy, and Siena Heights College, to examine first-hand the types of ethical instruction. Seventh, we received visitors at the Hastings Center from a wide variety of schools, such as Drexel University, New York University, Eastern Mennonite College, William Paterson College, the University of Illinois, Ohio State University, and St. Louis University, who gave us information about ethics teaching at their universities and colleges. Eighth, we conducted several meetings at which experts in various fields, such as law, journalism, business, engineering, public policy, medicine, science, theology, and philosophy, presented information about their own teaching activities, as well as activities in their disciplines and professions. Ninth, we commissioned monographs on the teaching of ethics in biomedicine, law, business, journalism, public policy, engineering, and the social sciences. These reports contained a great deal of empirical information on the nature and scope of ethical instruction in those areas. Finally, we collected previously published materials on the teaching of ethics, which surveyed various fields; these include the Society for Health and Human Values studies of medical ethics, and the Ethics and Values in Science and Technology Resource Directory[1] surveys of undergraduate and graduate programs in the areas of bioethics, professional ethics, and science and human values.

It might appear that such a varied base for empirical information would give a complete and comprehensive guide to ethics teaching in higher education in America. But this is simply not the case. The number of schools, programs, professions, and persons teaching in the broad area of ethics is very large. Much of our data on the teaching of ethics has come from professors actively engaged in such teaching. The dangers of this sort of self-reporting are patent—it is not always possible to assess a course or program on the basis of descriptions provided by those engaged in these enterprises. We have tried to compensate for exaggerations or distortions through personal interviews, site visits, and cross-checks with experts in the relevant academic and professional fields. In the end,

---

[1] *EVIST Resource Directory* (Washington D. C.: American Association for the Advancement of Science, 1978), and *Human Values Teaching Programs for Health Professionals,* 3rd ed. (Philadelphia: Society for Health and Human Values, 1976).

it seemed more valuable simply to present the data we have, given the dearth of factual information that is available. Indeed, it may well be that this initial survey of the state of ethics teaching in America will stimulate further empirical inquiry concerning this important subject.

THE RESULTS OF OUR CATALOGUE SURVEY

During the past decade, the field of ethics has experienced a resurgence as an area of study, not only in departments of philosophy and theology, but also in other departments and schools within the university. If this is indeed the case, it is a phenomenon that has occurred with unusual speed, given the inertia characteristic of the curricular offerings at most universities. To obtain a rough profile of the present state of the teaching of ethics, we conducted a survey of course listings in college, university, and professional school catalogues for the years 1977 and 1978. We examined the offerings at approximately one-fourth of all the accredited colleges and universities of higher education in the United States, 623 out of 2,270, and categorized 2,757 courses concerned with the teaching of ethics. Our general purpose was to see what kinds of courses were being offered, at what schools, to what audiences, and in which departments.

We decided to include in the category of ethics courses any course that included in its title the terms "ethics," "values," "moral," "responsibility," or any course whose description indicated a primary focus on ethics (e.g, "business and society," "journalism in a free society," "British intuitionists"). When in doubt, we included borderline cases as ethics courses.

This catalogue survey turned up a surprising amount of information. Eighty-nine of the colleges surveyed had no ethics courses listed at all. One medium-sized university, which lists in its catalogue its final objective for students as "the recognition of ethical ideas and the moral strength to put such ideas into daily living," listed only one course in ethics in its undergraduate philosophy department, and no courses at all in its graduate school. A common pattern appearing in many colleges is that a single course in ethics is offered in the philosophy department, with an additional course being given in a department of religion or theology, in schools that have them.

Of the courses falling into the ethics category, approximately one-fifth could be labeled as courses on professional ethics, and two-fifths as courses having ethics as their sole theme. The remainder have ethics as an important subtheme.

Our survey revealed a surprisingly large number of "applied ethics" courses: courses with distinctive and specific areas of concern, such as bioethics, business ethics, the morality of war, or ethics and human experimentation. These courses seem to concentrate on the application of moral theory to particular domains or problems, rather than on the history or rationale of morality and ethics *per se*. Approximately 50% of ethics courses fell into this category. However, the ratio of applied-ethics courses to traditional ethics courses varied considerably from university to university. In general, large, prestigious universities offer a larger number of traditional theoretical ethics courses than do smaller, less well-known universities. In many schools, the applied-ethics courses were concentrated in departments or professional schools outside of philosophy or theology departments, which tend to offer more theoretical courses. The topical concerns of applied-ethics courses ranged from "secretarial ethics" and "Christian business ethics" to "contemporary newspaper practices" and "pharmacy ethics."

In the applied-ethics category, the professions that seem best represented at both the graduate and undergraduate level are biomedicine, business, and law; and almost all of the universities surveyed offer a course in "bioethics" or "ethics and the life sciences." Approximately one-fourth of the ethics courses in the sample were taught by philosophy departments, while one-seventh of the total were taught by theology or religious-studies departments; the rest were scattered through almost every department.

By contrast, a comparative sampling of ethics offerings in philosophy departments from the period 1950–1965 revealed very few courses in "applied ethics." Moreover, a sample of thirty textbooks and readers used during that period confirmed the impression of an overriding emphasis on theoretical questions of ethics. An important change within the past decade in ethics texts has been an increasing focus on very concrete issues: abortion, truth telling, confidentiality, justice, war and peace, sexual ethics, and the like.[2] No less noteworthy has been the rapid proliferation of courses—almost all with an applied focus— in departments other than those of philosophy and religious studies. Some significant content changes do appear to be underway in those departments that have traditionally taught ethics, and the introduction of courses in ethics in other departments and divisions of the university is itself a new and notable phenomenon.

One of the most striking findings of the catalogue survey was the wide variation in the number of courses offered within different universities from state to state.[3] Arkansas, for example, has 20 colleges and universities; together, they offered 28 courses in ethics during the 1977–1978 period. In Kansas, by contrast, there are 23 colleges and universities, which offered 105 courses during that period. At some colleges of comparable size, nearly two or three times as many courses in ethics were offered as in others. We could not discern any systematic reason for these variations, and can offer no explanation for the dif-

[2] K. Danner Clouser, "Bioethics," in W. T. Reich, ed., *Encyclopedia of Bioethics*, vol. 1 New York: The Free Press, 1978: pp. 115–127.

[3] See also Jon R. Hendrix, "A Survey of Bioethics Courses in U. S. Colleges and Universities," *The American Biology Teacher* 39 (February 1977), pp. 85–92.

ferences. Our rough estimate is that somewhat more than 12,000 courses in ethics are offered in American undergraduate colleges and professional schools.

The Teaching of Ethics at the Undergraduate Level

Although we make no claim whatever to scientific completeness, on the basis of our meetings, correspondence, surveys, visits, and consultations we were able to reach some tentative conclusions about the teaching of undergraduate ethics. One of those has already been mentioned—that, in traditional departments of philosophy and religion, courses with an emphasis on applied ethics are much more common now than they were a decade ago, and seem to be increasing with great rapidity. Beyond that, we had a particular interest in new programs with an explicit focus on ethics that were either outside of traditional departments altogether, or jointly sponsored by different departments.

Ethics is receiving more systematic curricular attention than ten or twenty years ago, and the courses are attracting growing enrollments. This is particularly true in ethics courses based in departments other than philosophy or religion. But even the more traditional theoretical or historical survey courses seem to be attracting more students than they did a few years ago. It is of particular interest to note that though the number of students majoring in philosophy or religion has declined in recent years, the number of students who have encountered courses which emphasize ethics or ethical issues has increased. Since many of these courses fall outside traditional humanities-department offerings in ethics, it may be useful to summarize some of our findings and impressions concerning the newer courses and programs devoted to ethics.

1. Most new courses on ethics stress applied rather than theoretical concerns.

2. Most new courses and programs are financed by "soft" rather than "hard" money.

3. Most courses or programs explicitly concerned with applied ethics have been initiated within the past ten years.

4. Most new courses are interdisciplinary in content (i.e., medical ethics, environmental ethics, social-science ethics, etc.).

5. New courses on ethics or applied ethics are more likely to be team-taught than are older, traditional courses.

6. The majority of new courses at the undergraduate level appear to be located in science departments or in preprofessional programs.

7. Most ethics and values courses are elective rather than required.

8. Many newer courses in ethics tend to use novel pedagogical techniques, such as case studies, films, videotapes, panel discussions, visiting lecturers, class projects, etc.

9. Most new courses are explicitly oriented around specific ethical issues,

e.g., euthanasia, bribery, atomic power, whistleblowing, rather than broad ethical themes, e.g., justice, individualism, deontology.

10. A concern for ethics has manifested itself in the focus of required general education, humanities, and contemporary civilization courses.

11. The impetus for establishing new or applied-ethics courses and programs comes from many sources, including faculty, students, and concerned administrators.

12. It is most unusual for a student to major in ethics.

13. There is no uniformity of goal or method in teaching ethics to undergraduates. There is a wide diversity in pedagogical styles and approaches.

14. Most ethics courses are taught to groups or sections of students numbering 30 or less.

15. Schools with present or previous religious or denominational ties have initiated more ethics courses and programs than public institutions.

16. Small liberal arts colleges tend to give more attention to ethical concerns in courses than do large state schools.

17. A significant number of courses and programs exist in which ethics teaching has been linked to or inspired by social-scientific work on moral development.

18. New course offerings in philosophical or theological ethics tend to give greater emphasis to applied or practical issues.

19. A large body of literature has appeared in the past ten years on applied ethics. Course bibliographies in ethics courses tend to draw liberally from this literature.

It may also be useful to document some areas where worries, disagreements, or tensions exist concerning the teaching of ethics at the undergraduate level. Some key points of concern among teachers, administrators and students are the following.

1. The background and qualifications necessary for teaching ethics;

2. Disputes about the proper location for ethics courses within the curriculum;

3. The absence of "hard" financing, and scarce enrollments for new courses and programs;

4. Disputes about the appropriate content for an undergraduate ethics course—these involve disagreements over the goals, methods, and content of such courses;

5. Worries about the possibility of indoctrination occurring in the ethics classroom;

6. The best or appropriate modes of evaluating the teaching of ethics to undergraduates;

7. The worry that the current rebirth of interest in ethics may be more of a fad than a real shift in educational policy;

8. Worries about taking time from other areas in the curriculum to give to ethics;

9. Disputes about whether ethics should be taught as a part of other courses, or as a course in its own right;

10. Disputes about how "ethics" teaching should be defined, and over what actually counts as ethics.

One of the most surprising findings to result from our inquiry into the teaching of ethics at the undergraduate level is the degree to which persons involved in this enterprise feel somewhat isolated from colleagues and peers. No real mechanisms, outside of professional-society meetings in the humanities, exist for exchanging information and ideas about matters of pedagogy and methodology in this area. Many persons involved with courses in applied ethics are deeply concerned about their lack of experience in teaching courses in this subject.

In addition to concerns about the courses *per se,* many persons are worried about their ability to teach ethics effectively solely through formal courses or programs. Many instructors note that ethics education also occurs in the family, church, or dormitory, and they feel frustrated by the expectation that a course on ethics will promote or guarantee personal virtue or desirable behavior. Then, too, some educators worry that ethics education can easily be usurped by the political, theological, or ideological views of the instructors. Most educators feel torn between the conflicting demands, to effect behavioral change in students, but without indoctrinating them or prematurely biasing them against possible moral points of view. Students sometimes feel uncertain about the goals of ethics teaching, and about the standards of assessment that will be used in evaluating their performance in the classroom.

It is not easy to assess either the impact of ethics courses on students, or the reception of new courses by faculty and administrators. Factors that complicate such assessments include: the ambiguity as to what courses count or should count as ethics courses, the fact that newer pedagogical techniques are often utilized in ethics courses before they are tried elsewhere in the curriculum, disagreements as to the proper aims and goals of ethics teaching, the fact that a student does not come as a *tabula rasa* to an ethics course, and the fact that no agreement exists over the proper criteria for evaluation in ethics.

Despite these difficulties in assessing the impact of these courses and programs, it seems clear that there has been a resurgence of interest in the teaching of ethics at the college level. This resurgence can be characterized by the new and powerful presence of courses in "applied" or "professional" ethics at the undergraduate level. It remains to be seen whether this new emphasis on ethics, and the present concern with applied or practical issues in the ethics course, will continue. The precarious financial situation of many institutions may imperil the newer and less secure parts of the undergraduate curriculum.

THE STATE OF ETHICS TEACHING IN PROFESSIONAL SCHOOLS

Any attempt to put together a composite picture of the teaching of ethics in professional schools meets with difficulties. Although the available data on the number and extent of courses in ethics are far stronger at the professional than at the undergraduate level, there are nonetheless many gaps. It is often difficult to determine the background or original discipline of those teaching the courses, the extent to which their teaching of ethics represents a major scholarly or pedagogical interest (or is secondary only), and the extent to which the available courses are warmly or coolly received, both in terms of the quality of the teaching, and in terms of the status they have in the curriculum. Moreover, there are a number of fields, such as journalism and engineering, where professional degrees may be obtained solely by pursuing course work at the undergraduate level. This survey, in speaking about professional schools, will confine its attention almost exclusively to pedagogical efforts to teach ethics in schools that explicitly grant professional degrees in a particular field, or in postgraduate schools of professional education.

The generalizations and discussion that follow are based on a systematic study of seven areas of professional education, and on ancillary studies carried out in two other fields. The seven areas we studied in detail are law, business, public policy, biomedicine, journalism, engineering, and the social sciences. Additional data were also available on nursing and allied health fields.

We selected these particular areas for two reasons. First, given our limited resources, we felt that we had to confine our research to a small, manageable number of professional fields. Second, we wanted to study a diversity of fields which were representative of various levels of teaching activity in the ethics area. We hoped that enough areas of common concern and inquiry would emerge so that our findings would be of relevance to professionals teaching ethics in fields other than those reported here. Our findings in the professional areas we did study confirmed our hypothesis that there are many areas of overlap among the activities and teaching in the ethics domain among these rather diverse professions.

Little sense can be made of the teaching of professional ethics without an understanding of the character of professional schools. With the exception of graduate schools in the social sciences, their primary purpose is to provide students with those specialized skills, bodies of knowledge, and attitudes needed for them to work as professionals in society. Both the faculty and the administrations assume that their students have already had a general education, that professional schools neither are nor should be equipped to remedy deficiencies in that general education, and that the ultimate test of the value of the education is technical competence.

This is not to deny that there are many experiments and curriculum reforms at present underway in professional education. Some professional schools are more oriented toward broader social and political issues than others, and toward introducing their students to considerations which go beyond technical competence only. Many individual faculty members will have both scholarly and pedagogical interests that are broader than the merely technical. Still, professional education is strongly job- and profession-oriented: it transmits specific skills. That is what students expect when they enroll in such schools, what professors are trained and prepared to give them, and what employers who are going to hire the graduates will look for.

Given that context, the introduction of courses in ethics is rarely greeted with general enthusiasm, and their role in programs oriented in very different directions is uneasy. But the difficulties go beyond ethics teaching. It is striking how few professional schools offer students an opportunity to examine the nature of their profession in a general way—its historical roots, its function in society, its sociological characteristics, and its assumptions about the political and social order. Such questions will, of course, arise during a professional education, but few professional schools seem to think it valuable to confront them directly in a systematic fashion. If that is the case even within the professions themselves, it is easy to understand why courses in professional ethics, which inevitably involve the nature of the professions in question, find that they must operate in an atmosphere that is cool at best, and at times positively hostile.

With the exceptions of medicine and law, it is difficult in any of the professional-school areas to find more than a handful of faculty members for whom ethics (or "professional responsibility," as it is often called) is a major academic and teaching interest. It is equally rare to discover schools where courses on ethics have a central role in the curriculum—the overwhelming majority are elective courses, for instance. With only two exceptions that we could discern, scholarly work in ethics will not routinely assist younger faculty members in gaining tenure within traditional specialized departments; indeed, faculty members who desire to specialize in ethics will usually be seen as operating out of the mainstream of professional scholarship or education. One of those exceptions is law, where, if scholarship and professional responsibility are not exactly encouraged, they are nonetheless seen as substantive concerns. The other exception, just beginning to appear, is in those few professional schools that go out of their way to hire people to teach ethics, making it clear at the outset that their scholarship will be judged by the criteria appropriate in that field. This is happening in some medical and engineering schools, but remains rare in other schools.

In essence, then, the teaching of ethics in almost all professional schools can generally be characterized as follows.

1. It is seen as at best a secondary or tertiary function of the schools; those who teach such courses are likely to be seen as either outside of, or only barely on the fringe of, the main purposes of the schools.

2. Those attempting to introduce courses of ethics can expect considerable disinterest or resistance.

3. The curriculum of almost all professional schools is already overcrowded, and many are beginning to experience financial strains. Since professional schools are already subject to pressure either to increase the time given to subjects currently in the curriculum, or add still others of a technical nature, the teaching of ethics is hardly the most prominent feature of professional education in the United States.

At the same time, the current lack of sustained and scholarly attention to ethics in much of professional education is a source of considerable unease for many professionals, especially because professional schools have always claimed to take the moral role of professionals seriously. Professions in America are, in part, defined by the special moral duties, obligations, and rights of professional people. Because of this, and the level of public dissatisfaction with professional self-regulation and self-control, many educators see a special need for reemphasizing the moral elements of professional knowledge and behavior in the curriculum.[4]

A PROFILE OF SEVEN AREAS OF PROFESSIONAL ETHICS

All professions are showing new interest in the teaching of ethics, and are experiencing some degree of both external and internal pressure to introduce such courses. One helpful way of looking at the present status of the teaching of professional ethics is to begin with those professional fields where the teaching of ethics is fairly well advanced.

MEDICINE, NURSING

Among the strongest is that of medical ethics. Surveys undertaken in 1972 and 1974[5] revealed a significant growth and institutionalization of medical-ethics teaching in medical schools. Out of 110 medical schools in the United States, about 90% now offer at least some exposure to the subject. In the 1974 survey, 53 schools reported having faculty members with some specific responsibility in the area of medical ethics, and 31 faculty members were identified for whom the teaching of medical ethics is a primary task (e.g., one to which they

[4]Edmund Pellegrino, "Medical Ethics, Education, and the Physician's Image," *Journal of the American Medical Association* 235 (March 1976), pp. 1043–1044; and Derek C. Bok, "Can Ethics Be Taught?" *Change* 8 (October, 1976), pp. 26–30.

[5]Robert M. Veatch and Willard Gaylin, "Teaching Medical Ethics: An Experimental Program," *Journal of Medical Education* 47 (1972), pp. 779–785; and Robert M. Veatch and Sharmon Sollito, "Medical Ethics Teaching: Report of a National School Survey," *Journal of the American Medical Association* 235 (March 1976), pp. 1030–1033.

devoted at least half of their time). Although well over half the medical schools in this country still offer very little in the way of systematic training in ethics, practically all schools now feel the need to have at least some course, or sub-section of a course, devoted to the subject. Although there is still a tendency in medical schools to assign the teaching of ethics to those trained in medicine only, or occasionally in one of the social sciences, a number of medical schools in recent years have added philosophers or theologians to their faculties to teach ethics.

Most importantly, perhaps, the field of medical ethics, or bioethics, has become a major area of scholarly interest, drawing upon those primarily trained in ethics, but increasingly attracting those with medical or science degrees as well. A few universities are beginning to offer specialized graduate programs in the area (e.g., the University of Tennessee, Pennsylvania State University at Hershey), numerous summer workshops and intensive programs are offered in the field, and the many undergraduate courses in bioethics have stimulated students to request still more while in medical school. That so many of the moral dilemmas of contemporary biomedical research and clinical practice have received widespread exposure in the media—the Karen Ann Quinlan case, recombinant DNA research, the widespread introduction of prenatal diagnosis, psychosurgery—has given the status of ethical issues in medicine a dramatic focus unmatched in most other fields.

The fresh interest in ethics in graduate philosophy programs and in religious-studies programs (not to mention the critical shortage of traditional humanities teaching jobs) has drawn many to medical ethics in recent years. They are beginning to provide a reservoir upon which medical schools can and do draw. The development in a few schools of broad programs in the humanities in medicine[6] (approximately 20)—encompassing literature, history, some of the social sciences, political science, and economics—has given ethics a broader context than that of a single course or program in medical ethics alone. National debate over the quality and cost of medical care, the goals of health-care delivery, widespread concerns about an excessive emphasis on technology in medicine, and the desire to train more physicians who will go into family or general practice, all have stimulated a greater willingness to consider questions of ethics. If the teaching of ethics in medical schools still has a considerable distance to go, it is the one area we examined where there now exists some agreement upon methods for teaching ethics, and upon qualifications needed for the teaching of ethics; the one area, too, where solid and varied materials are available for use in the classrooms—films, textbooks, case books, and collected readings.

Schools of nursing show a considerable interest in the teaching of ethics. There appears to be neither hostility nor indifference toward the subject, and

[6]Thomas K. McElhinney, ed., *Human Values Teaching Programs for Health Professionals* (Philadelphia: The Society for Health and Human Values, 1976).

many of those teaching nursing ethics are working very hard to strengthen the courses, to improve their own background in the subject, and to develop a scholarly literature in the field. Nonetheless, for all of the enthusiasm, the literature on the subject is only beginning to develop. No published collections of cases exist, nor are there sophisticated readers in the field. In particular, those teaching nursing ethics frequently complain that they are forced to turn to the broader literature of medical ethics, much of which focuses on the ethical dilemmas of physicians, ordinarily very different in character from those confronted by nurses. As a result of a widespread movement on the part of nurses to see their profession accorded a higher social and professional status, and because of the desire for classroom material directed specifically to the problems of nurses, considerable interest has been shown in developing an adequate literature. With one exception, that literature has not appeared.

LAW

Many American law schools have traditionally offered and required of their students a separate course on legal ethics or professional responsibility.[7] Since 1974, the American Bar Association has mandated through accreditation standards that schools teach the "history, goals, structure, and responsibilities of the legal profession and its members, including the ABA Code of Legal Responsibility."

Although these traditions and new developments may suggest considerable strength in the field, the reality is less vigorous. A recent survey in the American Bar Association Journal showed that 133 of the 156 accredited law schools require completion of a course in professional responsibility.[8] Yet one-third of those courses comprise only about 15 hours of instruction, half the minimum-standard one-term law-school course. These courses are usually taught in the third year of law school, in seminars of 60–150 students. A survey conducted by Ronald Pipkin of over 1,300 law students from seven law schools discloses that the ethics course has an unusually low status in the curriculum hierarchy: it is perceived by students to be less valuable, to require less time and effort, and to be more poorly taught than other law school courses. Part of the problem may lie in the fact that most courses focus on the ABA Code of Professional Ethics, without giving any attention to ethical theory. Another problem may stem from the gulf between having a single course in ethics in a curriculum otherwise, by and large, not oriented to questions of legal theory. Over one-third of the teachers involved report using their own materials in class, rather than a standard textbook or compilation.

[7]Michael J. Kelly, *Legal Ethics and Legal Education* (Hastings-on-Hudson, N. Y.: The Hastings Center, 1980).
[8]*Ibid.*

Comparatively speaking, the field still lacks sophisticated writing in the areas of law, ethics, and professional responsibility, particularly in relation to what is available for other law school courses. Relatively few professors in law schools consider legal ethics their primary scholarly interest. Nevertheless, a new journal has been created—*The Journal of the Legal Profession*—and over ten new textbooks, as well as a considerable body of scholarly articles, have appeared in the past few years. There is every indication that a more theoretical and systematic examination of the legal profession and its responsibilities is underway.

In our own research, we found that most professors teaching legal ethics or professional responsibility have taught such a course for less than five years. There seemed to be no generally agreed-upon qualifications for teaching, and the course is usually taught by the youngest faculty members of the law schools. Nonetheless, the profession is interested in focusing more attention on the ethics of professional practice, and in some states questions on legal ethics are now part of the examination for admission to the bar.

BUSINESS

A somewhat different situation exists in schools of business.[9] Despite numerous discussions and conferences on ethics and business, the creation of special groups and centers to deal with the teaching of ethics in business schools, and a number of recommendations by professional groups that ethics be treated more systematically in the curriculum, the academic response has been meager. Most business schools do not have separate courses in business ethics, few include it as a required course, and few have faculty members whose primary responsibility or training is in ethics. The field of business ethics still lacks a coherent and scholarly body of literature, and is exceedingly short on people with experience and training in both ethics and business management.

Part of the difficulty in assessing the level of ethics teaching in business schools is that there are a number of courses which fall loosely in the ethics area. Courses in the social dimensions of business or business policy are often cited as indicative of an interest in teaching ethics. Approximately 60% of all business schools require at least one business-and-society course for graduation, and between 1,000 and 3,000 faculty members currently teach some aspect of corporate social policy. But, despite the recent emphasis on including course work on the environment of business, there are comparatively few courses that focus exclusively on business ethics. On the whole, ethics is most likely to be part of other courses, with little indication at present that separate courses in business ethics will be widely introduced. Few schools have hired faculty with

[9]Charles Powers and David Vogel, *Ethics in the Education of Business Managers* (Hastings-on-Hudson, N.Y.: The Hastings Center, 1980).

training in philosophical or theological ethics; and, where that has happened, those teaching have rarely had formal training in business or economics. In general, there is a dearth of persons sufficiently experienced in both ethics and business-management theory or practice to warrant full faculty status.

SOCIAL SCIENCE

A still different situation can be found in graduate schools of social science.[10] During the past decade there has been considerable discussion of the ethics of social-science research. It has turned on such issues as the use of deception in social-psychology experiments, the uses and abuses of surveys and opinion polls, moral problems posed by contract research, the legitimacy of cross-national studies such as Project Camelot, and the relation of social research to policymaking. Books have been published on these subjects, conferences run, and symposia organized. As a result of federal regulations, social-science research involving human subjects is now subject to the approval of Institutional Review Boards (IRBs). Yet, despite these developments, only a handful of courses is devoted wholly or substantially to ethics in the social sciences. We identified only ten courses explicitly devoted to ethics and social-science research. Discussions of ethics have made their way with increasing frequency into courses bearing other titles, especially research methods, and there are other signs that ethics is becoming an acceptable topic of discussion in these disciplines. We were able to identify about one hundred social scientists with some interests in ethics, but very few for whom it is a major area of teaching, research, or writing.

The attitude toward the teaching of ethics in anthropology, psychology, and sociology has shifted in recent years from outright hostility to wariness and skepticism. Some say that the teaching of ethics is basically irrelevant, that the ethical issues raised by the social sciences are too trivial to deserve scarce class time. Others regard the teaching of ethics as part of the larger assault on research freedom, personified by Institutional Review Boards. And a few are worried that ethics has become an outlet for ideological indoctrination. Nevertheless, the teaching of ethics in the social sciences is on the upswing, particularly in the form of lectures and readings in other courses. There is not a great deal of material available for classroom use, and the existing literature is especially weak on philosophical analysis, as distinct from issue raising. Still all signs suggest that there will be more activity in this area over the coming decade. To judge from work now in process, the prospects for an effective blending of disciplinary self-reflection with careful ethical analysis are improving. However, most social scientists apparently still believe that no special qualifications are requisite for

[10]Donald P. Warwick, *The Teaching of Ethics in the Social Sciences* (Hastings-on-Hudson, N. Y.: The Hastings Center, 1980).

the teaching of ethics. Moreover, there has been little enthusiasm for interdisciplinary teaching, or for special courses dealing explicitly with ethics.

ENGINEERING

With all the rapid proliferation of undergraduate courses in technology and society, relatively little has been done specifically in the area of engineering ethics, at either the undergraduate or the graduate level.[11]

In 1976, the National Society of Professional Engineers performed a survey of all the deans of accredited engineering schools. Out of 250 programs, 128 deans responded, and of these, only 13 indicated that professional ethics or professional responsibility received any special course attention in their school's curriculum. The bulk of the time in these 13 courses was spent in studying various codes of ethics developed by the engineering profession. Prior to 1976, there were almost no nonengineers involved in teaching courses in ethics or professionalism in schools of engineering.

This lack of attention to ethics has begun to change in the last three years. Rensselaer Polytechnic Institute was recently awarded a large grant from The National Endowment for the Humanities to assist in the development of more teachers in the field of engineering ethics, as well as case and other studies of ethics and engineering. There are presently over 100 individuals engaged in research and teaching in engineering ethics. Over half of these persons are nonengineers. In 1979, 30 to 40 courses were offered, and about 50 more were in various stages of preparation. In fact, there is some consideration being given by the accrediting organization for engineering schools—the ECPD—for mandating a required course in ethics and professionalism at all engineering schools.

This rapid burst of activity in the teaching of ethics in engineering has been stimulated by a number of forces. Various widely publicized "scandals," such as the Goodrich aircraft brake debate, The Bay Area Rapid Transit case, and the Firestone tire case, have focused attention on the professional obligations of engineers. NEH- and NSF-sponsored symposia have also stimulated interest in engineering ethics. Many engineers have noted the immediacy of moral issues in business and management for their work, and have tried to incorporate more types of policy issue in engineering education.

The quantity and quality of teaching materials for engineering ethics is still meager, and faculty members still tend to discourage student participation in "soft" courses such as ethics. There is a great reluctance to cede curricular time to ethical considerations, since most engineers believe that rapid advances in science and technology leave barely enough curricular time for achieving technical competence. It is unclear at present what direction ethical education will

[11]Robert J. Baum, *Ethics and Engineering Curricula* (Hastings-on-Hudson, N. Y.: The Hastings Center, 1980).

take in engineering for all the obvious increase in attention and concern for the subject.

JOURNALISM

A slightly different pattern again is manifested in schools of journalism, media, and communications.[12] Questions of media ethics have received considerable public attention of late. Important Supreme Court decisions have turned on the rights and privileges of journalists, and those who work in the journalistic media face a wide range of ethical issues. In a general sense, journalism schools have included courses in professional ethics within their curricula since the nineteen-twenties, though in some schools such courses broadened their focus in the forties and fifties into considerations of "professional responsibility," or of the relations of communications media generally with the larger society. At present, at least 25% of the schools offering training in journalism have specific courses in ethics. In addition to formal courses, ethical issues are discussed as well in the relevant contexts of other instruction in a majority of schools. However, when one looks for specific courses with the term "ethics" included in the titles, no more than a quarter of the schools of media or communication make such offerings. Those teaching the ethics courses usually have a background of professional experience, with formal training in law or history more likely than in ethics. And a number of courses focus attention on legal, rather than ethical, concerns.

The number of available books on journalism ethics have been, until recently, comparatively few; most are short on ethical theory, and solid casebooks are only beginning to appear. A number of older books on media and journalism ethics are being revised. Interest in the field is quickening, however; the subject has been a focus of interest at national meetings of journalism educators in the last few years, ethical requirements are being tightened in accrediting standards for schools generally, and several conferences focusing on ethics are now in the planning stages.

A noteworthy feature of most of the available literature on journalism ethics is that it is almost totally devoid of references to contemporary work in the fields of philosophical and theological ethics. In this respect, an analogous situation was found in some of the other professional fields we studied: a reasonably large body of literature on ethical and value questions, but a literature which makes little or no use of work done within the field of ethics itself. This is particularly true in the areas of social science, in the literature of business ethics, and in the literature of journalistic ethics.

[12]Clifford G. Christians and Catherine L. Covert, *Teaching Ethics in Journalism Education* (Hastings-on-Hudson, N. Y.: The Hastings Center, 1980).

PUBLIC POLICY

The teaching of ethics in schools of public policy and of public administration varies significantly from school to school.[13] At some schools a fairly important role is given to courses in ethics. In others, comparatively little interest is shown, and no opportunities for systematic ethical inquiry are provided. Is there any common denominator in these variations? Schools with strong political-science components and a pervasive interest in broad questions of public policy and society are much more likely to take ethics courses seriously than schools more heavily oriented toward economics, and such technical skills as the use of computers, cost–benefit analysis, microeconomics, and systems analysis. Schools with a heavy orientation toward quantification, decision theory, and other techniques designed to facilitate "rational" decision making often look upon ethics as "soft" and "subjective." Some see ethics as at most irrelevant, and at worst likely to interfere with the technical education of students. In this field, as in many others studied, there exist no casebooks on ethics, few scholarly books given over to the ethical issues of policy analysis, and only a relatively small supply of solid articles for classroom use. Yet the available literature does show a stronger component of ethical theory than is the case in other fields (e.g., nursing and communications media).

A number of faculty members in schools of public policy are working hard to see ethics given a stronger role in the curriculum. That most of them come from the field of political science, rather than economics, reflects a tension between these two disciplines in the schools. No comparable tension was discovered in the other professional schools that we studied, though in medical and engineering schools the teaching of ethics is frequently associated with the humanities, and thus well down on the list of the fields and disciplines that have prestige within those schools. Of 219 schools and programs in public policy, 77 reported that no ethics courses existed, 26 indicated that they had a required course, and 32 had one or more elective offerings. Distributive justice was a common theme in many of these courses.

---

[13]Joel L. Fleishman and Bruce L. Payne, *Ethical Dilemmas and the Education of Policymakers* (Hastings-on-Hudson, N. Y.: The Hastings Center, 1980).

CHAPTER 7

The Teaching of Undergraduate Ethics

BERNARD ROSEN

INTRODUCTION

Moral problems arise in every area of human concern. The decisions to punish a student for cheating on an examination, to release a faculty member because of lack of funds, to allow drinking in dormitories, or to authorize a family-planning clinic, are, at least in part, moral decisions facing members of the higher education community. As citizens we all know roughly our legal responsibilities, and we usually know our responsibilities to our fellow human beings. Sometimes, though, we are asked to break the law to fulfill our moral responsibility, as the abolitionists did in order to fight the immoral institution of slavery. We can agree that we have a moral obligation to obey the law, but also that we have an obligation to resist evil. Those who practice civil disobedience have usually decided that the evil of breaking the law is less than the evil of the action that the law requires. Recent examples include reporters who go to jail rather than reveal their sources, and antinuclear and antibusing demonstrators. We may disagree with those who think that their obligation to prevent nuclear power overrides their obligation to obey the trespass law, but we understand this sort of moral reasoning. The point is one with which we are all familiar: moral beliefs lead to action. Moral disagreements lead to confrontations, and moral agreements lead to powerful and effective alliances.

We learn our moral views just as we learn most other things, from the combined influences of family, friends, school, church, TV, and other such sources. We may be captured by an ideology or a novelist, or we may set about to study morality to decide which is the best view to hold. In recent years, the public has become much more aware of moral issues in government and the professions, partly because of such spectacular events as Watergate and corpo-

BERNARD ROSEN ● Department of Philosophy, Ohio State University, Columbus, Ohio.

rate bribery scandals. Institutions of higher education have been influenced by and have contributed to the level of awareness. Many new courses in moral problems have been introduced into the curriculum: courses, e.g., on ethical issues in medicine and biology, journalism, law, engineering, education, nursing, and other areas. These courses which examine the moral problems faced by professionals are based on the premise that it is better to wrestle with the problems before they become pressing. Some believe that professionals will behave in morally proper ways if they are "taught" what they should do, while others think that training in moral problem solving will lead each person to do what is morally right.

In addition to the courses on moral problems in specific areas, there continue to be courses that focus on moral problems, decision making, and action, without regard to specific subject matter. Usually taught by people trained in philosophy or theology, these courses frequently address some of the problems faced by professionals, but they also examine the moral dimensions of problems faced by all human beings. Such courses usually concentrate on the most general methods for analysing and resolving moral issues: those of such thinkers as Plato, Aristotle, Augustine, Aquinas, Kant, and Mill.

The coverage of normative ethical theories in undergraduate ethics courses has been relatively constant in America for the last two hundred years, though teaching techniques have changed, and authors have been added or subtracted with the emergence of new views and changes in intellectual fashion. A new and important development is the introduction of applied-ethics courses at both the undergraduate and the professional school level. Unlike general ethics courses, the applied-ethics courses focus almost exclusively on the moral problems that arise within a specific area or profession. The moral problems that arise for the health professional, for example, are the core of the medical-ethics course. Such a course will undoubtedly touch on problems about distribution of wealth in society, because one of the concerns of the health professional is the ability of patients to pay for health services; but it will not usually include a sustained analysis of alternative theories of distributive justice, or the morally proper way to distribute things of value in our society. In the general ethics course, by contrast, there is much greater emphasis on the comparison and critical evaluation of normative ethical theories. In applied-ethics courses there is usually no time for lengthy examination of competing normative ethical theories, and frequently the instructor is not trained for such an activity.

The applied-ethics courses have been introduced, in part, because of the increased concern about morally proper behavior. When bribes become standard in the practice of business, the public begins to lose confidence in institutions of business. Business people translate their concern about this situation into support for courses in business schools to discuss these sorts of problem. Many of these courses are taught within the professional area, but others are taught solely within philosophy or theology, or jointly by faculty from one of these areas and the professional area. In planning a general ethics course for undergraduates, the instructor must bear in mind that students frequently will take a course in applied ethics. When discussing the application of general normative ethical theories to specific problems in different areas, teachers of general courses must be careful not to duplicate the specific problems that will be covered in detail in the applied-ethics course.

Just as some professionals and members of the public think that the purpose of an applied-ethics course is to help the professional arrive at better moral decisions, there has long been a belief that a general ethics course does the same for students in their daily or ordinary affairs. There is a sense that students should be exposed to the main traditions of normative ethics in our culture, and that they should somehow learn how to arrive at moral decisions in a rational and responsible way. A general ethics course can provide preparation for an applied-ethics course, or, alternatively, an opportunity to pursue the interests in ethical theory that arise as the result of applied-ethics courses.

There are many levels of undergraduate ethics courses, ranging from the first general survey of normative ethics to considerations of abstract problems of the metaphysics of morals. This paper will focus on the first general course. It will address a variety of questions—What is the first course in ethics? What has been the recent history of undergraduate courses? What is ethics as a discipline? What is taught in such a course? What problems do administrators, parents, or trustees have with such courses? What is the relation between an ethics course and moral action?—in order to draw attention to the place and the problems of undergraduate ethics courses and teaching.

NATURE OF ETHICS

A normative ethical theory provides us with a general means of arriving at moral judgments that apply to specific situations, events, persons, actions, and things. For example, John Stewart Mill's theory[1] tells us that actions are right as they tend to maximize good consequences. Immanuel Kant's[2] version of the Golden Rule tells us to test our moral maxims by determining whether we can agree that everyone should act on them. W. D. Ross's[3] theory identifies factors, such as truth telling and promise keeping, that enter into our moral decisions, and suggests that these factors do not have a fixed weight, but are variable in weight depending upon the circumstances. Some people, including about a quarter of the students in ethics courses, claim that moral judgments are relative

---

[1] J. S. Mill, *Utilitarianism* (London: J. M. Debt & Sons, 1972), p. 6.
[2] Immanuel Kant, *The Moral Law*, trans. H. J. Paton (London: Hutchinson University Library, 1948), pp. 70–71.
[3] W. D. Ross. *The Right and the Good* (Oxford: The Clarendon Press, 1930).

to a society. The egoist maintains that actions are right as they tend to benefit the individual who does them.

In addition to normative ethical theories that offer a means of determining in specific circumstances whether an actual or proposed course of action is right, the subject of ethics can be approached through metaethics, the analysis of the meanings of crucial ethical terms as well as the logic of moral reasoning. The following are some key topics in metaethics.

- Freedom: In some sense and in some way, freedom is required for the performing of actions that are right and wrong.
- Action: There is, according to most, a close connection between accepting ethical judgments and acting upon them. We are inclined to do what we think is right, and avoid what we think is wrong.
- Meaning: What is the meaning or analysis of moral language?
- Moral predicates: Some thinkers suppose that moral predicates refer to properties, some claiming they are properties in the world and others in some nonempirical realm.
- Justification: Every theory has a basic means of arriving at moral judgments. Is this device, e.g., the principle of utility, justified by something in another area: by God, by society, or what?

A first ethics course for undergraduates will often cover the most important normative ethical theories, as well as the main problems in metaethics. Generally, the instructor will teach the students to evaluate the competing normative theories by presenting analyses of the applications as well as the problems of each theory.

Teachers of ethics are usually trained in either philosophy or theology. Theological ethics is, for the most part, the same as philosophical ethics. The great thinkers in ethics include Aquinas, just as the great thinkers in metaphysics include Bishop Berkeley. For most of the history of Western thought, there has not been any sharp division between the concerns of philosophers and those of theologians—especially with respect to ethics. Although emphases frequently differ, depending on training and school, the main positions covered are very much the same.

One difference between theological ethics and philosophical ethics is the metaphysical view that is used to complete an ethical theory. Those with a theological perspective have a greater tendency to assign a crucial role to God. Another difference is reflected in the role that a religious community plays in the moral life of religious persons. In general, however, the discussion of ethics in this paper should apply equally well to philosophical and theological ethics, and to those trained in either philosophy or theology.

Normative theories compete as to the best general means of arriving at normative judgments, e.g., judgments of right and wrong, in particular instances. Because they are competitors, and because there are criticisms of each view, the teacher must supply some guidance as to correctness. Discussion with many colleagues leads me to believe that the overwhelming majority of teachers of undergraduate ethics supply guidance, but do not think that their main function as teachers is to tell students which of the competitors is correct. Most teachers prefer one view, and will frequently argue for it vigorously, but they consider it much more important to impart critical and evaluative skills and foster understanding, than to inculcate belief in any particular normative theory.

To illustrate how each normative theory works, the instructor usually shows how it applies to specific or general problems. To apply utilitarianism, for example, to the question of abortion, the teacher would try to show that abortion on demand did or did not maximize the good: e.g., whether abortion on demand weakened society, and lowered appreciation for the welfare of others. One could then contrast the utilitarian approach with that of the egoist, to show how a different conclusion could very well be reached.

Since this procedure is so widely used in the teaching of ethics to undergraduates, these first courses are, to an extent, courses in applied ethics. However, one difference is that in most applied-ethics courses the problems are not used simply for illustrative purposes, and no great time is spent examining competing ethical theories. Most first courses in ethics are not purely theoretical, because the understanding of normative ethical theories requires some application. Some instructors will spend more time on application than others, but a mixture of application and theory will be found in almost every undergraduate ethics course.

Topics other than normative ethics and metaethics can have a place in ethics courses. These might include: the work of Jean Piaget and Lawrence Kohlberg on moral development; studies on moral education by Kohlberg and Sidney Simon; Louis Rath's work on Value Clarification; Matthew Lipman's studies in Philosophy for Children; the traditional concerns about the good life that are central in the writings of the Stoics and many Christian authors; and the exploration of non-Western approaches to problems of ethics. Most undergraduate courses, however, concentrate on normative ethics, with some exploration of topics in metaethics.

RECENT HISTORY OF ETHICS

Since Douglas Sloan has presented a detailed account of the history of the teaching of ethics courses in higher education,[4] I wish only to supplement his account with some observations about the separation of the social sciences from philosophy and ethics, plus the rise and dominance of logical positivism. I will

[4]Douglas Sloan, "The Teaching of Ethics in the American Undergraduate Curriculum, 1876–1976," this volume, Chapter 1.

also discuss the influence of the "relevance" movement, the growth of applied-ethics courses, and the rejection of positivism, in order to explain the present state of the teaching of undergraduate ethics.

Sloan has pointed out that the ethics course was frequently taught by college presidents. It was usually a general course with great scope, that encompassed many of the subjects that had been taught in previous semesters. It considered the place of human beings in their world, and analyzed the ends and goals that were characteristic of human nature. When the social sciences separated from philosophy, they took with them, in most instances, the moral issues that were part of those disciplines: for example, concerns about the urban poor, lack of health care, and substandard education. Such moral issues were identified with, and primarily discussed by, those in the social sciences.

The departure of these issues narrowed (some would say impoverished) the focus of many ethics courses, for they were topics on which the teacher frequently had strong opinions, opinions presented as the "correct" American or Christian views. Although there is little evidence that indoctrination was the goal of such teaching, it is true that the notion of allowing students to cultivate their own rational and critical faculties did not play the important role that it does today.

As Sloan has indicated, professionalism and the influence of positivism—first the positivism of Compte in the late 19th century, and then that of the Vienna Circle in the 1920s—led the social sciences to espouse an ideal of value neutrality. One would have thought that the value material—the moral concerns that were now dropped by the social sciences, the very issues they had taken when they separated from philosophy—would now return to philosophy. However, that did not occur, for the value-neutrality movement had its counterpart in philosophy. Although ethics did not become value-neutral in the same way as the social sciences, it did become almost entirely concerned with metaethical issues. G. E. Moore, surely one of the most influential writers in the English language in the twentieth century, set the tone very early in his *Principia Ethica:*

> This, then, is our first question: What is good? and What is bad? and to the discussion of this question (or these questions) I give the name of Ethics. . . . How "good" is to be defined, is the most fundamental question in all Ethics. If I am asked, "What is good?", my answer is that good is good, and that is the end of the matter. Or, if I am asked "How is good to be defined?", my answer is that it cannot be defined, and that is all I have to say about it.[5]

Teachers who attempted to raise actual moral problems to normative theories were often regarded as preachers, and as not engaged in their proper profession. And even when normative ethical theories were discussed, it was in regard to their claims about metaethical concerns. This was the mainstream of English-language ethics for the next fifty years or more. Philosophical analysis,

[5]G. E. Moore, *Principia Ethica* (Cambridge: Cambridge University Press, 1971), pp. 3, 5, 6.

analysis of meaning and language, became the primary subject matter of ethics, and of most other areas of philosophy as well.

The result was an academic life in which there were few forums for the discussion of normative issues, and almost no legitimate place for the discussion of normative ethical theories. To compensate for the lack of discussion of moral problems in ethics courses, these issues began to appear in other courses, especially those in literature and history.

The most dominant positions in ethics during this period were the various forms of noncognitivism. These ranged from the straightforward but simplistic view of A. J. Ayer to the sophisticated position of C. L. Stevenson. According to Ayer:

> We begin by admitting that the fundamental ethical concerns are unanalysable, inasmuch as there is no criterion by which one can test the validity of the judgments in which they occur. So far we are in agreement with the absolutists. But, unlike the absolutists, we are able to give an explanation of this fact about ethical concepts. We say that the reason why they are unanalysable is that they are mere pseudoconcepts. The presence of an ethical symbol in a proposition adds nothing to its factual content. Thus if I say to someone, "You acted wrongly in stealing that money," I am not stating anything more than if I had simply said, "You stole that money." In adding that this action is wrong I am not making any further statement about it. I am simply evincing my moral disapproval of it. It is as if I had said, "You stole that money," in a peculiar tone of horror, or written it with the addition of some special exclamation marks. The tone, or the exclamation marks, add nothing to the literal meaning of the sentence. It merely serves to show that the expression of it is attended by certain feelings in the speaker.[6]

Stevenson's position, though similar in some respects, is more complex:

> When you tell a man that he oughtn't to steal, your object isn't merely to let him know that people disapprove of stealing. You are attempting, rather, to get *him* to disapprove of it. Your ethical judgment has a quasi-imperative force which, operating through suggestion, and intensified by your tone of voice, readily permits you to begin to *influence*, to *modify*, his interests. If in the end you do not succeed in getting *him* to disapprove of stealing, you will feel that you've failed to convince him that stealing is wrong. You will continue to feel this, even though he fully acknowledges that you disapprove of it, and that almost everyone else does. When you point out to him the consequences of his actions—consequences which you suspect he already disapproves of—these *reasons* which support your ethical judgments are simply a means of facilitating your influence. If you think you can change his interests by making vivid to him how others will disapprove of him, you will do so; otherwise not. ...The difference between the traditional interest theories and my view is like the difference between describing a desert and irrigating it.[7]

[6] A. J. Ayer, *Language, Truth and Logic*, 2nd ed. (New York: Dover Publications, 1946), p. 107.

[7] C. L. Stevenson, "The Emotive Conception of Ethics and Its Cognitive Implications," *The Philosophical Review* 59 (1950), pp. 291–304. Reprinted in W. Sellars & J. Hospers, eds., *Readings in Ethical Theory*, 2nd ed. (Englewood Cliffs, N. J.: Prentice-Hall Inc., 1970), p. 257.

Ayer, a logical positivist, argues that, because moral claims are only pseudo-claims, one normative ethical theory cannot be better than another. In fact, he contends that there are no normative ethical theories in the sense that philosophers and theologians had thought. According to this conception of ethics, the teacher's task is to expose the errors of historical figures, and teach students how to avoid them. A main component of this view is that ethical utterances are nothing but the expression of attitudes. Stevenson's more sophisticated view allows for a kind of reasoning in moral matters, but only insofar as certain pieces of evidence are causally sufficient for the instilling of certain attitudes. On this view, gesturing hypnotically or speaking convincingly are as effective as any argument that a Kant or a Mill could present.

Several factors led to the decline in influence of noncognitivist theories and to the recognition that ethics is more than just attitudes. One was the severe criticisms of logical positivism by large numbers of philosophers, including pragmatists and Kantians. This criticism contributed to the displacement of logical positivism as the dominant philosophical movement in the English-speaking world. In addition, it became clear to increasing numbers of philosophers that the later Wittgenstein's philosophy was either not so different from the positivism that he helped to create with his crucially important work, *Tractatus Logical Philosophicus*, or that it was the beginning, and not the end, of a new direction.[8] Americans began to appreciate anew the pragmatism of Peirce, James, and Dewey. They began to see such thinkers as C. I. Lewis, not as reflections of English philosophy, but as original contributors to the American pragmatic tradition, in ethics as well as in theory of knowledge and logic. The displacement of positivism was also aided by new attitudes toward Marxism and existentialism; the positivists' contempt for what they regarded as the unclear claims of existentialism and Marxism now became subject to critical scrutiny. Pressing social issues—civil rights, the Vietnam war, and the political scandals of Watergate—reinforced the conviction that moral problems and their resolution were important. Successful efforts to attract older students, as the supply of younger students diminished, brought to the university a group who had mature moral concerns that they knew were not illusions. Faculty members with strong moral views began to express them, encouraged by and encouraging students to do the same. Finally, falling enrollments in institutions of higher education led academics, even those who continued to have contempt for ethics, to offer courses in which the concerns of students could be discussed. All of these factors combined to reduce significantly the influence of positivism and noncognitivism in ethics.

This story does not paint a picture of philosophers and theologians as the curators of ethics as a discipline. To be sure, normative ethics continued to be taught—one could not simply ignore Plato, Aristotle, Aquinas, Kant, and

[8]Ludwig Wittgenstein, *Philosophical Investigations* (New York: Macmillan, 1953).

Mill—but, to a large extent, the profession that gave rise to the discipline of ethics turned its back on normative ethics just as the social sciences had. Ethical concerns returned to the social sciences just when they again became legitimate in philosophy and theology. However, even at the height of positivism and non-cognitivism, students in philosophy and theology departments could not avoid the work of Aquinas, Mill, or Kant. Even if only to show the feebleness of their views, the instructor in philosophy or theology had to read the works carefully. The tools of critical reasoning, careful examination of arguments and evidence, and the attempt to show how views worked from the "inside," made the comeback of normative ethics courses much easier in philosophy and theological ethics than in other areas, where the tradition of critically evaluating normative issues was frequently lost.

Courses in ethics began to focus more and more on actual moral problems and issues. Abortion, euthanasia, war, marriage, racism, sexism, and capital punishment are typical problems in the compilations of the 1970s. These often give little attention to normative ethical theories; the problems were used to illustrate how normative ethical theories could be applied, but were themselves the primary or even total content of the courses. In a way, this was the analogue of the case-study method of teaching applied ethics. Syllabi and course outlines, however, show that, even when such compilations were used, the teacher presented the critical, historical, and rational framework in which the problems could be discussed. It now seems to me that the extremes of the "relevance" movement have been replaced by much better-balanced courses in undergraduate ethics.

Part of the explanation for the recent balance in ethics courses is that there are now many more specialized courses in which the more specific concerns can be addressed. These courses allow more problems to be examined without sacrificing rigor or coherence. It would be preferable to have a first course in normative ethics as a requirement for the more specific courses such as business ethics and bioethics, though I realize that that is not always possible. We have not attempted to recapture the purpose of the ethics course as taught by the college president, namely, to pull together all of the knowledge gained in undergraduate study. But though we no longer think of ethics as an all-embracing course, we have also come back from the depths of a positivistic ethics concerned only with the most abstract metaethical issues.

The Ethics Course and Its Teachers

Some institutions have one course in ethics, while others have ten. At some institutions, one person teaches the course in ethics as well as all the other philosophy courses, from symbolic logic to aesthetics. Occasionally the teacher of ethics is in a humanities division, and has no training in philosophical or theological ethics. Courses range from the intimate seminar with five to ten students to the lecture class with 250 and more. The teachers of ethics range in their personal behavior from the saintly to the wicked. At a few institutions, the ethics teacher is expected to present some one view, selected by the institution, as the correct view, and others as mistaken theories. At other institutions, a very few, no doubt, the defense of a particular view by an instructor is seen as evidence of incompetence. Presentations range from lectures with no applications to moral exercises within the classroom. These differences make it difficult to talk generally about the types and conditions of undergraduate ethics courses. Let me begin with a brief discussion of teachers (and institutions) as role models.

THE GOOD AND THE TEACHER WHO IS GOOD

The distinction between the morally wise person and the person knowledgeable about morality is easy to draw. The morally wise person is someone you would consult if you had a difficult moral problem: usually these are friends, or perhaps physicians or ministers. Such persons, on occasion, know something about normative ethics, but usually they are not formally trained in the subject. In contrast, someone may have extensive knowledge of normative ethical systems, but be insensitive to the actual needs of people, or not be a very good person. Students, of course, learn by precept as well as concept, and though we may hope that the teacher of ethics will be fit to serve as a role model, I do not think we can count on it. Certainly the instructor should know that one way to teach ethics is through personal example, though, as a teacher of ethics, one would have to generalize from one's own case, or abstract the general guidelines for the students. It is no exaggeration to say that moral lessons will be taught by the teacher of ethics, whether these lessons are intended or not, as a result of grading papers, responding to questions, handling difficult situations in class, and the like. Most (but not all) teachers of ethics recognize this, and act accordingly.

Students also learn from institutional behavior. If tenured faculty are fired, or competent Marxists not hired, or women discriminated against, the institution is conveying moral lessons to the students. Moral lessons are conveyed not only by the school, but also by family, friends, TV, and churches. This complicates the picture of what the teacher does, but it also dilutes the influence of that teacher.

Those who teach ethics are usually better able to justify or rationalize their actions than most, for their training and study has equipped them to marshal evidence. This means that the morally wise person trained in ethics is in a better position to do more good for more people, and the morally wicked person trained in ethics is in a position to do more harm.

MORAL PROBLEMS IN THE CLASSROOM

In his "Moral Principles in Education," John Dewey drew attention to the importance and pervasiveness of "moral habit":

> If we compare this condition with that of the well-ordered home, we find that the duties and responsibilities that the child has there to recognize do not belong to the family as a specialized and isolated institution, but flow from the very nature of the social life in which the family participates and to which it contributes. The child ought to have the same motives for right doing and to be judged by the same standards in the school, as the adult in the wider social circle to which he belongs. Interest in community welfare, an interest that is intellectual and practical, as well as emotional—an interest, that is to say, in perceiving whatever makes for social order and progress, and in carrying these principles into execution—is the moral habit to which all the special school habits must be related if they are to be animated by the breath of life."[9]

The teacher of ethics need not go beyond the classroom to discover moral problems for discussion and debate. Let me suggest a few problems that are well known, and a few that are not.

A typical moral problem, though it is not usually perceived that way by students, or even faculty, involves the student who wishes to pursue a point in which only he or she is interested, or who does not see a criticism of his or her own view that others think is obvious. For example, suppose that a student wishes to defend psychological egoism, the view that the only motive for voluntary action is self-benefit, as a way to defend ethical egoism, the view that actions are right as they tend to benefit self. Most students think that both views are "dumb," and want to do something else. The teacher now faces a moral problem: for the student can be put off by saying the concerns will be considered after class, but the occasion can also be used to show that sometimes we are justified in dealing with an issue because someone is deeply concerned about it. This is not to claim that there are no problems so obscure that we are not justified in saying that we will have to discuss them in private. It is to say that teachers frequently face a choice that is not easy to make, and that is, in part, moral. One cannot simply tell the other students that it is their obligation to listen to their fellow student, but one can try to awaken a sense of community by asking others to help clarify the question or problem. This helps to dispel the brittle individualism and competition that sometimes infects classrooms. You might talk about your own fallibility in pursuing topics; ask whether it is better to err on the side of supposing a question to be of importance and general interest. One can let answers to these questions emerge, show the ethical reasoning that they inevitably entail, and evaluate that reasoning by comparison with other models.

[9]John Dewey, "Moral Principles in Education," in *John Dewey: The Middle Works, Vol. 4, 1907–1909* (Carbondale and Edwardsville, Ill: Southern Illinois University Press, 1977), p. 274.

Every class has tests, or papers, or some other method of evaluating student performance. These exercises raise many moral issues. Should there be grades at all? Many students think that there should not, and when pressed will invariably present reasons concerning obligation and value. They will say that a university or college is better if there are no grades because ... No final evaluation of the reasons is needed to make this a worthwhile exercise in applied ethics. One of the topics that must come up, though, is the responsibility, usually a quasi-legal one, of the instructor to turn in grades. Should, morally, the instructor risk loss of job to uphold the value of a possible future university system? Should, morally, the students insist on this? What would Mill say about this? Kant?

In most of my ethics courses, I have a group project. Usually the group presents an oral report to the rest of the class, accompanied by an outline or paper. The latter is rewritten as a group paper, and is then handed in to be graded along with the other parts of the course work. A problem I pose for the students involves the grading of the group report; should each student in the group receive the overall grade given to the oral and written reports? In every group, some students contribute more: is it fair and just that everyone receive the same grade? How can one determine who gets what grade? Should the fellow group members have a say? How much of a say? These questions, their clarification, and their placement within the context of normative ethics, are an important part of the course.

Another topic that arises in class is student responsibility and attendance. Suppose a student exercises an option, given by the instructor, not to attend class (either a certain number of times per term, or whenever the student chooses), and thereby misses an assignment. Suppose that the assignment is a group of readings plus a quiz, or a short paper, and the student comes to class unprepared. Should the teacher allow the student a makeup? Require the student to take the quiz right then? Require the student to take it and not count it? These questions and others should all be raised before the problem arises, not only for the instructive value of the problems but also to protect the poor instructor.

These sorts of moral problems can profitably be raised in ethics classes. Although useful in applied-ethics courses, they are especially useful in undergraduate general ethics courses, because there is not the pool of actual moral problems that exists with the applied fields, and because there is often a sense among students that they don't have moral problems.

It would be possible to teach a first course in normative ethics totally within the context of the actual moral problems that arise in the classroom, by showing how the competing normative ethical theories apply to those problems. Alternatively, lectures on the major normative ethical theories could be illustrated with problems drawn solely from outside the classroom. With either format, students could learn how to recognize moral issues, become sensitized to them, learn how to examine them critically, etc. In short, the goals of the teaching of ethics outlined by Daniel Callahan[10] can be met using almost any method, if the teacher uses it well. My own inclination is to involve students as much as possible, because I agree with John Dewey that people learn best when they take an active part in the learning process. But this involvement or the use of discussion (or any method) depends upon the personality of the teacher, as well as the method itself.

TRICKSTERS

One problem faced by philosophers and theologians in teaching any course is that the students often come to regard them as tricksters, and perhaps sophists. Students come to believe that teachers can make any view look bad or good because they are trained to do so. The student may even conclude that his or her own view, that has just been shown to be inconsistent, or subject to seventeen separate fatal criticisms, is nevertheless correct. This attitude results, in part, from the mistaken notion that pluralism means that all views are equally justified or correct. It also results, in part, from the metaethical view that ethics (and perhaps all philosophy) is "soft," just a matter of selecting one view over another as a result of whim or impulse. Finally, students also perceive, quite correctly, that training in the tasks of marshalling evidence and evaluating arguments makes the teacher a very difficult opponent to defeat.

Perhaps the primary way to overcome this problem is to avoid the impression that the teacher is an opponent. This goal, very difficult because of the inevitable disagreements that arise in the teaching of ethics, is well worth achieving. It can be done by failing to take any stand; but then students think that you are wishy-washy, or get the impression that all views are equally correct. You can take a stand, but then claim that everyone has an equal right to his or her own opinion. This, however, simply confuses the distinction between pluralism and relativism. One way to reach the goal of nonopposition is to indicate that we are considering theories, and not people; we are engaged together in the enterprise of seeking a correct theory, or at least seeking the methods (reasoning, arguments, theory comparison, etc.) that will enable each of us to seek out the correct or best theory.

To help overcome the sense of being tricked, the teacher can present a problem or an issue concerning which the teacher does not have a solution. The teacher can present the issue, along with the proposed solutions or theories, and then try to show why each is unsatisfactory. This does not commit one to the view that there is no solution; indeed, I always indicate that I am confident that a solution will be reached. And it does give the students a sense that the teacher is not omniscient.

[10]Daniel Callahan, "Goals in the Teaching of Ethics," this volume, Chapter 2.

ACADEMIC FREEDOM AND UNPOPULAR VIEWS

Two different academic-freedom cases can arise in connection with the teaching of ethics. One occurs when a teacher holds a view that seems to preclude pluralism, and engages in indoctrination to inculcate that view. The second can arise when someone is hired to teach at a school, usually a religious institution, which officially endorses a specific ethical theory.

Suppose, as one occasionally hears, a Marxist is teaching an ethics course to undergraduates. Suppose also that the teacher pushes his view, demeans all other views, doesn't allow other views to be given a fair hearing, and uses sophistical techniques to silence critics in the classroom. This person, I would argue, is not a competent teacher, not because of the Marxist view, but because of failure to meet the goals of teaching ethics. A charge of incompetence must be supported by evidence that concerns the teaching, not the view that is held by the instructor. Everyone who teaches ethics thinks that some normative ethical theory is better than the others, and should be able to explain the reasons for support, whether the theory be utilitarian, Marxist, egoistic, or amoral.

The much more difficult case involves the institution with an official or even semiofficial point of view. On the one hand, it seems clear that once such an institution has hired a qualified individual to teach ethics, a person who did not hide his or her actual views in order to get the job, then academic freedom legitimately prevents the institution from dictating which view will come out "best" in the ethics class. On the other hand, suppose that an institution explicitly decides to hire a person of a particular ethical persuasion: e.g., Marxist, Thomist, libertarian, or utilitarian: Is this morally or legally permissible? If the individual were to change beliefs and adjust the ethics course accordingly, does the institution then have grounds to fire that person, without violating academic freedom?

PROBLEMS AND SOLUTIONS

Let us turn now to a brief consideration of the perhaps mundane but nonetheless perplexing problems that teachers of ethics face almost daily.

STUDENT CAPACITIES

The widely discussed decline of students' abilities to read and write makes the assignment of reading materials in ethics courses difficult. Most teachers of a first course in ethics want students to read at least some original material in the history of ethics. John Stuart Mill, one of the important figures, is widely admired by academics for his clear prose, though he wrote not for academics but for the educated public. Students, however, find Mill very difficult: they think the sentences too long, and frequently get lost in his arguments. (When students get lost in arguments, arguments that are usually quite straightforward, they describe this by saying that the author is "going in circles.") Students have considerably greater difficulty with Aquinas, Kant, and Aristotle. This is not to claim that most students cannot read these authors with understanding, but many cannot, and this poses a serious problem in the selection of course materials. It has led to a proliferation of easier works, many with cartoons, letters to the editor, and easy-to-read dramatic fiction.

A related problem is the age of most undergraduates in ethics courses, viz., usually between 18 and 21. Aristotle suggests that the study of ethics should not begin until after age 30, for people do not have sufficient maturity and experience. Young students are frequently unsympathetic to those who act out of fear, from the employee who agrees to cover up illegal activities to the person who betrays comrades to save his or her own life. They also tend to believe that they, as individuals, are not susceptible to moral corruption and temptation. This is a difficult issue to address in class, but almost all who teach ethics to undergraduates attempt to sensitize students to additional issues, those beyond their current experience.

AMORALISM AND SKEPTICISM

Teachers of undergraduate ethics courses often notice very early that a significant portion of the class does not recognize that they make moral judgments, act on the basis of ethical evaluations, or are enmeshed in a moral environment. Sometimes students think that the claim "I (or anyone) believe that an action is right" has the same meaning as the claim "An action is right." Although this equation can be used to express the sophisticated metaethical view of the noncognitivist, students usually do not use it in this way. Sometimes they suppose that there is no evidence available for moral claims, and that the only way to defeat moral skepticism is to equate the acceptance of a moral belief with its acceptability. Other students, seeing that the two are not generally the same, and thinking there is no way to show that one moral opinion is better than another, embrace amoralism; the view that nothing is right or wrong. Perhaps the most important way to overcome this problem is to discuss the actual moral problems that arise in the classroom. Another strategy is to set forth a number of normative ethical theories, and show how their acceptability is dependent upon the critical apparatus that the students are acquiring.

Students will frequently say, "I don't use moral terms such as 'right' and 'wrong.' I like some things and don't like others, but there is no such thing as morality." This is, in part, a verbal matter, though again there may be an underlying serious philosophical issue. Students who say such things will also claim that we should or should not have restrictive laws concerning abortion, gun control, and drugs. When asked why, they do not respond with preferences, but instead they give reasons. These turn out to be just the reasons that we all give to defend our moral views. In addition, it almost always turns out that the students hold some normative ethical theory, and are actually using it in the presentation of the reasons. Unfortunately, students often make use of two or more incompatible theories at the same time. One of the tasks of ethics teaching is to show that the views are incompatible, and why that is not something to be accepted lightly.

PLURALISM AND RELATIVISM

We pride ourselves on having a pluralistic society in which many different cultural subgroups flourish. The mix of elements from different cultures helps to make our society interesting, and gives it a vital mix of different ideas, cuisines, religions, music, literature, and dance. We tend to think that tolerance and appreciation of different cultures is the appropriate attitude, and to condemn the view that one of the subcultures is inferior to another. The old melting-pot idea was that each subculture would be swallowed up into a blend of cultures that was American culture. The new melting-pot idea seems to be that distinctness of cultural groups is a good thing to preserve, though those who wish to give up some aspect are free to do so. We may indeed be evolving a common culture that contains elements from the many subcultures, but many of the subcultures have remained distinct, and should, according to this view.

A problem in teaching ethics arises because of an ambiguous view of ethics and pluralism. Is a person's moral view (normative ethics) part of the subculture, or is it something else? To focus the problem more clearly, consider the following two statements.

1. All moral claims are equally correct.
2. All (seriously held) moral claims have an equal right to be heard.

If we substitute "subculture" for "moral claim," and "good" for "correct," then we have the claim of cultural pluralism. In fact, considered this way, there is no difference between (1) and (2), because (2) becomes the view that every subculture has an equal right to be lived by its members. When we consider morality, though, the situation seems to be quite different. If the Male Chauvinist Society, a fictional group (so far), claims that women are and ought to be the servants of men, we feel free to reject this view as being *incorrect*, though most of us would support the right of this view to be *heard*. Slaveholders believed that keeping slaves was morally permissible. We are generally agreed that they were mistaken, even though it was no doubt true that within the subculture of the slaveholders it was thought to be morally permissible.

Philosophers give many explanations of the difference between (1) and (2), as do social scientists, theologians, politicians, and others. Some maintain that (1) is true; this is one version of ethical relativism, a view held by a small number of philosophers and theologians. Many students confuse cultural pluralism with ethical relativism. As a result, teachers of undergraduate ethics must attend to the distinction, and convince students that it is neither un-American, antidemocratic, nor antipluralistic to suggest that not all moral views are equally correct. Most teachers of ethics also emphasize that views have an equal right to be heard, that every student with a seriously held view has a right to have that view aired and examined.

I would extend the right to be heard to views of subcultures in our society, but insist that not all the views heard are correct. For example, if many parents in a school system believe that special creation and not evolution is the explanation of life in its present form, I think that the view should be covered in a biology course. At the same time, the biology teacher has a professional obligation to evaluate the competing theories presented. Every biological view that is important to the community has a right to be heard, but they are not all equally correct. Professions in addition to philosophy and theology will have to learn to resist the public pressure to label a view as correct that in their own professional judgment is not correct.

INDOCTRINATION AND INDISPENSABILITY

Frequently those who reject the view that all moral claims are equally correct also reject the view that all moral claims have an equal right to be heard. They argue that moral issues and normative ethical theories are too important to leave to chance, or the ability of students to reason, so we must insure that our students (as well as all citizens) hold the "proper" moral views. The teaching that results from this kind of view is a form of indoctrination, discussed at length in Ruth Macklin's paper.[11] Indoctrination occurs when someone attempts to inculcate a view without the intended learner's exercising his or her own reasoning ability. The opposite of this is captured by several of the goals in the teaching of ethics that Daniel Callahan mentions: stimulating the moral imagination, developing analytical skills, and tolerating and resisting disagreement and ambiguity.

Dispensability is the goal of the teacher, to enable students to reason and reach decisions about moral problems and normative ethical theories without his aid. The teacher is needed, of course, to stimulate the student, impart basic skills, correct errors in reasoning, and show that options are available from great thinkers and traditions. Teachers of ethics must walk a fine line between the desire to insure that students are morally sensitive contributing members of our society, and what I consider the highest obligation of teaching, viz., to make oneself dispensable as a result of teaching.

It is easy to point out, once the distinctions have been drawn, that our aim

[11]Ruth Macklin, "Problems in the Teaching of Ethics: Pluralism and Indoctrination," this volume, Chapter 3.

is dispensibility, not indoctrination. We can resist the conclusion that indoctrination is an inevitable goal in the teaching of ethics if we reject the claim that all views are equally correct. We think that some views, both specific moral stands and normative ethical theories, are correct, and yet we believe that the competing views should be heard. My suggestion is that we understand this better when we recognize that indoctrination is undesirable, and dispensability is desirable.

EVALUATION

An ethics course can be evaluated from the perspective of the instructor, the student, the subject matter of discipline, the responsible administrator, or the community.[12] Let us cover the one that is easiest for me, as an instructor, to deal with, viz., the point of view of the instructor.

Any evaluation of a course depends on what you set out to accomplish. If you want students to be able to handle actual moral problems from the point of view of selected ethical theories such as utilitarianism, you determine the success of that by reading papers in which that is attempted. There is no essential difference in this process as it applied to ethics, or to economics or physics.

Since one of my goals is to equip students with the ability to evaluate and choose among competing normative ethical theories, I assign papers in which that is required. I, as instructor, can evaluate those papers. The standard of success is not that the students do original philosophy, or show great sophistication, but that they understand and sincerely attempt the task to marshal and evaluate evidence, and to choose on the basis of the findings. The students have to respond, as best they can, to the standard criticisms of their view, not because it is expected that they will turn out publishable philosophy, but because they are learning to be intellectually responsible for their views.

Student evaluation of teaching is important because it provides evidence of student attitudes toward the instructor and the subject matter. Since students are usually not in a position to evaluate what the subject matter ought to have been, one must take student criticisms of the course content with a grain of salt. However, if many students regularly think that the instructor is tyrannical and rude, or does not cover enough relevant and important topics, these evaluations should be taken seriously.

In evaluations I look for a variety of things: attitudes, expectations, a sense of having learned, a sense of having missed many things, signs that the course was too easy or too hard, and future plans. It is difficult to elicit reliable information, for the student who is "down" on the course is negative about almost everything. I ask a number of questions, twenty or so, and then have an open

[12]See Arthur Caplan, "Evaluation and the Teaching of Ethics," this volume, Chapter 5.

part of the evaluation. Students are asked to write about the things in the course that they would like to see retained, the things that they would like dropped, the things added, and the things changed. Not all students will write useful evaluations of this sort, but enough will so that you can make changes on the basis of the evaluations the next time you teach the course.

CHAPTER 8

The Teaching of Ethics in Undergraduate Nonethics Courses

SUSAN RESNECK PARR

In his first paper for me in an upper-level literature course, a graduating college senior argued that Meursault, the protagonist of Camus' *The Stranger,* should be seen as heroic. As he explained it, "Even though Meursault murdered someone, he is still a hero because he did it only in passing." In a conference the next day, the student verified that he had expressed himself accurately. The problem was not, as I had hoped, his writing.

In classes devoted to Tennessee Williams' *A Streetcar Named Desire* during the past three years, a majority of the students consistently have supported Stella Kowalski's decision to commit her sister Blanche to a mental hospital, rather than to believe that her husband, Stanley, had raped Blanche. They justified Stella's choice on the grounds that Blanche no longer could support herself and that her prolonged visit had interferred with Stanley and Stella's sex life. Although no one argued that Blanche was insane, several students did focus on her eccentricity, citing as their evidence her promiscuity and what they saw as the inappropriateness of her desire, at thirty, to be beautiful. Most were appalled at the rape itself, but a few students did condone it because Blanche had belittled Stanley.

Eventually, after discussions devoted to clarifying the issues involved, most of the students modified their responses. The apologist for Meursault came to realize that he didn't really condone murder as long as it was done casually, and those students who had justified Blanche's institutionalization didn't really believe, after some thought, that mental hospitals were appropriate dumping grounds for the indigent, the incovenient, or even the eccentric. Nor was any

This article also appeared in *Liberal Education,* Spring, 1980, Vol. 66, No. 1, pp. 51–66.

SUSAN RESNECK PARR ● Department of English, Ithaca College, Ithaca, New York.

one of them willing to argue that rape was an appropriate response to an insult, even an insult to the male ego. In other words, what had initially appeared to be moral callousness, in reality had been unreflectiveness.

But, as importantly, what also emerged from these discussions was the fact that many of the students believed, although for very different reasons, that such ethical considerations were not relevant either to their understanding of literature in particular or to their studies in general. Some of them were convinced that anything other than hard data was mere opinion and therefore of no significance. They assumed that the consideration of ethical problems for which there were no right and wrong answers was not learning at all. A second group insisted that any point of view, any interpretation, any response—however subjectively derived—was valid. They too did not equate an examination of ethical issues with learning.[1] Still others, without any special rationale, simply assumed that ethical questions had no place in liberal arts courses.

My experiences do not seem to be atypical. Although undergraduates and graduate students from across the country currently are flocking to applied-ethics courses, faculty from a wide variety of institutions and disciplines report that many of their undergraduate students seem either indifferent or resistant to ethical issues, particularly when such issues are raised in the context of nonethics classes. In other words, many students see ethical concerns as separate from educational ones.

The *Chronicle of Higher Education* survey, in the fall of 1978, of nearly 200,000 incoming freshmen, verifies that this is so.[2] For instance, when the students were asked to check off from a master list their reasons for seeking a college education, 75.4% indicated that they believed that going to college would enable them to get a better job. Seventy-four percent specified a desire to "learn about more things," and 68.3% saw the gaining of a general education as important. Yet, a great many of these same students did not connect questions of social and political values with the learning and the general education they said they sought. Specifically, only 31.1% considered "influencing social values" to be either an essential or a very important objective. Less than half that number, 14.6% judged "influencing the political structure" either essential or very important. Using the same scale, only 33.8% so ranked "promoting racial understanding," and only 27.5% so judged "helping to clean up the environment."

The *Chronicle* survey is illuminating in another way in that it also suggests that students may be indifferent to ethical questions because they place little value on individual belief. For instance, only a third of the students surveyed, or

---

[1]The increasingly popular values clarification, which has begun to permeate elementary and secondary education, reinforces both this sort of unreflective relativism, and this tendency to separate values and learning.

[2]"Characteristics and Attitudes of 1978–79 College Freshmen," *Chronicle of Higher Education* 4 (1979), pp. 14–15.

32.2%, agreed "strongly" or "somewhat" with the proposition that "people should not obey laws that violate their beliefs." It follows, then, that for those two-thirds of the students who believe that laws should be obeyed regardless of their validity, discussion of moral issues may well seem irrelevant.

Ethics and Individual Responsibility

The belief that individuals should not choose independently to break laws may be linked to another apparently widely held student attitude, that individual responsibility is an anachronism in today's world and that a concern with ethical issues is a meaningless academic exercise. In my own classes during the last several years, the message that I have heard more often than any other from my students about their sense of their place in the world has been that the world is so corrupt and social forces so powerful that they can make no impact on it. For instance, when an advanced class of hand-picked, academically responsible students saw Lina Wertmuller's film *Seven Beauties,* they easily accepted as both understandable and inevitable Pasqualino's choices of metaphorical and literal prostitution as well as his choice of murdering his friend in order to insure his own survival. It is true that they were horrified, but it is equally true that they saw Pasqualino as having no options. As several students patiently explained to me, Pasqualino was a product of an immoral and perverted world. He could be expected to be no better than that world. It had not occurred to these students that the film might be condemning Pasqualino for his failure to say no to the evil, nor did they recognize the other options the film suggested, however difficult those options were.

John Weiss, a history professor at Cornell, has had the same sort of experience with his students. After showing the film, *Battle of Algiers,* Weiss was astonished that many of his students so uniformly and readily accepted the film's stance that terrorism was the only option available to the Algerians. Because history had, in the end, happened in a certain way, Weiss's students believed that that way was the inevitable one.

Harvard government professor Richard Hunt has written eloquently about this phenomenon, which he has labeled a "no fault" view of history. After years of teaching a course on Nazism in a conventional way, "from a straight historical perspective," Hunt altered his approach, and called his new course "Moral Dilemmas in a Repressive Society: Nazi Germany." His goal was

> to present the Nazi phenomenon from the inside, so to speak, from the experience and testimony of those who lived through the period as victims, victimizers, bystanders, true believers, and members of the resistance, [giving] special attention to the real-life, sometimes life-and-death, moral dilemmas of specific individuals and groups.

What Hunt concluded was that his students held "depressingly fatalistic conclusions about major moral dilemmas facing the German people at their particular time and place in history." His even larger concern was that

> clearly some trends of our time seem to be running toward a no-fault guilt-free
> society. One might say the virtues of responsible choice, paying the penalty, taking
> the consequences all appear at low ebb today.[3]

ETHICS AND ILLITERACY

The conviction on the part of students that individuals can make no difference and that attempts to assume responsibility are futile is bound up with
the other crises in higher education: student ignorance and student illiteracy.
Although it is difficult to know for sure how pervasive these problems are, it is
nearly an academic cliché that large numbers of college students have little, if
any, knowledge of Western culture. Weiss's experience with an undergraduate
history class is all too common. When he alluded to the Book of Job, only
twelve of his fifty students recognized the reference. Of those twelve, nine had
learned about Job the semester before because their Western Civilization professor had talked about Job at length. In other words, only three of the fifty had
come to college knowing who Job was. When Weiss resumed his lecture with
an allusion to the Sermon on the Mount, a topic his predecessor hadn't discussed, only three students knew what he was talking about.

Others report similar experiences. Because he believes that his students are
ignorant of the Judaeo-Christain tradition, a colleague of mine has chosen not
to teach a seminar in Flannery O'Connor because he is sure that her fiction will
be inaccessible to them. Another colleague recently earned her students' censure
for "talking over their heads." The example cited most often was her allusions
to Othello. Students also seem ignorant of more recent historical phenomena
and are unable to discuss such events as the holocaust, Viet Nam, Selma, and
even Watergate. As one class insisted to me, they preferred not to read Norman
Mailer's *Armies of the Night* because it was about Viet Nam, an event that was
of importance only to my generation, not to theirs.

If a significant number of students really are as ignorant of and/or indifferent to the past as these anecdotes suggest, then their indifference to ethical
issues makes a new kind of sense. In other words, if students have no larger
context in which to place what they read, what they hear, what they write, even
how they behave and if they genuinely have no knowledge of tradition or of
precedents, it becomes more understandable, although not acceptable, why they
believe that only the immediate is of importance. Similarly, if they really do lack
a sense of the connection of events and of causality, it becomes understandable

[3]Richard M. Hunt, "No-Fault Guilt-Free History," *The New York Times*, February 16, 1976.

why they deny individual responsibility. By the same token, it also becomes clear why they seem so indifferent to learning the skills of careful and critical reading and of clear and logical writing. If individual action is of no significance in the world, then there is no real reason to try to understand others or to communicate one's own ideas.

It is, most of all, because of these student attitudes that the question of the place of ethics in the undergraduate curriculum ultimately must be seen as a part of the larger question of the goals and the ingredients of general education. Specifically, I have become convinced that faculty from all disciplines, but particularly the humanities, must be persuaded to give deliberate attention to the ethical dimensions inherent in the material of their courses. I also am convinced that an ethical focus can become an integral part of humanities courses without sacrificing either the traditional concerns of the disciplines in question or the critical detachment and rigor that is so much a part of our educational heritage. In fact, as I hope to demonstrate, infusing regular courses with ethical considerations is likely to enrich, not to weaken, those courses.

My own experience, for example, tells me that it is my students' involvement in Huck Finn's conflict between his instinct to free Jim and his socially induced belief that to do so will damn him to hell that motivates them to care about such conventional literary concerns as Mark Twain's choice of an innocent narrative stance for Huck, his use of irony, his device of disguises, his satiric treatment of religion, the implications of Huck's symbolic murder of himself, and the often-debated critical controversy over the effectivenesses or failures of the final third of the novel. In other words, by sensitizing students to ethical issues, by "exciting their moral imaginations," as Daniel Callahan puts it, those of us who teach may reinvigorate our courses. Even more importantly, by doing so we may begin to break into the circle of student ignorance and indifference.

There is also the possibility that inspiring students to think about ethical issues in nonethics courses is a more effective approach for motivating undergraduates to think about ethical dilemmas than either philosophy or applied-ethics courses. First, the ethical questions raised in literature, history, government, psychology, and sociology classes, for instance, often engage the students into considering ethical dilemmas that their own lives have not yet occasioned. At the same time, such a context allows them to confront more personal and sometimes threatening ethical dilemmas in a more detached and objective way than a direct discussion of those dilemmas might allow. For instance, white middle-class students who are made uncomfortable by a discussion of the Bakke case, of busing, and welfare, seem able to examine quite rationally the questions of racism, the meaning of human life, and the nature and limits of social responsibility after reading Richard Wright's *Native Son*. In great part, they are able to do so because the novel gives them a vivid sense of what it means to be trapped in a world of poverty, of no opportunity, and of self-loathing. They begin to understand the dangers for society when someone like Bigger, who has been given neither the knowledge necessary for self-understanding nor the language necessary for self-expression, turns to violence. They also begin to think about how language can become a tool to manipulate or to disguise reality as well as to communicate it.

But of equal importance is that, in order to discuss these issues fully, the students also must focus on the way in which the novel is permeated by blindness/sight and white/black imagery, on Wright's use of irony and Christian symbolism, and on Bigger's evolution as a character, particularly his change in consciousness. They are likely to argue about whether the novel, in the end, remains true to its literary mode or whether Wright chose propaganda rather than art. And finally, they understand that an awareness of history and philosophy also enriches their reading of the novel, since Wright was writing it at a time of ambivalence about the American Communist Party and at a time of sympathy for existentialsim.

In addition, there are compelling practical reasons for incorporating an ethical focus in nonethics courses. Since most ethics courses today are either applied-ethics courses located in professional and preprofessional programs or conventional philosophy- and religion-department courses devoted to the history of ethical theory or training in analytical skills, they primarily reach a self-selected audience, that is, students who already have an interest in ethics.[4] But it may well be the rest of the student population which would most benefit from a focus on ethics. Moreover, compartmentalizing ethics into separate programs and courses may trivialize it, suggesting to students that ethics is of importance only in professional, strictly intellectual, or religious contexts. This is not to say that such courses and programs are not in themselves important and necessary, but rather that something more may be needed as well.

FACULTY RESISTANCE

Faculty resistance to incorporating an ethical component in nonethics courses may be even more pervasive than that of the students. Indeed, many faculty members express genuine alarm at the prospect of any consideration of ethical issues in regular courses. Their reluctance, like that of their students, is the product of a broad set of educational values and of unreflectiveness as well.

To begin with, many relativists are resistant to a consideration of ethical issues. Rejecting any scheme of absolute values, they may embrace a stance of value-neutrality and argue that their disciplines, whatever they may be, are value-free. To many in this group, ethics is a matter merely of preferences and therefore not worthy of attention.

[4]Some special courses and programs, often interdisciplinary and experimental, have also been developed in recent years, but enrollment in these courses almost always is voluntary, and thus, once again, only reaches a self-selected group of students.

Those at the opposite end of the spectrum, those influenced by positivism, are even more likely to shun any deliberate examination of ethical questions, even those occasioned by their disciplines. Because they adhere strictly to a scientific, analytical methodology, wish to work primarily with the quantifiable, and accept as valid only that which can be proved, they judge ethical questions as being soft and subjective and therefore both unteachable, and unworthy of being taught. Similarly, for those whose pedagogy leads them to equate learning only with the transfer of information, the ambiguities and irresolutions inherent in ethical quandaries are bound to be uncomfortable.

This movement to the quasi-scientific has, in some important ways, changed the face of both the humanities and the social sciences, leading many teachers and scholars away from a consideration of meaning into a more limited attention to form. Certainly behaviorism, new criticism, and, more recently, structuralism are manifestations of this trend.

The valuing of specialization which has accompanied this shift in emphasis also tends to lead educators away from dealing directly with ethical issues. Specifically, a more narrow definition of areas of expertise has resulted in many faculty members' shying away from an interdisciplinary approach, which itself often occasions a discussion of ethical questions. For instance, the new critical rejection of anything but close textual analysis has encouraged many literature professors to ignore the social and historical context out of which a work emerged. Certainly, it was his new critical stance that led a colleague of mine from a reputedly excellent program to spend an hour-and-fifteen-minute class on a Flannery O'Connor short story, "The Displaced Person," talking only about patterns of imagery, linguistic nuance, and character development. Although the story is about a World War II Polish refugee who threatens to displace both the poor whites and the blacks on the Southern farm where he comes to live, not once during the class did the professor mention either World War II or the racial and class tensions within the story. It may have been a similar motive that led another colleague to spend an hour teaching *The Trojan Women* by emphasizing the pattern of shield imagery and ignoring the ethical torments confronting the women in a time of war.

Still, most faculty who profess to resist an ethical focus do in fact infuse their teaching with ethical considerations, even if unconsciously. Thus, few historians or political scientists would skirt the ethical implications of such events as the holocaust and the bombing of Hiroshima and Nagasaki, while literature professors seldom confine their classes only to matters of structure and language. Few would teach *Huckleberry Finn* by focusing exclusively on river symbolism and excluding Mark Twain's dramatization of the interplay between social and individual values.

Of course, there are those professors who do routinely raise ethical issues in their nonethics classes. As Princeton politics professor Dennis Thompson has suggested, these faculty members would wonder what is so problematic about raising ethical considerations since they do it all the time without thinking about it in any special way. But although many of this group probably are effective in incorporating an ethical focus in their classes, the problem of unreflectiveness remains. At the least, the phenomenon of some faculty members' dealing with ethical questions without being conscious of doing so and other faculty members' raising ethical issues "without thinking about it in any special way" gives students a potent message, that ethical questions are of only secondary importance and not worthy of the deliberate and detailed consideration given to more conventional scholarly research.

The question of whether an ethical focus should be an integral part of nonethics courses ultimately is part of the ongoing, larger debate about the nature of general education. If the goals of that education go beyond the transmittal of a body of knowledge and attempt as well to teach students to think critically and logically, to learn to support their ideas, and to express themselves clearly, then an ethical component is appropriate, if not inevitable. In turn, the incorporation of an ethical focus demands only what a conventional course with the same goals would require, that students be presented with a variety of perspectives, be taught the critical skills with which to analyze and evaluate those perspectives, and learn how to garner evidence in support of their own conclusions. It should be stressed that, though courses with an ethical focus share the particular goal of engaging students in the process of recognizing, and then learning to think critically about, ethical questions, they are not courses in moral reasoning, or applied ethics, or values clarification in the guise of literature, or history, or interdisciplinary courses. Since the ability to accomplish these goals ideally is among the tools of the academic trade, the often-cited question about faculty qualifications for such courses doesn't loom so large.

For the same reasons, the concern that faculty members will use such courses as forums for propaganda seems specious.[5] Although it is possible that ethics as a topic may seem to invite attempts at indoctrination more than other subjects, the fact is that the question of responsible faculty is one that academic institutions face all the time. Unhappily, most colleges and universities already harbor those instructors who impose on their subject matter their own biases and who reward with grades and praise only those students who become converts to their ideology. Thus, the safeguards for ethics-related courses are the same as for any others. Even more to the point, contrary to leading students astray, a more deliberate and reflective focus on ethics by responsible faculty throughout the curriculum might well enable students to judge more effectively the merits of that which is offered them in all their courses. A more overt focus on ethics might allow students better to resist the appeals of a proselytizer.

[5]See Ruth Macklin, "Problems in the Teaching of Ethics: Pluralism and Indoctrination," this volume, Chapter 3.

There is also the question of whether professional objectivity is ever possible. Can those who teach genuinely separate their personal values and beliefs from what and how they teach? The very selection of texts, the organization of a syllabus, the thrust of questions, and the nature of paper topics invariably reveal some sort of bias, however unconscious, as do such personal characteristics as tone of voice, facial expressions, and hand gestures. Even the act of professing not to teach ethics itself is a powerful statement to students of a professor's values and beliefs. Once again, a more deliberate consideration of ethical questions becomes desirable, because it encourages students and faculty alike to recognize their own biases and values so that they can adjust their angles of vision accordingly.

Humanities Courses with an Ethical Focus

The specific shape of humanities or interdisciplinary courses with an ethical focus inevitably will vary from faculty member to faculty member, from discipline to discipline, even from school to school. As is the case with all courses, these too will be dependent on such factors as the specific goals and teaching style of the professor; the backgrounds, abilities, and interests of the students; and the dictates of the discipline and course material. Nevertheless, since specific models may serve the interests of clarity and perhaps will provide useful starting points for others, I offer the following possibilities, based on my own experiences and those of Professors Hunt and Weiss.

The first model is the most obvious one, a course organized around a topic which has direct or indirect ethical implications. For example, I recently taught a seminar in deception and integrity in modern American literature.[6] The reading list included such classics as Fitzgerald's *The Great Gatsby*, Faulkner's *The Sound and the Fury*, Williams' *A Streetcar Named Desire*, Miller's *Death of a Salesman*, and Ellison's *Invisible Man*, as well as the more recent *Sula* by Toni Morrison, and Heller's *Something Happened*. Or an entirely different book list could be used. The focus, too, could be changed. It could be limited to deception and female characters, or to deception and male characters. It could be confined to acts of deliberate deception, to self-deception, or to acquiescence in the deceptions of others. In the end, as is true of all courses, the syllabi and the focus would be the product of professorial judgments.

Given the confines of the reading list, the broader topic of deception, and my other educational objectives, I began this course with *The Great Gatsby* and asked students to explore the thematic significance of the moment when the

---

[6]I taught this course in the Department of English, Princeton University, in the fall of 1979. My other models are based on my experiences at Ithaca College.

novel's narrator, Nick Carraway, dismisses the fact that his woman friend, Jordan Baker, "was incurably dishonest," by explaining, "It made no difference to me. Dishonesty in a woman is a thing you never blame deeply—I was casually sorry, and then I forgot." From there, we dealt with at least the following concerns, in the order the discussion gave birth to:

1. Nick, only paragraphs later, congratulates himself on being "one of the few honest people that I have even known," and he values Gatsby most when he believes Gatsby's version of events.

2. Nick's acceptance of Jordan's dishonesty serves to foreshadow his later acceptance of his cousin Daisy's more devastating deception when she allows Gatsby to assume the blame for killing Myrtle Wilson, a deception which leads to Gatsby's being murdered.

3. Daisy's deception suggests just how much she too has become corrupted by the same distorted values which Gatsby had so fully inculcated and which had finally destroyed him, that is, the pursuit of money and status at the expense of love, individual responsibility, and honesty.

4. Daisy, like Nick, has accepted a different set of expectations for women, as evidenced by her telling Nick that she hopes her daughter will be "a beautiful little fool" because "that's the best thing a girl can be in this world."

5. Nick's and Daisy's need for order and their valuing of male honesty have affected their response to Gatsby and their own evolutions as characters.

6. Deception in the novel not only is an outgrowth of social values and expectation, but that acts of deception, as in Daisy's case, perpetuate those same values and expectations which initially had victimized her.

Central to this approach to the novel are its more conventional thematic and formal concerns, such as Fitzgerald's vision of the American Dream, the meaning of the green light at the end of Daisy's dock, and the function of the image of Dr. Eckleburg overlooking the wasteland of ashes. But the difference between a regular literature course and this one is that the focus on deception makes it necessary, rather than merely optional, that the students think about the ways in which social expectations affect morality and whether, in the light of such expectations, an individual actually has free will. Additionally, these questions lead to a consideration of the nature of individual responsibility in general and American values in particular. A similar approach would be taken toward the other books in the course with an integration of thematic and formal concerns.

Courses might be structured around a variety of other topics which lend themselves to a consideration of ethical questions. For instance, during the past several years I have organized courses around the themes of blackness, masculinity, madness, absurdity, and the American Dream. Such topics as alienation, responsibility, fate versus free will, and good versus evil might be equally effective.

Richard Hunt's course on Nazism, "Moral Dilemmas in a Repressive Society," is an example of a history course organized around an ethical topic.[7] As Hunt explains in the syllabus, the course "explores significant 'moral dilemmas' confronting ordinary people living in a particular place during a specific time of recent history," Germany from 1918 to 1945. Drawing from historical texts, primary sources, literature, and film, Hunt uses a case-study method to examine such dilemmas as "who obeys and who resists and why"; "the 'sincerity' of belief in a New Nazi ideology and ethic"; and "war crimes, German and Allied bombing, and the Nuremberg judgments." He attempts to give his students the "perspectives of those actually living and suffering through the events of harsh history." In addition, Hunt uses the case studies "to illuminate the complexities of ethical decision making and the nature of morality, responsibility, and guilt."

John Weiss currently is developing a history course with the topic "Resistance and Collaboration, and Retribution in World War II."[8] As Weiss explains it, the course will combine an analytical approach with an ethical one. Thus, the students first will read Arthur Morse's *While Six Million Died* as preparation for an analytical examination of American foreign policy during those years. They will consider such factors as the political calculations behind American policy decisions and the training of American diplomats and others who made those decisions. Then, the class will turn to Philip Hallie's *Lest Innocent Blood Be Shed* as background for discussions of the moral issues involved in the choice either to resist or to collaborate. For instance, Weiss and his students will consider the moral implications of the choice of nonviolence.

Another model, which would be appropriate for a history course, an interdisciplinary humanities course, or a literature course, revolves around the relationship of literature to historical events and philosophical trends. For instance, I have twice taught a course centered around Ralph Ellison's *Invisible Man*. To begin with, we focused on how that novel explores the alternatives available to blacks throughout American history. As background, we read some of Frederick Douglass's speeches, Booker T. Washington's *Up From Slavery*, and Du Bois's reply to Washington. We examined the black nationalism movement, particularly as embodied by Marcus Garvey. We considered the place of blacks in the American Communist Party, both through historical texts and as presented in Richard Wright's *Native Son*. Then, because Ellison was writing out of an existential framework, we read Sartre. Because Freud was an important influence, some students read *Totem and Taboo*. By the end of the term, the students had confronted not only the novel in all its richness, but also the ethical choices

---

[7]Richard Hunt has offered this course several times in the Department of History, Harvard University.

[8]John Weiss offered this course at Cornell University in the Spring of 1980.

necessitated by the interplay between social and individual values. They had thought about the nature of individual freedom and individual responsibility, about the need for meaning, and about the problems of deception and self-deception.

Weiss's course, "Documenting the Depression: Literature, Film, and Memory," even more directly examines the relationship between art and history.[9] Although the documentaries are used as background material for a consideration of the depression itself, including the ethical dilemmas it occasioned, eventually the class focuses as well on the ethical problems inherent in documentaries themselves. For instance, they consider what Weiss calls the predatory nature of documentaries and discuss the conflicts between what may be the filmmaker's commitment to truth on the one hand and the exploitation of the documentary's subject on the other.

A final model is that of a course structured around a topic not directly related to ethics. Here, the material is dealt with in the terms it sets up, but with a particular eye to the ethical questions it occasions. For example, my seminar on Faulkner is infused with a consideration of the influence of cultural values (particularly as they relate to race and class) on individual action. This focus inevitably leads once again to the concomitant question of the nature of individual freedom and individual responsibility. A discussion of *Go Down, Moses,* then, requires that the class look at the ethical question the novel raises about its major character, Ike McCaslin, i.e., is it enough to repudiate a corrupt social system, as Ike does when he rejects his inheritance because it is tainted by slavery and incest, or is his repudiation merely an abdication of responsibility which, in the end, perpetuates the system?

NATIONAL EFFORTS NEEDED

There still remains the problem of convincing faculty and administrations that such an approach to undergraduate education is a valid and academically creditable one. Unless this happens, even those who wish to incorporate a focus on ethics may well avoid doing so because of a fear that any veering away from the more conventional pursuits of their disciplines might be a form of career suicide. Although foundations currently are supporting a number of ethics projects and programs, this funding is soft. Workshops and papers at professional meetings are positive efforts in that they provide the opportunity for faculty members with similar interests and goals to meet and to share ideas; but these generally reach a limited audience.

In the end, then, the effort must be made nationally. For this reason, a number of recent developments are encouraging. For example, whatever its spe-

---

[9]Weiss has taught this course at Cornell.

cific merits, Harvard's decision to require core courses has sparked reevaluation of curriculum on the part of scores of institutions. Educators once again are attempting to define the necessary and important ingredients of a general education. In the last year as well, two national commissions on the humanities— one funded by the National Endowment for the Humanities, and the other by the Rockefeller Foundation—have been set into motion; each is likely to address the question of the place of ethics and values in the undergraduate curriculum. Several foundations also have just joined together to fund the new American Association for the Advancement of the Humanities, a group which has as one of its goals the seeking of "fresh ways to explore and understand human existence."[10] The new Institute for Educational Affairs is a coalition of educators and business people which hopes to "restore to the traditional humanities their proper role as the source for moral reflection and education."[11] And recently, the Association of American Colleges, with a membership of 640 colleges and universities, announced a project the intent of which is to revitalize liberal education. As AAC president Mark H. Curtis argues, "Educators must stop emphasizing specialization and majors . . .and provide liberal learning that makes students 'responsible creatures in the wider world.'"[12]

In an "introduction to fiction" course I taught a year ago, my students were struggling to understand Graham Greene's novel, *Brighton Rock*. Because Greene's Catholic perspective, which is predicated on a belief in absolute good and evil, ran counter to the other modern literature we had read during the term, the students were confused by Greene's attack on relative social values of right and wrong. In an effort to focus the discussion, I asked them to try to explain, in the simplest terms, what the novel was essentially about. After a long silence, one of the better students in the class volunteered, "It's about values." Before I could ask her to elaborate, she then admitted, "I only know that because you're teaching the book." Initially, I was concerned that what I had been interpreting throughout the semester as an increased interest on the part of the students in ethical questions was after all only a new student canniness about "providing the professor with what she wants." But if what we as teachers do want is reflectiveness about ethical issues, then perhaps my student's response was in itself a promising beginning.

[10]Summary of a meeting of the Institute for Educational Affairs.

[11]Malcolm G. Scully, "Organization to Advance Humanities Sets up Shop," *Chronicle of Higher Education* 7 (1979), p. 7.

[12]Noreen McGrath, "Major Effort to Revitalize Liberal Education is Launched by Association of Colleges," *Chronicle of Higher Education* 15 (1979), p. 15.

CHAPTER 9

Professional Ethics: Setting, Terrain, and Teacher

WILLIAM F. MAY

Traditionally, when the professional hung out his shingle and declared himself ready to take clients, he professed or avowed a technical competence based on a tradition of learning; and, further, he declared himself to be morally accountable for this expertise, and ready in some measure to place it at the service of human need. The professional, to be sure, accepted pay for his work, but presumably he did not, in the fashion of other knowledge merchants—the magician or the wizard—use his knowledge primarily to acquire personal power, or to exhibit virtuosity. He joined knowledge and competence with moral substance, the power of knowledge with some measure of philanthropy. So goes the ideal.

After a period of rapid growth in knowledge, power, wealth, and institutional influence, the professions currently face difficulties. Many of them are oversupplied with personnel;[1] lay people have contested their authority, public scandal has shaken assumptions about rectitude in professional life; their power and wealth are often resented; their services are unevenly distributed; their guilds have shown an inability to keep their own houses in order; increasingly, they are held responsible for the failures and defects of those huge institutions which they serve, advise, and oftentimes control; and even their successes, their very considerable technical successes, have generated moral quandaries which professional training does not address.

---

[1] A 1963 issue of *Daedalus*, devoted to the professions, euphorically projected a limitless demand for professionals that could not possibly be met in this century. Within twelve years, all professions with the exception of medicine had experienced some oversupply.

WILLIAM F. MAY ● Kennedy Institute of Ethics, Georgetown University, Washington, D.C.

A response to these problems has to occur at a broader and deeper level than the introduction of mere course work in professional ethics. But one aspect of that response includes the question of university teaching in the field. This essay deals with that limited but important issue.

Since other essays in this project cover particular professions or specific moral issues facing their practitioners, I will forgo the attempt in this more general effort to report individually on the professions, and will propose rather a way of looking more comprehensively at the terrain. That requires sketching out a grid of concerns that ought to appear in all course work in the field, irrespective of the profession. It also requires some reflection on the vocation of the teacher who opens up the field for professionals and lay people alike. But, prior to a discussion of terrain and teacher, professional ethics must be located in its wider university setting. The twentieth-century university has responded handsomely to the challenge of providing the professional with technical training, but only marginally or not at all to questions of his or her moral sophistication. In the first part of this essay, I will have to show why this is the case, and why it must be otherwise if the university is to be faithful to its mission.

SETTING

If the professions are troubled in our times, then the university must bear some measure of responsibility for this state of affairs. The ethos of the professions has been largely shaped by the moral environment in our institutions of higher learning. This was not always the case. Earlier in Western history, the Church and the apprenticeship system successively sponsored or trained professionals, and imparted to them whatever moral substance they acquired. At the turn of the twentieth century in the United States, only about 30–35% of the Protestant clergymen, 10–12% of the physicians, and 15–20% of the lawyers had a college education. Thereafter, increasingly, the professions and the universities came to depend on another, with substantial consequences for the moral vision in which each operates.

The professions looked to the university chiefly because of its capacity to make good on one of the professional's two public claims about himself—his avowal of technical competence based on traditions of learning. They did not particularly expect from the university reflection on the moral issues young professionals would face, and certainly not on the moral problems that university training itself would create. The professional's extended university education had the indubitable result of raising standards of technical performance, but it also had the further effects of limiting the number of people who went into a profession, of creating a *de facto* monopoly for those who possessed university credentials, and of imparting to a profession as a whole the general prestige and rewards that regularized association with the university might bestow. For a mix of reasons, then, a lengthy university training program came to govern entrance not only into the traditional so-called learned professions, but also into the newer professions, such as engineering, accounting, and social work, and many others less obviously dependent upon a tradition of learning.

During the period of expanding professional education the university, for its own part, was not disposed to offer the professions more than they asked for. By its own dominant self-interpretation, it largely disclaimed moral reflection and nurture as part of its mission. At first glance, the university seemed to be engaged in a contradictory self-interpretation. When it sought to justify itself to the *outside* world (taxpayers, parents, donors, and employers), it made a somewhat utilitarian appeal to its capacity to produce professionals—skilled people who could provide the expertise that a society wants and needs. *Interior* to its own life, however, the university generated disciplines that deemed it their special vocation and glory to remain aloof from questions of value and utility in their disinterested pursuit of the truth. Since value judgments reflected only subjective and emotive preference, they had no place in the classroom. The university could offer objective information and analysis, that might be useful (or inconvenient, as the case may be) to those who for their own subjective reasons had chosen particular ends; but it could not itself criticize those ends, without descending into subjective propaganda and advocacy. Thus, the university became the institutional matrix that shaped the professions and their ethics at approximately the same time that many faculty members began to exclude questions of values from the university's domain.

The contradiction was only apparent between an interior commitment to objectivity and an external justification that was highly instrumental. Objectivism, instrumentalism, and careerism go together. Since the university did not offer an arena in which reasoned discourse, debate, and discriminative judgments could be made on the subject of ends or values without deteriorating into propaganda or advocacy, the information it offered was up for grabs to the highest bidder. Who was to say otherwise? Ends are only a matter of subjective preference. Since ends have no objective, public status, who is to deny the entrepreneurial claim that knowledge itself is not a public trust, but a private property to be sold for personal advantage? Professional skills, finely honed in the descriptive disciplines of the university, end up for hire. The vast resources and talents of the professions—from the academy through medicine, law, accounting and engineering—are largely at the disposition of the powerful. The moral substance of the professions gets obscured, and the professional occasion reduced to a commercial transaction.

It cannot be fairly claimed that the university ever conformed completely to this picture. Yet there was enough truth to it to make the subject of professional ethics a marginal enterprise. Many faculty members and administrators still express doubts about adding professional ethics to the curriculum. They argue that the subject lacks objective rigor; the curriculum is overcrowded; competent teachers are unavailable; and money is in short supply. Whether directly or indirectly, these objections reflect a sense of priorities. The primary business of the university is the development of technical competence, not moral reflection on those ends which that competence may serve.

Clearly, the subject of professional ethics will not take deep root in the curriculum if course work in the field is a grudging, marginal response to external pressure, or to current societal concerns. Only if faculty members and administrators see a more interior connection between moral reflection and the university's central mission will a path be found through the secondary issues: finding a place for professional ethics in an already overcrowded curriculum, and allocating the funds to make sure that it is taught, and taught effectively, by competent teachers. To do this, the university needs to recover and strengthen three aspects of its basic vocation. This recovery is possible because all three activities have had their continuing, though muted, life in the university, even during its burgeoning positivist years.

The university needs first to strengthen its sense of vocation in the training and cultivation of critical intelligence. Following World War II, the university in this country accepted as its chief responsibility the training of operational or technical intelligence. In the late 1960s, the counter-culture movement reacted against this, and opted in part for an anti-intellectualism that pressed for the affective component in learning. But during both periods there was too limited a notion of the work of the intelligence. The word "critical" has its roots in the Greek verb meaning to judge or decide. Accordingly, the task of criticism in the intellectual life includes making judgments as to worth and value in the spheres of politics, art, economics, religion, philosophy, and morals. Operational intelligence tells one how to get from here to there; critical intelligence raises questions as to whether the there is worth getting to. It asks what recently and incessantly has been called the question of values. The work of the intellect includes the task of normative as well as descriptive inquiry. This is precisely the activity of the intellect called for in professional life, but deemed by many professionals in the academic world to be merely subjective and emotive, and therefore an inappropriate intrusion in the classroom.

Critical inquiry belongs particularly, but not exclusively, to the mission of the humanities in the university. The subject matter of these disciplines is the creative works of humankind. They should be engaged in a twofold task: one, the work of understanding, a task which they share with the sciences; two, the equally disciplined work of interpretation and criticism. The latter evaluative work is not merely subjective in the sense of arbitrary. It is controlled by its object of inquiry—the creative works of humankind; it generates its own literature, community of inquirers, and standards of excellence. By the same token, the social sciences, insofar as they do not increasingly define themselves by their method, but by their subject matter—the social constructs of humankind—

should include not only descriptivists, but also those engaged in normative inquiry on policy issues. Finally, the professional schools should include not only their appropriate specialists on the recognized subdivisions of the legal and medical traditions, but also be open to the work of philosophers, theologians, ethicists, and those of their own practitioners who reflect on the substantive moral and policy issues which the professions raise.

Unfortunately, the humanities have tended to abdicate their ancient vocation, and to interpret themselves in the reflected light of scientific inquiry; the prestige of scholarship gets invested in descriptive work alone. Insofar as this has pervaded the university, it threatens the professions with moral impoverishment as they turn out technicians incapable of, or hostile to, critical thinking, and it diminishes the university itself in its intellectual life. The university is precisely the site where critical inquiry ought to occur, posing alternative goals for the society at large and the professions in particular. We concede too little to the range of the human mind, and grant too little to the capacity of the university to organize itself for civil and fruitful discourse, if we assume that the only alternative to objective inquiry is subjective advocacy. Critical inquiry is not only licit, but required, in the institution devoted to the cultivation of the whole of the human mind.

Second, the university has an ancient, related, and continuing responsibility for the cultivation of the civic self. The liberal arts college of the nineteenth and the early twentieth century tended to define its responsibility as the cultivation of the well-rounded person (to which end it imposed upon its students distribution requirements for the broadening of horizons). Subsequently, the twentieth-century university accepted as its ideal the training of the technically proficient person (to which end it stocked candidates for advanced degrees with esoteric knowledge, which each then proceeded to treat as a private acquisition, to be sold as needed and prized on the open market). Neither of these goals of education—the well-rounded, and the skilled person—should be disdained. But the quality-of-life and the careerist arguments, taken together, are still too narcissistic to be the sufficient aim of education. The university must recover its own early heritage, dating back to the Greeks, that accepted as part of its most comprehensive purpose the cultivation of the civic self.[2]

In the United States we have democratized education, but, at the same time, to our own disadvantage as a people, we have also privatized it, and justified it for what it can do in enlarging private opportunities. All of this is salutary in its own way, but extraordinarily fragile. Private opportunity, in the long run, flourishes only in the context of healthy institutions, and healthy institutions

---

[2]The privilege of civic education among the Greeks was, of course, much restricted: slaves and women were excluded, because they had only a private identity in domestic economy. Free men alone received an education; only those who were free from the quotidian burdens of earning a living could study the liberal arts. But in their freedom and in the house of leisure (the *scholē*) they prepared to take their place in the *polis* as citizens.

depend upon selves with some sense of public identity and responsibility. When the social covenant is weak and the professional thinks of himself as an entrepreneur alone, uninvested with a public trust, then our institutions suffer, and people get hurt when their institutions hurt. Both by its ancient traditions and by the terms of its modern social support, the university can ill afford to deny its public function and the civic destiny of its trained professionals.

This point would be trivialized if it were reduced simply to tacking onto the university curriculum courses in ethics and civics. Cultivation of the citizen requires a more fundamental change in the university, one that connects its life throughout to critical inquiry. Ultimately, the nurturing of the civic self and the encouragement of critical inquiry are part of one and the same enterprise, if value questions are not merely matters of private, subjective preference. To engage in critical inquiry is itself a social act, that teases the mind out of the bottle of private preference and opens it toward a community of inquirers. It makes a person publicly accountable and responsible for his judgments and decisions, and assumes these judgments and decisions to be interpretable in civil discourse. The classroom is a public place; the library, a commonwealth of learning; critical inquiry among peers, a kind of parliament of the human mind. Such inquiry is indispensable to a professional life that has more to offer than technical services for private gain.

Finally, the location of professional training within the university should not only nurture the professional as critic and citizen, but also cultivate him or her as teacher. The professional needs to be more than a dispenser of technical services; he must accept his role with his clients and patients as instructor. To the degree that the physician accepts his patient as partner or collaborator in the pursuit of health, he must perceive the truth as an important ingredient in that partnership. Generally, however, professionals underestimate the therapeutic value of teaching. The quarrel on this issue in medicine is very old. The "rough empirics" in classical Greece (who were familiar with treatments but not with the scientific reasons for their success) used to ridicule the more scientifically oriented physicians who sought to teach their patients. The empirics argued: patients don't want to become doctors, they want to be cured!

Yet the physician must function as teacher, if he would enlist his patients more actively in their own health maintenance. Words are to drugs what a preamble is to a constitution, argued P. Laine Entralgo, the distinguished Spanish historian of medicine. They help to interpret what is going on in the whole process. Teaching helps to heal the patient, to "make whole" the distracted and distressed subject. Other professions have a similar teaching obligation. The nurse and the social worker must engage in teaching their patients and clients, if they would do their work well. The lawyer has technical services to offer in drawing up contracts and appearing before the bar, but he must also teach his clients. Counseling is the functional equivalent of preventive medicine in the practice of the law. The very title, "rabbi," means teacher. In some Protestant denominations, the minister is defined as the teaching elder. Politicians, public administrators, and professional managers in corporations also find themselves teaching, if they would lead by persuasion.

If the professional must be a good teacher, then one needs to rethink the liberal-arts component in both undergraduate and professional education that cultivates the fundamental qualities of the teacher—a capacity for critical inquiry, a direct grasp of one's subject and a desire to share it, with verbal facility and sensitivity to one's audience. Theoretically, at least, requiring a liberal-arts background for professionals, and locating professional education in the university, should produce professionals who are more pedagogically skilled than the "rough empirics" of whom Plato complained. Unfortunately, however, academicians have assumed that only *some* of their graduates become teachers; the rest do not. Therefore, they have treated teaching as a segregated profession. Teaching is, of course, a special profession, but, at the same time, it ought to be the aim and purpose of a liberal arts education to turn out good teachers, whether students go into the teaching profession or not. The nonacademic professionals must teach, even as they dispense esoteric services. How else will they be bearers and transmitters of their cultural heritage and fit practitioners, and interpreters of their actions as professionals?

These several aims of a university converge in justifying professional ethics as a discipline. The uses to which the trained professional puts his knowledge are not merely a matter of emotional preference, they are themselves subject to that branch of knowledge which is the discipline of criticism; his professional judgments are not merely a matter of private predilection, they call for a public accounting, they are the choices of a citizen. Finally, reflection on these matters in the interdisciplinary ambience of professional ethics reminds the specialized professional that he does not preside over a hoard of mystifying knowledge, but must, in some degree, teach it and interpret it—to be effective through it and accountable for it.

THE TERRAIN

A preliminary look at the terrain actually covered in courses in professional ethics suggests that they often concentrate on what might be called quandaries in practice, especially those faced by the individual practitioner. This concentration has occured for understandable reasons. The great prestige of the case method of study in law and business schools, and the clinical method of training in medical school, tends to make practitioners divide the moral life into cases. The man in the street has also been—at least in part—quandary-oriented. The dramatic success (and potential dangers) of modern technology have lifted its dilemmas, especially those of medical technology, into the headlines, and attracted the attention of lay people and experts in ethics alike. Philosophers and theologians have responded with elegant work on the subjects of nuclear reactors, organ transplants, recombinant DNA research, technology assessment, and a host of other discrete but sensational problem areas. The cumulative result reinforces the view that ethics is chiefly a question of examining isolable issues, quandaries, and cases.[3]

In the following sketch of the terrain, I suggest that the teaching of professional ethics needs to go beyond individual quandaries and problems. It should also include institutional and structural criticism, the clarification of professional character and virtue, and the enforcement of professional standards and discipline. But, at the outset, attention must be paid to the kinds of moral questions that case study legitimately raises, and to the limitations of the method when used as the sole approach to teaching professional ethics.

QUANDARIES IN PRACTICE

In sorting out the moral questions he or she faces in a given case, the professional needs to ask at least five questions. Not all questions are germane to each case, but asking them sometimes helps to surface hidden problems.

1. *What is going on in the case?*   This question respects the link between the moral and the factual. The attempt to remake the world in the light of the prescribed requires knowing with some acuity the world of the described. Questions of fact are relevant to the moral disposition of a case.

The morally relevant facts, however, may include much more than the professional is accustomed to considering. In presenting a case for ethical review, a physician once reported in candor that his records were up-to-date on the technical, medical aspects of the case, but somewhat sketchy, after the first interview, on the patients's personal and social history—matters relevant to a wise decision. He observed wryly that a personal history usually gets updated only when a patient transfers to a new doctor. In retrospect, he conceded that a physician's failure to keep up this aspect of the patient's records affects his ability to make the best decision. Other professionals are similarly selective in extracting morally relevant information from a total factual complex. Engineers and professional managers have, until recently, attended only to "internal," as opposed to "external," costs, in assessing the value of a given industrial technology. Consequently, the total impact of a technology on air, water, and neighborhood simply did not appear as morally significant data. The anthropologist keeps voluminous notes on a host population in the course of field research, but tends to neglect those important alterations in his own personality, under the impact of the experience, that may be morally relevant to his decisions as a

<hr/>

[3]For a discussion and criticism of ethics devoted to dilemmas, see Edmund Pincoffs, "Quandary Ethics," *Mind,* 80 (1971) p. 552; and Stanley Hauerwas, *Vision and Virtue* (South Bend Ind.: University of Notre Dame Press, 1974).

participant observer. On the whole, a professional tends to emphasize those aspects of a case that his own technical skills allow to surface. A willingness to face neglected facts may be at least as important as any further step in attacking a moral problem. The apparently prosaic question—what is going on in a case—links up with the more conspicuously moral questions to follow.

2. *By what criteria should decisions be made?* This question poses the issue of rules, standards, principles, or reasons for acting in the attempt to resolve a quandary. A moral dilemma emerges in the first place because the practitioner senses some conflict between opposing goods (or matching harms) that cannot both be realized (or avoided) by a given course of action. He faces the tensions of life versus quality of life, client confidentiality versus the protection of others, the duty to publish versus the national interest, the promotion of the general welfare versus the rights of human beings made "subjects" in experimentation.

If the practitioner does not attempt to resolve the dilemma by shutting his eyes and leaping, or if the law has not already prescribed how he must act, he usually has recourse to one of three sources for moral criteria: the professional, the religious, and the philosophical. These overlap in their own complicated ways, and may figure, in varying degrees, in courses in professional ethics.

The professional source of criteria includes both the formal codes of the profession, and those informal patterns of behavior that get transmitted from generation to generation in a clinical or a practical setting. The physician's obligation to "do no harm," the lawyer's commitment to zeal for the client, the journalist's duty to protect his or her sources, and the accountant's duty to give a truthful presentation of a client's assets and liabilities are all instances of moral principles inscribed in the codes and reinforced in practice. But the formal codes have their defects as an exclusive source of criteria. Their rules sometimes conflict, thus generating their own quandaries. They occasionally collide with the laws that govern the society at large, thus requiring some principles of mediation between the two; and they are excessively self-protective of guild members at the expense of others, thus requiring criticism on the basis of moral principles lying outside the codes. Finally, most official statements, with the exception of the lawyer's *Code of Professional Responsibility,* lack a means for the development of a definitive body of case interpretation to help specify the scope and limits of a given rule. Lacking this, the codes become guidelines without lines to guide; they offer the client and the public too little protection, and leave unilluminated many of the quandaries and temptations that practitioners face.

Doubtless, those standards of performance informally transmitted in a clinical setting are the most important source of criteria for decision making. They have several advantages over written codes. At their best, they point professionals toward standards that exceed general minimums, while adapting principles to the complexities of individual cases. They particularly emphasize the moral importance of technical competence, and they back moral dicta with the force of example. But clinical ethics has its corresponding disadvantages as a sole source of criteria. It tends to emphasize technical competence at the expense of other values; and it fails to provide independent principles for the criticizing of peer leaders whose behavior may be less than exemplary. Ethics cannot be reduced to ethos; morals, to prevailing mores.

At first glance, it would not appear that religious traditions are a factor in professional decision making except in isolated issues (e.g., abortion). In the main, professional standands are confessionally indeterminate. The Hippocratic Oath has a religious root in ancient culture, but the pluralization of Western religious traditions created pressure on the modern professions to develop language about standards detached from religious source. One expects an accountant or an engineer to behave according to common norms, and not as a Presbyterian or a Reformed Jewish variant thereof. Even when moral principles tap the religious tradition (respect for life and personal liberty, passion for social justice, and loyalty to the client), philosophers and theologians alike often defend their ideals today in largely secular language.

A narrow look at professional standards, however, overlooks the broader impact of religion on practitioners and their ethics. Religious tradition is less likely to furnish a unique position on a given quandary than to provide a total vision in the context of which the quandary is resolved, or, if not resolved, borne. Quandaries in the law, for example, can pose the question whether the ideal of order or justice is the chief good that a legal system must serve. Liberals answer so automatically in favor of justice that they overlook the religious origin of this commitment in the Western notion of a righteous God. But an alternative religious conviction (that of the ancient Babylonians) would tend, in the way of the modern conservative, to link the law with the value of order, rather than justice. The horror of anarchy here takes precedence over injustice as the great evil from which a legal system protects us. Thus, a religious vision, in each case, provides a theoretical framework that may not differ greatly from a secular perspective in its resolution of a particular quandary. In some instances, a religious outlook may not agree with one party to a debate, but rather provide a somewhat more tragic perspective in which the conflict between two alternatives is not resolved, but suffered (Luther called it sinning bravely, politicians call it compromise); or it might provide a comic perspective (in the technical medieval sense of comedy) that relativizes the tensions of an imperfect world from the vantage point of transcendent good.[4] Whoever said that the moral life was easy?

The philosophical tradition is a third source of criteria in decision making. It has its reciprocal influences on the other sources, but, in one respect, it differs

---

[4]Other impacts of religious conviction on professional ethics have less to do with the decisions of the individual practitioner than with the cultivation of professional character, virtue, and style, and with the criticism of institutions and structures. For further discussion of the relationship of vision to decision, see the final section of this essay, on the teacher of applied ethics.

formally from them both. Professional and religious groups tend to invoke the particularities of a communal tradition, whereas philosophers, in the main, have sought to forge principles that recommend themselves irrespective of particular social groups and their formative experiences. Still, the philosophical literature itself constitutes a varied social tradition, and teachers of professional ethics make a somewhat selective use of it. Today, they tend to rely less on the classical moralists, Greek and Christian, who concentrated on the moral virtues, or on the recent philosophers on the Continent, who oppose prevailing structures. They emphasize, instead, a utilitarianism that orients ethics toward the production of the good, largely through cost/benefit analysis, or the formalistic ethics of Immanuel Kant, who appeals to those categorical principles of right and wrong (honesty, promise keeping and respect for persons) that should govern action irrespective of the goods and harms produced. Finally, current teachers of ethics for public policymakers acquaint practitioners with current debates between Nozick and Rawls on questions centering in the just distribution of goods and resources.

The professional decision maker looks to philosophy for a release from quandaries, but discovers often enough that the philosophical tradition keeps him in a bind. On the one hand, the practitioner needs a principle of beneficence—a principle and method for orienting action to future good, and avoiding future harm. On the other hand, the practitioner recognizes, uneasily, the force of moral principles that constrain action whether or not they can be justified on the basis of a cost/benefit analysis. Principles that oblige him to tell the truth, to respect other persons, and to distribute goods fairly have a kind of categorical force, irrespective of their vindication by an assessment of consequences.

Philosophy sometimes heightens quandaries, rather than releasing the practitioner from them. But not always; and even when philosophy has this effect, it is not without practical value in debates over values. Philosophical inquiry may help, even when it does not solve problems, to clarify responses, to subject them to critical scrutiny, to suggest others, and to allow all parties to a dispute to enter into the arena of public discussion, explanation, and debate. More subtly, it may, like theology, serve to place the problem itself in a new horizon. The alternative decisions may remain the same, but the horizon in which they are perceived alters the final meaning of a decision.

3. *Who should decide?* Around this question cluster the moral dilemmas of authority. These dilemmas are ticklish for the helping professions, even when the competence of the client is not in question. The client by definition needs services. He feels uneasy in his dependency. Suspicion of the overbearing professional dates all the way back to the Greeks. Plato wrote, "But the lawyer is always in a hurry; there is the water of the clepsydra driving him on." In Moliere's plays doctors are abusive; their procedures are invasive. Officious nurses and social workers appear regularly for criticism in popular literature.

Clients surrender to the professional, but feel uneasy about this surrender. This uneasiness lies in the background of the "consent issue." In medicine, the problem of consent emerges in a number of contexts: the right to refuse treatment, consent to high-risk therapy, abortion, the living will, telling the truth, and genetic screening and counselling. It emerges even more acutely in cases of behavior modification and control, especially when the patients in question— the young, the emotional disturbed, and the retarded—are incapable of giving consent, and the treatment may include incarceration or mind-altering drugs. The very setting in which the professional delivers services—the hospital, law office, court room, or social-service agency—tends to reinforce the layman's sense of inexpertness and powerlessness. He is on someone else's turf. It seems his duty to comply with what goes on there.

On the whole, the philosophical justification for informed consent usually gets stated on Kantian grounds. Irrespective of good intentions about outcome, professionals owe to their clients or their guardians an informed and uncoerced choice. They should not override rational and self-determining creatures. Utilitarian considerations may also enter into the argument secondarily. Informed consent, in this case, gets justified on the basis of the good it will produce. Thus, one may argue that informed consent helps generate the active collaboration of a client that is important to a successful outcome, and the favorable public reputation upon which a profession in the long run depends.

The issue of consent gets complicated when professional work affects large groups or third parties who are not the direct targets of the action or intervention. Engineers, professional managers, public policymakers, journalists, and researchers in the sciences and social sciences have impacts on more remote, but affected and diverse, constituencies. The use of consent forms in these cases hardly suffices. Consent requires more complicated negotiations with affected persons, or recourse to the courts or the political process. Professionals skeptical about consent procedures usually emphasize the inherent difficulties of informing affected persons (the technical nature of the knowledge; only professionals can handle it), or the likely adverse consequences of placing that knowledge in the hands of lay people (they will panic, or simply fail to approve the procedure).

In an increasingly litigious and rights-conscious society, the lawyer has a special role on consent issues. He becomes the special guardian of the rights of all clients in the hands of professionals. Professional power has increased today in scope, and questions about its legitimacy have proceeded apace. When authority gets laicized without social consensus over its speed and limits, then inevitably disputes end up in the hands of lawyers and the courts—from the rights of high school students to the criminally insane. There is a special irony in the lawyer's role as champion of clients against overbearing professionals, because lawyers themselves are not noted for their readiness to grant to their own clients much say in how they will conduct a case. A law school professor readily admitted that most criminal lawyers are willing to listen to their clients on only two issues of strategy: whether they will plead guilty, and whether they will take the stand in their own defense. Otherwise, lawyers tend to advise: leave the driving to us.

In the background of consent issues are rival concepts of the professional relationship—one paternalistic, in which the professional acts on behalf of the client as passive beneficiary; and the opposite, wholly instrumental, in which the client uses the professional as a hired gun. Well within those extreme limits, differences still surface between advocates of informed consent. In the more paternalistic version, the client consents, but the initiative clearly rests with the professional: Be it unto me according to thy word. In the second, the client engages in an active collaborative partnership with the professional in the pursuit of commonly defined aims.

Quandaries over "who decides" surface not only between professionals and clients, but also between professionals. The issue is particularly complex when the delivery of services requires team work among colleagues from different professions, or when professionals are hierarchically organized. The collegial strains against the bureaucratic. This topic, of course, extends beyond quandaries faced by the individual decision maker, and will have to be broached again in the discussion of institutions and structures.

4. For whose benefit does the professional act? Answers to the question of beneficiary spread across a spectrum from those professions that seem to announce their unconditional fidelity to the cause of a client (nursing, medicine, priesthood, counseling, and law) to those whose clients are often communities (social work, teaching) or institutions (law, accounting, engineering, architects, consultants), to those professionals who do not, strictly speaking, seem to have a client, but who work for institutions (some of the foregoing practitioners, but also, especially, professional managers and policy-makers).

The question of conflicting loyalties besets all professions across the spectrum, especially inasmuch as the professional who announces loyalty to the client may also work for an institution with its own purposes. In a case appropriately dubbed "The Psychiatrist as Double Agent,"[5] Willard Gaylin and Daniel Callahan commented on a practitioner on appointment at a medical school whose diagnosis (latent schizophrenia) of a student on medical leave led to an eventual refusal of readmission. What does a psychiatrist owe to his patient by way of confidentiality? What does he own to the institution that employs him, and to patients whom this physician-to-be might treat?

The problem of double agentry, of course, confronts the physician in many other situations: Whom does he serve when experimenting on human subjects—the patient, or medical progress? When screening and counselling in genetics—the needs and desires of the family, or some vision he has of the genetic future of the human race? When committing the disturbed—the patient,

---

[5] *Hastings Center Report* 8:2 (April 1978), pp. 1–23.

or the convenience of the family? When drugging the hyperactive child—the child, or the manager of a large school system? When delivering health care at a teaching hospital—the patient as the object of therapy, or the medical students whom the patients serves as teaching material?

The lawyer faces an analogous problem in double agentry. Just as the research physician is tempted to use his patients experimentally in ways that, as a pure therapist, he would not, so the cause-oriented lawyer may be tempted to develop a high-risk argument on behalf of a client, not because it serves best the client's interests, but because the argument may yield for the lawyer and his cause a landmark decision. Mindful of this temptation, the *Code of Professional Responsibility* prohibits the lawyer from being "more concerned with the establishment or extension of legal principles than in the immediate protection of the rights of the lawyer's individual client."[6]

The question of conflicting loyalties in medicine and nursing generally gets answered in favor of the patient. Only in exceptional cases does the apparent good (or interest) of the patient conflict with potential harm to others. But absolutely unconditional loyalty to the single client presents problems for the social worker who has competing obligations to other members of a family and to the family group as a whole. The principle of loyalty to the client has to be even more carefully limited for the lawyer and the accountant. Much of their work essentially involves the possibility of injustice to other parties. One has to have a mystical confidence in the outcomes of the adversary system to believe that unconditional loyalty to the client relieves the lawyer of all other obligations to justice.

5. *How should the professional decide and act?*   This final question is partly procedural, and partly a matter of style. A full-scale answer would have to deal with both. Since rules governing procedures (informed consent, deferential among colleagues, and the political process) follow from answers to the earlier question—who ought to decide—remarks in this section will be restricted to the aesthetic (and sometimes religious) question of style. The aesthetics of professional life usually gets lost in the quandary-oriented ethics. Moralists exhaust themselves on whether physicians ought to tell the truth, but spend little time on the not inconsequential question that bothers sensitive practitioners, as to *how* they ought to tell it—directly or indirectly, personally or with a sparing impersonality? As the saying goes, it is not only what you say, but how you say it and when you say it, that makes a difference. The theologian, Karl Barth, once observed that Job's friends were theologically correct but existentially false in their counsel, and therefore, ultimately, theologically incorrect. They chose a miserable time to sing their theological arias on the subject of suffering.

Style is a much deeper issue than how one packages what one has to say. Style is a matter of metaphysical perception, a sense for what the Stoics called

[6]Canon 5E C23.

the fitting, a discretion that is deeper than tact, more sensitive than rule, a feeling for what is congruent with reality. Without discretion the professional does not reckon with the whole of a case. He may tell the truth, but it is not the truth he serves when he tells it. He may be using the truth, to serve his own vanity, or to feed his craving for power, or to indulge himself in the role of nag, police-man, pedant, or judge.

With good reasons moralists have been suspicious of professional guilds that concentrate on questions of style and decorum. Style meant the eighteenth-century doctor with his gold-knobbed cane, the journalist with his note pad, the lawyer with his bulging briefcase, the engineer and the scientist with their laconic control of hard data. Style can be corrupted to mask incompetence, to present a false front to the world and cover one's cynical withdrawal from a client. But, in its uncorrupted state, style is the elegance of technical compe-tence, a fitness of bearing, and a personal attentiveness to all dimensions of a case.

In summary, the study of cases or quandaries has its obvious advantages in teaching professional ethics. It helps the student to recognize some moral issues; it links the specific questions that emerge in practice with abstract theory for the professional-to-be; and it provides a kind of test of rules in the moral life.

But exclusive attention to quandaries and cases has its deficiencies as a total definition of applied ethics. In the hands of the amateur ethicist, case dis-cussion sometimes produces little more than a rap session. It is secretly flattering to an audience that assumes that any and all intellectual resources for responding to an issue can be self-derived. Unfortunately, the professions, except for the law, have been slow to develop a literature and tradition that allows for the interpretation of cases. Sometimes philosophers and theologians, when they define their tasks as technical problem-solving alone, can run aground on the trivial. Exotic cases get studied to confound the moral rules of opponents or to vindicate one's own. So distracted, philosophers and theologians renounce the quest for wisdom, and settle for mere virtuosity. But, even at its best, case-oriented study has its defects as an exclusive method of teaching professional ethics. It tends to be reactive rather than proactive, reflexive rather than antici-patory. It resembles acute care more than preventive medicine. It insufficiently attends to the more enveloping defects of institutional structure; and, except as anticipated in the passing comments about professional style, it barely attends to questions of professional virtue.

INSTITUTIONAL AND STRUCTURAL CRITICISM

In addition to reflection on the discrete quandaries that practitioners face, professional ethics must analyze and criticize the social and economic structures within which the professional increasingly operates. Systems, institutions, and structures shape in advance the horizon in which the professional works, and the problems that surface as cases. Professional ethics fails to cover its subject if it restricts itself to quandaries alone. On these structural matters, the work of political theorists, sociologists, and social ethicists may be especially germane.

At a minimum, structural criticism must reckon with three issues: the distinctive services which each of the professions delivers in the context of larger social purpose; the institutional setting in which they generate what they deliver; and the justice of the delivery system.[7] A serious treatment of the first of these issues—the distinctive aims of a profession in the context of social good—requires a separate essay on each of the professions. Formally and ideally considered, all professions (except the academic) should serve the common good by applying theoretical knowledge to the solution of clients' (or institutions') practical problems. Materially considered, they differ from one another in the specifics of the practical problem addressed, the body of knowledge invoked, and the benefits delivered. (The academic profession differs still further from the rest in that it serves the common good chiefly through the discovery and transmission of knowledge rather than through its application.) More extended treatment of the social aims of seven professions is available in other essays in this project. The second and third issues, however, raise questions that cut across all the professions. As such, they are more manageable subjects for this more general essay.

The Institutional Setting

More and more professionals work for large-scale institutions, public and private, under whose authority they generate professional services. These institutions are of two kinds: those still controlled by the fundamental purposes of a profession (schools, universities, hospitals, law firms, newspapers, and consulting firms), and those that recruit professionals to their service, but whose organizational purposes are not wholly confined by the goals of the profession (most notably, the government, and the business corporation.).

Not only have more and more professionals come to work for large-scale institutions (the institutionalization of professionals), but, increasingly, professionals lead and control these organizations (the professionalization of institutions). Specifically, the task of management in these institutions has been professionalized. Corporations and public-service bureaucracies recruit leaders from a growing company of people who acquire their formal training at the universities in business and management programs. While it cannot be said that, outside a professional-school education, there is no executive job, mere amateur graduates of liberal arts colleges know, in fact, that by other routes few are chosen.

---

[7]Each of these subjects is huge, but the last two, on institutional setting and delivery systems, are more manageable in an essay of this compass. They admit of more generic treatment across professional boundaries. Full justice to the subject of professional purpose would require a separate essay on each of the professions. It can be no more than acknowledged in these pages.

This increasing concentration of professionals in huge and often commercial organizations has had a profound effect on practice. It permits professionals to specialize to a degree not possible before; it affects greatly the areas in which they specialize; and, in some cases, it allows for a stricter monitoring of technical performance. The financial incentives that the large organization offers influence mightily the distribution of professional talent, and complicate the very definition of the client served. Association with powerful institutions has probably increased the professional's influence in the society at large, but, at the same time, it has made him increasingly liable to criticism for the failures and defects of those institutions which he serves, and often controls. In facing these complexities, professionals find themselves equipped either with outmoded codes, which, in the words of a lawyer, were made for "downstate Illinois in the 1860s," or with no codes (in the case of most managers), or with professional societies, which (in the cases of engineering and nursing) exercise little power of sanction against offending institutions.

Some institutional issues that require attention may now be considered.

The Manager as Professional.   Abraham Flexner, whose influential Carnegie report on medical education (1910) gave him near judicial authority in the determination of professional status, denied it to managers—especially to those who managed business institutions. In Flexner's day, managers hardly drew on a tradition of theoretical knowledge available through a university education; they were motivated by cash incentives rather than the ideal of service, and whatever guild associations they established existed for purposes of self-promotion, rather than self-regulation. Measuring them against his checklist of traits, Flexner felt compelled to exclude business people and managers from the professional class.

But Flexner's clearcut line between the commercial and the professional has been somewhat obscured in our time, and from both sides. Professionals have learned how to convert their careers and guild organizations into instruments of commercial advantage and tribal self-protection. Managers, meanwhile, increasingly aspire to meet Flexner's standards. Although they have not established guilds with independent principles and enforcement powers, they increasingly emphasize the importance of a professional-school education, and they describe their enterprise as a "public service." It remains to be seen whether the service ideal will become a weighty component in corporate policy, or fly lightly as a banner in PR strategy;—in any event, professionals and managers seem to differ little from one another in intellectual and moral characteristcs.

The Columbia historian Walter Metzger has sought to distinguish the professional and the manager along different lines—by function, rather than intellectual and moral traits.[8] Both roles entail relationships that are asymmetrical; both exercise some power and authority as superordinates over subordinates: the professional over clients, and the manager over employees. But, in the

[8]W. Metzger, "What is a Profession?" *Seminar Reports,* Program of General and Continuing Education in the Humanities, Vol. 3, No. 1 (New York: Columbia University, 1975)

professional instance, the superordinate acts exclusively on behalf of the welfare of the subordinate; whereas, in the managerial mode, the superordinate exercises authority on behalf of the institution which both he and the subordinate serve. Clearly, the manager must be concerned for the welfare of workers under his or her charge, but the relationship does not exist—at least not primarily—for that purpose. It orients to the well-being of the institutions from which their own welfare mediately derives.

Metzger's view wrongly restricts the term professional to those who have clients. That restriction overlooks those important professions that invoke the ideal of service, and that rely on the competence of their practitioners, but that, strictly speaking, have no clients—the civil, military, and foreign services. Still, Metzger's distinction reminds us of the special problem faced by all professionals at work in an institutional setting. The professional *belongs to* the institution, even when he or she is in a position of top management and control. The institution is hardly subordinate to the professional as superordinate. The modern manager finds it difficult (almost as difficult as the civil servant and the military leader) to maintain a measure of independence, whether psychological or moral, from the institution and its imperatives.

The contrast in the sheer length of case studies in the fields of medicine and business symbolizes the difference between the traditional professional with clients and the manager. Cases in medical ethics are remarkably terse. Doctors usually have their patients dead by page two. In contrast, cases in management ethics are interminable. Some go on for 50 to 75 pages. This difference in length symbolizes an important difference in the moral problems each faces. The physician may have thousands of patients. Sheer numbers allows for, and indeed demands, some distance from each. The physician thus faces some of the moral problems of calloused detachment. But the manager must live, breathe, worry, and aspire, largely within the confines of the single corporation for which he works. It envelops him. It becomes his *de facto* world. This psychological envelopment does not confer upon managers the right to abandon either general moral constraints or the special constraints that they, as a professional class, may see fit to accept for themselves. But it does mean that moral constraints must largely be built into the very structure of the institution and its purposes. This task of moral construction is a central responsibility of management. It cannot depend entirely on the fitful efforts of individual persons.

The Public Purpose of Large-Scale Institutions. Huge institutions are inclined to define themselves exclusively by their stated primary mission (health, education, or the sale of products for a profit). This is acceptable in a specialized society. Anarchy would result if institutions tried to infinitize themselves and do everything. The educational institution must educate well; it cannot, in and of itself, respond to any and all moral and political challenges served up to it on any given day. Still, an institution must accept some further responsibilities to the welfare of its workers, and to the society at large, if it would preserve and strengthen the institutions whose protection it requires to do its primary work securely and well. Milton Friedman's monomania about profits leads to the spectacle of huge corporations claiming to be economic giants, while pretending to be social and political eunuchs. To their own long-range peril, they have done too little to arrest the decay of our cities upon whose health civilized life depends. The moral obligation of the professional and the professional manager includes not only their personal acceptance of the duties of citizenship, but their respect for the public responsibilities of the institutions they serve.

But the hierarchical pattern of corporate organization makes it difficult to develop in managers a sense of public responsibility. The structure itself—quite apart from the pressures of profitmaking—does not encourage the cultivation of public virtue. Most corporate managers are drawn from the lower ranks of the organization, or others like it. Although, as leaders of the corporation, they exercise enormous quasi-public powers, they are not usually well-prepared for this responsibility in the lower ranks of the enterprise. Admittedly, their advancement in the corporation depends not only upon their technical competence in a specialized area, but also on general social skills. They have to get along reasonably well with colleagues, superiors, and subordinates. Those social skills constitute a kind of political art, the ability to act in concert with others; but it is the art of politics shorn of its object, the common good. Only those at the apex of the organization have the right to act on behalf of the organization for the common good, either the common good of the organization or the still wider public good. Public virtue would be an anomaly in a corporate manager below the uppermost levels, and, for that reason, one would not expect to see it suddenly appear in those newly appointed eagles in the enterprise who were not previously trained to it in their formative years.

Tension between the Hierarchical and the Collegial Structures. The natural structure of the large-scale organization is hierarchical; the natural mode of organization among traditional professionals is collegial. Professionals historically have accepted patterns of super- and subordination among themselves only as temporary phases of training and education. The apprentice is subordinate to the master because he or she is not yet fully a professional. In attaining professional status, the apprentice acquires an independent relationship to sources of knowledge, and accumulates sufficient experience to apply this knowledge to specific cases. Thus, a primary mark of the professional is independence. The principle of collegiality expresses this independence within a community of professionals; colleagues act in concert with one another chiefly by persuasion, rather than command.

A hierarchically ordered corporation indulges in leadership by persuasion (teaching), but finally rests upon command, and upon sanctions vested in that command. The professional thus faces, in principle at least, serious potential conflicts between the imperatives of the organization and those derived from the aims and purposes of the profession. As a member of a bureaucracy, he is subordinate; as a professional, sometimes he must be, awkwardly enough, insubordinate. The conflict goes deeper than the occasional overt crisis when the professional must "blow the whistle": the collegial and the bureaucratic type of social organization establish somewhat conflicting notions of duty and modes of social identity, which one and the same person may suffer unresolved. Professional guilds vary greatly in their willingness and power to back members in valid challenges against the institutions for which they work. The American Association of University Professors has investigatory and legal defense funds for the protection of its members, and is willing to apply profession-wide sanctions against offending institutions. Other professions have proved timorous by comparison, leaving the individual professional to brave a conflict alone—which means, but rarely.

Bureaucratic Organization and the Professional Aspiration to Excellence. The large-scale organization has been called a device whereby people can accomplish great things without themselves being great.[9] It permits specialization, and therefore promotes excellence of a technical order. But it usually opts for a somewhat narrow, routinized, and quantifiable standard of excellence; it relies on efficient routines, rather than the heroics or charisma of its staff.

The professions resemble large organizations in their general impact on standards of performance; they fit into the same process of routinization. The very existence of the professions tends to regularize standards—in the selection of candidates for training, educational experience, and norms of performance. These standards, for the most part, spare the laity exposure to erratic and idiosyncratic treatment, whether at the hands of genius or fraud. Ideally, to be sure, professional ethics should press for more than the maintenance of minimal standards. The legal profession has recognized this—at least formally—in its *Code of Professional Responsibility*. It distinguishes between minimal disciplinary rules and maximal ethical considerations.[10] The distinction corresponds roughly to the categories Lon Fuller staked out (in *The Morality of the Law*) between a socalled ethics of duty and an ethics of aspiration. The first is largely minimalist, negative, and legislative in tenor—backed by sanctions. The second is maximalist, positive, and aesthetic in tone (as expressed in the phrase "a beautiful piece of work")—and backed by rewards and honors. The first establishes uniform standards; the second concedes a diversity in the forms of excellence. The first gets transmitted through rules; the second, largely through example. On the whole, however, a profession tends to settle into a minimalist understanding of moral obligations.

As professionals move into large-scale organizations, basic standards are more likely to get enforced, but, along with this, a tendency to minimalism gets reinforced. The teaching hospital, for example, can monitor more easily the

---

[9]See Sheldon Wolin, *Politics and Vision*, Chapter 10, for a discussion of the contemporary period as the age of organization.

[10]The American Association of Certified Public Accountants has adopted the same distinction in its Code of Professional Responsibility.

work of its staff members, compared with the solo practitioner who can largely escape the scrutiny of colleagues. But the large-scale organization also tends to flatten out the aspiration to excellence in its more daring forms. Predictable routines for handling cases are more convenient than bold and singular responses to assignments. Academic professionals, for example, aspiring to tenure, are ill-advised to undertake spacious, long-term projects that will not produce results in time to satisfy the quantitative standards of tenure committees. Minimal standards sometimes provide a ground floor in an organization that attracts the uninspired to that level of performance, and no more. Disciplinary sanctions can become a double-edged sword—necessary to cut out the grossly incompetent, but also effective in protecting the jobs of the mediocre.

These difficulties that the large-scale organization faces in maintaining its drive for excellence argue for critical reflection, and experiment with alternative modes or organization. But it does not persuade one to join the nostalgic who yearn for the days of the free-lance entrepreneur. It is a liberal fiction to assume that man is better in isolation than he is in society. Even the realistic Reinhold Niebuhr fell prey to liberal innocence when he titled his work *Moral Man and Immoral Society*. Men and women need community, not merely for the instrumental purpose of producing greater things than they can achieve by themselves, but for the moral reason of helping them to be better than they can be by themselves. One does not have to be a Puritan to respect the truth in the opposite assertion: immoral man and moral society. Men and women need the support, correction, and encouragement of their fellows; and professionals are no exception.

The Distribution of Professional Services

A cardinal principle of the helping professions has been the availability of services; no one who needs help should be denied it. Philosophically, one usually argues for the delivery of services to the whole community on the basis of a principle of distributive justice. Professional services deemed essential should be distributed, not according to merit alone, or the ability to pay, but according to need. This does not mean that professionals must treat everyone identically (needs vary), but that they (perhaps aided and abetted in their efforts by the society) should make an equal contribution to the goodness of the lives of others requiring professional service. This principle remains an ideal, which, in the midst of a *de facto* shortage of professional services, should be approximated by professionals and society.

The principle of service also springs from religious ideals (the Hebraic notion of covenant love—*chesed*—and the Christian ethic of *agape*) and an ecclesiastical reflection of those ideals in the notion of priestly vocation. A primary mark of the church (at least ideally) was its universality. It was an "ark of salvation," open to all creatures, familiar and strange, beautiful and grotesque, irrespective of shape, color, wealth, or size. A society may organize itself into the rich and the poor, but the religious professional, at least in principle, must make the word and the sacraments available to all who confess their need.

So also, the services of the lawyer, the physician, and others in the helping professions should extend beyond those parochial boundaries that ordinary life establishes. They should extend to the stranger and the needy. A profession is corrupt if it defects from this catholicity of spirit and mission, if it becomes captive to the interests of a particular family or class. The King's Chaplain may be an important post. But the priesthood reduced to a chaplaincy service alone has lost much of its independence, its dignity, its comprehensive mission, its covenant. Medicine, the law, and other latter-day professions lose much that belongs to their moral substance if they become hirelings in the service of a single class, if they lose the mark, as it were, of "catholicity."

The theologians, moreover, distinguish between two dimensions of catholicity; it has both external and internal marks. External catholicity refers to the church's mission to the whole of humankind; internal catholicity, to the church's obligation to meet the needs of the whole person, body and soul. The latter insistence became important in Roman Catholic polemics against an overintellectual Protestantism that seemed to neglect, in worship and sacrament, man's sensuous nature. Correspondingly, a profession has an obligation to meet the needs of the *whole public* (its external catholicity), but also the *whole needs* of the public (its internal catholicity). The first obligation requires the just distribution of professional services to the whole community; the second requires the development of the full manifold of specialized services. The two tasks are distinct, but related. When particular populations are unserved or underserved, a profession often fails as well to develop the full range of its resources. Until recently, some areas of the law (women's rights, adolescents' rights) remained relatively uncharted terrain, because these groups of people were underserved. Conversely, when a profession develops its resources lopsidedly, it fails to meet the needs of special populations. Engineers, as organized by industry, have lavished attention on the development of the automobile, at the expense of alternative modes of transportation. The underdevelopment of a specific area of professional expertise in this case left special populations underserved—the aged and the poor in cities—and threatens now to put the entire industrial world in jeopardy. The link between the uneven development of a profession and populations left unserved demonstrates the symbiotic relationship of professionals to clients. Clearly, clients need professionals to address their needs; but professionals just as surely need a full manifold of clients, if their profession and all its articulated services are fully to mature.

If these general principles are accepted, then the question remains as to the most adequate system for the delivery of services to the whole community.

Until this century, the professions relied partly on the ideal of service to attract people to the professions, and partly on their personal charity to extend services to all levels of society. These notions had their roots in Christianity, but they also had their social base in a class society. What the aristocratic principle of *noblesse oblige* was to the eighteenth century, the professional ideal of service was to the somewhat more bourgeois nineteenth century. The ideal of service, however, depended rather too heavily upon inherited sources of wealth, and produced somewhat arbitrary and demeaning results—depending as it did upon the conscience of each practitioner. To depend exclusively on personal charity in response to human need is to rely excessively on social imagination—the ability of a person or a class, preoccupied with its own needs, to keep steadfastly before its eyes the needs of others.

Some have argued, against the ideal of charity, that the professions would do a better job in delivering services to the wider community if they would renounce their moral pretensions to be more than commercial, and simply live up to the standards of competition in the marketplace. Ironically, the professional claim to be more than commerical has led to monopolistic practices, and conduct that falls below the level of commercial ethics. The practical effect of the strictures against advertising has been to eliminate services at less than monopolistic prices. The professions have tended, in effect, to combine the worst of several worlds. They have pretended to be more than commercial, while being commercial with a vengeance, yet without permitting commercial competition. No wonder the courts have proceeded recently to classify the professions with commerce, and forbidden them to engage in restraint of trade. The courts wished to hold the professions up to the minimal standards of the marketplace. For the sake of ethics, so-called professional ethics had to be challenged.

As salutory as the court decision may be in certain respects, contractualism will not alone solve the problem of maldistribution of services. The nation's most powerful law firms, with or without advertising, largely serve the corporations; they are overly Waspish (and Ivy League) in personnel; other ethnic groups concentrate disproportionately in solo practice. The medical profession has fared little better in serving the ghettos, minority groups, and rural areas. Neither personal charity nor the aggregate of individual commercial decisions suffices to produce that equitable distribution of services to which the professions have been ideally committed. Deeper structural changes are required.

Some would argue that the responsibility to deliver services to the whole community rests on the society at large, and not on the professional *per se*. The society should devise a system to provide these services, rather than rely on the *pro bono* work of professionals. This argument has the virtue of addressing the problem at a structural level. People should not depend upon charity for basic services. Obviously, neither a single professional nor a profession at large can meet the whole needs of the public, without forms of communal support and assistance. Society must respond.

Although conceding that society bears a basic responsibility for the comprehensive delivery of professional services, the professional and the profession cannot be wholly relieved of the responsibility for achieving that reform. Through *pro bono* work the professional is often strategically positioned to know better than anyone else in the society the distressful consequences suffered by the underserved or the unserved. No one knows better than the lawyer the disastrous results of incompetent or ruthless counsel. The nineteenth-century physician at work in Western cities helped catalyse social reform. He saw at first hand the devastating results of bad sanitation, malnutrition, and long hours of work for children, and could testify on behalf of specific structural changes required for the improvement of urban health. Quite apart from its strategic value in the achievement reform, the professional ideal of service has its intrinsic validity. Until the reform comes, there are still human beings with needs to be met, with broken bones to mend, with lives hopelessly snarled in the law. And after the reform comes, it is doubtful that the new structures, no matter how cleverly devised, will work if professionals lack strong moral commitments. Professionals have it within their power to undermine the best of systems. Although structural changes for the better will not occur in the first place without a *national* sense of obligation to meet the basic needs of an entire population, they will not be sustained for long without a *professional* sense of obligation to make good on those changes. The covenants of individual professionals will not of themselves provide a satisfactory distribution of services. That is the lesson of a system that relies on personal charity alone. But the professional's moral commitments, or lack of them, as repeated in hundreds of colleagues, can make or break the structures through which the society operates. That is the lesson of failed institutional reform.

So far, this discussion of problems in the distribution of professional services has kept within the limits of debates between conservatives and liberals. From a more radical perspective, their debates seem somewhat intramural. They merely differ on the degree to which professionals and the society at large have a responsibility to deliver professional services to all citizens. Radical critics have recently questioned the professional delivery system altogether. They find either the very relationship of the professional to clients demeaning, or the services delivered destructive. They oppose the medicalizing, the lawyerizing, and the technologizing of the society.

These moral radical critics resemble earlier opponents of the church's missionary activity, who criticized the church not for its failure to reach out to all people, but rather for the objectionable good it had to offer (Christianity), which it offered in an objectionable way (with condescension). For some radicals, the question about distributive justice must yield to prior questions. Is the good distributed truly a good, and can it be distributed, however equitably, without disabling or humiliating the recipient?

The classical example of this line of criticism is Ivan Illich's *Medical Nemesis*. Illich expands the medical term, "iatrogenic illness"—illness that has its origin in the very effort to heal—to cover the comprehensive clinical, social, and cultural destruction which the modern medical profession wreaks in the course of its efforts to cure. Illich believes that the destructive clinical effects of drugs, surgery, and other procedures exceed cumulatively, if genetic consequences are included, whatever good medicine has done. Further, Western medicine has a destructive social impact, in that it tends to relieve the patient of active responsibility for his own health. The patient becomes passive, the professional active, to the detriment of the goal of health. Finally, the habit of looking to the professional for rescue obscures from the patient the moral/cultural task of facing up to one's limits, and responding well to suffering, aging, and death. Thus, Illich repudiates the modern missionary liberal who would export Western medicine, with all its broadly destructive results.

Radical critics of the legal system similarly oppose efforts to extend legal services under a third-party payment system. The society is already too litigious, lawyers too numerous, their works mischievous. These critics would prefer a more radical reconstruction of the legal system—less adversarial, and more investigatory and participatory in mode.

Radical critics of religious institutions and the educational system have similarly challenged their professionals on the ground that they tend to discourage and obscure, rather than serve, the religious life or the intellectual life of the lay person. The professional is poisonous. Lay people should deal with him at best in small doses.

Finally, radicals have attacked engineers and scientists, and, more directly, the technology which they have helped to create, for their destructive impact on civilized life. Technology in the West has been developed in the context of an adversary system. Just as the doctor fights suffering and death, the lawyer his opponent in the courtroom, and the academician, ignorance, so the American engineer has operated in an adversarial ambience. W. H. Auden once expressed this metaphorically by observing that in Europe, nature is an animal to be trained; in America, a dragon to be slain. The poet had in mind the fact that America was a land of great distances, harsh extremes in climate, and a relatively small population, but a land of extraordinary riches if nature could be conquered. We therefore needed a hero, the scientist/technologist who would conquer distance, subdue the cold with central heating, the heat with air conditioning, and the rough terrain with the bulldozer. But once technology subdued the hostile environment, great riches would pour out of the dragon's belly.

We have come to an end of the era in which this myth prevails. We are as worried about the dragons that the technologist creates as we are about the dragon he fights. Worries over recombinant DNA research, nuclear reactors, and warheads are but symptoms of this uneasiness. Technology replaces nature as the mythic monster, and one looks for a different kind of bond with nature— the romantics, worshipful and adoring, and the cool heads, like Auden, more inclined neither to fear nor to worship nature, but to reduce it to a more comfortable, still disciplined, domestic scale.

This more radical criticism of the professions runs the danger of a blind, indiscriminate rejection of any and all things that the professional has to offer, and how he offers it. Since the revolution has not yet occurred, it produces the dubious result of giving a radical justification for an essentially conservative state of affairs. Why give tax money to support professional services to the poor? It will only worsen their condition, make them passive rather than responsible, and, where the doctor is successful, only exacerbate the population problem. Conservative skepticism and radical criticism join forces, and obscure the need for modestly conceived and modestly delivered professional services, and technologies built to a human scale. The slogan on French placards in the late 1960s, "Eliminate the Experts," no more solves the problems that people bring to professionals than smashing the machines solves the problems that nature poses for man. More interior, subtle transformations of the myths by which men and women live are more to the point.

PROFESSIONAL CHARACTER AND VIRTUE

Moralists make a mistake when they concentrate solely on the quandaries that practitioners face, or on the defects of the structures in which they operate. Inquiry into these matters already assumes specific dispositions of character, which themselves need to be clarified and criticized. The quandary-oriented professional tends to assume and prize the virtue of conscientiousness. The critic of structures often brings to the inquiry a specifically aroused moral indignation. Important to professional ethics is the moral disposition the professional brings to the structure in which he operates, and that shapes his or her approach to problems. The practitioner's perception of role, character, virtues and style can affect the problems he sees, the level at which he tackles them, the personal presence and bearing he brings to them, and the resources with which he survives moral crises to function another day. At the same time, his moral commitments, or lack of them, the general ethos in which he and his colleagues function, can frustrate the most well-intentioned structural reforms.

Unfortunately, contemporary moralists have been much less interested than their predecessors in the clarification and cultivation of those virtues upon which the health of personal and social life depends. Reflection in this area is likely to seem rather subjective, elusive, or spongy ("I wish my physician were more personal"), as compared with the critical study of decisions and structures. And yet, especially today, attention must be paid to the question of professional virtue. The growth of large-scale organizations has increased that need. Although bureaucracies offer increased opportunity for monitoring performance (and therefore would appear to lessen the need for internalized virtue), in another respect they make the society increasingly hostage to the virtue of professionals who work for them. Huge organizations wield enormous defensive power with which to cover the mistakes of their employees. Further, and more important, the opportunity for increased specialization which they provide means that few others—whether lay people or other professionals—know what any given expert is up to. He had better be virtuous. Few may be in a position to discredit him. The knowledge explosion is also an ignorance explosion; if knowledge is power, then ignorance is powerlessness. Although it is possible to devise structures that limit the opportunities for the abuse of specialized knowledge, ultimately one needs to cultivate virtue in those who wield that relatively inaccessible power. One test of character and virtue is what a person does when no one else is watching. A society that rests on expertise needs more people who can pass that test.

A short list of professional virtues should include at least the following.

Perseverence is a lowly virtue, but indispensable for the acquisition of technical competence in the course of lengthy professional training. A young physician once conceded that medical school required more stamina than brains. Most holders of Ph.Ds would have to confess the same about their own graduate-school education, though it takes the virtue of modesty to concede that fact.

Public-spiritedness orients the professional to the common good. The term, "profession," and the more ancient though less often invoked words, "vocation" and "calling," have a public ring to them that the terms "job" and "career" do not. Professionals are often licensed by the state; the society invests in their education; they generate their own public standards of excellence; and they are expected to conform to these standards, and to accept responsibility for their enforcement in the guild. Apart from public-spiritedness, the professional degenerates into a careerist, and his education becomes a private stock of knowledge to be sold to the highest bidder.

Integrity marks the professional who is upright or integral (whole). Integrity gets tested at the outset in the forward scramble for admissions to professional schools, and in the competition for grades and position. Uprightness has to do with moral posture: the upright professional refuses to put his nose to the ground, sniffing out opportunities at the expense of clients and colleagues; he equally refuses to bow before the powerful client, the influential colleague, and outside pressures. Integrity also signifies a wholeness or completeness of character; it does not permit a split between the inner and the outer, between word and deed. As such, it makes possible the fiduciary bond between the professional and the client.

The professional virtue of *veracity* requires more than truthfulness or the avoidance of lying. Professionals are the knowledge experts in our society. They can, of course, hoard what they know, and dispense it guardedly in the form of technical services. But the success of professional work often requires the active and intelligent collaboration of the client in the pursuit of professional purpose. As indicated earlier, the professional must be a teacher, to do his or her work well. Professional veracity, at this point, expands beyond the duty to tell the truth, and includes the enabling act of sharing it.

Although veracity has to do with sharing the truth, *fidelity* is a matter of being true to the client. It means keeping faith with the orignial promise to take the case, to keep confidences, and to work for the client's best interests, within the limits of the law and moral constraint. The philosopher J. L. Austin once distinguished between declarative and performative utterances. The first are statements that describe the world (it is raining), but the second are statements that change someone's world (I, John, take thee, Mary). A promise need not have the legal status of the marriage vow to qualify as a kind of performative utterance. Promises, to some degree, alter the world of the person to whom they are extended. The professional promise, "I will be your lawyer," alters importantly the client's world, even before the lawyer proceeds to do anything. That is why it is a serious matter when a professional agrees to take, or withdraws from, a case.

The professional transaction also depends upon a pair of virtues associated with giving and receiving—*benevolence* (or *love*), and *humility*. The virtue of benevolent service is the *sine qua non* of the professional relationship. The professional is giver; the client, receiver. The client depends upon the specialized service that the professional has to offer to meet his needs. The professional, of course, is paid for his work, and, like any seller, should be legally accountable for the delivery of goods promised. Compliance is essential; but the legal minimum should hardly be the norm. The professional transaction is giving and receiving, not just buying and selling. Contractualism based on self-interest alone suppresses the donative element in the professional relationship. It encourages a minimalism, a grudging tit for tat—just so much service for so much money, and no more. This minimalism is especially unsatisfactory in those professions that deliver help to persons with contingent, unpredictable, future needs, that can only be covered by the habits of service.

Humility is not a virtue that one usually associates with professionals. Quite the contrary; long training and specialized knowledge set them apart, and touch them with assumptions of superiority. In popular literature, the professional often takes liberties denied to others as a sign of skill and hard work. We are treated to the reckless, swinging style of the surgeons in "Mash," the final insouciance of the student lawyer in "The Paper Chase," or the authoritarian law professor who presides over language as an accomplished hostess, over her silver.

Clearly, the virtue of humility can have nothing to do with obsequiousness, or ritual expressions of self-doubt over competence. No one needs to see his lawyer nervous before the trial, or his surgeon shaky with doubt about his skill. Humility can only be understood as a necessary counterpart to the virtue of benevolence or love.

Idealistic members of the helping professions like to define themselves by their giving or serving alone—with others indebted to them. The young professional identifies himself with his competence; he pretends to be a relatively self-sufficient monad, unspecified by human need, while others appear before him in their distress, exposing to him their illness, their crimes, their secrets, or their ignorance, for which the professional as doctor, lawyer, priest, or teacher offers remedy.

A reciprocity, however, of giving and receiving is at work in the professional relationship that needs to be acknowledged. In the profession of teaching, to be sure, the student needs the services of the teacher to assist him in learning; but so also the professor needs his students. They provide him with regular occasion and forum to work out what he has to say, and to discover his subject afresh through the discipline of sharing it with others. The young rabbi or priest has more than once paused before the door of the sickroom, wondering what to say to a member of his congregation, only to discover the dying patient ministering to his own needs. Likewise, the doctor needs his patients; the lawyer, his clients. No one can watch the professional nervously approach retirement without realizing how much he needs his clients to be himself.

The discipline of receiving is important in still further ways. The successful client interview requires addressing, but also being addressed; giving, but also taking in; it means both speaking and hearing, the masculine and the feminine, the tongue and the ear. The professional's debts, moreover, extend beyond direct obligations to current clients; they also include public monies spent on education, the earlier contributions of clients upon whom he "practiced" while learning his craft, and the research traditions of his profession, upon which he daily draws. Humility, finally, is essential to professional self-renewal. No teacher stays alive if he or she does not remain a student. No preacher can preach the word if he no longer hears it. No physician can long dispense a range of professional services, if not serviced himself by the research arm of his profession.

This brief sketch of some of the virtues germane to professional life has, of course, its shadow side—the problems associated with professional incompetence and vice. Those problems bring us to the last subject that must be covered in the teaching of professional ethics, a subject that tests, however, the seriousness of the whole enterprise.

THE ENFORCEMENT OF PROFESSIONAL STANDARDS: SELF-REGULATION AND DISCIPLINE

The subject of professional self-regulation and discipline appears in the professional codes; it preoccupies the layman when he thinks angrily about professional behavior. But, unfortunately, academic ethicists largely ignore the subject, and the guilds themselves only too often neglect it. A self-protective code of ethics, a politics too narrowly defensive of guild interests, and monopolistic practices contribute to this neglect.

No one can doubt, however, the importance of the problem of lax professional self-regulation. A former president of the American Medical Association has conceded that some five percent of physicians and surgeons are incompetent, or otherwise unsuitable for practice. Surely the figure is conservative, if one considers the source, and reflects on the probable percentages in one's own line of work. Since there are 300,000–400,000 practicing physicians in the United States, a minimum of 15,000–20,000 are incompetent. Yet, on the average in recent years, only 65–75 physicians annually have had their licenses revoked. (Some have argued that the extent of self-regulation in the professions should not be measured entirely on the basis of the number of instances of revocation and disbarment. Subtler devices are available to a profession in disciplining its members. The incompetent or unethical practitioner can be blocked out of referrals. The reckless physician may have hospital privileges revoked, without being drummed out of the profession. Although such lesser disciplinary action must be considered in any total assessment of the extent of professional self-regulation, it hardly solves the problem. The practitioner who is driven out of a given referral system often relocates in another circle sufficiently mediocre or indifferent to put him beyond the reach of professional criticism.)

Given the importance of the subject of professional self-regulation, why have writers and teachers of professional ethics neglected it, and professionals ducked it? Academic ethicists, in my judgment, have ignored the subject for three reasons. First, they belong to the institution that nurtures and prepares the professional for certification; but the university, unlike the church in earlier centuries, has no license, as it were, for an extended life-time authority over the professional, and, even then, no authority that would extend to more than questions of intellectual competence. Teachers of professional ethics, therefore, tend to defer these disciplinary matters to the guild and the state. This does not mean that the university has nothing to do with subsequent professional standards. Continuing education is a positive of which disciplinary procedures are the negative. The research work of professional schools and their continuing-education programs contribute to the maintenance of standards of excellence. But continuing education touches on ethics only partially—as it works to improve technical competence.

Second, current writers in professional ethics prefer to concentrate on moral dilemmas or quandaries, rather than on flagrant wrongdoing, because the latter subject is somewhat awkward in the interdisciplinary and interprofessional settings where some of the basic work in professional ethics takes place. Quandaries are convenient for discussion among academics and professionals from various backgrounds, because they are psychologically impersonal, and secretly flattering. They assume that all parties to the discussion speak out of an indeterminate conscientiousness, a moral earnestness, as each attempts to offer the best solution to a quandary. Such discussions in an interdisciplinary setting do not require professionals to betray their kith and kin in front of outsiders. It relieves academic moralists of the necessity of talking about the sins of other professions while their own house is in a state of disorder. Social life, in general, depends upon etiquette, and interdisciplinary think tanks are no exception. The discussion of "dilemmas" conveniently serves the demands of courtesy.

Finally, and most important, questions of unethical behavior receive little attention from academic moralists because such problems seem intellectually uninteresting to them. The self-evident wrongness of such behavior encourages academicians to turn toward quandaries, where a moral bind arouses their intellectual curiosity. (The Vietnam war, in addition to its many other tragic features, had the bad luck to seem to be an intellectually uninteresting war. It seemed self-evidently wrong [or right] to protesters [or cold warriors]. It never produced a thinker of the stature of Reinhold Niebuhr, who was compelled to develop a fresh statement about human nature in order to justify American participation in World War II.) Academic moralists, on the whole, are drawn to intellectually interesting moral problems the way archeologists and historians are attracted to the study of civilizations that happen to have an abundance of preserved materials.

For a distinctive, and, I think, intellectually interesting set of reasons, practitioners are as loath to regulate themselves as academics are reluctant to discuss regulation. First, within any guild a network of friendship and courtesy develops that tends to make loyalty to colleagues take precedence over obligations to clients, or to the wider public that the guild serves. Inevitably professional colleagues exchange favors, information, and services. By comparison, the ties to clients seem transient. A profession organizes itself around certain ends—to serve a specific set of clients—but a sense of community develops among colleagues that becomes an end in itself. In the language of the sociologists: Every *Gesellschaft* (organization) tends to become a *Gemeinschaft* (community). Americans exacerbate the problem in that they do not distinguish (and separate) as clearly as Europeans the public order of work from the private order of friendship. It is extremely painful to bring charges against a colleague who is also a friend.

The peculiar source of authority in at least two of the professions (the law and medicine) adds to the difficulties in achieving self-regulation. These professions draw their power from fear—the patient's concern about suffering and death, the client's fear of the loss of property, liberty, or life. (No academic is engaged in a war on ignorance quite comparable to the physician's battle against disease.) This negative source of authority provides great prestige and/or financial reward for the physician and the lawyer in the modern world, but, at the same time, it renders their authority inherently unstable. Members of these professions are the object of great anger, and are subject to retaliation if through incompetence, greed, or thirst for power they help to impose on the patient/client what they were commissioned to resist. (The military profession also derives its authority from a negative, and suffers from the same instability of attitudes in the wider population it serves.) Since the stakes are so high, and since whole institutions (hospitals, clinics, and courts) can suffer from the publicized incompetence of a single practitioner, the temptation is strong to draw around the endangered colleague like a herd around a wounded elephant.

American professionals may also be reluctant to bring charges against their colleagues because of a morally wholesome, national aversion to officiousness. Unlike some of their European counterparts, Americans show little stomach for playing amateur policeman, prosecutor, and judge when they themselves are not directly or officially involved in an incident. Our libertarian and equalitarian instincts combine to produce a reluctance to interfere. In many respects, this is an admirable trait in the American character. Yet our distaste for officiousness cannot justify a laxness in enforcing professional standards. Professional status confers the duties of privilege, but not a limitless liberty; a respect for colleagues as equals, but not at the expense of clients in the inequality of their power.

In order to guarantee to the public that certain standards shall be maintained, the state limits the license to practice to those who have completed a course of professional education. Professionals as a group profit from this state-created monopoly. They fall short of their responsibilities for the maintenance of standards if they merely practice competently and ethically as individuals. The individual's license to practice depends upon the prior license to license which the state has, to all intents and purposes, bestowed upon the guild. If the license to practice carries with it the obligation to practice well, then the license to license carries with it the obligation to judge and monitor well. Not only the individual, but also the collectivity itself, is accountable for standards.

I understand the foregoing subjects to belong to the terrain to be covered by course work in professional ethics. The question remains as to its location in the university setting. Some would argue that professional ethics comes too late, no matter when or where it is taught. Moral habits are already set before a student leaves high school. Formal instruction in ethics cannot significantly alter the effects of earlier experience.

A limited truth lies behind this comment. Students are hardly born *de novo* from the forehead of a university. For eighteen years before coming there, they batten on the ethos of the society at large, and the special nurture of family, television, school, church, or synagogue. College-bound students get toilet trained, eat breakfast cereal, and organize their lives around root appetites just like everyone else. It would be an expression of gnostic *hubris* to assume that the university, and whatever ethics it has to offer, sets them apart from their fellows.

Still, the teaching of ethics has some value in the university and beyond. It can provide some measure of critical distance from the ethos, including the ethos of the university itself. Moreover, even though moral dispositions are largely formed, the goals to which these habits are directed can be subject to criticism and redirection. Habits can be reformed and redirected in the light of moral vision.

Some would argue that professional ethics should be deferred altogether to professional school, or, even better, to the early years of practice, when the young professional in the making has the experience to go with the concepts. Some academic ethicists prefer it that way, because it gives them a crack at more mature students.

There are strong arguments, however, for locating at least some course work in professional ethics in the undergraduate curriculum. Experience has its advantages, but conceptual tools in ethics are also important. Experience tends to establish an undertow in favor of already-established practice. There are advantages to acquiring some critical distance before immersion in the daily demands of a profession. Further, undergraduate courses in professional ethics (taught in the liberal-arts setting) are usually open to nonprofessionals as well as preprofessionals. This mixed constituency makes an important substantive statement. It suggests that professional ethics is not the property of professionals alone. The layman has a stake in the subject. Aggressive medical treatment versus allowing to die is not just a doctor's quandary, it is a patient's decision. Technology assessment is not just an expert's art; it poses for citizens the question of their destiny. To assume otherwise is to reduce the patient and the citizen to a moral nonentity. Nonprofessionals as well as preprofessionals and professionals belong in the total mix of students who reflect on the field. A course taught in the undergraduate setting reminds one that moral reflection about the professional transaction must include the ethics of the patient as well as the doctor, the client as well as the lawyer, the student as well as the teacher, the citizen as well as the policymaker. An exclusive preoccupation with the ethics of the professional (rather than with the professional/client relationship) obscures this fact. Finally, teaching professional ethics to a mixed audience serves to remind the preprofessional that he was a layman before he was a professional, and that he would be ill-advised wholly to suppress the layman in himself.

After having said all this in favor of undergraduate teaching in the field, one must concede the indispensability of instruction in the professional school setting. The specificity of the professional setting helps keep academic teachers disciplined by that experience. They see more accurately the bind of quandaries, the warp of institutional structures, and the strains on character that professional life imposes; the growing experience of students also provides teachers with a painful but rewarding test of their own ideas.

Some would argue that the subject of professional ethics is too important to be left to the academic specialist in a segregated course: it should leaven the work of already-established teachers in the conventional subdivisions of the professional curriculum. This so-called pervasive approach reflects an important truth. Ethicists do not have exclusive jurisdiction over ethics. All persons must reflect morally on their work. As Samuel Johnson once said, we are all moralists perpetually, geometers only by chance. Colleagues at work in other specializations can and must join the ethicist in the enterprise. But not to teach ethics somewhere, on the ground that it should be taught everywhere, more than likely condemns a school to teaching it nowhere—or teaching it badly, or teaching it conservatively by reflecting, and repeating in ethics the structural defects already built into the current subdivisions of the curriculum.

Professional ethics gets transmitted not merely through formal courses and codes, but also in clinical or practical settings. The exemplary behavior of outstanding practitioners teaches through performance. Some would use this phenomenon as a reason for not offering formal course work on the subject. But clinical ethics does not suffice. Much behavior is far from exemplary, merely customary; ethics is not ethos; morals is not reducible to mores. The formal ethicist offers some critical distance upon behavior, and encourages systematic reflection on quandaries and structures which otherwise might be neglected.

The apology for formal course work in ethics has its limits. Eager to make a place for themselves and the profession, ethicists sometimes neglect the fact that current formal ethics, in its own way, is reductive. It overlooks the inspiration of exemplary performance. It tends to reduce the moral life to universalizable rules; it loses sight of the similarities between the moral life, professional performance, and the work of the artist. All three kinds of practice involve rules; but they bear fruit in works that reflect more than rules; they aspire to an excellence often multiple in its forms, and communicable only in practice.

THE TEACHER

Recruits for teaching professional ethics come from two groups: those with primary training in philosophical or theological ethics, who acquire a secondary competence in the basic problems of a profession, and those with primary training in a profession, who, either by reason of moral zeal or course assignment, or both, are willing to develop sufficient competence in ethics to teach a course in professional responsibility. A few rare persons have terminal degrees in both ethics and a profession, but one cannot expect that preparation to be normal or usual. Where faculty members lack secondary competence in the opposite field, they often compensate for their deficiency by team-teaching a course with a partner who can supply the missing theoretical or practical base for competence. Team-teaching is costly in faculty time, and, depending on personal interactions, may not always provide the best of courses. But it may be especially useful in a transitional period, as faculty members help one another to acquire the requisite secondary competence.

Those teachers who currently patrol the terrain of professional ethics face a problem of credibility not only in the area of their secondary competence, but also in their home discipline. Professional-school faculty in the so-called "hard" disciplines often have little taste for teaching a course in professional responsibility. By default, the course gets assigned to an untenured junior colleague whose fate depends on his research in another field. If, as argued earlier, professional schools need to reckon with ethical issues as central to their enterprise, faculty members who teach in this area should acquire standing with their colleagues for this work.

But "applied ethics" has similar problems of credibility in the eyes of some basic theorists in the fields of philosophy and theology. It seems a second-rate enterprise, compared with foundational work. The task remains, then, in this closing section, to show why applied ethics is a worthy enterprise.

Rightly or wrongly, today the very term "applied" encourages a somewhat misleading view of the task of the teacher. It assumes a sharp distinction between ethical theorists, who do the truly foundational work (more highly prized by tenure and promotion committees), and applied ethicists, who relate abstract principles to practical problems of the kind that the professions generate. One immediately thinks of the corresponding distinction between pure and applied science, or between fundamental and mission-oriented research directed to the development of specific technologies.

Applied ethics, so conceived, at once claims too much and too little for the discipline. It claims too much to the degree that it implies to the professional community that it offers some kind of rescue and salvation from moral problems. The ethicist in this view functions as a kind of professional's professional. He specializes in a peculiar class of problems, called "moral problems," that the success of the professions have helped to generate, but cannot solve. This superprofessional, it is hoped, has access to rules and modes of reasoning that will eliminate moral problems. With some such hope, professionals attend seminars on ethics, and foundations support them. But, of course, moral problems prove to be a peculiar class of problems—chronic rather than periodic, hardy perennials rather than occasional. This leads moralists, in the fashion of the governor of California, to want to lower expectations.

Alternatively, applied ethics can claim too little for itself if it suggests that "applications" have a merely deductive, derivative, and dispensary relationship to theory. The truly serious moralist, from this perspective, does abstract, foundational work; the applied ethicist, at best, lives parasitically off this basic research, and relates it to specific problems which, alas, he knows less well than the experts in the field. His competence is constantly at risk. He carries water from wells he has not dug to fires he cannot find. He does not appear to be an intellectually serious figure.

This condescending view of the applied ethicist overlooks a more heuristic possibility for the vocation. Wrestling with specific issues may help one see theoretical problems in a fresh way. Through the effort to reach some kind of clarity about "applications," one may not merely package what is already known, but discover what is unknown, or barely known. To this degree, the applied ethicist becomes more than a taxonomist who classifies already-established moral systems and applies them to specific issues. He or she works as a constructive moralist who offers fresh theoretical insights in the course of interpreting and criticizing a specific world of practice.

If the teacher of applied ethics does not merely do retail work between the producer/theorist and the consumer/practitioner, what is his or her essential task, and how does it relate to theory? I propose that the essential task of the applied-ethics teacher is what might be called corrective vision.[11] The metaphor of vision links the teaching of ethics with the organ most associated with cognition. It implies that ethics in the classroom has as its primary and direct intention not the bending of the will, the stirring of the feelings, or the manipulation of behavior, but the illumination of the understanding. It is directed to insight and vision.

The vision that concerns the ethicist differs from the seeing available to the senses or through the instruments of science. Ethics is a type of corrective vision. That is why ethics relies heavily on the distinction between the descriptive and the prescriptive, between what is and what ought to be. It throws the accepted world into a new light, an unexpected horizon: it opens up new possibilities for action, so that behavior that a moment ago seemed so plausible and imperative now loosens its hold and its power to compel. In ethical reflection, the world as it once appeared gets stretched and rearranged; other modes of behavior and social structure, previously deemed unacceptable, now seem more inviting.

Corrective vision, however, challenges not the world of the descriptive sciences so much as the world as it gets distorted through the bias of institutional structures, or through the prism of human imperfection and vice. The seductive feature of immoral behavior is that it always seems plausible. Although warped and distorted, the world so perceived makes it demands upon men and women. An older tradition called this plausibility the temptation of evil. Immoral behavior usually presents itself as world-compliant rather than defiant. No one is so much the scoundrel that he does not think of his behavior as justified, as conforming to the world as it is. The man who hates believes that there are enemies out there to be hated. The greedy man thinks that his avarice is necessary because he has bills to pay, and a future to make secure. The ruthless believe that, except for their aggressiveness, the world would engulf them; it defeats the weak. Immoral behavior is tempting because it seems the most reasonable response to the vision of the world which vice itself presents. The Nixon people sought to invoke plausibility with the phrases "at that point in time," or "in that time frame." They responded to what they perceived to be the imperatives of the world as it was, and not as it ought to be.

[11]Sheldon Wolin applies this term to the work of the classical political theorists, who, of course, were partly engaged in moral criticism of their societies. See Chapter 1 in his *Politics and Vision*.

Applied ethics, then, entails a knowledgeable revisioning of the world that human practice presents. In this task, the ethicist is a theorist—quite literally. Unfortunately, the word "theory" suggests, to the practical person, a remote and abstract enterprise, lacking in relevance and payoff, blindly distant from the world of practice. But, classically understood, the moral theorist engages in a fresh envisioning of the world. So Plato understood it, when he cast the *polis* that he knew in the light of the ideal state. And so even Machiavelli understood it, when, in his dedication to *The Prince*, he compared the political theorist to the landscape painter who views the political leader from a distance, the distance of insight and perspective. The very word, "theory," in its Greek root refers to vision. Appropriately enough, the word "theater" also derives from *theoria*, because the theater, like theory, presents us with a world to see. I have suggested earlier that evil, in its temptingness, establishes a link between some specific vision of the world and its responsive vice. Correspondingly, the movement from evil to good, from wrong to right, from worse to better, from indecision to action, requires a corrective vision, a vision that exposes the stupidity in the plausible, the wrong in the apparently right, and the confusion in unwarranted indecision. Thereby the world loses some of its intractability, and the will its ground for intransigence.

Through this cognitive penetration, the ethicist serves, in some limited way, the human capacity for resolution and decision. Ethical theory may not always eliminate quandaries, but it opens up a horizon in which they may be seen for what they are, and thus become other than they were. The ethicist does not simply issue a blind call for a particular decision, or attempt to overwhelm the innate appetites of students, or strive to indoctrinate without illuminating. He or she opens up a way of envisioning the world that implies its own ordering of the appetites, reordering of structures, and fitting sense of decision. Such is the link between vision and virtue, cognition and the criticism of structures, knowledge and decision, moral insight and the pain of professional self-regulation.

PART III

Topics in the Teaching of Ethics

CHAPTER 10

Paternalism in Medicine, Law, and Public Policy

DENNIS F. THOMPSON

"If protection against themselves is confessedly due to children and persons under age," John Stuart Mill asks, "is not society equally bound to afford it to persons of mature years who are equally incapable of self-government?"[1] Mill answers his own question negatively, rejecting paternalism toward adults absolutely. "Because it would be better for him" or "because it will make him happier" can never, in Mill's view, justify restricting the liberty of a sane adult.[2] Many modern liberals, also committed to individual liberty, abandon Mill's absolutist stand against paternalism, and in fact Mill himself does not maintain it consistently. But, more than Mill, these later liberals stress that some adults always, and all adults sometimes, are incapable of exercising liberty.

The problem of paternalism thus becomes that of how to protect or help such individuals without renouncing the principle of liberty. If a paternalistic intervention restricts only decisions that are already unfree, if it is limited in scope, and if the person whose decisions are restricted accepts in some sense its purpose, the paternalism can be consistent with the principle of liberty. Liberty is preserved insofar as individuals are not coerced to act according to a conception of the good that they do not hold.[3] This approach does not completely resolve the problem, however. In many instances where we seek to justify pater-

---

[1] John Stuart Mill, *On Liberty*, in John Robson, ed., *Collected Works*, vol. XVIII (Toronto: University of Toronto Press, 1977), p. 280.
[2] Ibid., pp. 223–224, 282.
[3] Cf. Ronald Dworkin, "Liberalism," in Stuart Hampshire, ed., *Public and Private Morality* (Cambridge: Cambridge University Press, 1978), p. 127.

DENNIS F. THOMPSON ● Department of Politics, Princeton University, Princeton, New Jersey.

nalism, the ways in which a decision is unfree and the intervention limited, and the sense in which an individual accepts the purposes of the intervention, remain problematic. To bring out the complexities of the problem of paternalism, I shall examine the concept, and consider the conditions under which paternalism may be justified. This framework will then be applied to some examples in the fields of medicine, law, and public policy.

Because the problem of paternalism arises in many different areas of professional and public life, it serves well to illustrate how one might proceed in the teaching of ethics in courses in professional schools and in the study of public policy. The problem also combines philosophical and practical concerns in a way that makes it a suitable topic for undergraduate courses in applied ethics. The examples I consider are intended to suggest how paternalism could be explored in any of these kinds of course. Moreover, the teaching of ethics itself raises the problem of paternalism, since the teacher in some contexts may take a paternalistic stance toward his or her students. In a concluding section, I shall discuss briefly the pedagogy of paternalism.

THE CONCEPT OF PATERNALISM

Paternalism involves the imposing of constraints on an individual's liberty for the purpose of promoting his or her own good.[4] This definition points to three elements of paternalism, each of which may be controversial: the locus of the constraints, their form, and their purpose.

The locus of paternalism refers to the question of who imposes the constraints on whom. The issues raised by paternalism partly depend on the kind of relationship that exists between the individual whose liberty is restricted and the individual or institution who imposes the restriction. The paradigm of paternalism—the relationship between the parent and the child—presupposes that we can distinguish a class of persons, defined only by their chronological age, whose liberty may be constrained for their own good. This presupposition raises the problem not only of how to justify the criterion of chronological age, but also of how to determine who (parents, guardians, the state or no one?) has the

---

[4]This definition is consistent with those proposed by most recent writers, though my interpretation of it does not always agree with theirs. See Gerald Dworkin, "Paternalism," in Richard Wasserstrom, ed., *Morality and the Law* (Belmont, Calif.: Wadsworth Publishing Co., 1971), p. 108; Joel Feinberg, "Legal Paternalism," *Canadian Journal of Philosophy* 1 (1971), p. 105; Jeffrie G. Murphy, "Incompetence and Paternalism," *Archiv für Rechts-und-Sozial-philosophie* 60 (1974), p. 465; Rosemary Carter, "Justifying Paternalism," *Canadian Journal of Philosophy* 7 (1977), p. 133; Francis Schrag, "The Child in the Moral Order," *Philosophy* 2 (1977), p. 169; and Albert Weale, "Paternalism and Social Policy," *Journal of Social Policy* 7 (1978), pp. 160, 163.

right to restrict a child's liberty.[5] More commonly in the literature, paternalism refers to relationships between two adults. Here it is important—but not so common—to distinguish between relationships in which the persons are more or less equal in status and power, and relationships in which one person, by virtue of his social role or institutional position, has greater status or power than the other person. What constitutes a restriction on liberty in the latter kind of relationship (such as that between a professional and his client) may, as we shall see, differ from what counts as a restriction in the former kind of relationship. A third locus of paternalism is the relationship between individuals and the state. To avoid turning the problem of paternalism *tout court* into the problem of democracy, we should distinguish paternalistic restrictions that are not sanctioned by democratic procedures from those that are so sanctioned. A president who for the public good withholds information acts undemocratically as well as paternalistically if his action violates constitutional norms, but acts only paternalistically if his action conforms to such norms. Only the latter kind of action poses the distinctive problem of paternalism, since any objection to the former kind of action rests on a general argument for democratic government. A legislative act in a democracy can also be paternalistic; a law prohibiting the use of certain drugs is paternalistic with respect to anyone, including legislators themselves, who might want to use the drug. Notice, however, that legislation requiring contributions to some cooperative scheme (such as medical care) or legislation regulating wages and hours of work is not necessarily paternalistic, so long as its purpose is to give effect to the desires of a democratic majority, rather than simply to coerce a minority who do not want the benefits of the legislation.[6] Legislation is paternalistic only if the majority could promote their own good in some other (fair) way without coercing the minority, and if the justification for the legislation depends in part on an appeal to the good of the minority.

The second element of the concept reminds us that paternalism needs justification because it is a restriction of liberty. Even if an individual in some way consents to a restriction of his liberty for his own good, the restriction remains paternalistic if he wishes to perform the proscribed action while the restriction is in effect. (The classical example is Odysseus' request to be bound to the mast so that he cannot succumb to the Sirens' song.) It would not be helpful, I think, to broaden the concept of paternalism, as some writers propose, to include all

---

[5]See Schrag, "Child in Moral Order," pp. 167–177. More generally, see Onora O'Neill and William Ruddick, eds., *Having Children: Philosophical and Legal Reflections on Parenthood* (New York: Oxford University Press, 1979).

[6]Carter, "Justifying Paternalism," p. 145; G. Dworkin, "Paternalism," p. 112; and Mill, *Principles of Political Economy*, in John Robson, ed., *Collected Works*, vol. III (Toronto: University of Toronto Press, 1977), p. 956.

cases in which a moral rule is violated to promote an individual's good.[7] Violations of moral principles other than liberty are at most incomplete instances of paternalism, since they do not alone prevent an individual from choosing or acting on his own conception of the good. If for your own good I break a promise to you, but do not restrict your liberty in any way, then I do not actually impose my conception of your good on you. Moreover, the instances that these writers wish to count as paternalism—for example, a doctor deceiving his patient—can be properly considered as restrictions on liberty insofar as deception is a kind of coercion.[8] If a restriction on liberty is a feature of paternalism, we must avoid construing the concept of liberty so broadly that the problem of paternalism dissolves, or so narrowly that some important examples of paternalism fall beyond its scope. We can avoid the first consequence by rejecting a strong positive conception of liberty (the liberty to do what is good or worthwhile); with this conception, restrictions on an individual for the purpose of making him better off would not be a constraint on his liberty at all.[9] We escape the second consequence by recognizing that restrictions on liberty may take the form not only of physical or legal coercion, but also of more subtle impediments that arise from unequal power in some kinds of relationship. A patient's liberty may be restricted, for example, when a doctor fails to give him certain information that would be likely to incline him to choose a different course of action.[10] In this and other instances, the paternalist imposes his conception of the good on someone by limiting, in some way, actions which that person wishes, or might wish, to perform.[11]

The purpose of paternalism—the protection or promotion of an individual's own good—is also open to a variety of interpretations. Although we may wish to say that paternalism is justified only when the good is one that the individual himself can accept, the *concept* of paternalism includes goods ranging from prevention of immediate physical harm to the promotion of a whole style

---

[7]Bernard Gert and Charles M. Culver, "Paternalistic Behavior," *Philosophy and Public Affairs* 6 (1976), p. 49. For an even broader definition, see N. Fotion, "Paternalism," *Ethics* 89 (1979) pp. 194–198.

[8]Sissela Bok, *Lying: Moral Choice in Public and Private Life* (New York: Pantheon Books, 1978), pp. 18–19.

[9]Cf. Hillel Steiner, "Liberty," *Journal of Medical Ethics* 2 (1976), pp. 147–148.

[10]Cf. Allen Buchanan, "Medical Paternalism," *Philosophy and Public Affairs* 8 (1978), pp. 371–372.

[11]In a comment on this paper, Gerald Dworkin, though agreeing that paternalism involves imposing a conception of good on someone who does not want to be so treated, objects that paternalism should not always be regarded as a restriction of liberty. However, it seems to me that to say that you impose something on someone is normally to imply that you restrict or constrain his actions in some way, and that he is therefore less at liberty to do what he wishes to do, or would have wished to do.

of life.[12] Even so, we should distinguish paternalism from the legal enforcement of morality. Many writers agree with Mill that morality should not be legally enforced, but disagree with his claim that paternalism is never justified.[13] Harm or good, to be sure, cannot be determined without the invoking of some kind of moral theory or some standards of evaluation, but the harm or good with which paternalism is concerned must be experienced by the specific individual whose liberty is restricted; paternalism does not encompass the harm or good that the individual may cause to others, or to society in general. Contrary to what many assume, paternalism remains a distinctive problem, even if Mill's dichotomy between self-regarding and other-regarding actions cannot be sustained.[14] Even if it is impossible to say of any particular action that it affects only one person in the way that for Mill makes the action self-regarding, we can still offer, among the reasons for restricting an individual's liberty, the claim that the restriction promotes his own good. In this way, paternalism refers not to a distinct class of *actions*, but to a class of *reasons* that we may use to justify or condemn restrictions even on actions that harm other people, as well as the individual himself. The problem of paternalism becomes most salient when the claim that an action harms other people turns out on inspection to be tenuous, and a constraint on liberty cannot be defended without showing harm to the individual whose liberty is being restricted.[15] Absolute opponents of paternalism typically try to invoke every possible kind of social harm, however remote or speculative, to justify an intervention that would otherwise have to be supported on paternalistic grounds. But even if social harm can plausibly be demonstrated, we may often not only wish to appeal to paternalistic reasons as an additional

---

[12]Notice that even "negative" paternalism, which aims to prevent only bad consequences, has different implications, depending on whether the purpose is prevention of harm, or of suffering; the former might prohibit euthanasia, while the latter would permit or even require it [Christine Pierce, "Hart on Paternalism," *Analysis* 35 (1975), p. 206].

[13]H. L. A. Hart, *Law, Liberty and Morality* (London: Oxford University Press, 1963), pp. 30–33. See also C. L. Ten, "Paternalism and Morality," *Ratio* 13 (1971), pp. 56–66.

[14]See, e.g. Feinberg, "Legal Paternalism," p. 106n. Mill defends the distinction in *On Liberty*, pp. 223–224, 276–277, 292, and esp. 280 (where he anticipates the standard objection to the distinction). For analysis of the distinction, see Alan Ryan, *The Philosophy of John Stuart Mill* (Boston: Routledge & Kegan Paul, 1974), pp. 246–251.

[15]Some writers argue that most so-called paternalistic legislation can be justified on grounds of harm to others; e.g., Donald H. Regan, "Justification for Paternalism," in J. Roland Pennock and John W. Chapman, eds., *The Limits of Law, Nomos XV.* (New York: New York University Press, 1974), p. 201 ff. However, when courts have followed this approach, they have often ended up construing "harm to others" so broadly that individual liberty begins to disappear (e.g., when they count any diminution in an individual's economic productivity as a harm to society); see Comment, "Limiting the State's Police Power: Judicial Reaction to John Stuart Mill," *University of Chicago Law Review* 37 (1970), esp. pp. 620–622. Mill himself of course objects strongly to this approach. (*On Liberty*, p. 280).

justification for the intervention, but we may also need to call upon these reasons to establish an adequate justification for the intervention.

The Justification of Paternalism

It is difficult to maintain that a person's own good is never a justification for the restriction of his liberty. The law, for example, does not permit anyone to agree to being killed or mutilated, to engage in dueling or other forms of mutual combat, or to conclude a contract to sell oneself into slavery; no one is allowed to take drugs of certain kinds without a doctor's prescription.[16] Those few writers who have held that paternalism is never justified either have limited their claim to certain kinds of paternalism (such as that enforced by the criminal law), or have narrowed the definition of paternalism so that a restriction of liberty that may appear to be paternalistic is not.[17] More commonly (and more clearly, I think) our qualms about paternalism can be acknowledged by establishing stringent conditions for justifying paternalism.

Mill offers the following example that may be taken as a paradigm of justified paternalism:

> If either a public officer or anyone else saw a person attempting to cross a bridge which had been ascertained to be unsafe, and there were not time to warn him of his danger, they might seize him and turn him back, without any real infringement of his liberty; for liberty consists in doing what one desires, and he does not desire to fall into the river.[18]

Mill seeks to preserve his antipaternalism by denying that this is a case of paternalism at all; but though the person who is restrained does not desire to fall into the water and drown, he does desire to cross the bridge, and anyone who intervenes for the person's own good thwarts this desire, and restricts his liberty for paternalistic reasons. The intervention, nevertheless, seems justified, because of special features of the example; and these features suggest three conditions that must be satisfied if paternalism is to be justified in any particular case.[19] First,

---

[16]Feinberg, "Legal Paternalism," pp. 105–106. See also *Paris Adult Theatre I* v. *Slaton* 93 Sup. Ct. 2628, 2641 (1973).

[17]Michael Bayles, "Criminal Paternalism," in J. Roland Pennock and John W. Chapman, eds., *The Limits of Law* (New York: New York University Press), pp. 179–188; and Tom L. Beauchamp, "Paternalism and Biochemical Control," *Monist* 60 (1977), p. 71 ff.

[18]Mill, *On Liberty*, p. 294.

[19]For various versions and combinations of these necessary and sufficient conditions, see G. Dworkin, "Paternalism," pp. 122–126; Feinberg, "Legal Paternalism," p. 113; Ten, "Paternalism and Morality," p. 65; Murphy, "Incompetence and Paternalism," p. 479; John Rawls, *A Theory of Justice* (Cambridge, Mass.: Harvard University Press, 1971), pp. 248–250; Carter, "Justifying Paternalism," pp. 136–138; Weale, "Paternalism and Social Policy," pp. 170–172;

the decision of the person who is to be constrained must be *impaired;* in this case, the would-be bridge-crosser is ignorant of a crucial fact about the situation in which he acts. We assume that his desire would be different if his decision were fully free or voluntary. Second, the restriction is as *limited* as possible. In this case, the intervention is temporary and reversible; the person could, after learning that the bridge is unsafe, continue across it. Finally, the restriction prevents a serious and irreversible *harm;* we may have good reason to believe that the harm is one that the person wishes to avoid more than he wishes to cross the bridge.

It is tempting to view all of these conditions as a way of founding the justification of paternalism on the idea of consent, and up to a point this view can be helpful. The three conditions, taken together, might be seen as justifying paternalistic restraints on liberty at a particular time by appealing to consent at some other time; an objection to a current interference with liberty may in this way be overcome by the providing of a free choice in the future. That a decision is impaired justifies our not securing consent when we impose the restriction; that the intervention is limited creates an opportunity for consent in the future; and that the harm is serious provides a good reason for expecting consent at some other time. Paternalism is thus justified insofar as each of the three conditions establishes that the person whose liberty is restricted will, or could, consent to the restriction. For the paradigm case, the justification seems plausible enough; but when we try to generalize it, we run into difficulties of interpretation. The three conditions do not apply in any simple way to many instances of paternalism, and, as a result, in some cases we are forced to abandon any appeal to actual consent.

Many decisions that we may wish to restrict are not impaired in so temporary and easily correctible a way as that of the person who does not know that the bridge is unsafe. The variety of possible impairments is great, including not only ignorance, but also psychological compulsion.[20] Even ignorance may go beyond lack of knowledge of a specific fact; a person may be unaware of a general body of knowledge (such as medical or legal doctrine) that substantially affects his decision. He may be incapable of appreciating what facts are relevant to his decision because he weighs evidence incorrectly, does not recognize what counts as evidence at all, or is totally devoid of reason (e.g., a comatose patient). Psychological compulsions range from physiological necessity (such as drug addiction), which may be irresistible in most circumstances, to mere temptation

---

and John D. Hodson, "The Principle of Paternalism," *American Philosophical Quarterly* 14 (1977), pp. 62–65. For a different approach, see Bernard Gert and Charles M. Culver, "The Justification of Paternalism," *Ethics* 89 (1979), pp. 199–210.

[20]The best short discussion of the relation between such impairments and paternalism is by Murphy, "Incompetence and Paternalism," pp. 468–475.

(such as a conflict of interest), which may be compelling only under unusual circumstances.[21] Some of these impairments are sufficient to count as part of a justification for paternalism, and some are not, but there does not appear to be any categorical difference between them that would distinguish those that warrant intervention from those that do not. Most writers refer to degrees of impairment (whether it is "severe" or "serious"), thus deliberately leaving the distinction indeterminate. However difficult it may be to identify the impairments that would justify intervention, we should not say that a decision is impaired simply because an individual chooses a course of action that appears to us irrational (for example, refusal of life-saving surgery, or profligate expenditure of a trust fund). To justify paternalism, we must identify some impairment that can be described independently of the end or good an individual chooses.[22]

Because of the difficulty of formulating any general criterion for distinguishing the kinds of impairment that justify intervention, we should, especially when faced with doubtful cases of impairment, seek restrictions on liberty that, like those in Mill's bridge example, are temporary or easily reversible. But it is not always possible to limit the restrictions in this way. In the first place, if the impairment is not temporary, the restriction, to be effective, cannot be temporary either. A senile or comatose person may never be able to decide voluntarily whether a constraint on his liberty was warranted; even a perfectly normal person's ignorance of medical or legal knowledge is, for all practical purposes, permanent. In the second place, the intervention itself can change a person so that his future choice, though unimpaired, differs substantially from what he would have chosen if the intervention had not taken place. A person might subsequently consent to an intervention, but only because the intervention itself caused him to approve of the restriction on his liberty. Extreme examples of this self-justifying kind of paternalism are brainwashing and hypnosis, but milder and sometimes desirable forms, such as drug-education programs or compulsory counseling in welfare programs, also change a person's fundamental attitudes, and create difficulties for any attempt to justify paternalism by appealing to subsequent consent.[23] Nevertheless, the requirement that the constraint on liberty be as limited as possible does imply that we should choose the least restrictive alternative. The constraint should not extend, in scope or time, beyond the action specifically affected by the impairment in question. Hence, insofar as it

[21]Some theorists distinguish "strong paternalism" (restriction of voluntary choice) from "weak paternalism" (restriction of nonvoluntary choice), and hold that only the latter is justifiable. This view is consistent with my analysis only if one adopts, as Feinberg does ("Legal Paternalism," pp. 110–111, 124), a broad concept of voluntary choice corresponding to the notion of deliberate choice.

[22]Cf. Murphy, "Incompetence and Paternalism," pp. 482–483; and Feinberg, "Legal Paternalism," pp. 114–115.

[23]See Murphy, "Incompetence and Paternalism," pp. 482–483; Carter, "Justifying Paternalism," pp. 136–137; and Weale, "Paternalism and Social Policy," pp. 171–172.

is possible, society should regulate rather than proscribe harmful activities, and should always provide for the possibility of future consent—for example, by an enforced waiting period, rather than a permanent prohibition.[24] If future consent is impossible, we must have compelling grounds for believing that the individual would accept the good achieved by the paternalistic intervention, if his decision were not impaired.

The harm or benefit sought by the paternalist, however, is not always so obvious as it is in Mill's bridge example. More often, paternalism prevents an individual from choosing a course of action that *risks* harm instead of pursuing a safer course that he might not at the moment prefer. When the harm or benefit is not certain, we can be less confident that all individuals would or should accept the imposition of the same degree of risk. Furthermore, the comparative seriousness of the harm or benefit itself may be controversial. Even so obvious a harm as death is not one that all individuals should always want to avoid; surely one ought to be able to shorten or end one's life rather than indefinitely suffer a humiliating and painful illness. In a pluralistic society, judgments about the quality of life, and about the acceptability of means necessary to preserve life, are bound to differ; a Jehovah's Witness, for example, may reject a blood transfusion even if it is necessary for saving his life.[25] Neither can we clearly identify a class of harmful actions that should be restricted simply because they prevent the exercise of free choice in the future. Mill thought that a contract to sell oneself into slavery should be absolutely prohibited on these grounds, but, as many commentators have noted, we sacrifice future liberty when we make almost any kind of contract; a slavery contract is simply an extreme case, and could not be prohibited (at least on paternalistic grounds) without also proscribing many other kinds of contract.[26] (Society of course may regulate all such contracts to make sure they are freely entered into, and may wish for nonpaternalistic reasons to ban some kinds of contract completely.)

The problem of determining the kind of harm or benefit that would justify paternalism becomes most acute when the impairment is relatively permanent, and the restriction on liberty is relatively unlimited; in such cases, the individual whose liberty is constrained may never have a chance, even in the future, to accept or reject the appraisal of the harms or benefits that supposedly justifies the paternalism. But even where the individual will have such an opportunity, we still need criteria to specify what harms the individual would wish to avoid, or what benefits he would wish to enjoy, if his decision were not impaired.

[24]Murphy, "Incompetence and Paternalism," p. 479; G. Dworkin, "Paternalism," pp. 125–126; and Feinberg, "Legal Paternalism," pp. 116–117.

[25]Bayles ("Criminal Paternalism," p. 181) criticizes G. Dworkin for failing to deal with the problem of social pluralism. For some cases, see footnote 59.

[26]Mill, *On Liberty*, pp. 229–300; Mill, *Principles of Political Economy*, pp. 953–954; G. Dworkin, "Paternalism," pp. 117–118; and Feinberg, "Legal Paternalism," pp. 116–117.

These criteria sometimes can be based quite firmly on the individual's own settled preferences or his own life plan; if we know the individual well, if we can consult his family and friends, or if he has declared his wishes in advance (as, for example, in a "living will"), we may have good reason to assume that he would wish to avoid certain harms. Unfortunately, in some cases we cannot readily determine what a particular individual would wish; his friends and family may not be reliable sources, and his previous declarations may not be relevant to current circumstances. Furthermore, paternalistic legislation, which applies to an entire society, cannot easily be tailored to the settled preferences or life plans of particular individuals. We are thus driven to invoke a theory of the good that derives, not from the life plan of only one person, but from the plans of virtually all persons in the society. The problem then becomes to formulate a theory of the good that, insofar as is possible, imposes on individuals only values that all rational persons can accept.[27]

John Rawls offers a theory of primary goods to deal with this problem: "As we know less and less about a person, we act for him as we would act for ourselves from the standpoint of the original position. We try to get for him the things he presumably wants whatever else he wants."[28] Primary goods are "things that every rational man is presumed to want. These goods normally have a use whatever a person's rational plan of life." They include rights and liberties, powers and opportunities, income and wealth, and self-respect.[29] Although Rawls provides perhaps the most promising basis for the criteria that liberal paternalism needs to identify primary goods, his theory does not supply a completely neutral perspective that anyone, whatever his conception of the good, could accept. Rawls's primary goods, as critics have pointed out, are not equally valuable for all life plans. These goods, Thomas Nagel argues, are

> less useful in implementing views that hold a good life to be readily achievable only in certain well-defined types of social structure, or only in a society that works concertedly for the realization of certain higher human capacities and the suppression of baser ones, or only given certain types of economic relations among men.[30]

To escape this kind of objection completely, we would have to step outside of liberal theory altogether. Consider, for example, a Marxist theory, where

---

[27]It is difficult to avoid appealing to some kind of theory of the good, as Hodson discovers. After criticizing other theorists for in effect using such a theory, he proposes a concept of a "hypothetical unencumbered decision," which in some cases permits an appeal to a "rational will" ("The Principle of Paternalism," p. 63–68). See also Murphy, "Incompetence and Paternalism," pp. 481–483; G. Dworkin, "Paternalism," pp. 121–122; and Weale, "Paternalism and Social Policy," pp. 171–172.

[28]Rawls, *A Theory of Justice*, p. 249.

[29]Ibid., pp. 62, 90–95, 396 ff.

[30]Thomas Nagel, "Rawls on Justice," in Norman Daniels, ed., *Reading Rawls* (New York: Basic Books, 1975), pp. 9–10.

the notion of "false consciousness" plays a role formally analogous to an individual's misconception of his own good that justifies paternalism in liberal thought. As liberal individuals do not always know their own best interests, and must be guided by paternalistic measures, so Marxist classes do not always know their own good, and must be moved by a vanguard, a revolution, or some other means of transforming their consciousness. Just as the liberal seeks an objective standpoint from which to identify a good for individuals, so the Marxist attempts "to infer the thoughts and feelings which men would have in a particular situation if they were *able* to assess both it and the interests arising from it in their impact on immediate action and on the whole structure of society."[31] With Marxist theory it becomes possible to transcend the conception of primary goods that Rawls and other theorists attribute to individuals in a liberal society. But Marxism attains this transcendence at a cost. It severs the conception of the good completely from "what men *in fact* ... [want] at any moment in history,"[32] even when their choices are not impaired in the specific ways that we have already noted, and it therefore places no limit on the extent to which individual choices may be overridden, thus radically discounting the value of individual liberty.

Although a liberal doctrine of paternalism cannot always appeal to the actual choices that individuals make, the three conditions for justification warrant a paternalistic intervention only if an individual's choice is specifically impaired; the intervention is the least restrictive possible; and, when possible, the individual accepts the goal of the intervention, and, when that is not possible, the intervention satisfies a theory of primary goods that excludes relatively few life plans. The three conditions apply most directly to relationships between and among individuals, but suitably generalized they can also be used to appraise institutional relationships, as in legislative paternalism. Here we would look for impairments that arise from social structures or affect large numbers of people in similar ways, and would seek institutional limitations, such as hearings and appeals procedures, that in individual cases could partially override general prohibitions in the legislation. We would also insist that any paternalistic legislation conform to a theory of primary goods that virtually all members of society could accept, and we would further need to provide some institutional means of exempting individuals who might rationally reject even this theory. Despite the difficulties of interpreting each of the three conditions in the context both of individual and of institutional relationships, they provide a framework that creates a presumption in favor of individual liberty, and can encourage a critique of paternalistic practices in modern liberal society.

[31]Georg Lukás, *History and Class Consciousness*, trans. Rodney Livingstone (London: Merlin Press, 1971), pp. 51–54, 64–65, 72. The classical sources are Karl Marx and Friedrich Engels, "The German Ideology," in Robert Tucker, ed., *The Marx-Engels Reader*, 2d ed. (New York: W. W. Norton & Co., 1978), pp. 154–155, 163–175.

[32]Ibid., p. 51.

PROFESSIONALISM AND PATERNALISM

It may be argued that the relationship between a professional and a client is justifiable paternalism if it is paternalism at all. By enlisting the help of a professional, the client demonstrates that he lacks essential knowledge that only the professional can provide; the professional intervenes in limited and foreseen ways, and promotes a good, such as health or legal redress, that the client obviously accepts. Since a client voluntarily chooses the professional, can refuse his advice, and can go to another professional, we may suppose that the client, in effect, consents to whatever restrictions on his liberty the professional may impose.

This voluntaristic portrait of the relationship between a client and a professional neglects some features of professionalism that can give rise to paternalism. A profession is characterized, *inter alia*, by claims to a body of knowledge and specialized training; a monopoly over the training and practice of the profession (including self-regulation); and a social prestige that further enhances the authority of its members.[33] The client's ignorance that sometimes justifies paternalism also restricts his ability to choose among professionals, and to decide whether to follow professional advice. Abetted by the profession's claim to superior knowledge, a professional may be inclined to intervene in ways less limited than are actually called for by the client's circumstances. Professionals, for what they believe to be their client's own good, may, for example, withhold certain information, prescribe treatment, or provide services without the client's knowledge.[34] Although the client usually agrees with the general goal promoted by the profession (health, justice, welfare), professionals pursue these goals in many different ways, some of which a particular client may not accept, but is powerless to defy. To seek a second opinion, to engage another professional, or to charge malpractice is often very difficult. The client must challenge not merely an individual professional, but an institutionalized profession that in principle claims to be the exclusive arbiter of its members' competence, and in practice rallies to protect its members from criticism. Given the unequal roles of the professional and the client, it is not surprising that professionals restrict their client's liberty sometimes in ways that go beyond the limits and purposes of justifiable paternalism. This excessive paternalism is not a logically necessary consequence of professionalism, however, and in recent years many people, including professionals

[33]Ernest Greenwood, "The Elements of Professionalization," in H. M. Vollmer and D. L. Mills, eds., *Professionalization* (Englewood Cliffs, N. J.: Prentice-Hall, 1966), pp. 12–16, Richard Wasserstrom, "Lawyers as Professionals: Some Moral Issues," *Human Rights* 5 (1975), p. 2n; and Magali Sarfatti Larson, *The Rise of Professionalism* (Berkeley: University of California Press, 1977), p. x.

[34]Greenwood, "Elements of Professionalism," p. 12; Larson, *Rise of Professionalism*, pp. 220–225; and Everett C. Hughes, "Professions," in Kenneth Lynn *et al.*, eds., *The Professions in America* (Boston: Beacon Press, 1963), pp. 2–3.

themselves, have urged changes in the relationship between professionals and their clients, to reduce or eliminate paternalism.[35]

The salient feature of the traditional model of the relationship between doctor and patient is, according to many writers, "paternalistic benevolence."[36] The doctor's superior professional knowledge and altruistic intentions, on this view, warrant acting in a patient's interest without fully informing the patient of the nature of the diagnosis or the treatment, if the doctor believes that the health of the patient is best served in this way. In extreme cases, the doctor may use deception and even subtle forms of coercion to secure a patient's compliance. The traditional model has been challenged on both normative and empirical grounds.[37] A doctor who adopts a paternalistic attitude may violate a patient's liberty by restricting the range of choices that he can make. Although the doctor may know best what treatment is most appropriate for a specific pathology, he or she does not necessarily know best how information or treatment will affect a patient's whole well-being. Although the doctor may find it difficult to explain to a patient the diagnosis and the options for treatment, he can usually give much more complete and honest explanations than the traditional model demands.[38] Similarly, the notion that the relationship between doctor and patient rests on a contract in which the patient at least temporarily surrenders his autonomy to the doctor has been criticized for, among other things, implying that the doctor is accountable to no one but himself and the standards of the profession.[39] Furthermore, several empirical studies have shown that, the more fully a doctor explains a diagnosis and treatment, the more likely a patient is to comply with the doctor's instructions, and to be satisfied with the treatment.[40] Proponents of a more participatory model of the doctor–patient relationship propose measures such as a Patient's Bill of Rights, a Patient Rights Advocate, and changes in professional education and standards to encourage doctors to con-

---

[35]Matthew P. Cumont, "The Changing Face of Professionalism," *Social Policy* 1 (1970), pp. 26–31.

[36]Bernard Barber, "Compassion in Medicine: Toward New Definitions and New Institutions," *New England Journal of Medicine* 295 (1976), pp. 939–940; and Note, "Restructuring Informed Consent: Legal Therapy for the Doctor–Patient Relationship," *Yale Law Journal* 79 (1972), pp. 1535–1537.

[37]See Buchanan, "Medical Paternalism," pp. 370–387; and Edmund Pellegrino, "Medical Ethics, Education, and the Physician's Image," *Journal of the American Medical Association* 235 (1976), pp. 1043–1044.

[38]On truth telling in medicine, see Bok, *Lying,* pp. 220–241, and the essays in Stanley Joel Reiser *et al., Ethics in Medicine* (Cambridge, Mass.: M.I.T. Press, 1977), pp. 201–240.

[39]Roger D. Masters, "Is Contract an Adequate Basis for Medical Ethics?" *Hastings Center Report* 6 (1975), pp. 26–28; and William F. May, "Code, Covenant, Contract, or Philanthropy," *Hastings Center Report* 6 (1975), p. 36.

[40]David D. Schmidt, "Patient Compliance: The Effect of the Doctor as Therapeutic Agent," *Journal of Family Practice* 4 (1977), pp. 853–856; R. Duff and A. Hollingshead, *Sickness and Society* (New York: Harper & Row, 1968), pp. 280 ff.; and Thomas F. Plaut, "Doctor's Order and Patient Compliance," *New England Journal of Medicine* 292 (1975), p. 1043.

sult more openly with their patients, and recognize their professional ethics to be part of a universal ethics that creates a presumption against paternalism.[41] It has also been suggested that the traditional interpretation of "informed consent" should be altered. Instead of appealing to the "professional standard of care" (what would a reasonable doctor in this community have told the patient?), we should invoke a layman's standard (what would a reasonable patient need to know in order to make an intelligent decision?).[42] All of these proposals seek to foster a doctor–patient relationship in which a patient's ignorance and a doctor's unilateral actions and neglect of a patient's own views about his welfare are kept to a minimum—in short, a relationship that is as little paternalistic as possible.

The relationship between lawyers and clients also manifests paternalistic tendencies.[43] One survey of the attitudes of lawyers found that many "seem to need and gain pleasure from being paternalistic and dominating."[44] A manual on "How to Handle a New Client" advises that the lawyer give some clients what they want—"the calm reassurance of a good, wise parent."[45] It might be supposed that the conduct of a paternalistic lawyer is less pernicious than that of a paternalistic doctor, since a client's needs are less urgent than a patient's, a client can more easily change lawyers than a patient can change doctors, and a client can more readily understand legal options than a patient can comprehend medical alternatives. But, in many circumstances, the lawyer is the client's last hope of protection against severe deprivations of liberty, and often the client, especially if he or she is indigent, scarcely has any choice among lawyers.[46] The law can appear as mysterious as medical doctrine, and the criterion for what should count as a successful outcome of a legal dispute can be less clear than that for an outcome of medical treatment. Moreover, insofar as paternalism warrants a professional's favoring a patient or client over other individuals, the

[41]Joseph Margolis, "Conceptual Aspects of a Patient's Bill of Rights," *Journal of Value Inquiry* 12 (1978), pp. 126–135; George J. Annas and Joseph M. Healey, "The Patient Rights Advocate: Redefining the Doctor–Patient Relationship in the Hospital Context," *Vanderbilt Law Review* 27 (1974), pp. 243–269; and Robert Veatch, "Medical Ethics: Professional or Universal?" *Harvard Theological Review* 65 (1972), pp. 531–559.

[42]Note, "Restructuring Informed Consent," pp. 1555–1556; Benjamin Freedman, "A Moral Theory of Informed Consent," *Hastings Center Report* 6 (1975), pp. 34–36; and Marcus L. Plante, "An Analysis of 'Informed Consent,'" *Fordham Law Review* 56 (1968), pp. 649–650.

[43]Wasserstrom, "Lawyers as Professionals," pp. 16–22; Douglas Rosenthal, *Lawyer and Client: Who's in Charge?* (New York: Russell Sage Foundation, 1974), pp. 143–177, and Andrew S. Watson, *The Lawyer in the Interviewing and Counselling Process* (Charlottesville, Va.: Michie Co., 1976), pp. 133–135, 143–158.

[44]Rosenthal, *Lawyer and Client*, p. 172.

[45]Mirta T. Mulhare, "How to Handle a New Client," *The Practical Lawyer* 21 (1975), pp. 20, 22.

[46]See Marvin E. Frankel, "Experiments in Serving the Indigent," *American Bar Association Journal* 51 (1965), p. 461. A more radical view of the practice of poverty law is Stephen Wexler, "Practicing Law for Poor People," *Yale Law Journal* 79 (1970), pp. 1049–1067.

social consequences of lawyers' paternalism may be more harmful than those of doctors', since winning a client's case, unlike curing a patient, is not an intrinsic good.[47]

The paternalistic model of legal practice not only can have undesirable social consequences, but also may not serve the best interests of the client. A study of 60 New York lawyers litigating personal-injury claims found that "clients who actively seek information about their problems and participate in and share responsibility for dealing with them" are likely to get better results than "clients who trustingly and passively delegate responsibility."[48] Legal reformers have urged changes that would discourage paternalism in the lawyer–client relationship, including simplification of legal language, and training in more participatory styles of legal practice. Some have also proposed guidelines, perhaps enforced by law, that would require lawyers to consult more extensively with their clients; specifically, a lawyer should discuss with the client any delegation of part of the case to another lawyer, the terms offered or accepted in any out-of-court settlement, how much time should be devoted to the case, whether to go to trial, and important decisions about courtroom strategy (e.g. use of expert witnesses).[49] Some have suggested that the lawyer should be required to secure the client's written approval every time he makes an important decision in the case.[50] The participatory model itself is not without problems. Carried too far, it could absolve the lawyer of all responsibility for the advice he gives, and could restrict the liberty of a client who, with full knowledge, wishes to delegate authority for some major decisions to his lawyer.[51] Similar consequences could ensue from applying the model to the doctor–patient relationship. It would be unfortunate if the effort to guard against paternalistic intrusions succeeded only in eroding liberty in other ways.

Yet another kind of professional relationship—between social worker and client—has been criticized for excessive paternalism.[52] Added to the paternalistic tendencies of professionalism are further effects that flow from the social

---

[47]Cf. Wasserstrom, "Lawyers as Professionals," p. 14.

[48]Rosenthal, *Lawyer and Client*, pp. 148–149.

[49]Ibid., pp. 153, 156–157, and Wasserstrom, "Lawyers as Professionals," pp. 23–24.

[50]Lester J. Mazor, "Power and Responsibility in the Attorney–Client Relation," *Stanford Law Review* 20 (1968), pp. 1138–1139.

[51]The American Bar Association's Code of Professional Responsibility gives the attorney a right to control "certain areas of legal representation not affecting the merits of the cause or substantially prejudicing the rights of a client" (EC 7-7). See also Vern Countryman, Ted Finman and Theodore J. Schneyer, *The Lawyer in Modern Society*, 2d ed. (Boston: Little, Brown, & Co., 1976), pp. 80–81.

[52]Henry Miller, "Value Dilemmas in Social Casework," *Social Work* 13 (1968), pp. 32–33; Marie R. Haug and Marvin B. Sussman, "Professional Autonomy and the Revolt of the Client," *Social Problems* 71 (1969), pp. 156–159; and Ira Glasser, "Prisoners of Benevolence: Power Versus Liberty in the Welfare State," in Willard Gaylin *et al.*, eds., *Doing Good: The Limits of Benevolence* (New York: Pantheon Books, 1978), pp. 107–108, 118–119.

worker's position as an agent of the government. Because the social worker must follow general policies set by government, he or she may not be able to define the client's good exclusively as the client might.[53] In the process of helping the client, the social worker may also change "the client's attitudes and conduct so that he conforms more closely to expected and accepted patterns of behavior."[54] The process bristles with the dangers of self-justifying paternalism. Furthermore, because clients are typically poor, and members of minority groups, the inequalities of class and race exacerbate the inequalities of professionalism. To counter what has been called "welfare paternalism," reformers have urged greater participation by clients in the agencies that social workers and other professionals now dominate, stronger statements of the rights of clients, various legal protections, including welfare rights advocates, and the separation of income maintenance from the other services, so that a citizen may obtain the former without the latter.[55] Many have welcomed the growth of self-help organizations, such as the Mobilization for Youth, as a way to provide counseling and other social services for the needy while avoiding the paternalism that professional social workers might foster.[56] One writer has even proposed that social workers serve clients on a fee-for-service basis, subsidized by the government, but otherwise independent of government authority, so that the social worker may, without conflict, pursue the good of the client.[57] Others have warned that these reforms may go too far. In their efforts to exorcize the baleful aspect of paternalism, the reformers have forgotten that the paternalism of social work has a benign side. At least ideally, the social worker brings professional skills and a sense of caring that can genuinely benefit clients—most successfully when the relationship is not adversarial.[58] Here, as in other professional relationships, the problem is not to embrace or eradicate paternalism totally, but to locate its justifiable limits.

[53]Irving Piliavin, "Restructuring the Provision of Social Services," *Social Work* 13 (1968), pp. 35–37.

[54]Nina Toren, "The Structure of Social Casework and Behavioral Change," *Journal of Social Policy* 3 (1974), pp. 343.

[55]Joseph E. Paull, "Recipients Aroused: The New Welfare Rights Movement," *Social Work* 12 (1967), p. 104 ff.; Ad Hoc Committee on Advocacy, "The Social Worker as Advocate," *Social Work* 14 (1969), pp. 19–20; Miller, "Value Dilemmas in Social Casework," pp. 30–31, 33; and Glasser, "Prisoners of Benevolence," p. 146 ff.

[56]Alfred H. Katz, "Self-Help Organizations and Volunteer Participation in Social Welfare," *Social Work* 15 (1970), pp. 52–53; and Anthony J. Vattano, "Power to the People: Self-Help Groups," *Social Work* 17 (1972), pp. 13–14.

[57]Piliavin, "Restructuring Provision of Social Services," pp. 36–37.

[58]See Willard Gaylin, "In the Beginning: Helpless and Dependent," in Gaylin *et al.*, eds., *Doing Good: The Limits of Benevolence* (New York: Pantheon Books, 1978), pp. 32–33; and Donald Feldstein, "Do We Need Professions in our Society? Professionalization versus Consumerism," *Social Work* 16 (1971), pp. 5–11.

So far, we have concentrated on the paternalism that professionals foster by permitting clients little control over decisions made in their behalf. Typically, this paternalism takes the form of restricting opportunities for action by withholding certain information. Now we shall consider some cases where paternalism involves prohibiting specific actions, either by directly forcing benefits on an individual, or by imposing sanctions if the individual acts contrary to what others consider to be his own good.

COMPULSORY MEDICAL TREATMENT

Courts have generally held that adults of sound mind have the right to decide what is done to their body, and have therefore, in principle, rejected the paternalistic imposition of medical care.[59] Courts have recognized the right of patients to decline lifesaving treatment under emergency and nonemergency conditions, both where the prognosis is poor, and where it would be favorable if the treatment were administered. A patient can be compelled to accept medical care if it is necessary to prevent harm to other people, especially children, or to protect public health, but the patient's own harm cannot justify interference, even on grounds that patient has contracted with the doctor to preserve his health, or that the doctor has a legal and ethical obligation to do everything within his power to save the patient's life.[60] The patient's liberty takes precedence over both of these claims.

Although the general principle is strongly antipaternalist, it has been eroded by exceptions of three kinds. First, the doctrine of "therapeutic privilege" permits a doctor to withhold information if he thinks that the information would harm the patient, and thus may allow a doctor to administer treatment without the patient's full knowledge. I have already suggested that most instances of the withholding of information cannot be considered to be justifiable paternalism. Similar objections often apply to the use of placebos, which is, in effect, a form of compulsory nontreatment.[61] More difficult to judge is a second kind of exception: cases in which the patient does not simply reject treatment, or even request that treatment be discontinued, but asks the doctor

---

[59]Note, "Informed Consent and the Dying Patient," *Yale Law Journal* 83 (1974), p. 1632 ff.; and Robert M. Byrn, "Compulsory Lifesaving Treatment for the Competent Adult," *Fordham Law Review* 44 (1975), pp. 1–36.

[60]Byrn, "Compulsory Lifesaving Treatment," pp. 20–35. The question of compulsory sterilization illustrates poignantly some of the difficulties in distinguishing the paternalistic justification for intervention from one based on avoiding harm to others and to society. See "Sterilization of the Retarded: In Whose Interest?" *Hastings Center Report* 9 (1978), pp. 29–41.

[61]On the ethics of administering placebos, see Reiser *et al.*, *Ethics in Medicine*, pp. 240–252; and Bok, *Lying*, pp. 61–68, 97.

to administer a treatment that is likely to bring death. A physician may refuse to take such an active role, not purely for paternalistic reasons, but on the grounds that he or she ought not to be responsible for the death of another person.[62] Whether agreeing to administer treatment that causes death differs fundamentally from agreeing not to administer treatment that would preserve life depends on how one resolves some controversial problems (such as the status of the distinction between acts and omissions) in the theory of action and ethics more generally.[63] Although these problems cannot be settled by considering paternalism alone, we should notice nevertheless that the question of how far a doctor should go in helping a patient in these circumstances cannot be determined by medical criteria alone, such as the supposedly technical distinction between "ordinary" and "extraordinary" measures.[64]

A third class of exceptions—the most expansive—covers cases in which the patient is assumed to be mentally incompetent. It will often be difficult to determine whether a patient is, in fact, incompetent; physicians may disagree, and, in any case, they should not have the last word.[65] However, paternalism cannot be justified, as we have seen, if the chief criterion for mental incompetency is that the patient prefers an end (e.g. death) that the doctor regards as irrational. We may also wish to say that mere ignorance should not be sufficient, but even here "false belief" (such as in the much-discussed case of the otherwise rational woman who refused a hysterectomy because she did not believe she had cancer) may suggest qualifications; false beliefs may not warrant compulsory treatment, but they may call for extraordinary techniques of persuasion that would not otherwise be justified.[66] When there is no doubt that a patient is incompetent (if he is in a coma, for example), the problem then becomes to determine who should decide on the treatment, and according to what criteria of harm or benefit.[67] We are reluctant to give the parents or family full authority to make such decisions (their interests may differ from the patient's), but also hesitant to delegate responsibility solely to physicians, or to agents of the state (they too may have different interests, and also may understandably not wish to

[62]Note, "Informed Consent," pp. 1649–1650; and Byrn, "Compulsory Lifesaving Treatment," p. 8.
[63]See Charles Fried, *Right and Wrong* (Cambridge: Harvard University Press, 1978), pp. 201–204, 206–207, and citations therein.
[64]Buchanan, "Medical Paternalism," pp. 387–388.
[65]For some of the long-standing theoretical and practical problems in specifying criteria for mental incompetency in such cases, see Ronald Leifer, "The Competence of the Psychiatrist to Assist in the Determination of Incompetency," *Syracuse Law Review* 4 (1963), pp. 564–575.
[66]Ruth Faden and Alan Faden, "False Belief and the Refusal of Medical Treatment," *Journal of Medical Ethics* 3 (1977), pp. 133–136.
[67]For a criticism of one solution to this problem—the provision of "living wills"—see Marc I. Steinberg, "The California Natural Death Act: A Failure to Provide for Adequate Patient Safeguards and Individual Autonomy," *Connecticut Law Review* 8 (1977), pp. 203–220.

give professional or public sanction to the termination of life). In the case of Karen Quinlan, the New Jersey Supreme Court resolved—or evaded—this dilemma by requiring the consent of the parents, the attending physicians, and an Ethics Committee (the composition of which was also left vague). The Court, however, did stipulate that the criterion of harm or benefit should be what the patient herself would desire if she were "miraculously lucid for an interval . . . and perceptive of her irreversible condition."[68] This criterion is necessary for the justification of paternalism, but its application is not always clear, and it may yield conclusions in some cases (for example, involving Jehovah's Witnesses) that differ from what most people in similar circumstances would desire.[69] To justify paternalism, we cannot appeal to what rational persons in general would desire if we can determine what a particular person would want in the circumstances.[70]

THE LAW OF INVOLUNTARY GUARDIANSHIP

The law of most states provides that courts may appoint a guardian to manage the estate and the personal affairs of an individual who is not capable of doing so himself. The chief rationale is paternalistic: the guardianship is necessary to protect the individual from himself. Typically, the ward may not, without the guardian's approval, dispose of property, enter valid contracts, marry, change his domicile, or choose agents to act for him (doctors, lawyers, or even another guardian).[71] The practice of guardianship seems justified in many cases where the mental deficiency is clear (for example, severely retarded adults), but the courts and the state have also appointed guardians for persons who were deemed "improvident," "physically incapacitated," "excessive drinkers," "aged," "idlers," or "spendthrifts."[72] An Ohio court placed an 85-year-old man, other-

[68] *In re Quinlan*, 70 N. J. 10, 355 A. 2d 647 at 671 ff. (1976). See also Harold L. Hirsch and Richard E. Donovan, "The Right to Die: Medico-Legal Implications of *In Re Quinlan*," *Rutgers Law Review* 30 (1977), pp. 267–303; and the articles in "The Quinlan Decision: Five Commentaries," *Hastings Center Report* 7 (1976), pp. 8–19.

[69] See the cases in Byrn, "Compulsory Lifesaving Treatment," pp. 10–13; and Reiser et al., *Ethics in Medicine*, pp. 199–200.

[70] For a proposal that would establish such a standard in the law, see Note, "Informed Consent," p. 1642.

[71] Generally, see Richard C. Allen, Alyce Z. Ferster, and Henry Weihofen, *Mental Impairment and Legal Incompetency* (Englewood Cliffs, N. J.: Prentice-Hall, 1968), pp. 70–112, and Note, "The Disguised Oppression of Involuntary Guardianship: Have the Elderly Freedom to Spend?" *Yale Law Journal* 73 (1964), pp. 676–692. Similar issues arise when government agencies (the Social Security Administration or the Veterans' Administration) appoint a "representative payee" or "fiduciary" to receive someone's payments (see Allen et al., *Mental Impairment*, pp. 114–142).

[72] Allen et al., *Mental Impairment*, pp. 73–74, 236.

wise perfectly sane, under guardianship at the request of one of his potential heirs because he had given away a large portion of his estate (though he still had a trust fund that fully provided for all his own future needs).[73]

The broad reach of guardianship law, as it has often been applied, runs afoul of the conditions for justifiable paternalism—not only by invoking overly broad criteria of impairment, but also by restricting liberty beyond what would be necessary to protect a ward. Often commitment to a hospital is taken as a sufficient reason for appointing a guardian, though the ward may still be perfectly competent to manage his affairs in most respects. Courts and the state rarely monitor guardianships closely, and the procedure for terminating a guardianship is difficult, and seldom invoked by wards themselves.[74] Some of the dangers of guardianship might be alleviated if, as in the so-called Minnesota Plan, guardians were generally state officials; though this state paternalism brings problems of its own. Legal provisions for prior consent (e.g., designating guardians and specifying their authority in advance), and better procedures for hearings, reviews, and appeals in guardianship cases, might also help.[75] Whatever institutional reforms are contemplated, they should permit guardianship only if the impairment, the extent and duration of the guardianship, and the potential self-harm meet the conditions for justifiable paternalism.

THE DISTRIBUTION OF PUBLIC WELFARE

The general question of whether the government should redistribute income to the poor depends on what theory of social justice one adopts, not on what stand one takes on paternalism. Any restrictions of liberty that the government imposes to obtain the resources for redistribution do not fall on the recipients of welfare, but on the other members of society.[76] Even Mill would countenance such restrictions ("acts done for the benefit of others than the person concerned") as a legitimate exception to his presumption against government interference with individual liberty.[77] Once we accept a system of public welfare, however, the form in which the government distributes benefits can give rise to paternalism. Consistently with granting citizens a right to certain benefits, a welfare system may require that recipients satisfy certain conditions, or use the benefits in certain ways. Such requirements, in some circumstances, can be defended on grounds of administrative efficiency and social justice; but when they are primarily intended to promote the good of recipients, they con-

---

[73]Note, "The Disguised Oppression," pp. 680–681.

[74]Allen *et al.*, *Mental Impairment*, pp. 89, 92–93, 228–230.

[75]Ibid., pp. 99–112, 170–175.

[76]But see Weale, "Paternalism and Social Policy," pp. 164–165.

[77]Mill, *Principles of Political Economy*, p. 961.

stitute paternalism, preventing recipients from using the welfare payments as they might otherwise like to do. One kind of requirement—that the recipient accept any available job for which he or she is qualified—is sometimes proposed for paternalistic reasons, but it is also supposed to ensure that welfare goes only to those who most need it, and to keep the welfare rolls as small as possible.[78] Another kind of requirement—that a recipient accept counsel and scrutiny by social workers or welfare officials—encourages a paternalistic relationship of the kind that we have already examined.[79]

Some special problems of paternalism arise when the government requires that the welfare payments be used in certain ways by providing in-kind benefits (for example, food stamps, clothing, housing) instead of income.[80] Such a policy is sometimes defended on grounds of administrative efficiency: in-kind aid circumvents the problem of regional differences in prices of goods, and reduces opportunities for corruption. But, since the administrative arguments cut both ways (in-kind payments entail a more elaborate bureaucracy), the justification of in-kind aid must rest to a great extent on a paternalistic basis. The "underlying assumption" of such a policy is that "the poor need assistance because, unlike the rest of the population, they are unable to make the relevant choices by themselves."[81] If the government does not force recipients to use the benefits for purposes that will do them the most good, the recipients, inclined to satisfy present more than future desires, are not likely to act in their own best interests. The trouble with this rationale and the policy it promotes is that rarely do legislators and administrators have good evidence to show that the decisions of all or most recipients are impaired in the way required to justify paternalism. Moreover, in-kind aid is not, among practicable welfare policies, the one that interferes least with the liberty of recipients. A policy of a guaranteed income, or a negative income tax, many have urged, could accomplish most of the legitimate goals of a welfare system, while avoiding the more or less permanent restrictions inherent in a program of in-kind aid.[82] Unlike in-kind aid, a guaranteed-income policy gives recipients more opportunity to learn to manage their own affairs better, and eventually become less dependent on the direction of other people

[78]See Daniel P. Moynihan, *The Politics of Guaranteed Income* (New York: Random House, 1973), pp. 141–142, 218–220.
[79]See also Eveline M. Burns, "What's Wrong with Public Welfare?" *Social Science Review* 36 (1962), pp. 113–114.
[80]Weale, "Paternalism and Socialism," pp. 166–169; Lester C. Thurow, "Government Expenditures: Cash or In-Kind Aid?" *Philosophy and Public Affairs* 6 (1976), esp. 372–375; Lewis Coser, "What Do the Poor Need? (Money)," *Dissent* 18 (1971), pp. 485–491; Donald V. Fandetti, "Income versus Service Strategies," *Social Work* 17 (1972), pp. 87–93; and Moynihan, *Guaranteed Income*, pp. 116–124.
[81]Coser, "What Do Poor Need?" p. 488.
[82]Generally, see Larry D. Singell, "A Federally Guaranteed Minimum Income: Pros and Cons," *Current History* 65 (1973), pp. 62–87; and Moynihan, *Guaranteed Income*, pp. 17–59, 113–227.

and the state. The methods for distributing welfare range on a continuum, from the provision of cash through cash with advice, cash with compulsory advice, vouchers, in-kind payments, and dictated expenditures.[83] Any welfare system based on a paternalistic rationale should begin with the least restrictive policy on the continuum, and move to more restrictive ones only if they are necessary to make the system just, and only if they are consistent with the other conditions for justifiable paternalism.

THE REGULATION OF DRUGS

No paternalistic arguments need be marshaled to justify a large dose of regulation, or even prohibition, of harmful drugs. Mill prescribes the labelling of drugs "with some word expressive of [their] dangerous character," stringent controls on drugs that contribute to crime, and prohibition of the use of drugs by persons who while under the influence of drugs have previously committed crimes or otherwise harmed other members of society. Further restrictions would, on Mill's principles, be warranted to reduce the opportunities for fraud, and undue pressure on potential buyers of drugs.[84] To be sure, some forms of the argument from social harm tread precariously close to paternalism—for example, in proscribing the use of drugs by children and others in a "delirious state." Also, much of the crime associated with certain drugs occurs in the context of black-market operations made possible because a drug is illegal.[85] Furthermore, the decision that a drug is harmful involves a judgment about the degree of risk that a rational person should accept. Since no drug is completely safe, the government determines for society the various trade-offs between risks and benefits of drugs, and in the process may introduce paternalistic considerations.[86]

Nevertheless, in recent years it has been relatively harmless drugs that have generated the most controversy.[87] A 1962 amendment to the Food, Drug and Cosmetics Act mandated that the Food and Drug Administration require manufacturers to show that a new drug is not only safe, but also effective.[88] Some critics have assailed this amendment as opening the door to paternalism: "Freedom is the issue. The American people should be allowed to make their own

[83]Thurow, "Government Expenditures," pp. 372–375.

[84]Mill, On Liberty, pp. 294–297.

[85]Herbert L. Packer, The Limits of the Criminal Sanction (Stanford, Calif.: Stanford University Press, 1968), p. 332 ff.

[86]Cf. Hess and Clark, Div. of Rhodia, Inc., v. FDA, 495 f. 2d 975, 993–994 (D.C. Cir. 1974). On the FDA's proscription of saccharin, see "The Great Saccharin Snafu," Consumer Reports (1977), pp. 410–414.

[87]Generally, see David Boies and Paul R. Verkuil, Public Control of Business (Boston: Little, Brown & Co., 1977), pp. 720–741.

[88]21 U.S.C. 301 et seq., esp. 355(d).

decisions. They shouldn't have the bureaucrats in Washington, D. C. trying to decide for them what's good and what's bad, as long as it's safe."[89] If the government can prohibit the use of drugs because they are relatively ineffective, so the argument goes, the government could also on the same grounds ban any products (e.g. sugar cereals, frivolous games) that do not benefit individuals at all, or as much as some other products.[90]

In a controversy with curious political overtones, many of these arguments have been directed against the FDA's ban on Laetrile (also known as Vitamin B-17 or Amygdalin), a substance long touted as a cure or treatment for cancer. Scientific studies suggest that Laetrile is not effective in the treatment of cancer.[91] But since 1970 at least 15 states have legalized Laetrile, and several courts have overruled the FDA ban, implying that it constitutes unjustified paternalism.[92] For its own part, the FDA has not claimed any unqualified paternalistic authority, but rather has sought to show that the decision to use Laetrile is usually impaired. The cancer victim's choice between Laetrile and alternative therapies that are likely to be more effective cannot be free, because the victim decides in a "climate of anxiety and fear" created by the especially morbid nature of the disease and exacerbated by pecuniary and political pressures that the pro-Laetrile movement itself has produced.[93] Labeling Laetrile as ineffective would not be sufficient, because most people already know that fact, but cannot (as a result of "weakness of will"?) act on it.[94] By pointing to a serious impairment and a harm that a rational person would want to avoid, the FDA, in effect, seeks to meet the conditions for justifiable paternalism.

Insofar as the opponents of Laetrile can show that the decision to use the drug is substantially impaired, paternalistic prohibition of its use would be justified in many cases. However, this justification still must assume that the cancer victims would accept the goal of preserving their lives, and this assumption obviously does not apply to terminal patients. The FDA argues that we have no useful and reliable criterion to identify terminal patients, and that, even if we did, permitting them to use Laetrile would create enforcement difficulties, and tend to legitimize the drug for other patients.[95] Yet surely a person's decision to

---

[89]Representative Steven D. Symms (interview), "Legalize Laetrile as a Cancer Drug?" *U. S. News and World Report* 82 (1977), p. 51. For other evaluations, see Richard Landau, ed., *Regulating New Drugs* (Chicago, Center for Policy Study, University of Chicago, 1973).

[90]Boies and Verkuil, *Public Control of Business,* pp. 735–736.

[91]Generally, see FDA, "Laetrile: Commissioner's Decision on Status," *Federal Register,* Washington, D. C. August 5, 1977, pp. 39768–39805. The FDA case has concentrated on the inefficacy of Laetrile, but more recently some evidence suggests that the drug may be harmful also.

[92]Daniel B. Moscowitz, "Therapy Choice Increasingly Judged Layman's Domain," *Medical World News* 19 (1978), p. 80.

[93]FDA, "Laetrile," pp. 39803–39804.

[94]Ibid.

[95]Ibid., p. 39805.

risk death, if it is ever to be respected, should not be abridged in the face of a prognosis of virtually certain death, and the administrative objections raised by the FDA should not be decisive.[96] This is not to say that the government should not regulate, or under some circumstances prohibit, Laetrile even on paternalistic grounds, but only that an unqualified ban on the drug would not be as limited as the conditions of justifiable paternalism call for.[97]

THE REGULATION OF SAFETY

Like drug regulation, safety legislation can to a large extent be justified as necessary for preventing harm to others, or effecting collective goals efficiently. Thus, the Department of Transportation has not been charged with paternalism for recalling defective trucks and cars, or for mandating head restraints and other safety features on vehicles. The courts have generally upheld such regulations as a legitimate exercise of the police power of the state.[98] However, most of the regulations leave the consumer free not to use the safety devices, and thus differ from requirements that, for example, force drivers to use seat belts (as do ignition interlock systems and passive restraints). Laws that directly constrain drivers in this way have met with some judicial resistance and legislative reversal, partly on grounds that they constitute "an infringement on . . . personal freedom," thus implicitly raising the specter of paternalism.[99]

If such laws cannot be defended on grounds of social harm, they may not be justifiable at all, for a paternalistic rationale does not seem compelling here. It would be difficult to identify, independently of consumers' refusal to use safety devices, any specific impairment they suffer, and to show that they do not really want to accept the risks entailed by this refusal. Yet paternalistic arguments persist because the argument from social harm often appears even more tenuous. Laws requiring motorcyclists to wear protective helmets illustrate this strain toward paternalism. Many proponents of helmet laws, in defending the laws as necessary to protect society, stretch the concept of social harm to the point where it merges with paternalism. A leading advocate of such laws maintains:

> A society has a right to protect itself and its individual members from clear and
> present danger, and . . . requiring motorcyclists to protect themselves and all of

---

[96]"Ethical Dilemmas: The Laetrile Issue," *Medical Economics* (1977), pp. 162–169.

[97]Without considering the ethics of paternalism, the Supreme Court has upheld the authority of the FDA to ban Laetrile even for terminal patients; see *U.S.* v. *Rutherford,* 61 L Ed 2d 68 (1979).

[98]Boies and Verkuil, *Public Control of Business,* pp. 719–720.

[99]*Chrysler Corp.* v. *DOT,* 472 F. 2d 659 (6th Cir. 1972); and 15 U.S.C. 1397 (1974). See Comment, "Limiting the State's Police Power: Judicial Reaction to John Stuart Mill," *University of Chicago Law Review* 37 (1970), pp. 605–627.

us from this damage and this cost is completely within the right—and indeed the duty—of a compassionate community.[100]

No good evidence supports the claim that helmetless riders are more likely to injure others in accidents.[101] Insurance companies (and other members of society) could, in theory, avoid increased costs by refusing to compensate helmetless victims. If motorcyclists were willing, for their folly, to forgo making claims on society's medical resources, what further reason could society have to compel them to wear helmets? Even the courts, which have been reluctant to challenge a legislature's determination of social harm in these cases, have usually rejected the contention that "the State has an interest in the 'viability' of its citizens and can legislate to keep them healthy and self-supporting. This logic would lead to unlimited paternalism."[102]

If this excessive charity appears threatening, however, the cool indifference of extreme antipaternalism seems repellent. To resist resolutely any paternalism in regulation is to come close to embracing a conception of society in which each member owes nothing to others, except not to harm them. If an individual insists on taking risks that most citizens consider irrational and do not wish to pay the costs of, society may, on this conception, refuse to come to his aid if he harms himself as a result of taking these risks. In such a society, injured motorcyclists and other victims who had taken foolish chances would be left unattended on the streets and highways.[103] The antipaternalism that characterizes current policy does not follow this logic to such ruthless conclusions. Since 1976, when Congress told the Department of Transportation to stop withholding highway funds from states that had no mandatory helmet laws, more than 20 states have repealed these laws, but no state has taken steps to deny care to helmetless victims, or in any other way to treat them differently from other

[100]Ben Kelley, "Make Motorcyclists Wear Helmets?" *U. S. News and World Report* 82 (1977), pp. 39–40 (interview); and "Motorcycles and Public Apathy," *American Journal of Public Health* 66 (1976), p. 475. (More generally, see footnote 15).

[101]Although the claim that helmet *laws* reduce injuries has been challenged, all serious studies have confirmed the proposition that wearing helmets reduces injuries and fatalities. See, e.g., Jess F. Kraus *et al.*, "Some Epidemiologic Features of Motorcycle Collision Injuries," *American Journal of Epidemiology* 10 (1975), pp. 74–109.

[102]*American Motorcycle Ass'n.* v. *State Police*, 11 Mich. App. 351, 158 N.W. 2d 72, 75 (1968). Cf. *People* v. *Fries*, 42 Ill. 2d 446, 250 N.E. 2d 149 (1969); *Kingery* v. *Chapple*, 504 P. 2d 831 (Alas. 1972); *State ex/rel. Calvin* v. *Lombardi*, 104 R.I. 28, 241 A. 2d 625 (1968), aff'd. *State* v. *Lombardi*, 110 R.I. 776, 298 A. 2d, 141 (1972); and *Simon* v. *Sargent*, 346 F. Supp. 277 (1972).

[103]In an effort to justify helmet laws under a "harm principle," Regan suggests that even a motorcyclist who renounces his claim on society's resources still harms other people: he puts other people in a position where they must undertake some burden or expense to satisfy their general moral obligation to help others in need. But to sustain his argument, Regan is ultimately forced to propose a curious theory of personal identity, according to which a motorcyclist before an accident is a different person from the motorcyclist after the accident ("Justification for Paternalism," pp. 202–205).

victims. The way that current policy in many states thus combines antipaternalism and public benevolence may be theoretically strained, but it is practically desirable. Although rejecting paternalism, these states have nevertheless preserved the obligation to help those who harm themselves.

THE PEDAGOGY OF PATERNALISM

Although many of the issues in the teaching of paternalism also arise in the teaching of the ethics of other practical problems, three issues are especially pertinent to paternalism. First, there is the question of a satisfactory balance between case material and theoretical literature. The use of cases checks the temptation, particularly strong in discussions of paternalism, to assert that paternalism is never justified. This assertion may be defensible, but much less simply, once one has been forced to consider a range of cases, including some in which the person whose liberty is in question is unconscious, or otherwise unable to express his wishes. Examining a variety of cases is also an instructive way to convey the complexity of the notion of impairment as it is employed in justifications of paternalism. Each of the concepts that general classifications of impairment identify (e.g.,"mental illness," irrationality," "ignorance") embraces a wide assortment of cases, some of which call for paternalism, and some of which do not.

Nevertheless, a course dominated by cases is likely to leave students doubting that there are any general principles at all to be learned in the study of ethics. To transfer what they have learned about the cases in a course to other cases they later encounter, they must, wittingly or not, have recourse to general principles. These principles and their foundations therefore should be explicitly explored. Beyond the general principles of paternalism itself, the theoretical context of the problem of paternalism needs some attention. How far does the problem depend on assuming that an individual's conduct does not affect other people? Is an objective theory of the good, on which liberal paternalism sometimes relies, possible, and if so what content should it have? Questions of these kinds call for theoretical readings and discussions, for which cases can never substitute. One way (though certainly not the only way) to balance case material and theoretical literature is to devote the first part of a class to a discussion of philosophical readings on their own terms, and the second part to applications of these philosophical principles to several cases. (See the Appendix for an example of an outline of such an approach.)

Another pedagogical issue concerns the qualifications of the teacher of courses in practical ethics: Should the teacher be a philosopher with expertise in ethics, or a professional with knowledge of the field from which the practical problems are drawn?[104] The usual answers—team-teaching by a philosopher and a professional, or individual teaching by a philosopher trained in a profession, or a professional trained in philosophy—obviate the need to choose between kinds of qualifications. But when a choice is necessary, a philosopher seems the sounder appointment. At least in professional schools, students are likely to have more acquaintance with the context of the cases, and with the general doctrines of their profession, than with the principles and techniques of moral philosophy. That the students as well as the teacher stand ready to contribute their own special knowledge to the discussion creates an educational environment that diminishes the distance between student and teacher. Teaching about paternalism can thus take place in a setting that, insofar as possible, is free from paternalism.

The question of how far a teacher can and should assume a paternalistic stance brings us to the third and most general issue of pedagogy. It may be said that the process of education itself is paternalistic: the teacher requires a student, for his or her own good, to read certain works and to learn certain principles, even though the works and the principles may not be the ones the student would choose. Mill considered education to be another exception to his general presumption against interference with individual liberty, because "the want" of "education is least felt where the need is the greatest."[105] To be sure, at least older students have the opportunity (within limits) to decide whether to continue their education, and, if so, in what form. Even so, students are sometimes required to take a course in ethics (should they be?). Indeed, they may be prevailed upon, for their own good and against their will, to study the problem of paternalism. The techniques of teaching, moreover, may tend more or less toward paternalism. A standard format—the teacher imparting ethical knowledge through authoritative lectures—resembles the paternalistic model of professionalism that we have earlier criticized. The irony in this method might be exploited by asking students: Can you be taught paternalistically how to criticize paternalism? Perhaps further than many subjects, ethics calls for more egalitarian, participatory methods of teaching, that encourage students to develop their own moral views, rather than to adopt the views of their teacher; such methods, at least, would better accord with any conception of ethics that assumes, with Kant, that there are no experts in morals. Yet, whatever the format, the teacher claims, to some degree, to know what is good for students, and to be qualified to control how this good is achieved. The paternalism toward which these claims tend need not be pernicious. Ideally, the teacher, at

---

[104]For an illustration of this dispute, see the exchange between Amnon Goldworth and Ian E. Thompson, "The Implications of Medical Ethics," *Journal of Medical Ethics* 2 (1977), pp. 33–35.
[105]Mill, *Principles of Political Economy*, pp. 947–950.

each step of the process of education, exercises authority in a way that enables students to decide, autonomously and critically, which teachings to accept and which to reject. The classroom can thus serve as a microcosm of the problem of paternalism, as well as a possible model for the resolution of the problem.

Paternalism abounds in many different human pursuits; medicine, law, and public policy are exemplary, not exhaustive.[106] Sometimes the paternalism seems justified; more often, not. Even if we cannot arrive at definitive criteria that determine whether or not paternalism is justified in any particular instance, we can, in the quest for such criteria, learn a great deal not only about paternalism, but also about the application of ethical principles to practical problems.

ACKNOWLEDGMENTS

I am grateful to Marion Smiley for assistance with research for this article and also to her, Gerald Dworkin, Amy Gutmann, and Michael Kelly for helpful comments on an earlier version.

[106] Among the problems not considered here, the largest and most difficult concerns paternalism in cultures that subscribe to fundamentally different ethical and political principles, or stand at a different level of development, than the societies on which I have concentrated. Despite Mill's refusal to apply the principle of liberty to persons who live in "those backward states of society in which the race itself may be considered as in its nonage" (*On Liberty*, p. 224), some recent writers on political development have suggested that many programs in developing nations (such as "consciousness raising") constitute unjustified forms of paternalism. See, for example, Peter L. Berger, *Pyramids of Sacrifice: Political Ethics and Social Change* (New York: Basic Books, 1974), pp. 111–131.

Appendix

This outline suggests readings and discussion topics for a unit on paternalism in a course on ethics and medicine, law, or public policy. Although it would be possible to devote a whole seminar to paternalism, the outline assumes that paternalism will be only one among several topics in the course. The outline is divided into three sections, each of which should constitute about two hours of class.

I. The Theory of Paternalism

J. S. Mill, *On Liberty*, especially ch. IV–V. [An excerpt consisting of ch. IV appears in R. Wasserstrom (ed.), *Morality and the Law* (Belmont, Calif., 1971), pp. 10–23.]

Gerald Dworkin, "Paternalism," in Wasserstrom (ed.), *Morality and the Law*, pp. 107–126.

1. What is paternalism? Does it necessarily involve the restriction of individual liberty? If so, in what sense of "liberty"?

2. Why should paternalism be justified for all children even though many children are at least as "rational" as some adults who would not generally be treated paternalistically?

3. Is paternalism ever justified for adults? (A negative answer to this question is usually a sign that the criteria for justifiable paternalism have been built into the definition of paternalism.) If so, under what conditions? What kinds of impairment warrant paternalistic intervention? What kinds of goods are justifiable goals of paternalism?

4. Analyze Mill's discussion of these examples: prohibition of manufacture and sale of alcohol; taxation of liquor; sale of poisons; contracts in perpetuity (e.g. slavery); education. Does Mill consistently maintain an antipaternalist position?

II. Professionalism and Paternalism

Bernard Gert and Charles M. Culver, "Paternalistic Behavior," *Philosophy and Public Affairs* (Fall, 1976), pp. 45–57.

Richard Wasserstrom, "Lawyers as Professionals: Some Moral Issues," *Human Rights* (1975), pp. 1–24.

1. In what ways (if at all) is the relationship between a doctor and patient, or between a lawyer and a client, paternalistic? If the professional-client is paternalistic, to what extent is the paternalism justifiable? How can excessive paternalism be avoided?

2. Is a doctor ever justified in withholding from a patient information that concerns the patient's diagnosis and treatment? Is a doctor ever justified in deceiving a patient? If so, under what conditions?

3. Is a lawyer ever justified in withholding from a client information that concerns the client's case? In deceiving a client? If so, under what conditions?

4. Although the role of the public official is not the same as that of a doctor or lawyer, it has been claimed that the official's stance toward citizens can be paternalistic in ways similar to that of professionals. To what extent is this claim true? Are there other characteristics of the public official's role that manifest paternalism? [Except for the articles on social workers (cited in Notes), I have not found any suitable article explicitly dealing with paternalism and the role of public administrators. A brief discussion of legislative paternalism is in Rosemary Carter, "Justifying Paternalism," *Canadian Journal of Philosophy* (March, 1977), pp. 144–145. The classic debate about administrative responsibility indirectly raises the question of paternalism; see the articles by Friedrich and Finer in Francis Rourke (ed.), *Bureaucratic Power in National Politics*, 3rd edition (Boston, 1978), pp. 391–421.]

III. The Practice of Paternalism

Stanley J. Reiser *et al.* (eds.), *Ethics in Medicine* (Cambridge, Mass., 1977), pp. 199–200, 253–254, 517–528, 549.

"The Disguised Oppression of Involuntary Guardianship: Have the Elderly Freedom to Spend?" *Yale Law Journal* (March, 1964), pp. 676–692.

Albert Weale, "Paternalism and Social Policy," *Journal of Social Policy* (1978), pp. 164–169 [on welfare payments].

HEW, "Laetrile: Commissioner's Decision," *Federal Register* (August 5, 1977), pp. 39768–39769, 39797–39798, 39803–39805.

Donald H. Regan, "Justifications for Paternalism," in J. Roland Pennock and John W. Chapman (eds.), *The Limits of Law, Nomos XV* (New York, 1974), pp. 201–206; and "Make Motorcyclists Wear Helmets?" *U.S. News and World Report* (July 18, 1977), pp. 39–40.

1. Is a doctor ever justified in administering a treatment for a patient's own good but without the patient's consent? Under what conditions? If a patient is comatose, who should decide what treatment to administer or terminate? According to what standards?

2. For what kinds of persons is a legal guardianship justified? What safeguards would you incorporate in the law of guardianship and in agreements authorizing individuals to act as guardians?

3. In what ways (if any) is a welfare system that provides in-kind benefits instead of cash payments paternalistic? Is such a system justifiable?

4. On what grounds (if any) may the government prohibit the use of a nontoxic drug (such as Laetrile)? Can drug regulation ever be a justifiable form of paternalism?

5. Is the protection of motorcyclists from self-harm a sufficient reason to require them to wear helmets? Critically analyze the argument that such a requirement is justified to prevent social harm. May society legislate to preserve the viability or the productivity of some of its members against their will?

CHAPTER 11

Whistleblowing and Professional Responsibilities

SISSELA BOK

RESPONSIBILITIES IN CONFLICT

"Whistleblowing" is a new word in the glossary of labels generated by our increased awareness of the ethical conflicts encountered at work. Whistleblowers sound an alarm from within the very organization in which they work, aiming to spotlight neglect or abuses that threaten the public interest.

The stakes in whistleblowing are high. Take the nurse who alleges that physicians enrich themselves in her hospital through unnecessary surgery; the engineers who disclose safety defects in the braking systems of a fleet of new rapid-transit vehicles; the Defense Department official who alerts Congress to military graft and overspending: all know that they pose a threat to those whom they denounce, and that their own careers may be at risk.

Moral conflicts on several levels confront anyone who is wondering whether to speak out about abuses or risks or serious neglect. In the first place, he must try to decide whether, other things being equal, speaking out is in fact in the public interest. This choice is often made more complicated by factual uncertainties: Who is responsible for the abuse or the neglect? How great is the threat? And how likely is it that speaking out will precipitate changes for the better?

In the second place, a would-be whistleblower must weigh his responsibility to serve the public interest against the responsibility he owes to his colleagues and the institution in which he works. This conflict between responsibilities is reflected in conflicting messages within many professions: the

---

This paper draws in part on a chapter on whistleblowing in government service that I have prepared for a forthcoming book on ethics and government service edited by Joel Fleishman and Lance Liebman.

professional ethic requires collegial loyalty, while the codes of ethics often stress responsibility to the public over and above duties to colleagues and clients.

Thus the United States Code of Ethics for government servants[1] asks them to "expose corruption wherever uncovered," and to "put loyalty to the highest moral principles and to country above loyalty to persons, party, or government." Similarly, the largest professional engineering association requires members to speak out against abuses threatening the safety, health, and welfare of the public.[2] And a number of business firms have codes making similar requirements.

A third conflict for would-be whistleblowers is personal in nature, and cuts across the first two: even in cases where they have concluded that the facts warrant speaking out, and that duty to do so overrides loyalties to colleagues and institutions, they often have reason to fear the results of carrying out such a duty. However strong this duty may seem in theory, they know that, in practice, retaliation is likely. As a result, their careers, and their ability to support themselves and their families, may be unjustly impaired.

Government service offers an insight into the variety of forms that retaliation can take. A handbook issued during the Nixon era recommends reassigning "undesirables" to places so remote that they would prefer to resign. Whistleblowers may also be downgraded, or given work without responsibility, or work for which they are not qualified; or else they may be given many more tasks than they can possibly perform.[3]

Another risk—devastating from the point of view of career plans—is that an outspoken civil servant may be ordered to undergo a psychiatric fitness-for-duty examination. Congressional hearings in 1978 uncovered a growing resort to such mandatory examinations, and found that they frequently result from conflicts between supervisors and employees.[4] A person declared unfit for ser-

---

[1]Code of Ethics for Government Service, passed by the U. S. House of Representatives in the 85th Congress, and applying to all government employees and officeholders.

[2]Code of Ethics of the Institute of Electrical and Electronics Engineers, Article IV.

[3]For case histories and descriptions of what befalls whistleblowers, see Rosemary Chalk and Frank von Hippel, "Due Process for Dissenting Whistleblowers: Dealing with Technical Dissent in the Organization," *Technology Review* 81 (1979) pp. 48–55; Alan F. Westin and Stephan Salisbury, eds, *Individual Rights in the Corporation* (New York: Pantheon Books, 1980); Helen Dudar, "The Price of Blowing the Whistle," *The New York Times Magazine* (October 30, 1979, pp. 41–54; John Edsall, *Scientific Freedom and Responsibility* (Washington, D. C.: American Association for the Advancement of Science, 1975, p. 5; David Ewing, *Freedom Inside the Organization* (New York: E. P. Dutton, 1977); Ralph Nader, Peter Petkas, and Kate Blackwell, *Whistle Blowing* (New York: Grossman Publishers, 1972); and Charles Peters and Taylor Branch, *Blowing the Whistle* (New York: Praeger, 1972).

[4]"Forced Retirement/Psychiatric Fitness for Duty Exams," Subcommittee on Compensation and Employee Benefits, Committee on Post Office and Civil Service, House of Representatives, Nov. 3, 1978, pp. 2–4. See also the Subcommittee Hearings, February 28, 1978.
Psychiatric referral for whistleblowers has become institutionalized in government service, and is not uncommon in private employment. Even persons who make accusations without being "employed" in the organization they accuse have been classified as unstable, and thus as

vice can then be "separated," as well as discredited from the point of view of any allegations he may be making. The Chairman concluded that:

> There was general agreement ... that involuntary psychiatric examinations were not helpful to the Government, unfair to employees, and that the agencies placed psychiatrists in an impossible situation.

Outright firing, finally, is the most direct institutional response to whistle-blowers. One civil servant, reflecting on her experiences and on that of others, stated:

> The reactions of those who have observed or exposed the truth about Federal Agencies have ranged from humiliation, frustration, and helpless rage to complete despair about our democratic process.[5]

Add to the conflicts confronting individual whistleblowers the claim to self-policing that many professions make, and professional responsibility is at issue in still another way. For an appeal to the public goes against everthing that "self-policing" stands for.

The question for the different professions, then, is how to resolve, insofar as it is possible, the conflict between professional loyalty and professional responsibility toward the outside world. The same conflicts arise to some extent in all groups; but professional groups often have special cohesion, and claim special dignity and privileges. The strain between the ideals of public service and collegiality in the professions can therefore be especially strong; they add to the pressure on would-be whistleblowers.

The plight of whistleblowers has come to be documented by the press, and described in a number of books. Evidence of the hardships imposed on those who chose to act in the public interest has combined with a heightened awareness of professional malfeasance and corruption to produce a shift toward greater public support of whistleblowers. Public-service law firms and consumer groups have taken up their cause; institutional reforms and legislation have been proposed to combat illegitimate reprisals.[6] Some would encourage ever more employees to ferret out and publicize improprieties in the agencies and organizations where they work.

Given the indispensable services performed by so many whistleblowers—as during the Watergate period and after—strong public support is often merited. But the new climate of acceptance makes it easy to overlook the dangers of whistleblowing: of uses in error or in malice; of work and reputations unjustly lost for those falsely accused; of privacy invaded, and trust undermined. There

---

unreliable witnesses. See, for example, Jonas Robitscher, "Stigmatization and Stone-walling: the Ordeal of Martha Mitchell," *Journal of Psychohistory* 6 (Winter 1979), pp. 393–408.

[5]Carol S. Kennedy, *Whistle-blowing: Contribution or Catastrophe?:* Address to the American Association for the Advancement of Science, 15 February 1978, p. 8.

[6]For an account of strategies and proposals to support government whistleblowers, see *A Whistleblower's Guide to the Federal Bureaucracy*. Government Accountability Project, Institute for Policy Studies, 1977.

comes a level of internal prying and mutual suspicion at which no institution can function. And it is a fact that the disappointed, the incompetent, the malicious, and the paranoid all too often leap to accusations in public. Worst of all, ideological persecution throughout the world traditionally relies on insiders willing to inform on their colleagues or even on their family members, often through staged public denunciations or press campaigns.

No society can count itself immune from such dangers. But neither can it risk silencing those with a legitimate reason to blow the whistle. How, then, can we distinguish different instances of whistleblowing? A society that fails to protect the right to speak out even on the part of those whose warnings turn out to be spurious obviously opens the door to political repression. But, from the moral point of view, there are important differences in the aims, messages, and methods of dissenters from within.

THE NATURE OF WHISTLEBLOWING

The alarm of the whistleblower is intended to disrupt the status quo: to pierce the background noise, perhaps the false harmony or the imposed silence of "affairs as usual." For the act to be completed successfully, in the eyes of the person sounding the alarm, listeners must be aroused by the message, and capable of response. A signal must be sent, a voice raised, to an audience that gains new insight and takes action.

Three elements, each jarring, and triply jarring when conjoined, lend acts of whistleblowing special urgency and bitterness: dissent, breach of loyalty, and accusation.

DISSENT

Like all dissent, whistleblowing makes public a disagreement with an authority of a majority view. But, whereas dissent can concern all forms of disagreement with, for instance, religious dogma, government policy, or court decisions, whistleblowing has the narrower aim of shedding light on negligence or abuse: of alerting to a risk, and assigning responsibility for this risk.

Would-be whistleblowers confront the conflict inherent in all dissent: between conforming and sticking their necks out. The more repressive the authority they challenge, the greater the personal risk they take in speaking out; at exceptional times, as in times of war, even ordinarily tolerant authorities may come to regard dissent as unacceptable, and even disloyal.[7]

[7]See, for example, Samuel Eliot Morison, Frederick Merk, and Frank Freidel, *Dissent in Three American Wars* (Cambridge: Harvard University Press, 1970).

BREACH OF LOYALTY

The whistleblower hopes to stop the game; but since he is neither referee nor coach, and since he blows the whistle on his own team, his act is seen as a violation of loyalty. In holding his position, he has assumed certain obligations to his colleagues and clients: stepping out of channels to level accusations is regarded as a violation of these obligations. Loyalty to colleagues and to clients comes to be pitted against loyalty to the public interest, to those who may be injured unless the revelation is made.

Because the whistleblower is an insider in the very organization he criticizes, his act differs from muckraking and other forms of exposure by outsiders, as when reporters expose corruption within a government agency. Such acts are expected, sometimes even required of outsiders, and do not produce in them the same conflicts of loyalty. (Needless to say, the desire for "scoops" and for personal publicity presents moral conflicts all their own to critics from the outside.)

Pressure from within the institution adds to the internal conflict of loyalty. Fidelity to one's agency, to one's superiors, and to colleagues is stressed in countless ways. It may be supported by a loyalty oath, or a promise of confidentiality.

Not only is loyalty violated in whistleblowing; hierarchy as well is often opposed, since the whistleblower is not only a colleague, but a subordinate. Though aware of the risks inherent in such disobedience, he often hopes to keep his job.[8] At times, however, he plans his alarm to coincide with leaving the institution. If he is highly placed, or joined by others, resigning in protest may effectively direct public attention to the wrongdoing at issue.[9] Still another alternative, often chosen by those who wish to be safe from retaliation, is to leave the institution quietly, secure another post, and then blow the whistle. In this way, it is possible to speak with the authority and knowledge of an insider, without the vulnerability of that position.

Whistleblowing resembles civil disobedience in its openness; it differs from the anonymous warning as much as civil disobedience differs from covert breaches of the law.[10] Unlike civil disobedience, however, whistleblowing is usually not a breach of explicit rules and laws; rather, it is often protected by the

---

[8]In the scheme worked out by Albert Hirschman, in *Exit, Voice and Loyalty* (Cambridge: Harvard University Press, 1970), whistleblowing then represents "voice" accompanied by a preference not to "exit," though forced "exit" is clearly a possibility, and "voice" after or during "exit" may be chosen for strategic reasons.

[9]Edward Weisband and Thomas N. Franck, *Resignation in Protest* (New York: Grossman Publishers, 1975).

[10]There are great variations in the degree of furtiveness or anonymity of any one message. Thus, a leak through a newspaper may be made by a person known to the reporter, but unknown to the readers—disguised, perhaps, as a "highly placed official," or even wrongly characterized in order to mislead those seeking to identify the source of the leak.

right to free speech, but challenges unspoken bonds and loyalties. Its purpose, moreover, is narrower than that of civil disobedience; it aims for change through bringing to light new information of an accusatory nature, rather than through more general political disobedience.[11]

ACCUSATION

It is the element of accusation, of calling "foul," that arouses the strongest reactions on the part of the hierarchy. The accusation may be of neglect, of willfully concealed dangers, or of outright abuse on the part of colleagues or superiors. It singles out specific persons or groups as responsible for threats to the public interest. If no one could be held responsible—as in the case of an impending avalanche—the warning would not constitute whistleblowing.

The accusation of the whistleblower, moreover, concerns a present or an imminent threat. Past errors or misdeeds occasion such an alarm only if they still affect current practices. And risks far in the future lack the immediacy needed to make the alarm a compelling one, as well as the close connection to particular individuals that would justify actual accusations. Thus, an alarm can be sounded about safety defects in a rapid-transit system that threaten or will shortly threaten passengers; but the revelation of safety defects in a system no longer in use, though of historical interest, would not constitute whistleblowing. Nor would the revelation of potential problems in a system not yet fully designed, and far from implemented.[12]

Not only immediacy, but also specificity, is needed for there to be an alarm capable of pinpointing responsibility. A concrete risk must be at issue, rather than a vague foreboding or a somber prediction. The act of whistleblowing differs in this respect from the lamentation or the dire prophecy.

An immediate and specific threat would usually be acted upon by those at risk. But the whistleblower assumes that his message will alert listeners to something that they do not know, or the significance of which they have not grasped. The reason that the danger is not known or understood is often that it has been kept secret by the organization, or by certain members within it who are at fault.

The desire for openness inheres in the temptation to reveal any secret:

[11]I rely on the definition of civil disobedience offered by John Rawls: A public, nonviolent, conscientious, yet political act, contrary to law, usually done with the aim of bringing about a change in the law or the policies of the government. See his *A Theory of Justice* (Cambridge: Harvard University Press, 1977), p. 364. See also Hugo Bedau, "On Civil Disobedience," *Journal of Philosophy* 58 (1961), pp. 653–661. A *combination* of whistleblowing and civil disobedience occurs when, for instance, former CIA agents publish books to alert the public about what they regard as unlawful and dangerous practices in the intelligence community, and in so doing openly violate and thereby test the oath of secrecy that they have sworn, but that they now regard as having been unjustly required of them.

[12]Future developments can, however, be a cause for whistleblowing if they are seen as resulting from steps being taken, or to be taken soon, that render them inevitable.

sometimes also the urge to self-agrandizement and publicity, and the hope for revenge for past slights or injustices. There can be pleasure, too—righteous or malicious—in laying bare the secrets of co-workers, and in setting the record straight at last. Colleagues of the whistleblower often suspect his motives: they may regard him as a crank, as publicity-hungry, wrong about the facts, eager for scandal and discord, and driven to indiscretion by his personal biases and shortcomings.

EFFECTIVE WHISTLEBLOWING

Given the internal and external pressures exerted by the elements of dissent, disobedience, and accusation in whistleblowing, it is little wonder that such acts are the exception rather than the rule; little wonder that, once entered upon, most are destined to fail.

For whistleblowing to be effective, it must arouse its audience. Inarticulate whistleblowers are likely to fail from the outset. When they are greeted by apathy, their message dissipates. When they are greeted by disbelief, they elicit no response at all. And when the audience is unfree to receive or to act on the information—when censorship or fear of retribution stifles response—then the message rebounds to injure the whistleblower himself.

Whistleblowing requires *some* larger context, where secrecy, corruption, and coercion are less solidly entrenched, for the alarm to be possible—some forum where an appeal to justice can still be made. It also requires the possibility of concerted public response: the idea of whistleblowing in an anarchy is therefore merely quixotic.

Coercive regimes render whistleblowing an entirely different, often heroic practice, by their control over what is spoken, written, and heard. If not only are internal institutional protests blocked, but even national warnings thwarted, international appeals may be the only remaining possibility. Depending on the severity of repression, only the most striking injustices may then filter through with sufficient strength to alert ordinarily indifferent foreigners. Alarms, like rings in the water, weaken as they move away from their point of origin; if forced to go below the surface to emerge later, they may be further attenuated.

Such characteristics of whistleblowing, and strategic considerations for achieving an impact, are common to the noblest warnings, the most vicious personal attacks, and the delusions of the paranoid. How can one distinguish the many acts of sounding an alarm that are genuinely in the public interest from all the petty, biased, or lurid revelations that pervade our querulous and gossip-ridden society? Can we draw distinctions between different whistleblowers, different messages, different methods?

We clearly can, in a number of cases. Whistleblowing can be starkly inappropriate when in malice or error, or when it lays bare legitimately private matters having to do, for instance, with political belief or sexual life. It can, just as clearly, be the only way to shed light on an ongoing unjust practice, such as drugging political prisoners, or subjecting them to electroshock treatment; it can be the last resort for alerting the public to an impending disaster.

Taking such clear-cut cases as benchmarks, and reflecting on what it is about them that weighs so heavily for or against speaking out, we can then work our way toward the admittedly more complex cases in between these extremes: cases in which whistleblowing is not so clearly the right or wrong choice, or where different points of view exist regarding its legitimacy: cases where there are moral reasons both for concealment and for disclosure, and where judgments conflict.

Consider the following three cases, chosen from the fields of government, business, and engineering:

> "This material might not be earth-shaking, but I thought you might be interested." With that modest opener, John Samuels (not his real name) proceeded to reveal the fruits of his private, unauthorized investigation into government corruption ... to the Government Accountability Project (GAP) in Washington, D. C.
>
> The corruption Samuels disclosed was pervasive. As a construction inspector for a federal agency, he had personal knowledge of shoddy and deficient construction practices by private contractors. He knew his superiors received free vacations and entertainment, had their homes remodeled, and found jobs for their relatives—all courtesy of a private contractor. These superiors later approved a multimillion no-bid contract with the same "generous" firm.
>
> Samuels also had evidence that other firms were hiring nonunion laborers at a low wage while receiving substantially higher payments from the government for labor costs. A former superior, unaware of an office dictaphone, had incautiously instructed Samuels on how to accept bribes for overlooking subpar performance. Whether all of this information would have sparked a congressional investigation, captured the attention of the public, or initiated a cleansing of his agency will never be known. Samuels decided to remain silent.
>
> As he prepared to volunteer this information to various members of Congress, he became tense and uneasy. His family was scared and the fears were valid. It might cost Samuels thousands of dollars to protect his job. Those who had freely provided Samuels with information would probably recant or withdraw their friendship. A number of people might object to his using a dictaphone to gather information. His agency would start covering up, and vent its collective wrath upon him. ... As for reporters and writers, they would gather for a few days, then move on to the next story. He would be left without a job, with fewer friends, with massive battles looming, and without the financial means of fighting them.[13]

> An attorney, working for a large company supplying medical products, becomes aware of practices of falsifying inventories by adding nonexistent sales, and of attempts to influence federal regulatory personnel. She suspects, in addition, that machinery, sold by the company to hospitals for use in kidney dialysis, is unsafe. She brings these matters up with a junior executive, who assures her he'll look into the matters, and convey them to her chief executives if necessary. When she questions him a few weeks later, however, he answers her that all the problems have been taken care of, but without offering any evidence, and considerably irritated at her desire to learn exactly where the matter stands. She does not know

---

[13]From Louis Clark, "The Sound of Professional Suicide," *The Barrister* (Summer 1978), p. 10.

how much further she can push her concern without jeopardizing her position in the firm.

Engineers of Company "A" prepared plans and specifications for machinery to be used in a manufacturing process, and Company "A" turned them over to Company "B" for production. The engineers of Company "B," in reviewing the plans and specifications, came to the conclusion that they included certain miscalculations and technical deficiencies of a nature that the final product might be unsuitable for the purposes of the ultimate users, and that the equipment, if built according to the orginal plans and specifications, might endanger the lives of persons in proximity to it. The engineers of Company "B" called the matter to tbe attention of appropriate officials of their employer who, in turn, advised Company "A".... Company "A" replied that its engineers felt that the design and specifications for the equipment were adequate and safe, and that Company "B" should proceed to build the equipment as designed and specified. The officials of Company "B" instructed its engineers to proceed with the work.[14]

INDIVIDUAL MORAL CHOICE

What questions might those who consider sounding a public alarm ask themselves? How might they articulate the problem they see, and weigh its injustice before deciding whether or not to reveal it? How can they best try to make sure that their choice is the right one?

In thinking about these questions, it helps to keep in mind the three elements mentioned earlier: dissent, breach of loyalty, and accusation. They impose certain requirements: of accuracy and judgment in dissent; of exploring alternative ways to cope with improprieties, thus minimizing the breach of loyalty; and of fairness in accusation. For each, careful articulation and testing of arguments are needed to limit error and bias.

Dissent by whistleblowers, first of all, is expressly claimed to be intended to benefit the public. It carries with it, as a result, an obligation to consider the nature of this benefit, and to consider also the possible harm that may come from speaking out: harm to persons or institutions, and ultimately to the public interest itself. Whistleblowers must therefore begin by making every effort to consider the effects of speaking out versus those of remaining silent. They must assure themselves of the accuracy of their reports, checking and rechecking the facts before speaking out; specify the degree to which there is genuine impropriety; consider how imminent is the threat they see, how serious, and how closely linked to those accused of neglect or abuse.[15]

---

[14]Case 5, in Robert J. Baum and Albert Flores, eds., *Ethical Problems of Engineering* (Troy, N.Y.: Rensselaer Polytechnic Institute, 1978), p. 186.

[15]In dissent concerning policy differences rather than specific improprieties, moreover, whistleblowing, with its accusatory element, is an inappropriate and dangerous form of warning. It threatens the public interest, in that it so easily derails into ideological persecution. Many other forms of dissent exist when there is reason to voice policy disagreement or ideological differences.

If the facts warrant whistleblowing, how can the second element—breach of loyalty—be minimized? The most important question here is whether the existing avenues for change within the organization have been explored. It is a waste of time for the public, as well as harmful to the institution, to sound the loudest alarm first. Whistleblowing has to remain a last alternative because of its destructive side effects: it must be chosen only when other alternatives have been considered and rejected. They may be rejected if they simply do not apply to the problem at hand, or when there is not time to go through routine channels, or when the institution is so corrupt or coercive that steps will be taken to silence the whistleblower should he try the regular channels first.

What weight should an oath or a promise of silence have in the conflict of loyalties? There is no doubt that one sworn to silence is under a stronger obligation because of the oath he has taken. He has bound himself, assumed specific obligations beyond those assumed in merely taking a new position. But even such promises can be overridden, when the public interest at issue is strong enough. They can be overridden if they were obtained under duress, or through deceit. They can be overridden, too, if they promise something that is in itself wrong or unlawful. The fact that one has promised silence is no excuse for complicity in covering up a crime or a violation of the public's trust.

The third element in whistleblowing—accusation—raises equally serious ethical concerns. They are concerns of fairness to the persons accused of impropriety. Is the message one to which the public is entitled in the first place? Or does it infringe on personal and private matters that one has no right to invade? Here, the very notion of what is in the public's best "interest" is at issue: "accusations" regarding an official's unusual sexual or religious experiences may well appeal to the public's interest, without therefore being information relevant to "the public interest."

Great conflicts arise here. We have witnessed excessive claims to executive privilege and to secrecy by government officials during the Watergate scandal, in order to cover up for abuses the public had every right to discover. Conversely, those hoping to profit from prying into private matters have become adept at invoking "the public's right to know." Some even regard such private matters as threats to the public: they voice their own religious and political prejudices in the language of accusation.

Such a danger is never stronger than when the accusation is delivered surreptitiously: the anonymous accusations made during the McCarthy period regarding political beliefs and associations often injured persons who did not even know their accusers, or the exact nature of the accusations.

In fairness to those criticized, openly accepted responsibility for blowing the whistle should therefore be preferred to the secret denunciation or the leaked rumor: the more so, the more derogatory and accusatory the information. What is openly stated can more easily be checked, its source's motives challenged, and the underlying information examined. Those under attack may otherwise be hard put to defend themselves against nameless adversaries. Often they do not even know that they are threatened until it is too late to respond. The anonymous denunciation, moreover, common to so many regimes, places the burden of investigation on government agencies, that may thereby gain the power of a secret police.

From the point of view of the whistleblower, on the other hand, the choice is admittedly less easy. The anonymous message is safer for him in situations where retaliation is likely. But it is also often less likely to be taken seriously. Newspaper offices, for example, receive innumerable anonymous messages without acting upon them. Unless the message is accompanied by indications of how the evidence can be checked, its anonymity, however safe for the source, speaks against it.

In order to assure transmission for the message—through the press for instance—yet be safe from reprisals, the whistleblower often resorts to a compromise: by making himself known to the journalist, he makes it possible to check the evidence; by asking that his identity not be given in the printed article, he protects himself from the consequences.

From the public's point of view, accusations that are openly made by identifiable individuals are more likely to be taken seriously. Since the open accusation is felt to be fairer to the accused, and since it makes the motives of the whistleblower open to inspection, the audience is more confident that his message may have a factual basis. As a result, if the whistleblower still chooses to resort to surreptitious messages, he has a strong obligation to let the accused know of the accusation leveled, and to produce independent evidence that can be checked.

During this process of weighing the legitimacy of speaking out, the method used, and the degree of fairness needed, whistleblowers must try to compensate for the strong possibility of bias on their part. They should be scrupulously aware of any motive that might skew their message; a desire for self-defense in a difficult bureaucratic situation, perhaps, or the urge to seek revenge, or inflated expectations regarding the effect that their message will have on the situation.[16]

Likewise, the possibility of personal gain from sounding the alarm ought to give pause. Once again, there is then greater risk of a biased message. Even if the whistleblower regards himself as incorruptible, his profiting from revelations of neglect or abuse will lead others to question his motives, and to put less credence in his charges. If the publicity gained through his act matters

---

[16]Needless to say, bias affects the silent as well as the outspoken. The motive for *holding back* important information about abuses and injustice ought to give similar cause for soul-searching. Civil servants who collaborate in the iniquities of so many regimes; businessmen who support them through bribes and silent complicity; and physicians the world over who examine the victims of torture, and return them to their tormentors: all have as much reason to examine *their* motives as those who may be speaking out without sufficient reason.

greatly to him, or if speaking out brings him greater benefits at work or a substantially increased income, such risks are present. If, for example, a government employee stands to make large profits from a book exposing the iniquities of his agency, there is danger that he will, perhaps even unconsciously, slant his report in order to cause more of a sensation. If he supports his revelation by referring to the Code of Ethics for Government Servants urging that loyalty to the highest moral principles and to country be put above loyalty to persons, party, and government, he cannot ignore another clause in the same Code, specifying that he "ought never to use any information coming to him confidentially in the performance of government duties as a means for making private profits."

Sometimes a warning is so clearly justifiable and substantiated that it carries weight no matter how tainted the motives of the messenger. But scandal can pay; and the whistleblower's motives ought ideally to be above suspicion, for his own sake as well as for that of the respect he desires for his warning. Personal gain from speaking out raises a presumption against it, a greater need to check the biases of the speaker.

A special problem arises in this regard whenever there is a high risk that the civil servant who speaks out will have to go through costly litigation. Might he not at least justifiably try to make money on his public revelations—say through books or public speaking—to offset his losses? In so doing, he will not, strictly speaking, have *profited* from his revelations: he merely avoids being financially crushed by their sequels. He will nevertheless still be suspected at the time of his revelation, and his message will therefore seem more questionable.

To weigh all these factors is not easy. The ideal case of whistleblowing—where the cause is a just one, where all the less dramatic alternatives have been exhausted, where responsibility is openly accepted, and the whistleblower is above reproach—is rare. The motives may be partly self-serving, the method questionable, and still we may judge that the act was in the public interest. In cases where the motives for sounding the alarm are highly suspect, for example, but where clear proof of wrongdoing and avoidable risk is adduced, the public may be grateful that the alarm was sounded, no matter how low its opinion of the whistleblower himself.

Reducing bias and error in moral choice often requires consultation, even open debate:[17] such methods force articulation of the moral arguments at stake, and challenge privately held assumptions. But acts of whistleblowing present special problems when it comes to open consultation. On the one hand, once the whistleblower sounds his alarm publicly, his arguments *will* be subjected to open scrutiny: he will have to articulate his reasons for speaking out, and substantiate his charges. On the other hand, it will then be too late to retract the alarm, or to combat its harmful effects, should his choice to speak out have been ill-advised (in both senses of the word).

---

[17]I discuss these questions of consultation and publicity with respect to moral choice in Chapter 7 of *Lying* (New York: Pantheon Books, 1978).

For this reason, the whistleblower owes it to all involved to make sure of two things: that he has sought as much and as objective advice regarding his choice as he can *before* going public; and that he is aware of the arguments for and against the practice of whistleblowing in general, so that he can see his own choice against as richly detailed and coherently structured a background as possible.

Satisfying these two requirements, once again, has special problems because of the very nature of whistleblowing: the more corrupt the circumstances, the more dangerous it may be to seek consultation before speaking out. And yet, since the whistleblower himself may have a biased view of the state of affairs, he may choose not to consult others when, in fact, it would have been not only safe, but advantageous to do so; he may see corruption and conspiracy where none exists. Given these difficulties, it would be especially important to seek more general means of considering the nature of whistleblowing, and the arguments for and against different ways of combating abuse: to take them up in public debate and through teaching.

The public debate over whistleblowing is already under way. In the press, in articles and books, these problems have been described, and a number of remedies proposed. Institutional and legislative proposals are being made. Still lacking is work of a fact-finding, comparative, and analytical nature, on which practical decisions might be based; as well as the opportunity for individuals to give careful thought in advance to how they might respond, in their own working lives, to the conflicts where whistleblowing is one of the alternatives. To what extent can these needs be met through teaching?

WHISTLEBLOWING AND THE TEACHING OF ETHICS

Case studies of the dilemmas individuals face with respect to whistleblowing are attractive from the point of view of teaching applied ethics. They are concrete, striking, and reminiscent of experiences all have had from childhood on with conflicts of loyalty, and the burden of deciding whether or not to "tell on" a friend. A careful study of the moral arguments for and against whistleblowing in individual cases, and of the possible alternatives, will allow a better understanding of what is at issue in such situations, and of how they arise; it can allow a more considered choice of what stance to take if similar situations should arise at work, as well as an inquiry into what might be done at an earlier stage to achieve the desired result without the costs of whistleblowing.

Such teaching, moreover, may contribute to a broader analysis of practices of dissent and of conflicting responsibilities. It can allow both a problem-solving approach to immediate conflicts and a critique of long-standing practices and of the assumptions that underlie them.

These broader purposes are best served by going beyond the dilemmas presented for individual agents, discussed above, and looking, as well, at whistleblowing from the perspective of organizations and of professions. Such an inquiry can be undertaken, either in a particular institutional or professional perspective—say in a business school, or a school of engineering—or else in a still more general perspective that cuts across all forms of work.

What questions might such a broader inquiry raise? And how might they be approached in teaching and in research? What institutional arrangements might best cope with the uncovering of wrongdoing and neglect? And how might the different professions best cope with the need to reconcile professional loyalty and professional responsibility toward the public interest?

INSTITUTIONAL QUESTIONS

What changes, outside and inside business organizations, government agencies, and other places of work, might serve to protect the right of dissenters, cut down on endless breaches of loyalty and on false accusations, while assuring public access to needed information?

The more far-reaching set of changes, and the hardest to implement, involves the cutting down on legitimate causes for alarm. Reducing practices of corruption and cover-up, as well as opportunities for errors to go undiscovered, would reduce also the need to call attention to them. The needed changes in review procedures, incentives, and obstacles go far beyond the scope of this paper; but so long as improprieties remain serious and frequent, whistleblowing will remain a last resort for calling attention to them.

The need to resort to whistleblowing can be reduced by providing mechanisms for taking criticism seriously before it reaches the press and the courtroom. These mechanisms must work to counteract the blockage of information within an organization, and the tendency to filter out negative information so that those who must make decisions ignore it.[18] The filtering process may be simple or intricate; well-intentioned or malevolent; more or less consciously manipulated. David Ewing gives examples of how it works:

> During 1976 and 1977, hundreds of newspapers gleefully reported the seamy and sexy ways used by Southwestern Bell to manipulate regulatory officials. The scandle came to light after the suicide of T. O. Gravitt, an executive in San Antonio, and the firing of James Ashley, one of Gravitt's colleagues. It is difficult to think of any practice that Ma Bell frowns on more (as demonstrated by the prompt and decisive action by national headquarters once the lid came off the scandal). However, would-be whistleblowers were discouraged so firmly at the scene of the crimes that no early warmings seem to have found their way to New York. If they had, the company could have been spared a severe setback in public relations,

---

[18]John C. Coffee, in "Beyond the Shut-eyed Sentry: Toward a Theoretical View of Corporate Misconduct and an Effective Legal Response," *Virginia Law Review,* 63 (1977) pp. 1099–1278, gives an informed and closely reasoned account of such "information blockages," such "filtering out," and of possible remedies.

to say nothing of the multimillion dollar damage suits it appears to have lost to Ashley and Gravitt's family.

A couple of years ago, when the Alaska pipe line was being built, some managers began ordering construction crews to take shortcuts in order to reduce costs and meet time deadlines for construction. According to reports confirmed by *The Wall Street Journal* and other sources, many batches of X rays of weld joints were falsified so that flaws would not be detected. Some workers who objected were told to shut up. Nevertheless, news about the cover-up seeped out, and investigators were hired to look into the problem. Attempts were made to frustrate the investigation (one of the investigators died under mysterious circumstances), but the dreary mess finally came to the attention of responsible officials. It then became necessary for thousands of welds to be rechecked, and a great many corrected. This great extra cost in time and money, to say nothing of the bad publicity for the construction firms, can be charged to the lack of suitable mechanisms for whistle blowing.[19]

Ewing argues that industry has much to gain by not discouraging internal criticism. A number of managements do welcome the views of dissenters, and promise that no one will be unfairly dismissed or disciplined for having made their revelations.

Such an "open door" policy may suffice at times; but it is frequently inadequate, unless further buttressed. In the first place, the promises of protection given by top management cannot always be fulfilled. Though an employee may keep his job, there are countless ways of making his position difficult, to the point where he may be brought to resign of his own volition, or stay, while bitterly regretting that he had spoken out. Second, it would be naive to think that abuses in industry or in government are always unknown to top management, and perpetrated against their will by subordinates. If the abuse—the secret bombardment of Cambodia, for instance, or the corporate bribing or conspiracy to restrict trade—is planned by those in charge, then the "open door" policy turns out to be a trap for the dissenter.

For these reasons, proposals have been made to protect dissenters in more formal ways. Independent review boards, ombudsmen, consumer or citizen representatives on boards of trustees, bills of rights for employees: these and other means have been suggested to protect dissenters while giving serious consideration to their messages.

These methods of protection spring up and sometimes die away with great rapidity. They are often instituted without careful comparison between different possibilities. Teaching and research could do much to study them, to compare their advantages and disadvantages and their differing suitability under different circumstances. The benefits from these methods, when they work, are strong. They allow for criticism with much less need for heroism; for a way to deflect the crank or the witch-hunter *before* their messages gain publicity; for a process

[19]David W. Ewing, "The Employee's Right to Speak Out: The Management Perspective," *The Civil Liberties Review* 5 September-October (1978), pp. 10–15.

of checking the accuracy of the information provided; for a chance to distinguish between urgent alarms and long-range worries; and for an arena for debating the moral questions of motive and of possible bias, of loyalty and responsibility to the public interest.

Many of these methods work well; others fail. They fail when they are but window dressing from the outset, meant to please or exhaust dissenters; or else they fail because, however independent at the outset, they turn into management tools. Such is the fate of many a patient-representative in hospitals; their growing loyalty to co-workers and to the institution once again leaves the dissenter little choice between submission and open revolt.

Still another reason for the failure of such intermediaries is their frequent lack of credibility. No matter how well-meaning, they will not be sought out if they cannot protect from retaliation those who turn to them for help. Even if they can give such protection, but cannot inspire confidence in those with grievances, their role will be largely a ceremonial one.

A comparative study of such intermediaries and means of protection would have to seek out the conditions of independence, flexibility, separateness from management, institutional good will, fairness, and objectivity needed for success. Moreover, in looking at the protection given to dissenters, the entire system must be kept in perspective, so that changes in one area do not produce unexpected dislocations elsewhere. To what extent will increased due process make the entire institution more litigious? To what extent will protection in one place put increased pressure on another? Is it not possible, for example, that the increasing difficulties of firing incompetent federal employees have led to the growing resort to psychiatric fitness-for-duty examinations (mentioned above), and that these, in turn, have become a new weapon with which to combat critics?

A different method for reducing the tension and risk of whistleblowing is to state conditions expressly under which those who learn about an abuse *must* blow the whistle: times when to do so, far from being disloyal, is not only right, but obligatory. Laws or other regulations can require revelations, and thus take the burden of choice off the individual critic.

Such requirements to report already exist in a number of places. The Toxic Substances Control Act, for instance, enacted in January, 1977, requires companies producing chemicals to instruct their employees and officials to report chemicals that pose a substantial risk to health or to the environment. Once again, these requirements open up fields for study and for comparison. There is much to learn about how effective they are, how they may be combated within an industry, and how they compare with other ways of reducing neglect and abuse.

In order to be effective, requirements to report must be enforceable. It is, therefore, not appropriate for them to be as open-ended and exhortative as the U. S. Code of Ethics in urging government employees to "expose corruption wherever uncovered." Such requirements must be more specific than provisions in codes of ethics. They must be limited to clear-cut improprieties, and used as a last resort only. Once again, here the lines must be firmly drawn against requiring reporting on religious or political belief, or purely personal matters. In many societies, citizens are asked to report "deviations," fellow workers to spy on one another, and students to expose the subversive views of their teachers. No society can afford to ignore these precedents in its enthusiasm for eradicating corruption.

PROFESSIONAL RESPONSIBILITIES

Requirements to disclose deserve careful study in courses on professional ethics, as do the corresponding parts of the various codes of ethics. What role do such codes play with respect to the conflicts engendered by dissent? How have they changed, made more specific, or provide for exceptional cases? The weighing of responsibilities—to colleagues, to the profession itself, to clients, to innocent bystanders, and to the public—presents unusually difficult problems for most professions; these problems are still far from being resolved.

Teaching can also explore the different conceptions of such responsibilities in the different professions. Some place the highest value on service; others on profit; still others on accountability to the public. How do these differences affect the view of the legitimacy of whistleblowing and dissent? Do some positions limit this legitamacy? To take a recent example, General John K. Singlaub lost his post for denouncing President Carter's policy in South Korea in 1977. He argued that the President's announced intention to withdraw ground forces in four or five years was foolishly dangerous, and that it would lead to war. *The New York Times*, in a lead editorial on May 24, 1977, supported the President, arguing that

> a policy in Korea cannot be entrusted to those who would destroy it. The general was a necessary example. . . . The price of democracy and of the nation's capacity to hold elected officials acccountable, is obedience within bureaucracy and above all in the military.

The question of obedience and dissent is receiving increased attention in classes in ethics in the military academies. It is clearly not enough to insist on obedience at all times in the various bureaucracies and in the military. Obedience cannot be the right response to requests to cover up for the use of deficient machinery, or for a planned usurpation of power, or for the bombing of a neutral country. More careful distinctions will have to be drawn, and, once again, the codes and documents setting forth professional standards may have to be revised in the light of these distinctions.

The comparison between different types of work when it comes to whistleblowing forms part of a larger set of issues (recently highlighted in a number of articles)[20] that ought not to be ignored in courses in professional ethics: Must a professional sometimes act in such a way as to breach his personal ethical standards? May professional and personal ethics actually *conflict?* John Noonan phrased the question as follows, for lawyers:

> Can an honest person practice regularly as a criminal defense lawyer in the United States? Can a decent person serve as prosecuter for the state or federal government? Can an honest, decent person teach other persons to be criminal defense lawyers or prosecutors in the American system of criminal justice?[21]

Such questions are not addressed to those who argue that professionals assume particular obligations to serve their clients as they do not serve all others, by protecting, say, their confidentiality more forcefully than would be their right were they *not* in a professional relationship with these clients. Such practices can be openly set forth and defended. Rather, Noonan's question addresses the means of acting as a professional: it asks whether professionals have special privileges of breaking common moral standards surreptitiously. Should they allow themselves to lie and cheat for their clients, for example? Should public officials overcome scruples about the covert use of force to further what they take as their nation's long-term interest? And at what point of threat to innocent bystanders should psychiatrists abandon their privilege of keeping confidential the plans of their patients?

These questions merit serious debate, not only in courses in professional ethics, but in preprofessional courses. Students should have an opportunity to think in advance of what will be expected of them, and of how it may conflict with what they expect of themselves. Such consideration will in turn without a doubt affect the professional practices themselves—if in no other way than to draw distinctions in what is now all too often an impossible tangle of diverging views. These distinctions will be clarified, too, if they are looked at from a perspective that includes a number of kinds of work; there is danger, otherwise, that the sense of mission and high purpose within any one calling may serve to undercut criticism, and reinforce the status quo.

TEACHING METHODS

The conflicts of whistleblowing can hardly be discussed in the absence of case material and practical considerations. For this very reason, the temptation

---

[20]Benjamin Freedman, "A Meta-Ethics for Professional Morality," *Ethics* 89 (1974), pp. 1–19; Stuart Hampshire, "Public and Private Morality," in Stuart Hampshire, ed., *Public and Private Morality* (Cambridge: Cambridge University Press, 1978), pp. 23–53; Thomas Nagel, "Ruthlessness in Public Life," in Stuart Hampshire, ed., *Public and Private Morality* (Cambridge: Cambridge University Press, 1978) pp. 75–91; Richard Wasserstrom, "Lawyers as Professionals: Some Moral Issues," *Human Rights* 5 (1975), 1–24; and Bernard Williams, "Politics and Moral Character," in Stuart Hampshire, ed., *Public and Private Morality*, (Cambridge: Cambridge University Press, 1978), pp. 55–73.

[21]John T. Noonan, Jr., "Professional Ethics or Personal Responsibility?" *Stanford Law Review* 29 (1977), p. 363.

might be strong to go no further in seeking how best to convey these conflicts in the classroom. The result would be a lively discussion; but very little light would be shed on the problems themselves. It is more important than ever, when striking cases lie near at hand, to consider the order in which they should be taken up, their scope and variety, the kinds of reasoning that should be employed in dealing with them, and the theoretical background without which they will have but a scattered impact.

The cases themselves should vary, so as to permit the consideration of how elements in whistleblowing vary: the degree of certainty about facts, for instance, or the degree of anonymity of the messengers, or the risk of retaliation, or possible differences in obligations to superiors. These elements can then be explored much more systematically, so that they are perceived with more discrimination, and weighed with greater care.

I have already mentioned the importance, too, of broadening the perspective so as to show how related problems arise in many different kinds of work. Such a broadened perspective serves to counteract the biases that affect all reasoning about professional ethics. And it reduces the sense of isolation that a student often feels with respect to particular professional structures: it allows a student to step outside the professional perspective, and consider the effect of problematic practices on those with whom he will work, on himself as a moral agent, and on the respect in which his profession is held, as well as on outsiders.

Perspective will be gained, too, if the class discussion of whistleblowing is placed in the context of the larger political and moral issues that I have referred to in this paper: issues of dissent and free speech, of fairness in accusation and refuge in anonymity, of institutional changes and professional responsibilities.

Such issues may be raised at all levels of training, be they general, preprofessional, or professional. But, at every level, it is important that instructors who take up questions of whistleblowing do not do so in ignorance of the contexts in which such conflicts spring up. It would be helpful, too, especially in courses preparing for a particular professional experience, if practitioners could join the students at times to convey a sense of the practical difficulties that arise, as well as of the problems that seem excruciating on paper, but can, in fact, easily be averted.

Whistleblowing is a new word for a very ancient practice. It is becoming more prominent now, as we learn to spot it in very different circumstances, and as organizations grow in size and number. It stands in need of careful study, and offers the opportunity for a close look at individual choices, as well as possible institutional changes and professional standards. The teaching of ethics can benefit from and contribute to such inquiries, and can help to seek ways of protecting dissent and encouraging criticism, while cutting down on erroneous or harmful resorts to the panic button.

PART IV

Summary Recommendations on the Teaching of Ethics

CHAPTER 12

Hastings Center Project on the Teaching of Ethics: Summary Recommendations

American higher education is in the throes of many difficulties at present. They include declining enrollments, increasing financial pressure, the inability of many promising teachers and scholars to gain employment or tenure, and some degree of public criticism. It may not be an auspicious moment to urge the introduction of new courses and programs, whether in ethics or in any other subject. Nonetheless, we do not hesitate to propose that the teaching of ethics be given a far more central role in the curriculum than it has had in recent decades. Although many of the current problems of higher education are practical and financial, others bear on the nature and role of the university itself. Few would openly contend that the main purpose of higher education, even of an explicitly professional education, is simply that of preparing students for better jobs and higher incomes. Yet, for many students, that is the perceived reality. Nor would many contend that questions of ethics and values should have no place in the university. Most would in a very general way assert just the opposite. Yet, the formal opportunities to pursue moral questions are often scant and episodic. Few would argue that the professions do not have moral purposes and traditions, or deny that professionals ought to serve goals that transcend the merely technical. Yet, the opportunities to examine the nature of the professions and their moral purposes are scanty.

Those discrepancies were a stimulus for our project. Much more importantly, the same discrepancies underlie a general public uneasiness about the directions of higher education, and a no less strong uneasiness within the academic community itself. One need look no further than the variety of curriculum-reform movements and faculty-renewal programs now under way to gain

This material has been taken from *The Teaching of Ethics in Higher Education: A Report by The Hastings Center*, (Hastings-on-Hudson, N. Y.: The Hastings Center, 1980).

credence for that assertion. We have centered our attention on one aspect only of the current ferment: that of the role of ethics instruction in the university. But it is an aspect that reflects a more general concern about the university and the way it is preparing students to manage their own lives, their life in community with others, and their vocational or professional roles. More and better courses in ethics will by no means solve the larger problems facing the university, nor will a focus on moral issues guarantee it a new purpose and vitality. Our only claim is that a "higher education" that does not foster, support, and implement an examination of the moral life will fail its own purposes, the needs of its students, and the welfare of society. The university offers a unique context for a careful examination of moral claims and moral purposes. We ask only that such an examination be made formal and explicit, and that sufficient imagination, energy, and resources be invested in the teaching of ethics that its importance will become manifest, both within and outside of the university.

We have already set forth the substance of our findings, our recommendations, and our suggestions, and we hope that those who desire a fuller discussion will turn to the other publications prepared as part of our project. Nonetheless, it may serve an additional purpose if we summarize those recommendations that we believe to be the most important.

1. *Goals in the teaching of ethics.*   The general purpose of the teaching of ethics ought to be that of stimulating the moral imagination, developing skills in the recognition and analysis of moral issues, eliciting a sense of moral obligation and personal responsibility, and learning both to tolerate and to resist moral disagreement and ambiguity. Those purposes ought to mark all courses in ethics; they should be supplemented by the examination of those specific topics appropriate to particular areas of personal, social and professional concern.

Courses in ethics ought not explicitly seek behavioral change in students. They should seek to assist students in the development of those insights, skills, and perspectives that set the stage for a life of personal moral responsibility reflecting careful and serious moral reflection.

The undergraduate teaching of ethics ought to assist students in the formation of their personal values and moral ideals, introduce them to the broad range of moral problems facing their society and the world, provide them contact with important ethical theories and moral traditions, and give them the opportunity to wrestle with problems of applied ethics, whether personal or professional.

The teaching of ethics in professional schools ought to prepare future professionals to understand the types of moral issues they are likely to confront in their chosen vocations, introduce them to the moral ideals of their profession, and assist them in understanding the relationship between their professional work and that of the broader values and needs of the society.

2. *Pluralism and indoctrination.*   Courses in ethics should respect the pluralistic principles of our society, acknowledging the variety of moral per-

spectives that mark different religious and other groups. Indoctrination, whether political, theological, ideological, or philosophical, is wholly out of place in the teaching of ethics. Although students should be assisted in developing moral ideals and fashioning a coherent way of approaching ethical theory and moral dilemmas, the task of the teacher is not to promote a special set of values, but only to promote those sensitivities and analytical skills necessary to help students reach their own moral judgments.

3. *Evaluation of the teaching of ethics.* The most appropriate methods of evaluation are those traditional to the humanities: an assessment on the part of teachers (and in some cases outside examiners) about whether their students understand key concepts, are able to fashion coherent moral arguments both orally and in writing, and can display an ability sensitively to recognize moral problems and examine them in a rational way. Although empirical and other test instruments may have value in measuring changes in student judgment of moral issues, it is doubtful that they can be either useful or illuminating as the ordinary means of evaluating the progress made by students in courses in ethics.

4. *Qualifications for the teaching of ethics.* An advanced degree in philosophy or religion is the minimal standard for ethics courses taught within the disciplinary perspectives of those fields. As an ideal, those teaching applied and professional ethics—where knowledge of one or more fields is necessary—ought to have the equivalent of one year of training in the field in which they were not initially trained. Team-teaching, in addition to its other values, can often help fill the gap when one or more of the instructors has been trained in one field only. Courses in applied and professional ethics ought not to be introduced into the curriculum unless those proposing to teach such courses either have the necessary training, or are in the process of getting it. As a general rule, the more deeply a teacher proposes to go into the subject matter of applied and professional eithics, the greater the degree of training that will be necessary. By the same token, extensive training will not ordinarily be necessary for those who propose only to give over a short segment of a course to one or more issues in applied or professional ethics.

5. *Training programs in applied and professional ethics.* The most important general need in the field of applied and professional ethics is the development of training programs. At present, there are very few opportunities for those trained in one field to gain the equivalent of the one year of additional training proposed above. Training programs of two kinds are needed: first, programs to assist those with no training in ethics to gain a basic knowledge of that field, and, second, programs for those trained in ethics that will allow them to work for the equivalent of a year in another field. While a few joint Ph.D. programs, providing degrees in two fields, would be helpful, the more critical need is for one-year programs, or for a series of summer programs of workshops that would, over a period of time, provide the equivalent of one year of training. Our research for this project indicates that there would be a significant audience for such programs.

6. *The placing of ethics in the curriculum.* Every undergraduate should have a systematic exposure to both ethical theory and applied ethics. The minimal standard ought to be that of a one-semester course, with other opportunities available for more advanced work in ethical theory, or work in different areas of applied or professional ethics. Every professional student should have a systematic exposure to the ethical problems of his or her chosen profession. At least a one-semester course should be available, and further course opportunities should exist for those interested in advanced work.

Although moral problems ought to be faced when they arise in the context of other courses, at the undergraduate or professional-school level, reliance should not be placed upon such sporadic encounters as a substutute for the availability of well-organized, full courses. No other serious subject is taught in the curriculum by what has been called the "pervasive method," and ethics ought not to be the outcast.

7. *Establishing a climate for courses in ethics.* Those proposing to teach courses in ethics should fully inform their colleagues and pertinent administrators of the purposes and expectations of their courses. It should not be assumed that others will automatically understand the explicit purpose of such courses. Special efforts should be made to explain to the university or professional-school community what courses in ethics hope to achieve, and what means are to be used in the endeavor.

Bibliography

In addition to this book, The Hastings Center's Project on The Teaching of Ethics has issued a report, *The Teaching of Ethics in Higher Education* (Hastings-on-Hudson, N. Y.: The Hastings Center, 1980), and the following monographs.

Baum, Robert J. *Ethics and Engineering Curricula.* Hastings-on-Hudson, N. Y.: The Hastings Center, 1980.

Christians, Clifford G., and Covert, Catherine L. *Teaching Ethics in Journalism Education.* Hastings-on-Hudson, N. Y.: The Hastings Center, 1980.

Clouser, K. Danner. *Teaching Bioethics: Strategies, Problems, and Resources.* Hastings-on-Hudson, N. Y.: The Hastings Center, 1980.

Fleishman, Joel L., and Payne, Bruce L. *Ethical Dilemmas and the Education of Policymakers.* Hastings-on-Hudson, N. Y.: The Hastings Center, 1980.

Kelly, Michael J. *Legal Ethics and Legal Education.* Hastings-on-Hudson, N. Y.: The Hastings Center, 1980.

Powers, Charles W., and Vogel, David. *Ethics in the Education of Business Managers.* Hastings-on-Hudson, N. Y.: The Hastings Center, 1980.

Rosen, Bernard, and Caplan, Arthur L. *Ethics in the Undergraduate Curriculum.* Hastings-on-Hudson, N. Y.: The Hastings Center, 1980.

Warwick, Donald P. *The Teaching of Ethics and the Social Sciences.* Hastings-on-Hudson, N. Y.: The Hastings Center, 1980.

The following references are meant to provide an introduction to the topics found below. These references represent a selected list from a literature that ranges from quite extensive in some subject areas to almost nonexistent in others. Annotations have been provided only in those cases where the title may not fully reveal the contents.

GENERAL ARTICLES ON THE TEACHING OF ETHICS

Archambault, Reginald D. "Criteria for Success in Moral Instruction," *Harvard Educational Review* 33 (Fall 1963): 472–483.

Bennett, William J., and Delattre, Edwin. "Moral Education in the Schools," *The Public Interest* No. 50 (Winter 1978): 81–98.

Bereiter, Carl. "The Morality of Moral Education," *Hastings Center Report* 8:2 (April 1978): 20–25.

Bok, Derek. "Can Ethics be Taught?" *Change* 8 (October 1976): 26–30.

Bok, Sissela, and Callahan, Daniel. "Teaching Applied Ethics," *Radcliffe Quarterly* 69:2 (June 1979): 30–33.

Callahan, Daniel. "The Rebirth of Ethics," *National Forum* LVIII: 2 (Spring 1978): 9–12.

Frankena, William. "Towards a Philosophy of Moral Education," *Harvard Educational Review* 28 (Fall 1958): 300–313.

Montefiore, Alan. "Moral Philosophy and the Teaching of Morality," *Harvard Educational Review* 35 (1965): 435–449.

Peters, R. S. "Moral Development and Moral Learning," *Monist* 58 (1974): 541–68.

Ryle, Gilbert. "Can Virtue Be Taught?" in R. F. Dearden, P. H. Hirst, and R. S. Peters, eds., *Education and the Development of Reason*. London: Routledge & Kegan Paul, 1972.

Trow, Martin. "Higher Education and Moral Development," *American Association of University Professors Bulletin* (Spring 1976): 20–27.

Walzer, Michael. "Teaching Morality," *The New Republic* 178:23 (June 10, 1978): 12–14.

MORAL PHILOSOPHY

Baier, Kurt. *The Moral Point of View: A Rational Basis of Ethics*. New York: Random House, 1968.

Berlin, Isaiah. *Four Essays on Liberty*. Oxford: Oxford University Press, 1969.

Bok, Sissela. *Lying: Moral Choice in Public and Private Life*. New York: Pantheon Books, 1978.

Brandt, Richard B. *Ethical Theory*. Englewood Cliffs, N.J.: Prentice-Hall, 1959.

Donagan, Alan. *The Theory of Morality*. Chicago: University of Chicago Press, 1977.

Feinberg, Joel, ed. *Moral Concepts*. New York: Oxford University Press, 1969.

Frankena, William K. *Ethics*. 2nd ed. Englewood Cliffs, N.J.: Prentice-Hall, 1974.

Fried, Charles. *Right and Wrong*. Cambridge, Mass.: Harvard University Press, 1978.

Harmon, Gilbert. *The Nature of Morality*. New York: Oxford University Press, 1977.

MacIntyre, Alasdair. *A Short History of Ethics*. New York: Macmillan, 1966.

Mackie, J. L. *Ethics: Inventing Right and Wrong*. New York: Penguin Books, 1977.

Nozick, Robert. *Anarchy, State, and Utopia*. New York: Basic Books, 1974.

Rachels, James, ed. *Moral Problems: A Collection of Philosophical Essays*. New York: Harper & Row, 1971.

Rawls, John. *A Theory of Justice*. Cambridge, Mass.: Harvard University Press, 1971.

Sellars, W. S., and Hospers, John, eds. *Readings in Ethical Theory*. 2nd ed. New York: Appleton-Century-Crofts, 1970.

Smart, J. J. C. and Williams, Bernard. *Utilitarianism: For and Against*. New York: Cambridge University Press, 1973.

Taylor, Paul, ed. *Problems in Moral Philosophy: An Introduction to Ethics*. 2nd ed. Belmont, Calif.: Dickinson Publishing Co., 1971.

Toulmin, Stephen Edelston. *An Examination of the Place of Reason in Ethics*. New York: Cambridge University Press, 1950.

Williams, Bernard. *Morality: An Introduction to Ethics*. New York: Harper & Row, 1972.

THEOLOGICAL ETHICS

Fox, Marvin, ed. *Modern Jewish Ethics: Theory and Practice*. Columbus, Ohio: Ohio State University Press, 1975.

Gustafson, James. *Protestant and Roman Catholic Ethics.* Chicago: University of Chicago Press, 1978.

Gustafson, James. *Can Ethics Be Christian?* Chicago: University of Chicago Press, 1975.

Gutierrez, Gustavo. *A Theology of Liberation.* Maryknoll, N.Y.: Orbis Books, 1973.

Haring, Bernard. *Toward A Christian Moral Theology.* Notre Dame, Ind.: University of Notre Dame Press, 1966.

Haring, Bernard. *Morality is for Persons.* New York: Farrar, Straus & Giroux, 1970.

Kellner, Menachem Marc, ed. *Contemporary Jewish Ethics.* New York: Sanhedrin Press, 1978.

Maguire, Daniel C. *The Moral Choice.* Garden City, N.Y.: Doubleday, 1978.

McCormick, Richard A. *Ambiguity in Moral Choice.* Milwaukee: Marquette University Press, 1973.

Niebuhr, H. Richard. *The Responsible Self.* New York: Harper & Row, 1978.

Niebuhr, Reinhold. *An Interpretation of Christian Ethics.* Cleveland: The World Publishing Company, 1963 (1935).

O'Connell, Timothy E. *Principles for a Catholic Morality.* New York: Seabury Press, 1978.

Outka, Gene H. *Agape: An Ethical Analysis.* New Haven: Yale University Press, 1972.

Ramsey, Paul. *Basic Christian Ethics.* Chicago: University of Chicago Press, 1978.

Tillich, Paul. *Morality and Beyond.* New York: Harper & Row, 1963.

EDUCATION AND MORALITY

Astin, Alexander. *Four Critical Years: Effects of College on Beliefs, Attitudes and Knowledge.* San Francisco: Jossey-Bass, Inc. 1977.

Beck, C. M., Crittenden, B. S., and Sullivan, E. V., eds. *Moral Education.* Toronto: University of Toronto Press, 1971.

Bruneau, William. "A Resource Bibliography for the History of Moral Education in Western Europe 1850–1939," *Moral Education Forum* 4:3 (Fall 1979): 8–15, 18–20.

Carter, Jack L. "The Anatomy of Controversy: Freedom and Responsibility for Teaching," *BioScience* 29:8 (August 1979): 481–484.

Delattre, Edwin J. and Bennett, William J. "Where the Values Movement Goes Wrong," *Change* 11 (February 1979): 38–43.

Grant, Gerald, and Riesman, David. *The Perpetual Dream: Reform and Experiment in the American College.* Chicago: The University of Chicago Press, 1978.

Hall, Robert T., and Davis, John V. *Moral Education in Theory and Practice.* Buffalo, N.Y.: Prometheus Books, 1975.

Kirschenbaum, Howard, Simon, Sidney, and Howe, Leland. *Values Clarification.* New York: Hart Publishing Co., 1972.

Kohlberg, Lawrence. *Collected Papers on Moral Development and Moral Education.* Cambridge, Mass.: Center for Moral Education, Harvard University, 1973.

Langford, Glenn, ed. *New Essays in the Philosophy of Education.* London: Routledge & Kegan Paul, 1973.

Lickona, Thomas, ed. *Moral Development and Behavior.* New York: Holt, Rinehart, & Winston, 1976.

McGrath, Earl J. *Values, Liberal Education and National Destiny.* Indianapolis: Lilly Endowment, n.d.

Mischel, Theodore. *Cognitive Development and Epistemology.* New York: Academic Press, 1971.

Perry, William G. *Forms of Intellectual and Ethical Development in the College Years: A Scheme.* New York: Holt, Rinehart & Winston, 1970.

Peters, R. S., ed. *The Philosophy of Education.* Oxford: Oxford University Press, 1971.

Rudolph, Frederick. *Curriculum: A History of the American Undergraduate Course of Study Since 1636.* San Francisco: Jossey-Bass, Inc., 1972.

Schwarzlose, Richard A. "Socratic Method Adds Zest to Ethics, Law Classes," *Journalism Educator* 33:1 (April 1978): 9–24.

THEMES AND ISSUES IN THE TEACHING OF ETHICS

INDOCTRINATION

Caws, Peter. "On the Teaching of Ethics in a Pluralistic Society," *Hastings Center Report* 8:5 (October 1978): 32–39.

Paske, Gerald. "Education and the Problem of Indoctrination," *Proceedings of the Philosophy of Education Society* No. 50 (Winter 1978): 92–100.

Schleifer, Michael. "Moral Education and Indoctrination," *Ethics* 86:2 (January 1976): pp. 154–163.

Snook, I. A., ed. *Concepts of Indoctrination.* London: Routledge & Kegan Paul, 1972.

PATERNALISM

Dworkin, Gerald. "Paternalism," in Richard A. Wasserstrom, ed. *Morality in the Law.* Belmont, Calif.: Wadsworth Publishing Co., 1971.

Feinberg, Joel. "Legal Paternalism," *Canadian Journal of Philosophy* 1 (September 1971): 105–124.

Gert, Bernard, and Culver, Charles. "Paternalistic Behavior," *Philosophy and Public Affairs* 6 (Fall 1976): 45–57.

Mill, J. S. *On Liberty.* David Spitz, ed. New York: W. W. Norton, 1978.

Weale, Albert. "Paternalism and Social Policy," *Journal of Social Policy* 7:2 (April 1978): 157–172.

WHISTLEBLOWING

Chalk, Rosemary, and Van Hippel, Frank. "Due Process for Dissenting Whistleblowers," *Technology Review* 81:1 (June/July 1979).

Edsall, John. *Scientific Freedom and Responsibility: A Report of the AAAS Committee on Scientific Freedom and Responsibility.* Washington, D. C.: American Association for the Advancement of Science, 1975.

Ewing, David. *Freedom Inside the Organization.* New York: E. P. Dutton, 1977.

Morison, Samuel Eliot, Merk, Frederick, and Freidel, Frank. *Dissent in Three American Wars.* Cambridge, Mass.: Harvard University Press, 1970.

Nader, Ralph, Petkas, Peter, and Blackwell, Kate, eds. *Whistle Blowing.* New York: Grossman, 1972.

Weisband, Edward, and Franck, Thomas M. *Resignation in Protest.* New York: Grossman, 1975.

LAW

Countryman, Vern, Feinman, Ted, and Schneyer, Theodore. *The Lawyer in Modern Society.* Boston: Little, Brown & Co., 1976.

Feinberg, Joel, and Gross, Hyman, eds. *Philosophy of Law.* Encino, Calif.: Dickenson Publishing Co., 1975.

Frankel, Marvin E. "The Search for Truth: An Umpireal View." *University of Pennsylvania Law Review* 123:5 (May 1975): 1031–1059.

Freedman, Monroe. *Lawyer's Ethics in an Adversary System*. New York: Bobbs-Merrill, 1975.

Freedman, Monroe. "Professional Responsibility of the Criminal Defense Lawyer: The Three Hardest Questions," *Michigan Law Review* 64 (June 1966): 1469–1484.

Freund, Paul A. "The Moral Education of the Lawyer," *Emory Law Journal* 26:1 (Winter 1977): 3–12.

Gorovitz, Samuel, and Miller, Bruce. *Professional Responsibility in the Law: A Curriculum Report from the Institute on Law and Ethics*. College Park, Md: Council for Philosophical Studies, 1977.

Hazard, Geoffrey C. *Ethics in the Practice of Law*. New Haven: Yale University Press, 1978.

Kaufman, Andrew L. *Problems in Professional Responsibility*. Boston: Little, Brown & Co., 1976.

Lawry, Robert. "Lying, Confidentiality, and the Adversary System of Justice," *Utah Law Review* 4 (1977): 653–694.

Meltsner, Michael, and Schrag, Philip G. "Report from a CLEPR (Council on Legal Education for Professional Responsibility) Colony," *Columbia Law Review* 76:4 (May 1976): 581–632.

Noonan, John T. "Professional Ethics or Personal Responsibility?" *Stanford Law Review* 29 (1977): 363.

Schwartz, Murray. "The Professionalism and Accountability of Lawyers," California Law Review 66 (1978): 669.

Wasserstrom, Richard A. *Morality and the Law*. Belmont, Calif.: Wadsworth Publishing Co., 1971.

Wasserstrom, Richard A. "Lawyers as Professionals: Some Moral Issues," *Human Rights* 5 (Fall 1975): 1–24.

Weinstein, Jack. "On the Teaching of Legal Ethics," *Columbia Law Review* 72 (1972): 452.

Weinstein, Jack. "Educating Ethical Lawyers," *New York State Bar Journal* 47 (June 1975): 260–263.

PUBLIC POLICY

Arendt, Hannah. "Lying in Politics," in her collection *Crisis of the Republic*. New York: Harcourt, Brace & Jovanovich, 1972.

Barry, Brian. *Political Argument*. London: Routledge & Kegan Paul, 1965.

Beauchamp, Thomas L., ed. *Ethics and Public Policy*. Englewood Cliffs, N.J.: Prentice-Hall, 1975.

Calabresi, Guido, and Bobbitt, Philip. *Tragic Choices*. New York: W. W. Norton & Co., 1978.

Cohen, Marshall, Nagel, T., and Scanlon, T., eds. *Equality and Preferential Treatment*. Princeton: Princeton University Press, 1976.

Glover, Jonathan. *Causing Deaths and Saving Lives*. New York: Penguin Books, 1971.

Hampshire, Stuart, ed. *Public and Private Morality*. Cambridge: Cambridge University Press, 1978.

Held, Virginia. *The Public Interest and Individual Interest*. New York: Basic Books, 1970.

Jonsen, Albert, and Butler, L. H. "Public Ethics and Policymaking," *Hastings Center Report* 5:3 (August 1975): 19–31.

Price, David. "Public Policy and Ethics," *Hastings Center Report* 7:6 (December 1977): 4–6.

Rohr, John. *Ethics for Bureaucrats: An Essay on Law and Values*. New York: Dekkar, 1978.

Self, Peter. *Econocrats and Policy Process: The Politics and Philosophy of Cost-Benefit Analysis*. London: Macmillan, 1975.

Strauss, Leo. *What is Political Philosophy?* Westport, Conn.: Greenwood, 1973 (1959).

Thurow, Lester. *Generating Inequality*. New York: Basic Books, 1975.

Tribe, Laurence. *When Values Conflict: Essays on Environmental Analysis, Discourse and Decision*. Cambridge, Mass.: Ballinger, 1976.

Walzer, Michael. *Just and Unjust Wars*. New York: Basic Books, 1977.

Walzer, Michael. "Political Action: The Problem of Dirty Hands," *Philosophy and Public Affairs* 2:2 (Winter 1973): 160–180.

Wolin, Sheldon. *Politics and Vision: Continuity and Innovation in Western Political Thought*. Boston: Little, Brown & Co., 1960. Especially Chapter Ten.

BUSINESS

Ackerman, Robert, and Bauer, Raymond, eds. *Corporate Social Responsiveness: The Modern Dilemma*. Reston, Va: Reston Publishing Co., Inc., 1976.

Barach, Jeffrey, ed. *The Individual, Business, and Society*. Englewood Cliffs, N.J.: Prentice-Hall, 1977.

Beauchamp, Thomas, and Bowie, Norman, eds. *Ethical Theory and Business*. Englewood Cliffs, N.J.: Prentice-Hall, 1979.

Brenner, Steven N., and Molander, Earl A. "Is the Ethics of Business Changing?" *Harvard Business Review* 55:1 (January–February 1977): 57–71.

DeGeorge, Richard T., and Pichler, Joseph. *Ethics, Free Enterprise, and Public Policy: Original Essays on Moral Issues in Business*. Oxford: Oxford University Press, 1978.

Donaldson, Thomas, and Werhane, Patricia, eds. *Ethical Issues in Business: A Philosophical Approach*. Englewood Cliffs, N.J.: Prentice-Hall, 1979.

Epstein, Edwin, and Votaw, Dow, eds. *Legitimacy, Responsibility and Rationality*. Santa Monica: Good Years, 1978. A collection of original essays that addresses both ethical and social issues.

Ermann, M. David, and Lundman, Richard J., eds. *Corporate and Governmental Deviance: Problems of Organizational Behavior in Contemporary Society*. Oxford: Oxford University Press, 1978.

Henderson, Hazel. "Should Business Tackle Society's Problems?" *Harvard Business Review* 46:3 (May–June 1968): 77–85.

Luthans, Fred, and Hodgetts, Richard M., eds. *Social Issues in Business*. New York: Macmillan, 1976.

Nicholson, Edward A., Litschert, Robert J., and Anthony, William P., eds. *Business Responsibility and Social Issues*. Columbus, Ohio: Charles E. Merrill Publishing Co., 1974.

Purcell, Theodore. "A Practical Guide to Ethics in Business," *Business and Society Review* 13 (Spring 1975): 43–50.

Sethi, S. Prakash. *Up Against the Corporate Wall*. Englewood Cliffs, N.J.: Prentice-Hall, 1977.

Steiner, George A., and Steiner, John F., eds. *Issues in Business and Society*. New York: Random House, 1972.

Stone, Christopher. *Where the Law Ends*. New York: Harper & Row, 1975.

SOCIAL SCIENCE

Bermant, Gordon, Kelman, Herbert, and Warwick, Donald, eds. *The Ethics of Social Intervention*. Washington, D. C.: Hemisphere Publishing Company, 1978.

Bogart, Leo. *Silent Politics: Polls and the Awareness of Public Opinion*. New York: Wiley-Interscience, 1972.

Bower, Robert T., and de Gasparis, Priscilla. *Ethics in Social Research: Protecting the Interests of Human Subjects*. New York: Praeger Publishing Co., 1978. More than half of this book is devoted to an annotated bibliography on ethics in social research.

Denzin, N. K., and Erikson, Kai. "On the Ethics of Disguised Observation," *Social Problems* 15 (1968): 502–506.

Diener, Edward, and Crandall, Rick. *Ethics in Social and Behavioral Research.* Chicago: University of Chicago Press, 1978.

Erikson, Kai T. "A Comment on Disguised Observation in Sociology," *Social Problems* 16 (1967): 366–373.

Gouldner, Alvin. "Anti-Minotaur: The Myth of Value-free Sociology," *Social Problems* 9 (1962): 199–213.

Katz, Jay. *Experimentation with Human Beings: The Authority of the Investigator, Subject, Professions, and State in the Human Experimentation Process.* New York: Russell Sage Foundation, 1972.

Kelman, Herb. *A Time to Speak: On Human Values and Social Research.* San Francisco: Jossey-Bass, Inc., 1968.

Macrae, D., Jr. *The Social Function of Social Science.* New Haven: Yale University Press, 1976.

Mead, Margaret. "Research with Human Beings: A Model Derived from Anthropological Field Practice," *Daedelus* 98 (1969): 361–386.

Rivlin, Alice M., and Timpane, P. Michael, eds. *Ethical and Legal Issues of Social Experimentation.* Washington, D. C.: Brookings Institution, 1975.

Ruebhausen, O. M., and Brim, O. G. Jr., "Privacy and Behavioral Research," *Columbia Law Review* 65 (1965): 1184–1211.

Sjoberg, Gideon, ed. *Ethics, Politics, and Social Research.* San Francisco: Jossey-Bass, Inc., 1968.

ENGINEERING

Baum, Robert J., and Flores, Albert W., eds. *Ethical Problems in Engineering.* Troy, N. Y.: Rensselaer Polytechnic Institute, Human Dimensions Center, 1978.

Bonnell, John A., ed. *A Guide for Developing Courses in Engineering.* NSPE Publication #2010, Washington, D. C.: National Society of Professional Engineers, 1976.

Ethics, Professionalism & Maintaining Competence: Proceedings of a Conference held at The Ohio State University, March 10-11, 1977. New York: American Society of Civil Engineers, 1977.

Florman, Samuel. *The Existential Pleasures of Engineering.* New York: St. Martin's Press, 1976. In this volume, Florman explores the nature of the engineering profession and its obligations to society.

Fruchtbaum, Harold, ed. *The Social Responsibility of Engineers* (Annals of the New York Academy of Sciences, Vol. 196, Part 10), New York: Scholarly Reprints, 1973.

Layton, Edwin T., Jr. *Revolt of the Engineers: Social Responsibility and the American Engineering Profession.* Cleveland: Case Western Reserve University Press, 1971.

Oldenquist, Andrew G. and Slouter, Edward E. "Proposed: A Single Code of Ethics for All Engineers," *Professional Engineer* 49:5 (May 1979): 8–11.

Perrucci, Robert, and Gerstl, Joel E. *Profession Without Community: Engineers in American Society.* New York: Random House, 1969.

Weil, Vivian M. "Moral Issues in Engineering: An Engineering School Instructional Approach," *Professional Engineer* 47:10 (October 1977): 45–47.

JOURNALISM

Carty, James W. "Ethics: A Lost Concept," *The Collegiate Journalist* 8 (Spring 1971): 11–18.

Christians, Clifford G. "Fifty Years of Scholarship in Media Ethics," *Journal of Communication* 27 (Autumn 1977): 19–29.

Christians, Clifford G. "Problem-Solving in a Mass-Media Course," *Communications Education*

BIBLIOGRAPHY

28 (May 1979): 139–143. Describes a teaching methodology aimed at helping students develop analytic skills.

Diggs, Bernard J. "Persuasion and Ethics," *The Quarterly Journal of Speech.* 50:4 (December 1974): 359–373.

Kelley, Frank K. "Ethics of Journalism in a Century of Change," *Nieman Reports* 22 (June 1968): 12–15.

Rivers, William L., and Schramm, Wilbur. *Responsibility in Mass Communication.* rev. ed. New York: Harper & Row (1957), 1969.

Rubin, Bernard, ed. *Questioning Media Ethics.* New York: Praeger Special Studies, 1978.

Sanders, Keith, and Chang, Wong. *Freebies: Achilles' Heel of Journalism Ethics.* Columbia, Mo.: Freedom of Information Foundation, University of Missouri, 1977. An investigation of professional reactions to ethics codes.

Swain, Bruce M. *Reporter's Ethics.* Ames: Iowa State University Press, 1978.

Thayer, Lee, ed. *Communication: Ethical and Moral Issues.* New York: Gordon & Breach, 1973.

Thomson, James C. "Journalistic Ethics: Some Probings by a Media Keeper," Bloomington,: The Poynter Center, Indiana University Press, January 1978.

BIOETHICS

Aroskar, Mila A. "Ethics in the Nursing Curriculum," *Nursing Outlook* 25 (April 1977), pp. 260–264.

Aroskar, Mila A., and Veatch, Robert. "Ethics Teaching in Nursing Schools," *Hastings Center Reports* 7 (August 1977): 23–26.

Beauchamp, Tom, and Walters, LeRoy, eds. *Contemporary Issues in Bioethics.* Encino, Calif.: Dickenson Publishing Co., 1978.

Davis, Ann, and Aroskar, Mila. *Ethical Dilemmas and Nursing Practice.* New York: Appleton-Century-Crofts, 1978.

Gorovitz, S., Jameton, A., Macklin, R., O'Connor, J., Perrin, E., St. Clair, B., and Sherwin, S., eds. *Moral Problems in Medicine.* Englewood Cliffs, N.J.: Prentice-Hall, 1976.

Gustafson, James M. *The Contributions of Theology to Medical Ethics*: Milwaukee.: Marquette University Theology Department, 1975.

Heitowit, Ezra D., Epstein, Janet, and Steinberg, Gerald. *Science, Technology, and Society: A Guide to the Field.* Ithaca, N. Y.: Cornell University Press, 1976.

Hendrix, Jon R. "A Survey of Bioethics Courses in U. S. Colleges and Universities," *American Biology Teacher* 39 (February 1977): 85–92.

Humber, James M., and Almeder, Robert F. eds. *Biomedical Ethics and the Law.* New York: Plenum Press, 1976.

Hunt, Robert, and Arras, John, eds. *Ethical Issues in Modern Medicine.* Palo Alto, Calif.: Mayfield Publishing Co., 1977.

Jakobovits, Immanuel. *Jewish Medical Ethics.* New York: Bloch Publishing Co., 1959.

Purtilo, Ruth B. "Ethics Teaching in Allied Health Fields," *The Hastings Center Report* 8:2 (April 1978): 14–16.

Ramsey, Paul. *The Patient as Person.* New Haven: Yale University Press, 1970.

Reich, Warren T., editor-in-chief. *Encyclopedia of Bioethics.* New York: The Free Press, 1978.

Sollitto, Sharmon, Veatch, Robert, and Singer, Ira. *Bibliography of Society, Ethics, and the Life Sciences 1979-80.* Hastings-on-Hudson, N.Y.: The Hastings Center, 1979.

The Teaching of Bioethics: Report of the Commission on the Teaching of Bioethics. Hastings-on-Hudson, N.Y.: Institute of Society, Ethics, and the Life Sciences, 1976.

Veatch, Robert. *Case Studies in Medical Ethics.* Cambridge, Mass.: Harvard University Press, 1977.

Walters, Le Roy, ed. *Bibliography of Bioethics.* Detroit: Gale Research Co., 1975.

PROFESSIONAL ETHICS

Bledstein, Burton. *The Culture of Professionalism*. New York: W. W. Norton, 1976.

Boley, Bruno A. *Crossfire in Professional Education: Students, the Professions, and Society*. New York: Pergamon Press, 1977.

Collins, Randall. *The Credential Society*. New York: Academic Press, 1979.

Freidson, Eliot. *Professional Dominance: The Social Structure of Medical Care*. New York: Atherton Press, Inc., 1970.

Larson, Magali S. *The Rise of Professionalism*. Berkeley: University of California Press, 1977.

Merton, Robert K., ed. *Authority and the Individual*. New York: Arno Press, 1974.

Index